≺ ≻

DEVISING LIBERTY:
PRESERVING AND CREATING FREEDOM
IN THE NEW AMERICAN REPUBLIC

THE MAKING OF MODERN FREEDOM

General Editor: R. W. Davis

DEVISING LIBERTY

PRESERVING AND CREATING FREEDOM
IN THE NEW AMERICAN REPUBLIC

≺ ≻

Edited by David Thomas Konig

STANFORD UNIVERSITY PRESS
STANFORD, CALIFORNIA
1995

Stanford University Press
Stanford, California
© 1995 by the Board of Trustees of the
Leland Stanford Junior University
Printed in the United States of America

CIP data appear at the end of the book

Stanford University Press publications
are distributed exclusively by
Stanford University Press within
the United States, Canada, Mexico, and
Central America; they are distributed
exclusively by Cambridge University
Press throughout the rest
of the world.

≺ ≻

Series Foreword

THE STARTLING AND MOVING events that swept from China to Eastern Europe to Latin America and South Africa at the end of the 1980s, followed closely by similar events and the subsequent dissolution of what used to be the Soviet Union, formed one of those great historic occasions when calls for freedom, rights, and democracy echoed through political upheaval. A clear-eyed look at any of those conjunctions—in 1776 and 1789, in 1848 and 1918, as well as in 1989—reminds us that freedom, liberty, rights, and democracy are words into which many different and conflicting hopes have been read. The language of freedom—or liberty, which is interchangeable with freedom most of the time—is inherently difficult. It carried vastly different meanings in the classical world and in medieval Europe from those of modern understanding, though thinkers in later ages sometimes eagerly assimilated the older meanings to their own circumstances and purposes.

A new kind of freedom, which we have here called modern, gradually disentangles itself from old contexts in Europe, beginning first in England in the early seventeenth century and then, with many confusions, denials, reversals, and cross-purposes, elsewhere in Europe and the world. A large-scale history of this modern, conceptually distinct, idea of freedom is now beyond the ambition of any one scholar, however learned. This collaborative enterprise, tentative though it must be, is an effort to fill the gap.

We could not take into account all the varied meanings that freedom and liberty have carried in the modern world. We have, for example, ruled out extended attention to what some political philosophers have called "positive freedom," in the sense of self-realization of the individual; nor could we, even in a series as large as this, cope with the enormous implications of the four freedoms invoked by Franklin D. Roosevelt in 1941. Freedom of speech and freedom of the press will have their place in the narrative that follows, certainly, but not the boundless calls for freedom from want and freedom from fear.

We use freedom in the traditional and restricted sense of civil and political liberty—freedom of religion, freedom of speech and assembly, freedom of the individual from arbitrary and capricious authority over persons or property, freedom to produce and to exchange goods and services, and the freedom to take part in the political process that shapes people's destiny. In no major part of the world over the past few years have aspirations for those freedoms not been at least powerfully expressed; and in most places where they did not exist, strong measures have been taken—not always successfully— to attain them.

The history we trace was not a steady march toward the present or the fulfillment of some cosmic necessity. Modern freedom had its roots in specific circumstances in early modern Europe, despite the unpromising and even hostile characteristics of the larger society and culture. From these narrow and often selfishly motivated beginnings, modern freedom came to be realized in later times, constrained by old traditions and institutions hard to move, and driven by ambition as well as idealism: everywhere the growth of freedom has been *sui generis*. But to understand these unique developments fully, we must first try to see them against the making of modern freedom as a whole.

The Making of Modern Freedom grows out of a continuing series of conferences and institutes held at the Center for the History of Freedom at Washington University in St. Louis. Professor J. H. Hexter was the founder and, for three years, the resident gadfly of the Center. His contribution is gratefully recalled by all his colleagues.

R.W.D.

Contents

<>

Acknowledgments

Several foundations have generously supported The Making of Modern Freedom series, and two in particular have supported this volume. The National Endowment for the Humanities provided funding for planning meetings and also sponsored the autumn 1990 conference where the volume was first discussed. It largely took shape in the fourth of our annual Institutes in the spring semester of 1991. The Institutes, which bring the authors together as Fellows of the Center for the History of Freedom, have been fully funded by the Lynde and Harry Bradley Foundation. We are grateful for all the support we have received, including the strong backing we have always enjoyed from Washington University.

R.W.D.

CONTRIBUTORS

Lance Banning
University of Kentucky, Lexington

Norma Basch
Rutgers University

Richard D. Brown
University of Connecticut, Storrs

Paul A. Gilje
University of Oklahoma

Nathan O. Hatch
University of Notre Dame

David Thomas Konig
Washington University

Jan Lewis
Rutgers University

Peter S. Onuf
University of Virginia

Alan Taylor
Boston University

DEVISING LIBERTY:
PERSERVING AND CREATING FREEDOM
IN THE NEW AMERICAN REPUBLIC

≺ ≻

Introduction

DAVID THOMAS KONIG

THE PREAMBLE TO THE federal Constitution made explicit the purpose of the nation's republican government in 1789: "to form a more perfect Union, establish Justice, insure domestic Tranquility, provide for the common defence, promote the general Welfare, and secure the Blessings of Liberty to ourselves and our Posterity." These goals, now formed by our national history into a seamless web, stand as inseparable from one another. Without union, the common defense is imperiled; without justice, the blessings of liberty are elusive; without domestic stability, the public welfare is endangered. From the perspective of the late twentieth century, these goals appear mutually necessary, each as indispensable to the others as it is to the larger enterprise.

Their successful fusion over two centuries, however, obscures that fact that in 1789 a disturbing contradiction lay deep within these ambitious generalizations. A federal union of the size created in 1789, capable of defending itself from external enemies and preserving social order at home, would defy the canons of political orthodoxy if it were also expected to honor and protect liberty. Free, republican government, it was conventionally believed, could not survive in a geographically extended sovereignty, for the power needed to govern such an immense nation would inexorably overwhelm individual liberty and create a despotism of enormous proportions. In urging the ratification of the Constitution in *The Federalist*, James Madison had labelled this dilemma "the great difficulty": "You must first enable the government to controul the governed; and in the next place, oblige it to controul itself."[1] Madison had identified one of the central problems of eighteenth-century American political philosophy—the rivalry of power and liberty.[2] How might freedom be preserved in a complex, expanding, and increasingly commercial republic without creating the coercive (and inevitably corrupting) state power that history and theory had shown necessary in such circumstances?

It is the purpose of this book, one volume in the series *The Making of Modern Freedom*, to understand how Americans attempted to define "freedom" and then to establish the social and material conditions through which they might become, in John Jay's words, a "people free, contented, and united."[3] To be "free" brought to mind a plurality of meanings to eighteenth-century Americans. It meant different things to the peoples of the different regions in an extended republic, and it suggested different goals or purposes for the various— even competing—groups that constituted American society. Nevertheless, this "discourse and the communities that formed around it"—to borrow the apt phrasing of intellectual historian David A. Hollinger—drew upon a fund of ideas that Americans could employ in generating a politically and socially creative conversation. He explains: "Participants in any given discourse are bound to share certain values, beliefs, perceptions, and concepts—'ideas,' as these potentially distinctive mental phenomena are called for short— but the most concrete and functional elements shared, surely, are *questions*."[4] Their central question—what Hollinger would call their "discourse-defining question"—was "freedom." Conditioned by premises of political thought and buffeted by many unexpected historical contingencies, they probed its causes, its creation, and its preservation. Answers in the quarter century after 1789 were not the same; in many cases, they directly contradicted each other. Nonetheless, they arose in "a historically and socially specific context of public discussion"[5] that shaped and guided the discussion of a fundamental, pressing question of immense practical immediacy.

Much of this discussion—that of political institutions, especially—is well known.[6] With the Constitution and the Bill of Rights, the Founders devised a national government they hoped would be sufficiently energetic to advance freedom yet so constituted as to place that power within the constraints needed to protect liberty. Their product, an unfinished structure that reflected an ongoing contest of political thought in the new republic, rejected both history and theory in a number of ways. Recasting the concept of sovereignty, they rejected the notion that *imperium in imperio* ("two sovereign authorities in the same state")[7] was a solecism of politics; instead, the new national government and the states shared a hitherto indivisible sovereignty. Next, the constitutional structure of representation transformed the extensive nature of the republic—which, theory dictated, must produce a monolithic juggernaut state—into a federal union of dispersed and diverse local units more likely to compete with one another than consolidate themselves. Should the assembly of states and districts manage to form themselves into a monolithic bloc, the Constitution divided state power in a way never before attempted—into functionally distinct branches, each capable of checking the errant action of another. Finally, the Founders included a list of specific prohibitions which the state "shall" not—rather than merely "ought" not—do. Altogether, in the period of twenty-eight months between the first gavel at the Philadelphia convention and Congress's submission of the Bill of Rights to the states, "We the people" had achieved a sustained creativity unmatched in political annals.

"Devising" liberty, however, involved more than that word connoted in its common usage of contriving or inventing. Many nations had created systems of free government, but their political efforts had, ultimately, ended in the loss of liberty. The real challenge was to "devise" liberty in a sense closer to the more technical legal sense of the word: namely, to make a testamentary gift of real property as a legacy to the future. "[T]he Blessings of Liberty," it must be emphasized, were to be secured "to ourselves *and our Posterity.*" Only with difficulty had that legacy been identified and claimed by the generation of 1776. To preserve and bequeath it to future generations, political institutions—even of the most creative sort—might not suffice. Madison reflected a widely held caution when he stated that government, as "but the greatest of all reflections on human nature," was vulnerable to human corruption. Structural political mechanisms, though necessary to restrain the state from discrete abuses, were ultimately only "auxiliary precautions." "A dependence on the people," he insisted, "is no doubt the primary controul on the government."[8]

As the chapters in this volume make clear, the founding generation had to go beyond the public sphere of politics to the people themselves in order to assure the legacy of freedom to future generations. It was, after all, the people in whom sovereignty lay and who constituted government. They might alter or deform it at their will, or they might abuse the authority vested in them. Thomas Paine had struck a resonant chord in *Common Sense* when he had identified "the constitution of the people," rather than "the constitution of the government," as the source of freedom.[9] Madison, therefore, sought the solution to his "great difficulty" in "that honorable determination, which animates every votary of freedom, to rest all our political experiments on the capacity of mankind for self-government."[10]

The chapters in *Devising Liberty* attempt to examine the intellectual premises and the historical contingencies that conditioned the debate on assuring self-government by creating a "new order for the ages," a *novus ordo seclorum*. They reveal that Americans in the quarter century after 1789 recognized that this new order must be a social one as well as a political one, for without a firm social and material basis self-government was impossible and no free government could survive. Once the structure of government was established and state institutions created, the goals set forth in the Constitution's preamble would be promoted by a society conducive to them.

Such a society depended on certain known preconditions. A broad distribution of property among male freeholders, for example, was necessary to assure the material independence of the citizen and thereby support his resistance to corruption. Entrusting the freedom and stability of a republic to the possession of property was not new, of course; as a staple of Anglo-American political discourse it was at least as old as James Harrington's *Oceana* (1656). But the manner of implementing this ideal provoked debate. As Lance Banning shows, Madison's political economy of a republic of freeholders initially led him to share Alexander Hamilton's quest for an invigorated federal system, but Madison expected to employ this system to prevent a headlong rush into development and thus into a set of "social circumstances undesirable for liberal republics." Hamilton, while welcoming Madison's support, saw other conditions for the success of the republic—a more traditional English-style political economy in which property assured stability in a much different way. The incompatibility of these two positions—"barely glimpsed by their respective spokesmen" in the 1780s—divided Americans until Hamilton's old party collapsed and the Jeffersonians "appropriated part of the design that they had once perceived as inconsistent with the health of a republic."

The West figured prominently in the plans of the founding generation, for its lands promised the availability of untold acreage for yeoman farms. Yet territorial expansion had its perils and, to many, actually endangered liberty and union. According to these fears, expansion would diffuse the already limited authority of the federal government, increase localist particularism, and permit interstate rivalries to escalate into crises. As Peter Onuf demonstrates, however, such apprehensions rested on an outdated, European balance-of-power conception of relations among sovereign states, which the events and contests of the 1780s gradually led the Founders to reject. Instead of coexisting uneasily as full sovereignties in precarious balance, the states would yield many of their sovereign powers and vest them in a "Center of Union." No longer fearing one another and thereby freed of the need to tax themselves heavily for defense, they could devote more of their energies to securing property rights, protecting civil liberties, and fostering economic development and population growth—all necessary preconditions for a secure, enduring republic.

Onuf reminds us that in the scheme of a new order the West meant more than land: it meant an opportunity for adding new states and creatively reconfiguring the relationship among the constituent elements of the union. Alan Taylor shows us that land itself took on new meaning as a foundation of that order. Indeed, it took on three new meanings that vied with one another. For whites, two visions competed—that of squatters and that of national government officials. For the former, land meant political independence, to be sure; but it also led to a reconfiguring of social relationships among the people. The squatter's access to free land gave him not only political independence, but social autonomy, too. Moreover, land meant liberty of an entirely different sort—an entrepreneurial opportunity "to claim, use, develop, and, perhaps, ultimately to sell wilderness land." To officials of the national government, that vision offered too much independence, for it threatened relations with the Indians and jeopardized the vital revenues that would flow from an orderly system of land sales. The West also offered opportunity to Indians in the post-Revolutionary era. "One people's freedom," writes Taylor, "came at another's expense." Emphasizing the role of the Indian as an active player in the contest for the West, he describes how the fertile expanse of the Northwest Territory presented the Indians who lived there with a vision of their own freedom and independence. To them, possession of these lands constituted a declaration of independence from what had become a tradition of "debilitating dependence on treaty annuities bestowed by white authorities."

The call for free land and squatters' rights echoed the cry for free trade and sailors' rights as described in Paul Gilje's chapter. For seafaring workers in the waterfront communities of the early republic, "revolutionary ideas of equality seeped into the forecastle" and, it might be added, fueled their support for a strong national authority capable of protecting their interests on the high seas. Political leaders, in turn, were acutely aware of the indispensable role that a vigorous maritime community played in the nation's efforts to establish a sound basis for the republic's survival. Both ashore and at sea, the workers who inhabited the waterfront identified their own independent way of life with the basic impulse of the Revolution and demanded their "liberty." The term, of course, more commonly referred to a sailor's spree ashore. But it also reveals to us the legitimation of an anti-authoritarian outlook proudly assumed as a right and a necessity. Though it would certainly be too much to argue that the average Jack Tar thought of himself and his unruly way of life as a necessary foundation of a free republic, the widespread sympathy for his cause and his popular identification with defiance of Great Britain—both before 1776 and after—became a rallying cry for the nation.

Not all Americans viewed the waterfront population quite so positively. The swaggering defiance of unjust British power might easily become violent, anti-social contempt for all duly constituted authority. Seeking to elevate Jack Tar to respectability and virtue, evangelicals urged Bibles and sobriety upon him. But the evangelicals' mission was not limited to the benighted, nor was it alone as an attempt to educate the masses and transform them into the kind of citizens needed in a free republic. As Richard D. Brown explains, the movement for universal literacy was characteristic of Revolutionary-era reform in that it included both public and private endeavors. The effort to equip the citizenry for its republican responsibilities revealed that the Revolution, whose public phase enlisted the best efforts of a generation, had a private dimension, too: voluntary, localistic, and decentralized, the literacy movement embodied qualities destructive of the old hierarchical social order that supported monarchy.

In the volume editor's chapter on jurisprudence, Madison's injunction that government must "guard one part of the society against the injustice of the other part"[11] emphasizes the importance of private law as a basis for a new type of social unity essential to a free republic. The effectiveness of private law, it was believed, enabled Americans simultaneously to protect their individual rights and the peace of their communities without the aid of the coercive state institutions traditionally thought necessary. But private law was to do more to preserve liberty than protect citizens from one another. By fostering the growth and vitality of private institutions, it helped erect barriers that stood between the individual and the state. Moreover, by harmonizing discrete interests, the law unified society and empowered it as a counterweight against the power of the state.

The legal authority to form voluntary associations also involved the ability to dissolve them when they, in turn, might become oppressive of their members. From the right to dissolve the political bands that Jefferson's Declaration of Independence asserted, to the right to dissolve the marriage bond was a link easily made in the minds of many Americans. As Norma Basch makes clear, the "chronological convergence between the legal reordering of marriage as a social institution and the political reordering of the society at large" produced significant divorce reform in the early republic. Proper relationships in the state had to reflect proper relationships among contracting private individuals, and the new republic would no longer base its security and freedom on the corporatist bonds that sustained monarchy.

So, too, did the quest for "gospel liberty" presuppose the necessity of freely associating individuals. With religion removed from the purview of the state, Nathan Hatch argues, a vital foundation of a free society was privatized and allowed to flourish on its own, supported by the voluntary efforts of private groups joined together by nothing other than their conviction that free religion was essential to a free society. The Methodists epitomized the proliferation of new sects, by which a "battery of young leaders without elite pedigree constructed fresh religious ideologies around which new religious movements coalesced." Hatch challenges the conventional historical wisdom that portrays the evangelical revivals of the Second Great

Awakening "as a profoundly conservative force, an attempt by traditional religious elites to re-impose social order upon a disordered and secularized society," as an attack on the market economy, and as "expressions of resistance to bourgeois individualism." To the contrary, he argues, groups such as the Methodists were celebrating and exploiting the fluidity, openness, and commercialization of society that enabled Christians to seek "gospel liberty" and to create new denominations in such bewildering number that no orthodoxy could rule. Viewing "politics, religion, and society as different facets of a common reality," the advocates of popular religion self-consciously undermined hierarchy and deference and sought to replace them with democracy and self-expression. In that way, the people would be freed of control by church or state.

As an agent of privatization, evangelicalism removed broad areas of American life from state control, and in almost all cases it served to liberate those sectors of American life where the intrusive hand of government had protected privilege and had acted to impede individual advancement. The one glaring exception was slavery, which was already governed by a private law system of contract and property rights against attack by the state, and which would be strengthened by the rise of evangelical religious thought. Contrary to the thesis that slavery survived the Revolution owing to the ideological support of republicanism, Jan Lewis convincingly demonstrates that the Anglo-American reverence for property rights protected slavery in the earliest years of the republic when that system was under fierce attack. Only much later—in the second quarter of the nineteenth century—did proslavery advocates dust off and reshape republicanism to justify slavery as necessary to white freedom. In between, evangelicalism, with its emphasis on a community of believers joined as well by affection and familial intimacy, "domesticated" slavery and removed it from attack as a public evil.

Lewis's chapter points up the enormous value placed by Americans on private relationships in a free society. Just as importantly, however, it reveals the fragile balance between the public and private dimensions of the Revolution. With slavery removed from the public purview, or at least with its public dimension much diminished, one of the most important debates of the Revolution moved to a new and different stage. Perhaps most importantly of all, however, Lewis wisely leads us to appreciate the vital fact that the founding generation's revolutionary vision of liberty was itself the product of historical contingency, competing philosophies, and political competition. The concept of liberty as articulated in the first years of the republic combined many different and potentially incompatible strands of thought. Devised amid conflict and responding to ever-changing needs, the founding ideal remains so today.

Political Economy and the Creation
of the Federal Republic

LANCE BANNING

AS RECENTLY AS 1980, there was little reason to expect a reinvig-
oration of intensive interest in the Founders' economic thinking. Federalist opinion, nearly everyone agreed, was socially conservative, yet strongly pro-developmental: determined to defend the
rights of property, to create a national market, and to raise a legal
framework in which private enterprise might thrive. Since 1980,
much has changed, though we are just beginning to appreciate the
implications. In the aftermath of a remarkable resurgence of intense
investigation,[1] the enduring image of the Federalists as champions
of economic liberty and growth (and of their foes as narrow-minded
or heroic friends of agricultural and populistic values) has come to
seem, not altogether wrong, but certainly too simple. A subtler understanding would insist that the creation of the federal republic did
not represent the triumph of a single economic vision, which competed with a single Antifederalist perspective. Rather, it resulted
from a temporary union of opposing views whose presence and development were central to the story of the rise and subsequent division of the movement which secured the Constitution.

The middle 1780s, recent scholarship suggests, witnessed a convergence in support of sweeping constitutional reform by men with
quite distinctive views about the economic policies and circumstances necessary to secure a permanent foundation for the nation's
freedom. Two conflicting visions of a sound political economy can
be detected, in their embryonic forms, in a congressional dispute of
1783. Both were deeply rooted in the British thought and practice
that were starting points for late-colonial opinion. Each, in different
ways, expressed the highest aspirations of the Revolution. Though

neither was articulated fully in the arguments of 1783—and their intrinsic incompatibility was barely glimpsed by their respective spokesmen at that time—both received a fuller formulation during the depression of the middle eighties, and both required a more effective federal system. Thus, the major architects and most impressive spokesmen for the two distinctive visions, James Madison (in his continual collaboration with Thomas Jefferson) and Alexander Hamilton (with early help from Robert Morris), were able to cooperate effectively in constitutional reform. The deepest differences between them were not among the topics which they needed to pursue in their impressive exegesis of the Constitution.

Still, for Madison and Hamilton alike, the Constitution was a means toward larger ends, not an end within itself; and shortly after its adoption, their conflicting wishes split the Federalists of 1789 into two clashing parties. Competing visions of political economy were not the only reasons for this split, but they were certainly among its most important causes. As Hamilton completed the articulation of his vision and attempted, piece by piece, to have it written into law, Madison and Jefferson responded with a more specific formulation of a program of their own. By 1792, the two conflicting visions were essentially mature; and although both would undergo important further evolution—partly in response to changing times and partly in response to other actors—the two competing programs were a central feature of political disputes until the War of 1812 produced a short-lived synthesis of elements of each. Popular opinions and the changing shape of popular divisions can be wrapped into a narrative which treats these clashing visions as essential elements of an extended argument about the founding of a liberal republic.[2]

≺ I ≻

Country, Court, and the Republican Revolution

In December 1782, in the midst of growing rumors that a peace agreement had been reached, a deputation from the continental army came to Philadelphia to seek immediate provision for the unpaid private troops and firm assurances from Congress that the continental officers would actually receive the peacetime pensions promised them two years before. Soon thereafter, believing that the final weeks of war might also prove the final opportunity for doing justice to the army, for restoring public credit, and for laying the foundations for the nation's post-war economic growth, Robert Morris, the Confederation's superintendent of finance, initiated an intense campaign for independent federal taxes. On 17 January, he told the deputation from the army that the funds for one month's pay could be provided by a final draft on overdrawn accounts abroad, but that additional provisions for the military and civilian creditors could not be made without approval of new taxes. Then, on 24 January, without preliminary warning, Morris threatened to resign in four months' time if no provision had been made by then for managing the federal obligations, declaring that he would not serve as "the minister of injustice." By February, when the news of a preliminary treaty was confirmed, rumblings from the army's winter camp at Newburgh were becoming truly ominous in tone; and at the seat of Congress, Morris's supporters, some of whom were widely feared to be intriguing with the army, were pressing for his program in an atmosphere of crisis. At the camp, the agitation culminated in anonymous addresses of 10 and 12 March, calling on the soldiers to refuse to be disbanded while their needs remained unmet.[3]

For Morris, the arrival of the deputation from the army was, at once, a reason and an opportunity for forcing the Confederation Congress to initiate a serious consideration of a sweeping program of reform. Since taking his position, in the spring of 1781, the superintendent had supplied the army as it marched to victory at Yorktown. He had instituted valuable administrative changes at the Office of Finance, secured creation of a national bank, and urged a settlement of the accounts between the central government and states as an initial step toward managing the public debt. But peace was not yet certain, and Rhode Island still refused to ratify the impost, a congressional request of 1781 for power to impose a modest tax on foreign imports. The states were greatly in arrears on their congressional requisitions, and the public creditors were growing ever more impatient for their pay. On 29 July 1782, Morris had delivered an important paper on the state of public credit, insisting that a whole new set of independent federal taxes would have to be combined with the receipts anticipated from the impost and from sales of western lands in order to meet current expenses and pay the interest on the debt. He recommended the addition of a land tax, a poll tax, and an excise. By fall, however, Congress had been able to agree on nothing more than further requisitions on the states.[4]

With the arrival of the deputation from the army, there was little room for long, additional delays. Congress hurriedly deputed a committee to travel to Rhode Island for a personal appeal for ratification of the impost. These delegates were barely on the road, on Christmas eve, when a humiliated Madison was forced to tell the fundless Congress that his own Virginia had rescinded its approval of the measure, destroying all remaining hope that this amendment would provide the answer to the army's pleas.[5] As Congress turned its full attention to provisions for the debt, some of Morris's supporters took his threatened resignation as a signal for a concentrated effort to enlist extra-congressional pressure for independent federal funds. Through most of February, Congress battled over Morris's proposals in an atmosphere of mounting crisis.[6]

By 28 January, when Madison assumed strategic leadership of the proponents of reform, its advocates were making modest progress. Even the Virginia delegation, which included three of Morris's most bitter foes, seemed willing to renew the recommendation of an impost; and Congress was proceeding toward a plan for commutation of the half-pay pensions, a compromise which continental officers were willing to accept in light of fixed republican hostility to lifetime grants. Still, many congressmen were willing to depart no further from the requisition system than was absolutely necessary to fulfill the federal obligations. Shortly after the receipt of news of the preliminary peace, John Rutledge (SC) and John Francis Mercer (VA) moved to apply the proceeds from a new impost (if this amendment should be ratified by all the states) exclusively to the debt due to the army. Madison helped to defeat this proposal on 18 February, only to be startled by a motion by Alexander Hamilton (NY) and James Wilson (PA), Morris's staunchest allies in the Congress, to open the deliberations to the public when the members were debating matters of finance. Sharing in the general dislike of this surprising motion, which was greeted by a quick adjournment, Madison asked his Pennsylvania colleagues to explain it. They replied that they had put themselves in a delicate position with their legislature by persuading it to drop its plans for a state assumption of a portion of the federal debt and only wanted their constituents to see that they were doing everything they could. "Perhaps the true reason," Madison suspected, was that they hoped that "public creditors, numerous and weighty in

Philadelphia, would have an influence" from the galleries on the congressional proceedings.[7]

Congress had already heard one speech in which the brilliant but incautious Hamilton had urged an independent federal revenue on grounds that worried several members: "As the energy of the federal government was evidently short of the degree necessary for pervading and uniting the states, it was expedient to introduce the influence of officers deriving their emoluments from and consequently interested in supporting the power of Congress."[8] "This remark," wrote Madison, "was imprudent and injurious to the cause which it was meant to serve," since fears of just this sort of influence were among the most important reasons why the states resisted revenues that were to be collected by the officers of Congress. All the members most opposed to independent federal revenues had "smiled," Madison noted, "at the disclosure"; Arthur Lee and Theodorick Bland, two Virginia colleagues, told him privately that Hamilton "had let out the secret."[9] Now, the obvious attempt to throw the doors of Congress open to a potent lobby reenforced the gathering impression that several of the advocates of general funds were hoping that the army and the public creditors would join to pressure both the state and federal governments into a grant of independent general taxes. Madison himself was patently uneasy over what his allies seemed to have in mind.

At just this point, the pressure from the army neared its peak, encouraged, if not deliberately provoked, by some of the Philadelphia advocates of general funds. On the morning after Hamilton's attempt to open the debates, with congressmen referring openly to pressure from the army, Rutledge renewed the motion to appropriate the impost exclusively to the soldiers' needs. Hamilton again denounced "such a partial dispensation of justice," suggesting that "it was impolitic to divide the interests of the civil and military creditors, whose joint efforts in the states would be necessary to prevail on them to adopt a general revenue." Wilson seconded the young New Yorker, adding that "by dividing the interest of the civil from that of the military creditors provision for the latter would be frustrated." But Virginia's Mercer still opposed "a permanent debt supported by a permanent and general revenue." He believed that "it would be good policy to separate instead of cementing the interest of the army and the other public creditors."[10]

On the following evening, 20 February—after another day of angry debates—Madison and several others went to dinner at the home of Congressman Thomas FitzSimons. Here, Hamilton and Richard Peters, former officers whose military contacts kept them well informed about conditions in the camp, told the gathering that it was certain that the army had decided not to put away its arms until its just demands were met. A public manifesto, they revealed, would be forthcoming soon, and "plans had been agitated if not formed for subsisting themselves after such a declaration." General Washington, the two ex-officers announced, had come to be "extremely unpopular among almost all ranks from his known dislike to any unlawful proceeding," and "many leading characters" were working to replace him with the more compliant Horatio Gates. Hamilton had written the commander, he reported, in order to alert him to these schemes, urging him to lead the army in any plans for redress, "that they might be moderated."[11]

Why Hamilton and Peters chose to make these revelations at this moment is impossible to know. Perhaps the course of conversation simply led them to divulge their latest information. For if they wanted to intensify the pressure for new taxes, the strategy could not have been more misconceived. With only Hamilton dissenting, the gathering agreed that Congress was unlikely to approve any general revenues except the impost, and several of the diners seem to have concluded that the temper of the army would permit no more delay.

For Madison, there is no doubt, the dinner at FitzSimons's home was a critical event. On the morrow, he was on his feet again in Congress for a speech in which he still defended general revenues as consistent with "the principles of liberty and the spirit of the constitution." Now, however, he "particularly disclaimed the idea of perpetuating a public debt," and he admitted that he was convinced that Congress would be forced to limit its recommendations to the impost and a "call for the deficiency in the most permanent way that could be reconciled with a revenue established within each state separately and appropriated to the common treasury."[12] Before this speech, Madison had worked in close cooperation with the financier and his congressional spokesmen. From this point forward, he was bent upon a compromise of which they disapproved. On 26 February, he outlined a proposal that he hoped would end the crisis, together with a list of the responses he expected from each state.[13] By early April he believed that his proposals, reported from committee on

6 March, would be substantially approved. They were, indeed, accepted in amended form on 18 April 1783, and Madison was asked to draft an explanation to the states. Already, on 22 March, Congress had received George Washington's report on the collapse of the conspiracy at camp.[14]

Madison's departure from the other advocates of general revenues has usually been seen, when it is mentioned, as a simple consequence of his conclusion that nothing but a compromise could end an urgent crisis. More was certainly involved. In the first place, the Virginian's plan of 26 February was not intended merely to provide as permanent a fund for managing the debt as Congress and the states seemed likely to approve. Madison intended something much more comprehensive. Congress would renew its call for power to impose an impost. This amendment to the Articles, together with additional, though individual, state appropriations for the debt, would be combined with several lesser measures meant to put an end to nearly all of the recurring conflicts that had troubled Madison throughout his years in Congress, ranging landed states against the landless, small against the large, the South against New England. This was not the quickest or the simplest way to counteract the pressure from the army, but Madison believed that it might be the surest way to guarantee that all the public creditors would actually receive their dues. And he was seeking, now, not only to avert a national disgrace, not only to conciliate the soldiers, but also to repair the fundamental fractures that appeared increasingly to threaten the very survival of the union.[15]

The long and often bitter argument about the funding of the debt had sharpened nearly all of the divisions that had marked the Continental Congress through the last three years. Sectional disputes about apportioning the obligations of the states were older than the separation from Great Britain. Any general tax—and almost any mixture of a set of general taxes with an impost—still appeared to threaten unfair burdens. Jealousies between the landed and the landless states had been intensified again by news of the preliminary peace, in which America had won the West and a potential treasurehouse of future revenues before Virginia and the other landed states had completed their western cessions. Moreover, the debates had made it evident that Morris and his allies aimed at something vastly broader than a firm provision for the debt; and Madison, beginning with his speech of 21 February, had quite deliberately tried to disassociate himself from Hamilton's suggestion that a funded debt could be a useful tool for strengthening the union. While he was still convinced that funding and a commutation of the half-pay pensions could not be less consistent with "our republican character and constitutions than a violation of good faith and common honesty," he insisted that he "was as much opposed to perpetuating the public burdens as anyone" in Congress.[16] He would thus concur "in every arrangement that should appear necessary for an honorable and just fulfillment of the public engagements and in no measure tending to augment the power of Congress which should appear unnecessary."[17] Madison was out of sympathy by now, not only with the tactics, but also with the ultimate objectives of Hamilton, Wilson, and Morris. As some of their opponents had suggested, those objectives seemed to squint at a conception of the future which was much at odds with many revolutionaries' thoughts about the sort of nation the United States should be.

Morris's July report had advocated general revenues that would be adequate to meet the ordinary operating costs of Congress as well as to assure the steady payment of the interest on the debt. These revenues would be collected by the officers of Congress, and they would be conterminous with the existence of the federal obligations. Though Madison insisted that such revenues accorded with "the spirit" of the Articles of Union—they would make "the federal constitution" more "efficient"—he was also perfectly aware that independent federal taxes would entail a fundamental change in the relationship between the central government and states.[18] This alteration of the federal balance was precisely what opponents disapproved, and it was just what Morris, Hamilton, and Wilson found so difficult to relinquish. It was this that Madison first favored, then abandoned in his speech of 21 February. But he did not surrender it because he was inherently more pliable than many of his allies. He gave it up because it did not seem to him, as it did to many of them, an object worth the risks it came to entail. He gave it up because it had become apparent that the other advocates of general funds had motives and objectives he had never really shared.[19]

All of the original supporters of independent general funds regarded a dependable federal revenue as essential to the restoration of public credit and possibly to the continuation of the union. All of them regarded steady payment of the interest on the debt as a critical test of national character and an indispensable security against the day when it might be necessary to borrow again. Not all of them, however, actually wished to see the debt retired, nor did Morris's plan provide for payment of the principal as well as of the interest. Congressional opponents noticed this when they condemned a "permanent" or "perpetual" debt, and historians increasingly agree that several of the advocates of general funds were looking consciously beyond the reestablishment of public credit toward a funding plan that would promote the nation's post-war growth and foster a particular variety of political centralization. Properly funded, as Morris said in his report, the mass of "dead" certificates of debt (or paper promises too poorly backed to be exchanged on private markets) would rise in value, become "a sufficient circulating medium" for the country, and provide the capital for more intensive economic development.[20] Simultaneously, the obligations of the federal government would become a new "cement" of union. Looking to Congress rather than the states for their salaries, pensions, or other claims, civilian creditors, the discharged soldiers, and the officers appointed to collect federal taxes would join with merchants doing business with the national bank to "unite the several states more closely together in one general money connection." They would "give stability to government" by combining in its support.[21]

Hamilton, like Morris, had been thinking in this fashion for some years. His private correspondence and his anonymous newspaper series, "The Continentalist," had repeatedly insisted on the need to create among the nation's leadership a class of influentials tied to the federal government and capable of counterbalancing the influentials currently tied to the states. As he conceived it, an enduring and effective central government required the union of the general government's resources with those of a monied and officeholding class directly dependent on that government for the promotion of its economic interests.[22]

The implications of this thinking can be understood more clearly, in the light of recent scholarship, than was the case as recently as 1980. So can its opponents' reasons for alarm. Remembering the history of England in the decades following the Glorious Revolution of 1689, Hamilton and Morris and perhaps some other economic nationalists were thinking of a replication of Great Britain's path to national stability and greatness. They were thinking of combining certain segments of America's elite into a single interest intimately tied by fortune and ambition to the infant federal regime, much as standard histories said that the ministers of William III had once successfully created a "monied interest" loyal to the new succession and capable of counterbalancing the Tory gentry. It is not, in fact, a gross exaggeration to suggest that these American reformers hoped to use the national debt to build a single nation—or at least to forge a single national elite—where none was really present in 1783. They envisioned the emergence in America of a facsimile of those related interests—government, the military, commerce, and finance—which ordinarily united in support of British ministries and lent stability to that familiar system: interests that the English had in mind when they referred in general terms to the forces supporting the "court."[23] Imagining a national greatness predicated on an imitation of the economic and financial strengths of England, Hamilton and Morris were prepared to risk some further clamors from the army, if not to feed the agitation, for the sake of general funds. But Madison, who was preoccupied with the defense of a republican revolution—and who would never see Great Britain as a proper model for the new United States—was not. Although he did not quarrel with Morris's supporters or join with Rutledge, Lee, and Mercer, he knew what he implied when he deliberately disclaimed a desire to perpetuate the national debt.

Madison was not less continental-minded than the other advocates of general taxes. Educated at the College of New Jersey, he had been accustomed since his youth to thinking of the Revolution as a national movement, and the years in Congress had intensified these feelings.[24] Yet Madison had come to Congress deeply influenced by the thinking of the early Revolution, which itself was deeply influenced by a hundred years of strident criticisms of the eighteenth-century British system of administration and finance. By the seventh decade of the century, when trouble with the colonies began, condemnations of this system had become a standard tool for understanding an enormous range of national ills. And many of the most destructive of these evils seemed to have been born with the financial innovations introduced by the creators of the Modern Whig regime.[25]

Beginning in the middle 1690s, England had developed an unprecedented method of financing its involvement in recurring European wars. Central to this system was a firm commitment of specific revenues for steady payment of the interest on the national debt, together with a sinking fund which could be used for its retirement during peacetime. Tightly interwoven with this funding system were the Bank of England and the other chartered corporations, which purchased vast amounts of government certificates of debt in exchange for their exclusive right to certain sorts of trade.[26] Credit was the key to eighteenth-century warfare, and the new financial structure made it possible for tiny England to compete successfully with France in four great wars for empire. Thus, to Modern Whig defenders, the financial system seemed the very crux of national stability and international prestige.[27] But to the critics of its managers and builders—managers like Robert Walpole—the financial system seemed a vast, deliberate addition to the instruments of influence and corruption that were driving England rapidly to ruin.

British opposition thought was not intrinsically inimical to commerce, manufacturing, or liquid forms of wealth. Several of the greatest opposition writers were spokesmen for the city and its interests.[28] Yet eighteenth-century thinkers were as conscious of the new finance as of the growth of commerce strictly speaking, and opposition thinking started from a set of neoclassical assumptions that had been imported into English thought by Harrington and other thinkers of the Interregnum: that power follows property, that great extremes of poverty and wealth are incompatible with freedom, and that only those who live upon their own and do not owe their livelihoods to others are the masters of themselves and capable of virtuous participation in a healthy public life.[29] On all these counts, the new financial system and its creatures seemed inherently corrupt. Like parliamentary placemen, public pensioners, or representatives of rotten boroughs, dealers in the public funds or owners of the stock of chartered corporations were dependent on the treasury for their support. Their economic interests chained them to the will of an executive whose aims were always different from, and often hostile to, the will and interests of the body of the freemen. In Parliament, the tools of grasping ministers subverted legislative independence. Out of Parliament, the unearned wealth of creatures of the new finance spread habits of dishonesty, subservience, and waste to every corner of the kingdom. And while the placemen and the "monied interests" fattened on the public spoils, independent farmers, artisans, and tradesmen were impoverished by high taxation and demoralized by the example of the great. Under such conditions, the survival of the nation's ancient freedom seemed increasingly in doubt.

For colonials, it now seems clear, opposition accusations offered a compelling explanation of the crisis which impelled them into independence. Indeed, to a remarkable extent, the early revolutionaries tended to define their hopes and character as a distinctive people by contrasting their republican experiments with what the opposition writers said was wrong with eighteenth-century Britain. America *meant* virtue rather than corruption, vigor rather than decay. It meant a pleasing mediocrity of fortunes, citizens who lived upon their own resources, freemen who could fight or vote according to their own autonomous desires. It meant, in short, whatever seemed to have been lost with the appearance of the eighteenth-century system of administration and finance.[30]

Experience, of course, produced a certain disenchantment. Gouging, hoarding, and a growing weariness of war reminded everyone that even staunch republicans were human. In order to defeat the British, the militia had to be supported by a continental army. By the time the war was won, the powers of the central government were widely recognized to be unequal to its tasks. Still, the dream was stronger than the disenchantment, and the recollection of the evils of the old regime was too intense for many to be willing to abide its reconstruction, even in the most attenuated form.

By 1783, a handful of the strongest continentalists believed that national ills were so intractable that they demanded thoroughgoing reconstruction of the current federal system.[31] Madison, like the majority in Congress, was not prepared for a solution so extreme.[32] Though he was willing, unlike Lee or Mercer, to accept a centralizing change, he did not regard this as a principal objective in itself. He was willing to approve an alteration of the federal balance, but only in the sense and only to the point that he conceived it necessary for the preservation of the union; and this was not the least because he shared the critics' fears that certain federal measures might prove incompatible with what he called the "spirit" or the "principles" of a republican revolution. Thus, he carefully distinguished his desires from Hamilton's suggestion that a funding system might be used to foster national integration, to create what foes of Morris's proposals saw as a corrupting link between the government and officeholding and financial interests. Although he shared the economic nationalists' desire to reestablish public credit, Madison could not accept a program meant "to achieve political centralization by fiscal reform."[33] He did not articulate a systematic explanation of his disagreement with the other advocates of funding. This would await developments after 1789, when Hamilton's desires became the basis for a more specific program. It would require a further evolution of Madison's own views. By 1783, experience had taught him that congressional reliance on the states for revenues endangered both the character and the harmony of the Confederation. But he had yet to formulate a positive economic program of his own—a program incompatible, in many of its objects and assumptions, with the economic changes that Hamilton and Morris wanted to promote.

< II >

Commerce, Manufactures, Agriculture, and the Constitution

As the British army left New York, a new invasion was arriving. Merchants bringing British goods, on British credit, rushed to reestablish the connections broken by the war. American consumers, unsupplied for years, greeted the arriving ships with open arms and purses; the deficit in trade with Britain in the three years after the conclusion of the peace was more than £5,000,000.[34] Excluded from their most productive pre-war markets, native merchants were unable to correct this huge imbalance. Specie poured from the United States to cover the commercial obligations, but the wartime hoard was insufficient to prevent a crisis. As American importers struggled to repay their loans, pressing smaller debtors in their turn, the country entered a severe contraction.

The depth, duration, and extent of this depression have been matters for dispute, but recent findings generally suggest that it was sharper, longer, and more general than used to be believed. A downturn started in the fall of 1783 and lasted for at least two years. The impact and duration of the troubles varied greatly in the different economic regions. Suffering was slightest in the Chesapeake and greatest in New England and the lower South. Still, all along the seaboard, merchants failed, debtors were distressed, and seamen, artisans, and shipyard workers suffered unemployment. In all the north-

ern cities, there was growing pressure for protection. Everywhere, attention focused with new urgency upon the economic needs and
promises of independence.[35]

At the beginning of the war, when Congress threw American
commerce open to the world, the economic vistas opened by the end
of old restrictions had seemed as boundless as the prospects for political reform. Economic liberty would complement and be supported
by republican ideals. America's example of free trade would revolutionize the world and bring unparalleled prosperity at home. Few
other principles acquired such axiomatic status early in the Revolution. None was challenged more severely with the peace. On 2 July
1783, Orders in Council closed the British West Indies to American
shippers and barred the importation there of much American produce,
including salted meats and fish. Other British regulations barred the
vessels of one state from bringing in the products of another, prohibited the importation into Britain of whale oil, fish, and meat,
and placed prohibitive duties on American grain. Without protection
from the British, the Mediterranean trade became an easy prey for
pirates. Finally, in 1784, the Spanish masters of Louisiana prohibited
Americans from trading down the Mississippi.[36]

The newly independent states attempted to alleviate their citizens' distress. Seven issued paper money. Eight imposed retaliatory
duties on British ships or goods.[37] But states attempting separate actions of this sort were commonly defeated by the inconsistent regulations of their neighbors, paper money fell disastrously in North
Carolina and Rhode Island, and American commissioners in Europe
made almost no progress in their efforts to negotiate commercial
treaties. By the middle of the decade, in the midst of rising animosities among the several states, sentiment was moving overwhelmingly toward granting Congress power over trade. At least in northern cities, it was also moving unmistakably toward new support for
economic changes and commercial policies that early-Revolutionary
thought had generally condemned.

The early-Revolutionary doctrine of free trade had nicely managed
a profound, traditional ambivalence concerning commerce, which
was well expressed in Adam Smith's *The Wealth of Nations*, published in the very year of independence.[38] On the one hand, commerce seemed to nearly all enlightened eighteenth-century thinkers

an improving, civilizing force, the single feature which distinguished modern Europe most decisively from its medieval past and made it possible for moderns to surpass the comforts and achievements of the ancients. Carrying the bountiful productions of a modern specialization of labor, commerce softened manners, favored the refinement of the arts, promoted peaceful international relations, and supported larger populations at a higher level of material wellbeing than had any ancient civilization.[39] On these grounds, a few of its proponents carried their enthusiasm to the point of arguing that even private vices, such as selfishness and greed, promoted the collective good.[40] More commonly, however, as was true of Smith, enlightened thinkers recognized that growing commerce also had its costs. As nations moved from savagery through agriculture to the most advanced commercialization, the benefits to individuals proved dangerously unequal. Idleness and enervating luxury appeared among the rich, and independent craftsmen were replaced, as work was subdivided to its most productive point, by laborers whose narrow lives and straitened circumstances rendered them unfit as citizens or soldiers.[41] Among the British, not surprisingly, a humanistic condemnation of the growing role of commerce tended to be most pronounced among opponents of the oligarchic system of administration and finance, which favored foreign trade and manufacturing for export. Celebration of the benefits of commerce tended to be least restrained among the Modern Whig defenders of the mercantilistic system. Arguments for natural economic growth and unrestricted international exchange were something of a mean between these more extreme positions. Certainly, to Smith and to Americans alike, the "natural" policy appeared to be ideal for thriving, mostly agricultural societies that wanted the advantages of commerce, but without its social costs.[42]

Early in the Revolution, the dividing line between a civilized society and a debilitated one seemed relatively clear. Mills and shops and trading ships were not a threat to freedom. Indeed, increased domestic manufacturing of more of the necessities of life could lessen the dependence on expensive imports and promote republican simplicity and thrift, while growing native commerce would exchange America's extractive surplus for more of the amenities of life. The social fabric would be threatened only as the population grew so dense that there was no alternative to more intensive change or if the nation forced itself into a premature old age by following the mercantilistic policies of Europe.

In the post-war slump, the line began to blur. Hamilton had verged on heresy in 1782, when he denounced the "speculative" doctrine of free trade and argued that the policy of all enlightened nations was to keep the balance on their side.[43] But by the middle of the decade, nearly everyone agreed that the United States could not pursue free trade in the face of universal mercantile restrictions, and that only by united measures could the situation be improved. By then, moreover, there was growing sentiment for policies of just the sort that Hamilton had recommended in 1782, policies toward which the economic nationalists had glanced in the congressional debates of 1783.

Two changes were especially apparent. The stronger was a more insistent argument for native manufactures. Domestic manufacturing of coarser, simpler goods—from nails to homespun clothing—had long been seen as necessary to reduce dependence on expensive imports or even to produce necessities of war. Now, the advocates of manufactures added further arguments for their importance. The growth of native manufactures might provide alternative employment for the seamen, fishermen, and dockyard workers who were suffering from the collapse of foreign trade. It might enlarge the native market for the farmers whose commodities could not be shipped abroad. It might provide new objects for investors. Everywhere, as independence fostered new attention to the opportunities at home, there was a rising interest in improving roads and rivers and in building new canals. Some easterners were even thinking of the markets that would rise beyond the Alleghenies. Thus, the argument for manufactures looked increasingly beyond the current troubles toward the opportunities that their development might hold—even, it occurred, for foreign export.[44] And, with that, the case for manufactures could be fitted into a progressive, pro-developmental vision which had had few public advocates ten years before. The emergence of this pro-developmental vision was the second change encouraged by the economic troubles.

Like the argument for manufactures, uninhibited insistence on the benefits of an expanding oceanic commerce started with the post-war slump. As the depression deepened, prices fell, and specie disappeared, many revolutionaries blamed undisciplined consumers, who were running into debt and risking their autonomy by buying foreign luxuries on credit. In response, a scattering of voices blasted atavistic fears that commerce was inherently corrupting.[45] A few dispensed entirely with the old ambivalence and offered an unqualified defense of manufacturing and commerce in their highest forms, urging policies that would encourage rapid growth and arguing that even the pursuit of luxuries would further the collective good.[46]

The rise of pro-developmental sentiment was marked, and most of it supported federal reform. Indeed, until quite recently, the link between the two seemed so apparent that even those who disagreed most strongly with the Beardian interpretation of the Constitution did not doubt that constitutional reform was partly an expression of an enterprising, pro-developmental movement. Of all the forces pushing toward reform, none was stronger than the movement for a federal power over commerce. At the Federal Convention, the determination of the delegates to make America a single market—and to make that market safe for private property and private contracts— seems beyond dispute. And it has long been clear that in the contest over the adoption of the Constitution, coastal regions and the urban and commercial centers favored the reform more strongly than did the inland regions and the farmers who were less involved in raising crops for market.[47]

But visions of American development could come in a variety of forms; and recent scholarship has strongly challenged the convention which conflates these forms into a single, modernizing movement. Pro-developmental interests did support the Constitution, but it is by no means clear that all of the progressive and dynamic economic interests favored the reform.[48] And it is certain that the single most important architect of change supported it for very different reasons. For Madison, in fact, a more effective federal system was intended to *forestall* the very economic changes which a number of his allies wanted to promote.

Madison was not an early advocate of federal authority to regulate the nation's commerce. In 1781, he helped defeat a motion to amend the Articles to this effect.[49] As late as the spring of 1783, he was reluctant even to proceed with a commercial treaty with Great Britain, fearing that a pact, though eagerly desired by northern shippers, could be purchased only with concessions that would sacrifice the basic interests of the planting states.[50] Soon, however, Madison's ideas began to change. In August 1783, as he was finishing his term in Congress, he read the earl of Sheffield's *Observations on the Commerce of the American States*, which argued that Great Britain could maintain its dominant position in the trade with the United States without dismantling its restrictive navigation system.[51] By autumn, he had seen the British proclamation of July, which confined American commerce with the West Indies to British bottoms.[52] In 1784 and 1785, as the depression deepened and the states attempted futilely to counteract the British domination of their trade, Madison became increasingly committed to a federal power of retaliation.[53] Indeed, the inability of the confederated states to grapple separately with European regulations, their failure to achieve unanimous consent to federal supervision, the mutual animosities resulting from their separate legislation, and the "vicious" measures most of them pursued in order to relieve their citizens' distress were certainly the most compelling reasons for his new conclusion that nothing short of a complete reconstitution of the federal system could preserve the union and the Revolution.

To Madison, as to the great majority of revolutionary thinkers, the viability of the American experiment in popular self-governance depended on the moral fiber of the people. This, in turn, depended heavily on the conditions of their economic life, which would be prosperous or poor in close relationship to their ability to find sufficient outlets for the products of their work. Most Americans—and almost all Virginians—were agricultural producers; and as long as this was so, they either had to trade their surplus for foreign goods, stop buying foreign imports (and lapse into a primitive, subsistence mode of life), or risk their personal and even national independence by going ever deeper into debt. Lacking markets for their products, citizens could be demoralized by idleness, indebtedness, or want; and a demoralized majority could mean no end of trouble for a fragile, new republic.[54] "Most of our political evils," Madison was coming to believe—paper money, moratoriums on taxes, and laws protecting citizens from private suits for debt—"may be traced up to our commercial ones, as most of our moral may to our political."[55] Ideally, he wrote, he favored "perfect freedom" of commerce. "But before such a system will be eligible perhaps for the United States . . . all the other nations must concur." British policy especially, he pointed out, excluded American merchants from "the channels without which our trade with them must be a losing one." But how was a redress to be "extorted"? "Only by harmony in the measures of the states." Acting individually, the states could not compel the Europeans to relax their navigation laws, any more than they could "separately carry on war or separately form treaties of alliance or commerce." Thus, in 1785, when Congress proved unable to agree on a request for federal power over trade, Madison responded with his earliest admission that the crisis might require more drastic measures—even a complete replacement of the current Congress by a "medium" which might inspire more trust.[56] A few months later, when he proved unable to persuade Virginia's legislature to instruct its delegates to move again in Congress for a power to retaliate against the Europeans, he helped revive the resolution which initiated the Annapolis Convention and the course of extra-legal action leading to the Constitution.[57]

The story from this point is widely known. Responding to Virginia's call for a convention to consider better means of regulating interstate and foreign trade, delegates from Delaware, New Jersey, and Virginia, joined by one commissioner from Pennsylvania and two from New York, gathered at Annapolis early in September 1786. Though others were en route, the dozen members present waited seven days beyond the date appointed for the meeting. Then, confronted with the possibility of total failure, they unanimously agreed to turn their disappointment into yet another evidence of the necessity for bolder action, calling for a second general convention which would be empowered to consider *all* the defects of the current constitution. Spurred by Shays's Rebellion, which culminated during the succeeding months, every state except Rhode Island answered their appeal.[58]

The decision at Annapolis was once portrayed as something of a coup. A handful of committed continentalists, it was remarked, declined to wait for the arrival of the delegations from New England and recommended a procedure that could only speed the obvious decline in the authority of Congress. In fact, however, these reformers acted more in desperation than in confidence that their proposal would succeed; and careful reconstruction of the context of their resolution, which is not so well remembered as the act itself, is critical to understanding their decision. Although the fact is seldom emphasized as strongly as it should be, the Annapolis Convention met in the immediate aftermath of the most explosive sectional crisis of the Confederation years—a crisis which encompassed and exacerbated all of Madison's concerns and turned his thoughts in earnest toward the sweeping federal reforms that Hamilton had been encouraging for years.

Even at the darkest moments of the Revolutionary War, when British armies threatened Richmond and controlled two southern states, Madison had doggedly resisted motions to forgo American insistence on a right to navigate the Mississippi River if this sacrifice proved necessary to conclude a wartime pact with Spain.[59] Happily, as he conceived it, the United States did not complete a treaty of alliance with the Spanish, and Congress reinserted its insistence on a right to navigate the Mississippi in its new instructions for a postwar treaty. Still, Madison maintained an anxious watch on these negotiations. As Kentucky moved toward separation from Virginia and depression deepened in the East, the West loomed ever larger in his vision. When the masters of Louisiana closed the river to Americans in 1784, he urged both Jefferson and Lafayette to seek French intercession. The stakes, as he explained them to these friends, can help us understand the depth of his alarm when the depression influenced a majority in Congress, on the eve of the Annapolis Convention, once again to consider a surrender of this claim.

Madison had formed a special bond with Lafayette soon after learning of the closure of the river, joining the marquis for an adventure to the Iroquis negotiations on the Mohawk. If he spoke as freely to the Frenchman as he claimed, he probably repeated much of what he wrote to Jefferson before departing from Virginia. He could not believe, he said, that Spain could "be so mad as to persist" in policies that might "delay" the navigation of the Mississippi but could no more stop it, finally, "than she can stop [the current of] the river itself." The law of nations, human rights, and natural justice—all of which were "every day deriving weight from the progress of philosophy and civilization"—all suggested that the owners of a river's mouth might levy tolls on the inhabitants above, but had no right to bar their trade completely. These and other arguments, he thought, should influence France—and all of Europe—to support an open Mississippi. Certainly, they can reveal to us how indispensable the westward movement was to all of Madison's own ambitions for the nation. "By this expansion of our people," he believed, the growth of native manufactures would be long postponed, American demand for

European imports would continually increase, and the production of the agricultural commodities that the United States would trade for European manufactures would continually expand. "Reverse the case," he argued,

and suppose the use of the Mississippi denied to us, and the consequence is that many of our supernumerary hands who in the former case would [be] husbandmen on the waters of the Mississippi will on this other supposition be manufacturers on this [side] of the Atlantic; and even those who may not be discouraged from seating the vacant lands will be obliged by the want of vent for the produce of the soil and of the means of purchasing foreign manufactures, to manufacture in a great measure for themselves.[60]

Many easterners, it should be noted, feared the emigration to the West for just the reasons Madison touched on in this passage. Madison was thoroughly familiar with their thinking, deleting from the finished letter an admission that "the only sufferers" from westward emigration would be those who would "remain in the Atlantic states." The westward movement, he conceded, contributed to the depopulation of the eastern states, to the depreciation of their lands, and to their slowness in developing the naval strength "which must be their only safety in case of war."[61] Still, he never wavered in his course. When Lafayette returned to France and wrote that many of his correspondents in Virginia (probably including Washington himself) seemed far from eager for an open Mississippi, Madison replied that Lafayette was right to count him "out" of those who reasoned on "very narrow and very delusive foundations." He emphasized again that Europe had a choice between a maritime and manufacturing United States and growing commerce with its farmers. He warned again that the American affection for its major European ally could be threatened if it seemed that France supported Spain.[62]

Something very like a sense of providential purpose was involved in Madison's conception of the West. He calculated that the westward movement would increase the numbers and prosperity of all mankind. He saw the West as a frontier for all of Western Europe, as well as for the seaboard states, and he insisted that the Mississippi was the outlet "nature" had intended for its produce. It mattered, to his mind, that acquiescence in the closure of the river would be "treason" to these natural "laws."[63] It mattered, too, of course, that the ability of the Confederation to retire the public debt was universally believed to be dependent on the value of the western lands. By themselves, however, none of these considerations seems entirely to account for the intensity of Madison's commitment. A fuller explanation must incorporate the depth of his fraternal feelings for the westerners themselves, along with his conviction that beyond the mountains immigrants from all of the Atlantic states would meet and mingle and become a single people, forming new communities to which the older ones would each be bound more tightly, by "the ties of friendship, of marriage and consanguinity," than any of them were to one another. "On the branches of the Mississippi," he explained to Lafayette, there would develop not "distinct societies" but "only an expansion of the same one," not "a hostile or a foreign people" but a people who would more and more be seen as "bone of our bones, and flesh of our flesh," a people whose essential interests merited the same consideration as those of any other portion of the union.[64] A fuller explanation must return, as well, to his repeated warnings that the closure of the Mississippi could compel the West and East alike to turn from agriculture to intensive manufactures.

Madison's resistance to a turn toward manufactures may appear surprising, for there is nothing more ubiquitous in modern writings on his thought than the assertion that he was an advocate of "multiplying interests" in "an extended commercial republic."[65] Not, it seems apparent, if we are to judge by his position on the Mississippi. Here, he quite deliberately rejected much of what this language usually implies.[66] Madison agreed with the contemporary advocates of manufactures that rapid emigration to the West retarded more intensive economic change, but he supported it, in part, *precisely for this reason*. As Drew McCoy has argued, the Virginian hoped that the United States would long continue at a "middle level" of development. He dreaded the progression to the "higher" economic stage that others wanted to encourage.[67]

Madison was not an enemy of commerce—not, at least, if "commerce" meant the civilizing, comfort-raising benefits of trade, which he was doing everything within his power to encourage. But growing commerce had a second set of implications in contemporary thinking. It could also mean intensive economic change: the transformation of a largely agricultural economy into an urban, manufacturing society that could produce and even export many of the niceties and luxuries of life. And Madison, like Jefferson, responded with revulsion to the notion that the nation ought to move as rapidly as possible in this direction. Both of the Virginians knew that most Americans enjoyed a level of material prosperity that was the envy of the most "advanced" economies in Europe. Both were deeply influenced by those countervailing strands in eighteenth-century thought which warned that the transition to a manufacturing or heavily commercialized economy could render a society incapable of freedom.

It was Jefferson, of course, with his supreme ability to dress received ideas in gifted prose, who had reduced the argument to memorable phrases:

Those who labor in the earth are the chosen people of God, if ever he had a chosen people, whose breasts he has made his peculiar deposit for substantial and genuine virtue . . . Generally speaking, the proportion which the aggregate of the other classes of citizens bears in any state to that of its husbandmen is the proportion of its unsound to its healthy parts, and is a good enough barometer whereby to measure its degree of corruption. While we have land to labor then, let us never wish to see our citizens occupied at a workbench or twirling a distaff. Carpenters, masons, smiths are wanted in husbandry; but for the general operations of manufacture, let our workshops remain in Europe . . . The loss by the transportation of commodities across the Atlantic will be made up in happiness and permanence of government. The mobs of great cities add just so much to the support of pure government as sores do to the strength of the human body. It is the manners and spirit of a people which preserve a republic in vigor.[68]

Not until the early months of 1792 would Madison prepare a full equivalent to Jefferson's discussion of the proper population for republics.[69] And yet, if there is any doubt that the ideas expressed in 1792 already influenced his position of the middle eighties, this should be dispelled by the reflections he articulated in response to Jefferson's emotional denunciation of the poverty encountered on a trip through rural France.

Jefferson attributed the "wretchedness" of the majority in France to the excessive concentration of its landed property in great estates. Remarking that "the earth is given as a common stock for man" and that the combination of uncultivated lands and massive unemployment was a violation of this natural law, he recommended legislation like his own attacks on primogeniture and entail in Virginia, laws that would work gradually to level individual fortunes.[70] Madison's response probed deeper. "I have no doubt," he wrote, "that the misery of the lower classes will be found to abate wherever the government assumes a freer aspect and the laws favor a subdivision of property." Still, the greater comfort of the mass of people in the new American republics was as much a product of their smaller populations as it was of the "political advantages" received. "A certain degree of misery," he feared, might be inevitable in countries "fully peopled." For wherever this was so, a fraction of the people would suffice to raise a mighty surfeit of "subsistence," and there would still remain a greater number of inhabitants "by far" than would be necessary to produce all of the other needs and even comforts of existence. How would such societies employ their surplus people? "Hitherto," he answered, they had been divided into "manufacturers of superfluities, idle proprietors of productive funds, domestics, soldiers, merchants, mariners," and such. Yet all of these employments had been insufficient to absorb the surplus, and "most" of them would be reduced by the reforms that he and Jefferson desired. A better government would have less need for soldiers. "From a more equal partition of property must result a greater simplicity of manners, consequently a less consumption of manufactured superfluities and a less proportion of idle proprietors and domestics." There would thus be no exemption for republics from the pressures rising from the productivity of laborers and land. Republican ideals could speed developments that good republicans must fear.[71]

For the long run, Madison confessed, he had no answer to the problem of "a country fully peopled." Even North America would one day be as crowded as contemporary Europe, perhaps with all the misery that this implied. But this, he knew, was looking far into the future. For the present—and for years to come—the westward movement promised an escape. As long as it continued freely, the United States would not be forced to hurry toward intensive economic change. Its republics would be shielded from the inequalities and misery that more intensive changes would entail. Expansion to the West would multiply the agricultural societies that were the best foundations for republics. It would also, and continually, relieve the crowding that would otherwise propel the East into conditions that would threaten these foundations there.

But none of this would work without an open Mississippi. None of it would work without a freer trade between the old world and the new. Already at a middle level of development, Americans would never be content, as Madison explicitly admitted, to return to mere subsistence. If western farmers were unable to exchange their surplus for the comforts and conveniences of life, then either westerners would choose to manufacture for themselves or else potential migrants would remain in the Atlantic states, where growing population and a lack of foreign markets were already urging rapid economic change. The clock could only run one way, and in that way, in some respects, lay genuine improvements. Madison, accordingly, did not propose to turn it back, or even to arrest its progress. He wanted only to prevent its speeding uncontrollably toward social circumstances undesirable for liberal republics. This, however, he desired more desperately with every passing year. Afflicted by depression, all of the Atlantic states were being pressured into legislation he condemned. And with conditions in the East already weighing heavily on that imaginary clock, the closure of the Mississippi was a dangerous addition.

In 1786, the double weights combined to pull the country into crisis. As Madison was packing for his journey to New York and on to the Annapolis Convention, James Monroe reported that John Jay, the Confederation's secretary for foreign affairs, had asked to be relieved from his instructions to insist upon the right to navigate the Mississippi. Jay had been immersed in tedious negotiations with Diego de Gardoqui since the early summer of 1785. The Spanish envoy was prepared to recognize the borders claimed by the Confederation since the peace, especially if he could win a mutual guarantee of territorial possessions. He offered valuable concessions in the monarch's European ports, Spanish purchases of naval masts in the United States, and Spanish aid against the troublesome North African corsairs—all, however, only if the union would accept the closure of the Mississippi for a period of twenty-five or thirty years. On 29 May 1786, believing that these terms demanded only that the union should forebear a while from pressing its insistence on a claim of no great present consequence to the United States—a claim, in any case, that it was hopelessly unable to enforce—Jay initiated a request for new instructions.

The sectional collision sparked by Jay's request for new instructions is described in every standard study of the background of the Federal Convention.[72] Led by Massachusetts, whose representatives were eager to assist their struggling fishermen and shippers, seven northern states were willing to approve the change. But nine states were required to ratify a treaty; and marshalled by Virginia, all the

planting states were bitterly opposed. As Congress deadlocked on
the issue, ancient animosities between New England and the South
vented in a furious eruption. Leaders on both sides began to talk
about an end of continental union with an earnestness that they had
never shown before.

New Englanders were understandably infuriated by the stubborn
southern stand on Jay-Gardoqui. The people of the northern ports
were desperately in need of markets and employment, but the southerners, it seemed, were more concerned about protecting their investments in trans-Appalachian lands.[73] Privately, some eastern politicians wondered whether it would make more sense to form a smaller,
regional confederation homogeneous enough to have a set of common interests.[74] To southerners, of course, the selfishness seemed altogether on the other side. Indeed, Virginia's leading congressmen,
Monroe and William Grayson, both suspected that the whole attempt
to alter Jay's instructions was an eastern plot to either dominate the
union or destroy it. In 1786, the West was everywhere perceived as
an extension of the South. Western settlement was still almost exclusively on lands southwest of the Ohio, and as population moved
increasingly into this region, it was clear that the admission to the
union of new southwestern states could fundamentally affect the
federal balance.[75] While Grayson warned that westerners and southerners alike would be profoundly disaffected from the union if "they
saw their dearest interests sacrificed and given up [in order] to obtain
a trivial commercial advantage for their brethren in the east," Monroe warned Patrick Henry that the Jay-Gardoqui project was deliberately designed to damage western growth and keep "the weight of
government and population" in New England. Should they fail in
that, he thought, the men behind it would not hesitate to use that
failure to destroy the union.[76]

There is nothing to suggest that Madison accepted Grayson's or
Monroe's analysis of Jay's maneuvers. There is every evidence, however, that he fully shared their anger and alarm. Although he knew
that he would soon be leaving for New York and promised a complete
communication once he had arrived, he could not restrain the fury
and amazement prompted by Monroe's original report, delivering a
lengthy, livid blast as soon as he received it. Congress, he insisted,
had no better right to bar Virginia's western citizens from passing
down the Mississippi "than to say that her eastern citizens shall not

pass through the capes of Henry and Charles." He had forgiven Congress, he suggested, for considering this measure under the duress of war. But to adopt it now "would be a voluntary barter in time of profound peace of the *rights* of one part of the empire to the *interests* of another part. What would Massachusetts say to a proposition for ceding to Britain her right of fishery as the price of some stipulation in favor of tobacco?"[77] To Grayson and Monroe, the conflict was a struggle over sectional ascendancy within the union. To Madison, for whom the westward movement and the preservation of the union were alike essential if the Revolution was to be secured, the stakes were even higher.

Madison arrived in New York City early in the fourth week of July. He reached the seat of Congress just in time for some of the most serious deliberations of the summer. On 4 August, a grand committee on the state of the Confederation handed in the period's most sweeping recommendations for amendments to the Articles of Union.[78] On 3 August, however, Jay's address to Congress had initiated the debates that soon foreclosed congressional attention to any other subject. While he was in the city, Madison was thoroughly immersed in private talks on both of these great topics. What advice he gave, if any, is uncertain. What he learned is more apparent—and would deeply influence the decisions he would soon be called upon to make.

Madison returned to Philadelphia on 10 August, but as the argument in Congress neared a temporary resolution, Monroe kept him abreast of every new maneuver. He wanted Madison to probe the views of absent congressmen from Pennsylvania and "send them up" if they were likely to assist.[79] He wanted Madison's advice about a compromise designed to keep the Mississippi open as an avenue for western exports in exchange for an agreement that would close it to their imports for a time. Most of all, perhaps, he wanted Madison to understand that "Jay and his party are determined to pursue this business as far as possible, either as the means of throwing the western people and territory without the government of the U.S. and keeping the weight of population and government here or of dismembering the government itself for the purpose of a separate confederacy."[80]

Madison advised against the introduction of Monroe's compromise proposal.[81] The warning came too late. On 30 August, Monroe reported that a seven-state majority, from Pennsylvania north with-

out a break to Massachusetts, had swept aside the southern opposition and instructed Jay to yield the right of navigation through the
Spanish enclave if the claim would otherwise prevent conclusion of
a treaty.[82] On 3 September, he added that the foreign secretary was
determined to pursue his talks despite the dubious legality of these
instructions. Everything, he wrote, would now depend on Pennsylvania and New Jersey, where the pro-Jay forces were already working
to solidify their following or to prepare for a dismemberment of the
Confederation on the line of the Potomac if they could not keep
these states in line. Monroe expected Madison to counter these intrigues, especially among the Pennsylvanians. "If a dismemberment
takes place, that state must not be added to the eastern scale. It were
as well to use force to prevent it as to defend ourselves afterwards."[83]
Written on the eve of Madison's departure for Annapolis, the letter
reached him in that town.[84] It was a vivid, late reminder that the
union tottered on the very edge of fragmentation.

The bitter schism over Jay's negotiations with Gardoqui was by
no means all of what was on the minds of the commissioners at the
Annapolis Convention. As Hamilton would write in the fifteenth
Federalist, the country seemed to many of these men "to have reached
almost the last stage of national humiliation . . . There is scarcely
anything that can wound the pride or degrade the character of an independent nation, which we do not experience."[85] Nevertheless, to
all of these reformers, the commercial and financial troubles of the
middle eighties seemed a symbol and a centerpiece of most of these
debilities and dangers, which were soon to take the terrifying form of
Shays's Rebellion. To Hamilton, whom Isaac Kramnick has described
as "the premier state-builder in a generation of state-builders,"[86] a
more effective federal system had appeared for years to be a precondition for the economic and financial policies that could assure the
nation's greatness. And of all the nation's needs, a federal power over
trade now seemed to Madison the most essential, the more so as a
proper grant would carry with it the assurance of a steady source of
independent general taxes. Continental measures were the only ones
that might compel the Europeans to accept the sort of world that
would sustain America's new order. In their absence, ineffective separate regulations were producing rising animosities among the states
and growing talk of separate regional confederations. In their absence,
too, the inability to trade commodities for European imports drained
the country of its scarce supply of precious metals and provided "pre-

texts for the pernicious substitution of paper money, for indulgences for debtors, for postponements of taxes," and for other unjust legislation in the states. The Jay-Gardoqui crisis was another—and incalculably pernicious—consequence of these commercial evils. "An alarming proof of the predominance of temporary and partial interests over . . . just and extended maxims,"[87] it struck Madison as the final evidence that liberty and union were immediately at risk and could be rescued only by a central government which could be trusted with the powers necessary to create conditions under which the nation's revolutionary promises could be fulfilled.

Madison's and Hamilton's agreements were extensive and profound. Both of them believed that proper governments originate in the consent of the society they serve and are intended to secure the people's happiness and rights. Both maintained that private rights and popular consent could be successfully combined only by establishing effective checks and balances among distinctive governmental branches. To both, the Constitution seemed a safe and necessary remedy for pressing national ills.[88] For all of this, however, revolutionary promises were different things to different men, and underlying differences between the two collaborators were as real as their agreements.[89] Since early in the decade, Hamilton had taken Britain as an archetype of national success. Thoroughly emancipated from the early-Revolutionary condemnation of the Modern Whig regime, he saw the Constitution as an instrument that would permit a vigorous administration to construct the economic and financial props of national greatness.[90] For Madison, by contrast, the Constitution was the means by which the new world could *avoid* the European curses of professional armed forces, persistent public debts, powerful executives, and other instruments or policies that Hamilton associated with effective statehood.[91] Thus, when Patrick Henry cautioned the Virginia ratifying convention that "those nations who have gone in search of grandeur, power, and splendor have . . . been the victims of their own folly," Madison agreed that "national splendor and glory are not our [proper] objects."[92] Hamilton envisioned the creation of a "modern" state. Madison intended to perpetuate the Revolution.[93]

Still, the contest over the adoption of the Constitution was not primarily, or even very visibly, an argument concerning economic fundamentals. It did not pit capitalists against anti-capitalists, modern liberals against classical republicans, or progressive against conservative economic interests. Federalists and Antifederalists alike re-

garded private property and private enterprise as givens. Both preferred prosperity to economic hardships. There was little opposition
to the commerce powers granted by the Constitution, and little doubt
that they would be employed against the Europeans' mercantile restrictions. (In *The Federalist*, in fact, Hamilton seemed every bit as
sure as Madison that efforts to retaliate against the British would be
among the leading objects of the first administration.)[94] Many northern artisans and merchants did believe that constitutional reform
was in their economic interest. Many southern critics of the Constitution feared that it would be employed to institute a navigation system which would favor northern manufacturers and shippers at the
planting states' expense.[95] But there were other reasons for supporting (or opposing) the reform, and there were other northerners and
other southerners who thought in different patterns. Many enterprising Antifederalists from Pennsylvania or New York insisted that the
economic prospects and conditions of the country were by no means
as distressed as their opponents claimed, argued that the difficulties
could be overcome by enterprise and thrift, and feared that federal
powers over commerce would produce monopolies and other favors
for established economic interests.[96] On the other side, in the Virginia ratifying contest, Madison maintained that temporary burdens
on the planting states would be abundantly repaid by the protections
offered by the Constitution and argued that, in any case, from the
beginning and more certainly with every passing year, the agricultural majority within the federal Congress would protect the farming
interests from commercial domination.[97] For all these reasons, it is
very difficult to say to what degree the authors of *The Federalist* were
conscious of the underlying incompatibility of their objectives, which
had been articulated mostly in their private writings. For both of
them, the prime necessity of 1788 was the adoption of the Constitution. Only later would their different visions move into the forefront
of their minds and tear the Federalists apart.

≺ III ≻

From Collision to Consensus

Clashing visions of political economy were not the only reason for
the party conflict of the 1790s. They were, however, fundamental to

its origins and course, and they were tightly interwrapped with all its other aspects. On the first day of business of the first new Congress, Madison proposed discriminatory duties on the ships of nations having no commercial treaty with the union—a striking testimony to the hopes that he had had in mind throughout the course of constitutional reform.[98] Defeated in this effort, he revived it twice again, in 1790 and 1794, before a treaty with the British (which he bitterly opposed) forbade such measures for the next ten years. On both of these occasions, he was checked, in part, by Hamilton's determined opposition to a scheme that threatened to disrupt the revenues on which the funding plan depended and to end in a commercial conflict that, as he conceived it, the United States was sure to lose.[99]

Madison and Jefferson believed that the United States was capable of forcing Britain to accept a freer trade. Most American exports, as they saw it, were necessities of life: raw materials and food on which the British and their colonies in the Caribbean were vitally dependent. Most American imports, on the other hand, were "niceties" or "luxuries" that the United States could either do without or manufacture (at a shop and household level) on their own. America, accordingly, would suffer little from an economic confrontation with the British, while the British government would soon be faced with heavy pressure from the colonies and from the manufacturers and merchants who would find themselves deprived of an essential market. Independence, as the two Virginians understood it, was to be secured—for both the nation and the citizens of whom the nation was composed—by freeing trade to take its natural channels. The promise of the Revolution would be kept by opening the oceanic markets and the western lands that would preserve the mostly agricultural economy of the United States and, with it, the personal autonomy and relatively equal distribution of the nation's wealth that characterized a population overwhelmingly composed of independent farmers.[100]

Hamilton's ideas were altogether different. Influenced more by Hume and James Steuart than by Smith or eighteenth-century opposition thinkers, he believed that a developed state would win an economic confrontation with a less developed rival.[101] More than that, he reasoned from a different understanding of the current situation and the future prospects of the new republic. Though Madison and Jefferson were very much concerned with freeing oceanic commerce, their ambitions for the nation focussed on the West, where the regime of liberty could be continually revitalized as it expanded over space, and on the prospect that by force of sheer example the American experiment would revolutionize the world. Hamilton's concerns were markedly more European in their flavor. A Hobbesian or Machiavellian in his conception of the world, he faced toward the Atlantic and envisioned an arena of competing empires into which America must enter much like any other state. In time, as he conceived it, the United States could take a brilliant part in this arena. But to have this kind of future, it must first possess the economic and financial preconditions for successful competition. In the meantime, it must conscientiously avoid a confrontation with Great Britain, the nation that could threaten the United States most dangerously in war or (through investments in the new republic's economic growth) assist it most impressively toward greatness. Early in the new administration, he established close relationships with Britain's ministers to the United States and used these private channels to assure that good relations were maintained. Meanwhile, taking British institutions as a model, he set about to build a modern nation.[102]

Hamilton's design for national greatness may have been complete in its essentials when as secretary of the Treasury he answered Congress's instructions to submit a plan for managing the revolutionary debt. His first Report on Public Credit, delivered on 14 January 1790, recommended that the federal government assume responsibility for the remaining obligations of the several states, as well as those of the Confederation Congress, and fund them all at par. "If all the public creditors receive their dues from one source," Hamilton argued, "their interests will be the same. And having the same interests, they will unite in support of the fiscal arrangements of government."[103] For him, as clearly as for Robert Morris, proper management could turn the revolutionary debt into a positive advantage for the nation.

Of all the nationalists of 1783, Hamilton had had the clearest vision of a nation integrated on a British model and financially and economically equipped for national greatness. Now, he meant to put that vision into practice. Thus, the funding and assumption program was intended from the first to further major economic and political, as well as narrowly financial, goals. On one side, proper funding of the state as well as federal obligations would create a counterbalance to the state attachments that had always seemed the greatest danger to the union; it would tie the economic interests of a vital segment of America's elite to the success of national institutions.[104] On the other side, the funding program would become the principal foundation for the nation's future role in global competition. Even as it re-established the ability to borrow and attached the monied interests to the central government's success, funding would invigorate—the modern word is "monetize"—the public debt, transforming governmental obligations into liquid capital that could be multiplied again by using the certificates of debt to back the loans and notes of a new national bank. The bonds and banknotes could be used, in turn, to foster manufacturing and commerce, which would serve as pillars for the nation's economic independence. In effect, by simply pledging that specific revenues would pay the interest on its bonds, the nation could anticipate—and in the very process could assure—its future greatness. It would be capable, at once, of leaning on descendants who would benefit from its achievements and of drawing capital investments from abroad.[105]

The trouble with this magic, which did in fact accomplish much of what the secretary had in mind, was that it threatened other founders' visions of the sort of nation the United States should be. Although he planned to make the people prosperous and happy, Hamilton's concerns were focussed on the state, not upon the citizens of whom the public was composed. Although he was a champion of private liberties and economic freedom, insisting that a more complex economy would furnish "greater scope for the diversity of talents and dispositions,"[106] he was also as emancipated from traditional concerns about the civic virtue of the people as any statesman of his age. Accordingly, although he certainly believed that every group and every region would eventually enjoy the benefits of growth, he emphasized the quick development of manufacturing and commerce, which were critical to the correction of a chronic deficit of payments; and he dismissed as selfish the inevitable complaints about the temporary sectional and class inequities that would result. For Hamilton, as surely as for his opponents, the long-term goal was economic independence; but Hamilton defined this independence in a different way. He pictured a mature and largely self-sufficient economic system in which manufacturing would build a large domestic market for the farmers and the specialized activities of different economic regions would combine into a healthy whole.[107] To reach this goal, however, it was necessary in the short term to protect the revenues derived from British imports and to use these revenues in ways that favored certain men and certain regions more directly than some others. Such means were unacceptable to many; and the end itself, as it was clarified in Hamilton's succession of reports, was incompatible with Jefferson's or Madison's ideals.

Madison had favored Hamilton's appointment to his office. Hamilton had taken his position confident of Madison's support. Only gradually, as both articulated their ideas and tried to put them in the form of legislation, did the gulf between them come to seem abysmal. Madison objected from the start to the specifics of the plan for funding and assumption: to the prolongation of the debt and of the taxes necessary to support it; to the transfer of the nation's wealth from the productive to the non-productive classes; to the sheer injustice (as he saw it) of a program that did not discriminate between original and secondary holders and, in its initial version, favored certain states while risking the allegiance of some others. But Madison was overwhelmingly defeated on the issue of discrimination, and the argument about assumption was resolved by compromises that corrected the inequities with which he was especially concerned. Only as the funding plan was followed by reports suggesting the creation of a national bank (December 1790) and federal encouragement of manufactures (December 1791) did Hamilton's design assume an unmistakeable configuration. And only as he thought about the implications did Madison's uneasiness develop into thoroughgoing opposition.

From the first, the funding and assumption program stirred anxieties about corrupting links between the federal treasury and special-interest factions, together with concerns about its consequences for the distribution of the nation's wealth. The more apparent it became, however, that Hamilton was following a British model, the more opponents saw him as another Walpole: as a minister who was subverting legislative independence and endangering the social fabric by creating a corrupted following of men who lived upon the treasury at popular expense. By the fall of 1791, Madison and Jefferson believed that Hamilton intended to "administer" the new republic toward a government and a society that would, in time, subvert the revolutionary dream. At this point, they urged the revolutionary poet Philip Freneau to come to Philadelphia to start a paper that would rouse the nation to its danger. In that paper, during 1792, Madison and others built a systematic ideology of opposition.[108]

The party struggle of the middle nineties can be analyzed in a variety of ways. Like the conflicts in the old Confederation Congress, it pitted the New England states against Virginia and her neighbors. It ranged consolidationists against the principled proponents of a strict construction of the Constitution, enemies of popular disorders against the champions of popular participation in political affairs. After 1793, when revolutionary France began its twenty years of war with Britain, clashing attitudes about the European struggle intermeshed with the domestic conflict and with different judgments of the country's interests to produce the most ferocious party battle in the nation's annals. Throughout its course, however, different visions of political economy were near the center of this conflict, and conflicting economic policies contributed importantly to its directions.

Most of the American elite and most of those who lived by manufacturing or commerce had supported the adoption of the Constitution. Others had opposed it out of fear of the elite or out of a suspicion that a stronger central government would favor the commercial interests. After 1789, the apprehensions of the latter group were rapidly confirmed. The funding plan entailed enormous gains for secondary holders, mostly in the North and East, who had acquired their bonds at fractions of their value.[109] Many of these monied men were able to increase their profits once again by using their certificates to purchase bank stock. And all of this was paid for, many said, by impost duties weighing heaviest on southern planters, together with an excise tax on whiskey that provoked rebellion in Pennsylvania, Virginia, and North Carolina. It is not surprising, then, that by the end of 1792, a large majority of former Antifederalists were starting to support the Jeffersonian opposition, whose leaders were revolted by the massive transfer of the nation's wealth and thought of the perpetuation of the debt, the prolongation of the taxes necessary to finance it, and governmental privileges for special interests (typified by the creation of the bank) as policies which undermined the relative equality appropriate for a republic. These policies, Madison complained,

make it a problem whether the system of the old paper under a bad government, or of the new under a good one, be chargeable with the greater substantial injustice. The true difference seems to be that by the former the few were victims to the many; by the latter the many to the few . . . My imagination will not attempt to set bounds to the daring depravity of the times. The stock-jobbers will become the pretorian band of the government, at once its tools and its tyrants; bribed by its largesses, and overawing it by clamors and combinations.[110]

But many of the manufacturers and merchants who had hoped to
benefit from the adoption of the Constitution benefitted only indirectly, if at all, from Hamilton's financial and commercial programs.
Hamilton did very little to support the master craftsmen, journeymen, and workers who were actively involved in making manufactured goods and who had clamored for protection from the flood of
British imports. The funding system, in his thinking, was the indispensable foundation for political stability and economic growth. In
order to maintain it, he consistently opposed protective legislation
likely to disrupt the flow of (mostly British) imports. The tariff generated 90 percent of the federal revenues which paid the interest on
the debt. Accordingly, the plan for manufactures advocated bounties
rather than protective tariffs and was more concerned with the encouragement of large-scale manufacturing for export than with aid-
ing handicraft production, while Hamilton's Society for the Encouragement of Useful Manufactures was an unsuccessful scheme for
mobilizing large investors in a company that smaller manufacturers
regarded as a threat. By the middle of the decade, hundreds of mechanics, artisans, and small, aspiring tradesmen, who were often special targets for the Federalists' contempt for "mushroom politicians,"
were fleeing from the party for an opposition which encouraged popular participation and condemned monopolistic corporations.[111]

By the middle of the decade, also, many merchants were enlisting
in the Jeffersonian coalition. As France and Britain each attempted to
deny its enemy the benefits of neutral trade, Americans were peri-
odically at risk. Near the end of 1793, a secret Order in Council of
6 November resulted in the sudden seizure of 250 American vessels
engaged in trade with the French West Indies. The Federalists responded by defeating Madison's commercial resolutions and securing a negotiated resolution of the crisis. But John Jay's treaty with the
British, ratified on 24 June 1795, acquiesced in British definitions of
the rights of neutrals and provoked a naval war with France. Despite
these troubles, commerce burgeoned; but it burgeoned most dramatically with areas outside the British Empire, where, of course, the
traders suffered most from British seizures and the quasi-war with
France.[112] By 1800, many of these traders were profoundly discon-
tented with a foreign policy that left them most at risk and seemed
to render the United States commercially subservient to Britain. Merchants such as Samuel Smith of Baltimore, the Crowninshields of

Salem, James Nicholson of New York City, and John Swanwick and Stephen Girard of Philadelphia—all of whom engaged primarily in trade with Britain's foes—were staunch Republicans before the decade's end.[113]

Economic policies were not the only reason for the Federalists' defeat in 1800. They may not have been the most important. For a large proportion of the population—market farmers, shippers, and the hosts of laborers and craftsmen who were occupied in building ships, transporting goods, or packaging and finishing materials for export—the war in Europe was an economic windfall; and Hamilton may well have been correct that this prosperity would have collapsed abruptly in a confrontation with the British. After 1807, when the Jeffersonians resorted to commercial warfare, this is just what happened. Still, Hamilton's political economy *was* predicated from the first upon an intimate relationship between the federal government and well-established monied and commercial interests, which was just what many Antifederalists had feared. His policies delivered little to the handicraft producers who competed with imported manufactures. After 1793, when the financial plan encouraged a commercial policy that smacked of a subservience to Britain, it generated disaffection even in some merchants. In 1789, the Federalists had managed to appeal to an enormous range of economic interests. By 1800, much of this support had dropped away. And, naturally, as northern artisans and merchants shifted their allegiance, the Jeffersonians became a different party too.

The change within the Jeffersonians might best be seen as a beginning, not an end. Until the War of 1812, the economic policies of Jefferson's and Madison's administrations were consistent with the goals that both men had pursued since early in the 1780s: to retire the public debt; to sever the corrupting links between the federal government and special interests; to maintain the constitutional division of responsibilities between the federal government and states; and to pursue the freer trade and western growth that might perpetuate an agrarian and republican balance of property. The Jeffersonians did not dismiss their old suspicions of intensive economic change, nor did they heartily endorse the unrestrained pursuit of individual self-interest. Yet Jefferson and Madison had always thought that individual pursuits of private economic goods would harmonize most fully in a system free from governmental privileges or from "unnatural" incentives for the sorts of enterprise least suitable for a republic; and northern artisans and merchants, who were a growing portion of the party, may always have embraced the two Virginians' enmity toward privilege while never sharing fully in their reservations about rapid economic growth. After 1808, as economic warfare favored the development of native manufactures and as northern Jeffersonians and British immigrants defended economic change, the party as a party shifted even farther toward a pro-developmental stance.[114] Party leaders shifted with it.

Again, there is a danger (often run) of overemphasizing this transition. Jefferson and Madison had never stood at the agrarian extreme of opposition to the Hamiltonian system. Neither did they ever move wholeheartedly into the pro-developmental wing of Jeffersonian opinion. But changing times did foster a significant revision of the old ideas. In the crisis of 1794, many party spokesmen had objected to the building of a navy, an enormous object of expense which they believed was needed mostly to protect the carrying trade between the island colonies and Europe. Jefferson and many others long remained ambivalent about a commerce unrelated to the nation's "natural" needs and capable of dragging the United States into the European conflict. As late as 1816, Jefferson observed that

the exercise, by our own citizens, of so much commerce as may suffice to exchange our superfluities for our wants may be advantageous for the whole. But it does not follow that . . . it is the interest of the whole to become a mere city of London to carry on the business of one half of the world at the expense of eternal war with the other half . . . Our commercial dashers . . . have already cost us . . . more than their persons and all their commerce were worth.[115]

Nevertheless, both Jefferson and Madison committed their administrations to protection of this commerce, and both expressed an understanding of its role in the reduction of the chronic deficit of payments.[116] Then, as economic warfare failed—in part, as Madison conceived it, because the British found in Canada and South America alternative suppliers of the needed raw materials and food—both he and Jefferson conceded the necessity of an expanded role for native manufactures.[117]

The War of 1812 taught further lessons. Armies and supplies moved poorly on the primitive communications network in the West. Without a national bank, the federal government was a financial cripple. At the peace, the fragile manufactories that had developed during the preceding years were once again endangered. Accordingly, in 1816, Madison recommended and the Republican Congress overwhelming approved the first protective tariff, a second national bank, and an ambitious plan for internal improvements. With these measures, in effect, the Jeffersonians admitted that America could not compel the Europeans to accept the sort of world in which the new republic could escape the dangers of intensive economic change. With these measures, they accepted an essential portion of the Hamiltonian design.

Even this, it should be noted, hardly constituted a complete surrender of the party's old ideas. Republicans still hoped that education, proper leadership, and an enormous reservoir of western lands would limit or postpone the civic evils most of them still feared. They still had no intention of committing the United States to mercantilist economics, Hamiltonian finance, or other adjuncts of the European state. And yet the choice did seem to lie between increasing self-sufficiency and national dependence on external markets which could not be guaranteed. Under proper leaders, it could now be hoped, a national bank and moderate encouragement of native manufactures need not have the threatening effects that "monocrats" had once deliberately encouraged. Land had never seemed the *only* source of personal autonomy and civic virtue, and independent artisans and merchants had repeatedly displayed their fierce attachment to the nation's freedoms. Therefore, as the Federalists collapsed, the Jeffersonians appropriated part of the design that they had once perceived as inconsistent with the health of a republic, synthesizing elements from both of the competing visions that had shaped the nation's struggles. It was, of course, a fleeting moment of agreement. It would be quickly challenged by the Panic of 1819, which would reopen many of the old debates and set them near the center of a second party conflict. But, in that, which is a different story, both the Democrats and the Whigs would argue mostly over means. The fundamental ends—independence and the founding of a federal republic—now appeared secure.

The Expanding Union

PETER S. ONUF

NAPOLEON'S DECISION TO sell Louisiana to the United States in 1803 came as a stunning surprise to most American observers. Although the French had yet to take formal control of the colony from Spain according to the terms of the Treaty of San Ildefonso (1800), Napoleon's interest in extending his rule to the North American heartland was well known. Thus, when Spanish intendant Juan Ventura Morales suspended the American right of deposit at New Orleans in October 1802, angry Americans were convinced that he was acting on Napoleon's orders. The next French move, they believed, would be to close off the Mississippi completely and so gain effective control over the American frontiers. Efforts to vindicate American rights inexorably would draw the new nation into the vortex of European power politics. No one imagined that American negotiators would be able to persuade the French leader to part with New Orleans, much less with his vast new empire west of the river.

Before the Mississippi crisis was so suddenly, and unexpectedly, resolved, the future of the American union itself seemed in jeopardy. Bellicose Federalists urged a preemptive strike to prevent the French from occupying the region. President Jefferson hoped diplomatic maneuvers would defuse the crisis: given the apparently imminent collapse of the Peace of Amiens (1801) and the threat of Anglo-American rapprochement, the financially-strapped French leader might be willing to sell New Orleans or at least offer ironclad assurances of American navigation rights. But relying on the contingencies of European politics entailed high risks, for the failure to secure American rights on the river would be bound to alienate frontier settlers and foster disunionist schemes.[1]

Partisan controversy during the Mississippi crisis of 1803 revived key aspects of the great debate over the future of the union that a quarter century earlier had led to the drafting and ratification of the federal Constitution. Then too Spain's denial of American rights to trade freely on the Mississippi—and John Jay's controversial proposal to renounce those rights in exchange for commercial concessions— had exacerbated intersectional tensions. On both occasions a hostile foreign presence on the western frontier raised the spectre of disunion and threatened the new nation's future population, prosperity, and power.[2]

For the framers of the Constitution, "independence" and "union" were inextricably linked: the American states could not command the respect of old world powers, or avoid the entanglements of old world politics, until they forged a more perfect federal union. In 1803, the prospect of a powerful French colony on the Mississippi revived the founders' anxieties about the loyalty of western settlers, the durability of the union, and the future of republican government in America.

In 1803 the American negotiators Robert R. Livingston and James Monroe announced that with the acquisition of Louisiana "we separate ourselves in a great measure from the European world and its concerns, especially its wars and intrigues." "The bond of our Union will be strengthened," they promised, while "we make . . . a great stride to real and substantial independence."[3] At home, an enthusiastic chorus of publicists and orators echoed these themes. Instead of collapsing, the union would grow larger and stronger. "All obstructions are visibly removing," according to Vermonter Orasmus Merrill, as "immense fields" opened to American enterprise. The purchase thus offered "new excitements to union and independence." Under Jefferson's "mild, yet energetic administration," the United States would soon be "the wonder of the world, and more formidable to the irruptions of tyranny, than were Chinese walls to Tartar hordes."[4]

Pervasive anxieties about the survival of the union help explain the extraordinary outburst of patriotic enthusiasm unleashed by the Louisiana Purchase. Celebrations of the vast "prospects of increasing wealth, importance and national strength" opened up by the purchase testified eloquently to the almost claustrophobic sense of encirclement and entanglement that had dominated contemporary discourse.[5] With Louisiana, orators exclaimed, the Americans would surely be the happiest people on earth, while the failure to dislodge Napoleon from the Mississippi would have left them the most wretched. By dramatically illuminating—and exaggerating—these alternative futures, the Louisiana crisis forced statesmen and publicists to define what was distinctive and therefore worth cherishing about the American experiment in republican government. What did the American Revolution signify in the history of the world?

≺ I ≻

Old World and New World

While the Louisiana crisis remained unresolved, Republicans acknowledged the union's vulnerability but argued that the conquest of New Orleans would simply draw "us into the vortex of European politics and perpetual war."[6] They argued that a war of conquest would dissolve the crucial moral distinction between new world and old that played such a crucial role in American revolutionary ideology.[7] A protracted state of war, David Ramsay later explained, would undermine "our republican forms of government, and [pave] the way for the concentration of power in the hands of an hereditary monarch."[8] DeWitt Clinton agreed: when "free countries" go to war, "the power which wields the force will rise above the power that expresses the will of the people." The engorgement of federal executive power would also constitute a "severe shock" to the state governments. "Those stately pillars which support the magnificent dome of our National Government will totter under the increased weight of the superincumbent pressure."[9]

Federalists dismissed Republican scruples about the deleterious effects of warfare on republican government. Alexander Hamilton insisted that a swift strike against Louisiana was essential to the national interest. A powerful French presence on the Mississippi "threatens the early dismemberment of a large portion of our country: more immediately the safety of all the Southern States; and remotely the independence of the whole union."[10] A French colony would throw up an "insuperable mound to our future progress," novelist Charles Brockden Brown warned, spreading "the seeds of faction and rebellion" and inflicting a "fatal wound to the future population, happiness and concord of this new world."[11] The new nation was particularly vulnerable in the West. Once they had established their control over the Mississippi, explained Senator William Wells of Delaware, the French would "reduce under their influence the fairest portion of our empire."[12] According to Pennsylvanian James Ross, whose belligerent resolutions provoked controversy in the Senate and throughout the country, the westerners must "make the best bargain they can with the conqueror."[13] The survival of the union presupposed mutually beneficial, interdependent interests. What then would keep frontier settlers in the union if it was so clearly in their interest to look elsewhere?

Republicans and Federalists agreed that the new nation's safety would be jeopardized by the French occupation of Louisiana because the authority of the federal government was so weak on the southern and western frontiers. A volatile frontier was less likely to bother the French than to subvert the American union: "let the French be but once settled" along the Florida border, Wells warned the Senate, "and they will have the whole of your Southern States at their mercy. Unhappily," he need not have reminded his slaveowning colleagues, "there is an inveterate enemy in the very bosom of those States."[14] After the purchase had been completed, Congressman Samuel Purviance of North Carolina added the finishing touches to this ghastly scenario. Had the rapacious Napoleon gained control of New Orleans, "the tomahawk of the savage and the knife of the negro would confederate in the league, and there would be no interval of peace."[15]

The persistence of sectional tensions and party strife exacerbated fears about tenuous loyalties and permeable frontiers.[16] By exploiting divisions among the Americans, the two great European powers would be able to enlist American proxies in their ceaseless struggle for global supremacy. As the French extended their influence in the western settlements, Federalist Senator Gouverneur Morris predicted, the eastern states would tilt towards Britain: "the powerful influence of one nation on one great division of our country, and of another nation on the remainder, will tend to disunite us."[17]

A strong union, spokesmen for both parties agreed, was the essential condition for American independence. Yet, as Morris suggested, party divisions over how to meet the European threat made the new nation vulnerable to European interference. "We are *now* the happiest people on earth," Republican James Jackson of Georgia told the Senate, "and, *if united*, the force of Europe cannot injure us."[18] Disunion, it followed, was the greatest disaster that could befall the American people, a "Pandora's box" that no man could contemplate "without horror."[19] According to Republican publicist Gideon Granger, disunion meant "jealousies, wars, and the last dregs of human wretchedness." Disunited, America would become the image of Europe, the bloody scene of "perpetual wars" and "dreadful tragedies."[20]

The completion of the Louisiana Purchase extricated the Jeffersonians from their dilemma, and their sense of relief was palpable. Instead of a militarized frontier, Marylander Joseph Nicholson exulted, "the wilderness itself will now present an almost insurmountable barrier to any nation that may be inclined to disturb us in that quarter."[21] The purchase "secures us from the danger of ambitious neighbors and consequent wars," North Carolinia congressmen Joseph Winston told his constituents, and thus "rescues us in a great measure from European connexions and jealousies."[22] "All apprehensions on account of hostile neighbours, either civilized or savage," were miraculously dissipated.[23] The accession of Louisiana constituted "a perpetual guarantee" against further threats to national security in a "quarter, where we were weakest, and on many accounts most vulnerable." The American republics were now "insulated from the rest of the world."[24]

Maintaining the distance between new world and old—keeping Europe out of America—was crucial to the Republicans because of their belief in the distinctive character of the American federal republic. In conventional terms the United States was a weak power, perhaps no "power" at all. "We do not strike terror into the nations of Europe," editor William Duane remarked with considerable satisfaction, nor "do we affect the equilibrium of the balance of power."[25] But the union *among* the American states was growing ever stronger—because of interdependent interests, republican constitutions, and the delegation of sovereign powers to the federal government—and would soon be immune to external threats. The timely French withdrawal from the Mississippi guaranteed that the new nation would not be drawn into a great European power struggle while the union remained imperfect and therefore vulnerable. Americans "ought to be particularly thankful," Orasmus Merrill told a Vermont audience, "that the European Hydra, denominated the *Balance of Power*," could no longer "extend its baleful influence to the western shores of the Atlantic."[26]

The European system, the so-called "balance of power," was the antitype of the American federal union. "The history of that quarter of the world," wrote Kentuckian Allan B. Magruder, provided a "summary of the evils which America has escaped." "Europe is cut up into innumerable independent sovereignties," he explained, "some powerful and others feeble." Given their conflicting interests and disproportionate capabilities, "a balance of power" to prevent strong states from overwhelming the weak was "an object of absolute necessity." Tragically, however, the alliances that supposedly secured the balance instead simply spread the ravages of war, and "all Europe is sometimes then in a blaze at once." The "Gothic policy" of the old world thus guaranteed neither the integrity of states nor the liberties of their subjects.

Once the threat of a powerful and potentially hostile European power on the Mississippi had passed, American horizons again seemed boundless. Echoing the enthusiastic hopes of the Revolutionary generation, Americans could once more hold forth on the westward course of empire. "Never since the commencement of the annals of mankind," exulted "Sylvestris," "did any civilized nation possess so advantageous a position. Never was there a people who had their happiness so much in their own power."[27]

David Ramsay, historian of the Revolution, best captured the revived sense of American potency and purpose. If the destinies of new world and old were still linked, the terms were reversed: America would not become Europe; Europe would become America.

The happiness enjoyed under our new system, in this new world, has a direct tendency to regenerate the governments of the old, without the horrors and bloodshed of revolutions . . . The rulers of the eastern continent, who hold a great part of their fellow-men in bondage, and who are perpetually involving them in wars, will relax in their oppressions . . . know[ing], that our now extended limits afford an ample asylum for the poor of all nations.[28]

Ramsay and other celebrants of the Louisiana Purchase fashioned a continental vision of the American future out of the anxieties and forebodings of the Louisiana crisis. Here was a "new and luminous example of pacific and open negociation," the definitive answer to Federalist war-mongering.[29] Instead of being drawn into European wars, the union of American states would be a model and inspiration for the war-torn "eastern continent." Only by following the American example and establishing "one general republic to concentre in a point the whole will of society" would it be possible to "destroy those clashing interests and dissimilarities which beget wars."[30]

Americans projected their hopes onto the vast screen of the new western empire. Dangers to the republic from "clashing interests," slave revolts, or Indian reprisals were magically transcended—or at least displaced. Instead of imploding and collapsing, the union would expand across the continent. "What is to hinder our extension on the same liberal principles of equal rights," Ramsay asked, "till we have increased to twenty-seven, thirty-seven, or any other number of states that will conveniently embrace in one happy union, the whole country from the Atlantic to the Pacific ocean, and from the lakes of Canada to the Gulf of Mexico?"[31] Enthusiastic orators promised that a "more natural, more intimate and more permanent Union" would result from the accession of Louisiana.[32] "A new spring would be given" to American "enterprise," and the expanding realm of free trade would foster reciprocal and interdependent interests.[33] The ugly divisions glimpsed in the crisis debates would be suppressed. Finally secured in possession of the Mississippi, "the eastern and western people feel a strong reciprocal interest in the prosperity of each other, and a new bond of union is extended between the extremities of the continent."[34] Through the alchemy of free trade and interdependent interests, unity would emerge from diversity and the great promise of the American Revolution would be redeemed.

≺ II ≻

Crisis of the Union

Revolutionary Americans had sought to create a new world order. By avoiding "entangling alliances" and negotiating treaties on the basis of commercial reciprocity and free trade, the new nation would in-augurate a new diplomatic system that would extend peace and pros-perity throughout the world. With the destruction of Britain's colo-nial monopoly, the European states would compete freely for the American trade. As a result, preacher and educator Ezra Stiles told the Connecticut legislature in 1783, "all the European powers will henceforth, from national and commercial interests, naturally be-come an united and combined guaranty, for the free navigation of the

Atlantick." This new "commercial system," including the "maritime nations, on both sides" of the ocean, would "establish the *benevolence* as well as the *opulence* of nations, and advance the progress of Society to civil perfection."[35]

Stiles's paean to the new nation's future "Glory and Honour" constituted a virtual catalogue of liberal assumptions about political and economic development. The belief that commercial relations would promote rational and civilized behavior among sovereign states as well as among individuals was a staple of Enlightenment thought.[36] The sovereign's "savage" impulses toward conquest were curbed by calculations of long-term self-interest deriving from mutually beneficial exchanges. As these advantages became increasingly conspicuous, a "generous and truly liberal system of national connexion" was bound to emerge. Nations would combine, as in the case of the Armed Neutrality of 1780, to "disarm even war itself of hostilities against trade."

Stiles's vision of global peace and prosperity was complemented by, and ultimately depended on, optimistic projections of the future development of the new nation's vast hinterland. "It is probable that within a century from our independence the sun will shine on fifty million of inhabitants in the *United States*," he wrote—in what was to prove a remarkably accurate prediction. High rates of reproduction would be enhanced by the influx of useful immigrants attracted by the freedom and opportunity of republican America.[37]

As soon as independence was secured in 1783, friends of the Revolution began to draw flattering contrasts between the "savage state" of European politics and the rapid progress of "political civilization" in the new world. "The establishment of so many free states upon the purest principles of civil and religious liberty," wrote the Englishman Thomas Day, "affords the most consolatory prospects to every friend of humanity." As long as the Americans remained true to their republican principles, predicted Thomas Pownall, former royal governor of Massachusetts, "they will become a Nation *to whom all Nations will come*; a Power whom all the Powers of Europe will court to Civil and Commercial Alliances; a People to whom the Remnants of all ruined Peoples will fly . . . for refuge." Liberty was the best guarantee of prosperity: "*the riches of the sea will pour in upon them; the wealth of Nations must flow in upon them*; and they must be a populous and Rich People."[38]

With a vast continent to settle, the Americans would soon constitute a "world within themselves."[39] But the American world would
not be divided among contentious and hostile nations. Instead, wrote
Stiles, the "fermentation and communion of nations will doubtless
produce something very new, singular, and glorious."[40] The absence
of artificial social and political distinctions would foster the "natural" tendency of a free people to pursue harmonious, interdependent
interests. Wars of conquest would be superfluous, even when the
new empire of liberty challenged the remaining outposts of European
rule in America. The irresistible attractions of the American union
would inspire wars of liberation in Canada and other neighboring
colonies. Britain "may form new settlements," Thomas Paine asserted in 1782 when the Paris peacemakers were still deliberating
about the new nation's boundaries, "but they will be for us; they will
become part of the United States of America; and that against all her
contrivances to prevent it, or without any endeavours of ours to promote it."[41]

Yet Paine's bold vision betrayed the same anxieties about the future of American republicanism that were to characterize the Louisiana crisis of 1803. With a rapidly growing, land-hungry population,
the new nation's need for new lands was apparently boundless.[42] But
what if hostile imperial powers did not melt away? What if, to reverse
Paine's prediction, American settlers proved less loyal than their foreign counterparts?

The furor over John Jay's offer to forgo the navigation of the Mississippi in 1786 demonstrated the volatility of westerners' loyalties.
If the United States did not secure their economic interests, a Kentuckian warned, "our allegiance will be thrown off, and some other
power applied to."[43] Lord Sheffield, the leading British opponent of
commercial rapprochement with the former colonies, was convinced
that the interests of western settlers would drive them out of the
union. He turned Paine on his head: the rage for emigration "to the
interior parts of the continent" would retard the economic development of the depopulated eastern states while gaining Britain new
customers, if not subjects. In the event, "the authority of the Congress, can never be maintained over those distant and boundless regions, and her nominal subjects will speedily imitate and multiply
the examples of independence."[44]

American policy-makers recognized the need to coordinate frontier settlement with the establishment of effective national authority and the extension of transportation links and market relations. They also recognized that claims to "independence" in the new settlements jeopardized the integrity and independence of the union as a whole. Skeptical about the prospects for a natural harmony of interests, congressmen concluded that a durable union depended on the deliberate exercise of power to preserve the new nation's jurisdiction and property rights on the frontiers. The break with Britain was not, by itself, a sufficient guarantee of popular loyalty and enlightenment.

The great western hinterland offered the Revolutionaries the opportunity to create and sustain a new world order. At the same time, however, the success of the American experiment was most problematic in scattered frontier settlements where economic and political connections to the union were most tenuous. Paradoxically, the same vast spaces that provided scope for a new and enlightened "empire of liberty"—the antithesis of the old world's bloody balance of power—created conditions under which American republicans were most likely to behave like Europeans, or even to fall under the influence of European powers. In the boundless West, American republicanism would self-destruct. The precocious pursuit of self-interest and the premature assumption of the prerogatives of self-government threatened to unleash centrifugal forces that would destroy the union and Europeanize American politics.[45]

Western policy-makers recognized that the future of the union, and therefore of republican government in America, depended on its capacity to expand. In theory, as the English radical Richard Price told his American friends, there was no limit to the potential size of the union: "peace *may be* maintained between any number of confederated states." But the increasingly evident "imbecility" of the Confederation Congress, discordant state policies, and rising sectional suspicions suggested that the imperfect union of states under the Articles was much more likely to collapse than expand. Because "no provision is made for enforcing the decisions of Congress," Price warned, the new world would be condemned to recapitulate the unhappy experience of the old.[46]

Proponents of national constitutional reform exploited such predictions by European commentators, hostile and friendly alike. These

writers gave short shrift to the idea that the states' republican constitutions were a sufficient guarantee of harmonious union: "as you
have our vices," so "you will soon have our politics."[47] Dean Josiah
Tucker was convinced that "clashing interests" would seize control
of local governments, whatever their form, thus fostering an endless
cycle of "internal Disputes and Quarrels." With "no *Center of Union*
among them," it was the Americans' "fate" to be "A DISUNITED
PEOPLE . . . divided and subdivided into little Commonwealths, or
Principalities."[48]

Advocates of the new federal Constitution agreed that the chief
threat to the union was the dangerous and delusive idea of state sovereignty.[49] The exaggerated pretensions of the states subverted Congress's authority and left the new nation vulnerable to the depredations of foreign powers. As a result, explained Thomas Dawes in
the Massachusetts ratifying convention, we may be "independent of
each other, but we are slaves to Europe."[50] Yet even if these continuing external threats could be discounted, the disintegration of the
union promised to unleash the "dogs of war."[51] Without a strong
confederation, conflicts of interest among the states would soon escalate into war. "Every state would be a little nation," John Jay
warned his fellow New Yorkers; it would be "jealous of its neighbors,
and anxious to strengthen itself by foreign alliances, against its former friends."[52]

During the ratification controversy, Federalists argued that a
"more perfect union" was the only possible means of preventing the
imminent Europeanization of American politics. In republics the
rights of citizens were secured against their own governments, but
republics enjoyed no "natural" security against each other. "If we
should be disunited," wrote Alexander Hamilton, "we should be in a
short course of time, in the predicament of the continental powers of
Europe—our liberties would be a prey to the means of defending ourselves against the ambition and jealousy of each other."[53] Far from
being the universal solution to all political problems, republicanism—the Revolution's most precious legacy—was jeopardized by
the failure to establish a durable federal alliance among the states.

The interests of sovereign states were necessarily opposed, wherever the "sovereignty" was located. Chronic interstate conflict,
which was most notable over boundaries and trade, would weaken
the union and prepare the way for future wars. Most ominously, in

the absence of an effective federal union discrepancies in state size and power offered irresistible opportunities for the better-situated states to advance their interests at the expense of their weaker neighbors. Each American state must be able to defend itself, warned "Cato," lest it "expire under the sword of its foes, or sink into submission."[54] The dilemma, as Hamilton noted, was that such preparations jeopardized the new nation's independence of old world entanglements as well as republican liberty: threatened with extinction, small states might well look abroad for support.

Constitutional reformers insisted that there was no inherent distinction between the international behavior of republics and that of other polities. The first law of nature was self-preservation: for states this meant that all other considerations, including respect for the rights of other states as well as for the private rights of their own citizens, must give way when their survival was at stake.[55] America's republican revolution therefore was not in itself an adequate solution to the classic problem of international politics, of how to establish a stable, peaceful, and lawful regime among independent states.

The challenge was to construct a new world order on non-European principles. This meant, as the polemicist Joel Barlow later put it, that the American states would have to be "federalized"—subordinated to a perpetual, constitutional alliance—in order to preserve their republican character.[56] If, instead, the union collapsed and the states took on the attributes of independent sovereignties, the distinction between governors and governed that the Revolutionaries had sought to abolish would reemerge with a vengeance. Republican liberty would be the inevitable casualty.

Constitutional reformers argued that *republicanism* and *federalism* represented solutions to two logically distinct sets of problems, the organization of power and guarantee of rights *within* and *among* states, respectively. Insisting on this distinction, they dismissed the Antifederalists' contention that voters had to choose between the preservation of republican liberty in the sovereign states and the creation of a powerful, necessarily despotic national government. To the contrary, resolution of the crisis of the union was the essential condition for the survival of republican government in the states.

The crucial conceptual breakthrough in the development of American federalism was the recognition that "state sovereignty"—the monopolization of political power by the state governments—jeopardized republican government as well as the survival of the union. A strong federal alliance would protect the American republics from foreign interference and, no less importantly, from each other, thus securing their republican constitutions from the distorting effects of chronic conflict. Exercising their republican rights, Americans would move and trade freely across state boundaries, thereby strengthening the bonds of union. The vastly extended national domain would sustain the optimal conditions for private enterprise, republican government, and harmonious union among the states.

≺ III ≻

The Federal Republic

Before the ratification of the federal Constitution, nationalist reformers warned that the states' republican constitutions were jeopardized by the deterioration of the union under the Articles of Confederation. The new constitution would preserve the union; the "guarantee clause" in Article 4 specifically promised that the national government would uphold republicanism in the states, securing them against the establishment of monarchical regimes. Prospective new states would have to draft acceptably republican constitutions, approved by Congress, prior to their admission.[57]

The founders' solution to the crisis of the union was predicated on the interdependence of state and national governments. If a durable union depended on the republican character of its member states, they were equally convinced that the states as republics depended on a durable union. The American states were constitutionally compatible; defined in terms of their constitutional limitations, republican state governments were also compatible with an energetic national government.

Under the new dispensation, the states would continue to be the primary locus for republican self-government. But federal supremacy was supposed to guarantee that the corporate interests of state governments would always be subordinate to the rights of the sovereign people and that the states would not arbitrarily interfere with the free movement of trade and people across state boundaries. The American founders thus "established a union of interests and of states," Joel Barlow wrote. It was this double character of the union that he believed would secure a perpetually peaceful and ever-expanding new world order.[58]

The state governments could not invoke transcendent corporate interests, distinct from the people's, and the federal compact deprived them of coercive sanctions for asserting and enforcing their claims against other states. This circumscribed conception of statehood presupposed a mobile citizenry, not bound by irrevocable, unconditional obligations to particular governments. And if American citizens could move freely from state to state without compromising their rights, there was nothing sacred about any particular state's territorial pretensions. State boundaries were subject to change, just as the limits of the union itself could be extended to embrace new states.

Given the territorial monopoly of the original thirteen states, settlers in distant frontier regions could only hope to enjoy the benefits of reasonably convenient republican self-government if state boundaries could be redrawn. During the Confederation years, when the protracted struggle over conflicting state claims in the West immobilized Congress, the prospects of a jurisdictional settlement that would facilitate the expansion of the union remained extremely doubtful. But the completion of state land cessions, the establishment of a more energetic central government, and the consolidation of federal authority on the western frontiers transformed the new nation's prospects. Remarkably, British writer "Calm Observer" noted in 1794, "the American republics, in various instances, have even parted with territory and people close adjoining, allowing them to become independent states; and have then admitted these offsets to a proportional weight in the general confederacy."[59]

The expansion of the union began with the admission of Vermont in 1791 and Kentucky in 1792, districts formerly claimed by New York and Virginia respectively. In 1796, after a brief period under federal control, the western region of what had been North Carolina, a hotbed of separatist activity, joined the union as Tennessee.

The promise of statehood was also extended to settlers in the vast trans-Ohio hinterland ceded by New York (1782), Virginia (1784), Massachusetts (1785), and Connecticut (1786). After the resistance of the Ohio Indians was smashed at the Battle of Fallen Timbers in 1794, the rapid settlement of the southern part of the territory led to the creation of Ohio (1803), Indiana (1816), and Illinois (1818) under terms set forth in the Northwest Ordinance of 1787. In the south-

west, the Georgia cession of 1802, long delayed and complicated by
the Yazoo land scandal, confirmed federal authority in the Mississippi Territory (organized in 1798). Congress governed the region under a modified version of the Northwest Ordinance, eliminating the
ban on slavery in Article 6. Once American control was secured and
cotton began yielding fabulous profits, settlers poured into the region
and Congress created two more new states, Mississippi (1817) and
Alabama (1818). Louisianans, promised "incorporation in the union"
by Article 7 of the French cession treaty (1803), had gained statehood
in 1812.[60]

For Jeffersonian Republicans, the expansion of the union vindi-
cated the republican principle that states and their governments existed to serve the people, not the other way around. The union was
dynamic and expansive precisely because it was voluntary and un-
coerced. Settlers in frontier regions were drawn into the union by self-
interest, not fear of conquest. As one eastern writer explained, the
"prosperity and increasing importance" of the western settlements
depended on "the emigration of our youth and the introduction of
our capital."[61] Westerners did not need to be reminded, James Jackson of Georgia told the Senate, "that their independence, their rights,
their properties, depend . . . on union with their sister States."[62]

Contrary to Antifederalist predictions, the states' renunciation of
sovereignty and submission to a perpetual federal alliance did not
necessarily lead to the creation of an over-mighty, despotic central
government. The very existence of the federal government, *not* the
actual exercise of its potentially extensive powers, secured the states
against "war and foreign interference." As long as peace persisted,
the government of the union would remain a "weak fabric," its latent force only being called forth in the unlikely event of a serious
challenge to American independence.[63] "The spirit of their Government," a British admirer concluded, "encourages Commerce, and
discourages War."[64]

Because the states disclaimed the conventional prerogatives of
sovereignties, pretexts for serious conflict among them evaporated,
and the new federal government could govern with a light hand.
Under the new dispensation, proponents of ratification promised,
the delegation of sovereign powers to the central government would
eliminate the occasions for their use. And the most significant result
of this concentration of power, Vermonter Nathaniel Chipman in-

sisted, was to *strengthen* the states. "Solely an impression of the
efficiency of the federal government," he wrote in 1793, instantly
added "a degree of energy to the states governments, and put an end
to those factions and turbulent commotions"—such as Shays's Rebellion—"which made some of them tremble for their political existence."[65] The mere "impression" of the union's potential power
reenforced state authority and disarmed domestic dissidents. As a
result, Calm Observer agreed, the "separate states in general exhibit
prosperous and respectable governments."[66]

Strength or "energy," defined in conventional—coercive—terms,
was the *sine qua non* of union.[67] At the same time, however, the concentration of powers in the federal government would free the states
from the compulsions of force in their relations with each other.
Thus, even as Hamilton and his nationalist allies sought to give the
United States the tone and substance of a credible, if necessarily secondary, world "power," Republicans celebrated a new world order—
a union of states—from which power had been banished. Union,
they insisted, was grounded in voluntary limitations on power, not
in the fear of superior force: when the states embraced the new federal compact, they agreed to disarm themselves and submit to the
strictly limited authority of a general government within which they
continued to play an important role. The happy result was that the
states, confined to their proper sphere, gained new energy, while the
union of states grew larger, stronger, and ever more prosperous.

What "union" meant and entailed was still controversial. Was a
powerful national government set *over* the states essential to the survival of the union? Or was the strength of the union a function of
harmonious relations *among* states? For Jeffersonians like Joel Barlow, the answer was clear. Invoking federalism against the Federalists, Barlow argued that the continuing expansion of the union depended on securing the jurisdiction of the states against the central
government. "The interest we shall have in inducing new nations to
join our union, instead of being our rivals, is a strong argument," he
wrote in 1799, "for preserving at least as much power to our individual states as they now possess, and for not suffering any encroachment from the federal government." Particularly since "their feder-
alizing with us" was a matter of "choice," the terms of union had to
be favorable. The principle was equally applicable to settlements organized under federal auspices, but eminently capable of withdraw-

ing from the union whenever the central government's authority "becomes oppressive" or even "appears to be so." "We should not forget," Barlow concluded, "that the United States are to be held together by interest, not by force."[68]

The Jeffersonian idea of union implied unconventional conceptions of national power and security. Paradoxically, limitations on governmental power in America constituted the new nation's ultimate strength. Republican governments that guaranteed property rights and civil liberties—and taxed themselves lightly—fostered the growing wealth and population that would enable the United States to meet any crisis. Within "twenty years," Virginian George Nicholas promised the Senate in 1803, the growth of population would guarantee American security: "our united force will be such, that no nation at the distance of three thousand miles will be able to contend with us for any object in our neighborhood."[69] Three years later Tennessee congressman John Rhea also asked for "twenty years more" of "honorable peace," after which "the prosperity, happiness and power of the United States of America will remain fixed on a basis not to be moved by the united efforts of nations."[70]

The creation of new states guaranteed the "zeal and patriotic spirit" of a rapidly growing frontier population.[71] Westerners cherished the union because they participated in the federal government on an equal basis while enjoying the benefits of republican self-government in their states. This is why Napoleon's efforts to detach the western states would prove unavailing, Kentuckian John Breckinridge assured the Senate in 1803. His people would never willingly exchange "that exalted, that enviable rank of one of the independent States of United America" for the "degraded, dependent condition of a colonial department of a foreign nation."[72] By the same logic, the failure to extend republican institutions into new territories would jeopardize the union. "The standard of separation, would ere long be erected," warned David Ramsay in 1804, if the vast region acquired from France "was to continue to be governed as a dependency on the United States."[73]

Responsiveness to the political aspirations of frontier communities made good sense to Republican leaders anxious to build the party's strength. An expansionist policy also promised to promote private enterprise while establishing the foundations of national wealth and power. The prosperity and patriotism of a growing population would secure the new nation's sovereignty and independence against all threats. For the most enthusiastic expansionists, the rapid addition of new self-governing republics to the American federal union offered a still more edifying spectacle. "Upon this liberal plan of government," Allan Bowie Magruder exclaimed, "the whole world might be regulated in peace and harmony."[74]

Because of the principle of state equality—and the absence of a dominant metropolitan core—new states could join the federal alliance without fear of being overwhelmed by powerful neighbors.[75] The security offered to small and weak states by the federal constitution was a major incentive for frontier communities to seek membership in the union, "the ark of their safety."[76] According to Allan Bowie Magruder, "a remote state of the Union is placed upon the same ground of equality with the one bordering immediately on the seat of empire. In proportion to its strength it has the same weight in the national councils of the Federal Union. Each state has a government of its own, independent of the whole confederate power of the nation." Outside of the union, each state would be "too weak" and "too small" to secure "its own immediate sovereignty"; in union, "all the qualities of strength, wisdom and virtue, move in one consolidated mass to the accomplishment of every great measure upon which our happiness depends."[77] "Our present form of government is the very best on earth for a great country," Ramsay agreed. "It combines the freedom and convenience of the smallest, with the strength and protection of the largest."[78]

Rhetorical assaults on the balance of power, the "political phantom" that so conspicuously failed to secure the "liberties" of European states, underscored the Americans' belief in the superiority of their federal system.[79] Rather than contracting and imploding, the union extended the benefits of peace and security by adding new states. American federalism thus represented the antithesis of the European system, where peaceful states were routinely "subjugated and divided between their more warlike neighbours."[80]

The behavior of the American republics under the Confederation had convinced the framers of the federal constitution that disunion would unleash such forces of state particularism. They did not expect an American balance of power to secure the sovereignty and independence of their separate republics. Instead, they imagined for a disunited America a future very much like Europe's during the French

Revolutionary and Napoleonic Wars. Unchecked by federal obligations, fully sovereign states would exploit their relative advantages:
the resulting *imbalance* of power would provoke a cycle of wars that
would only cease when "the arm of tyranny" finally "impose[d] upon
us a system of despotism."[81] The wisdom of the framers in constructing a true federal union thus was thrown into sharp relief by Napoleon's quest for "universal monarchy." "The lamentable picture of
European wretchedness would serve as a mirror to explain and prog-
nosticate" America's "future destiny" if their own union collapsed.[82]

≺ IV ≻

New States

The survival of the American union did not depend on a balance of
power or spontaneous harmony of interests among the states, or on
their natural affinity as self-governing republics. To the contrary,
the framers of the Constitution insisted, the balance, harmony, and
peaceful coexistence of the American republics depended on union.
Congress's policy for governing and distributing the new national domain, set forth in a series of ordinances from 1784 to 1787, anticipated and illuminated this conceptual reversal. The interests of the
union would be secured *before* frontier settlers assumed the prerogatives of self-government and formed new states. Like James Madison
and his fellow constitutional reformers, the authors of congressional
western policy saw republicanism as a *problem*, not a panacea: Revolutionary Americans were not naturally virtuous, nor could they always be expected to know where their true interests lay.[83]

Western policy-makers sought to guarantee the orderly expansion
of the union by circumscribing the scope of political activity on the
frontiers. Under the terms of the Northwest Ordinance, Congress
governed frontier regions through appointed officials during the for-
mative stages of settlement; settlers only began to govern themselves
as their communities gained political maturity and became more
fully integrated into the national economy. Only at this point, congressmen concluded, was it safe to assume that the pursuit of private
interests was compatible with the public good.

The new system for governing the national domain reflected
Congress's determination to suppress unauthorized separatist move-

ments and uphold the jurisdictional pretensions and property rights of the original states. Even Vermont, the only self-proclaimed new state to survive the Revolutionary era, had to negotiate a settlement with New York before its admission.[84] Meanwhile, policy-makers hoped, direct congressional rule in the Northwest Territory would eliminate the conditions that had fostered rudimentary experiments in self-government and statehood applications.

During the waning years of the Confederation, frontier settlers proclaimed their "independence" of the old states in order to defend their settlements from external threats, drive Indians off coveted lands, secure their own (often dubious) titles, and enjoy the benefits of law and order. Separatists had few illusions about the "sovereignty" of their new states. When they called for "the protecting arm of the federal government" and asked Congress to exercise its "paternal guardianship," petitioners acknowledged their political weakness and immaturity.[85] Anxious easterners naturally saw portents of incipient anarchy in these new state movements, but for westerners the inability or unwillingness of the old states to govern effectively created the anarchic conditions that justified appeals to Congress. Self-government was the last resort of vulnerable frontier settlements, or perhaps a threat to wield against unsympathetic and unresponsive easterners, but rarely an end in itself.

The territorial system relieved frontier people of the need to provide for their own security and thus eliminated a primary impulse for political activity. Settlers in the national domain did not at first resist or resent Congress's avowedly "colonial" rule: a strong federal presence was precisely what new state proponents had long demanded. While their numbers remained small and scattered, settlers were content to forgo the benefits—and costs—of self-government and to defer their claims to a place in the union. When territorial citizens did become politically active, the scope of their activity was much more narrowly defined than it had been for separatists during the Revolutionary era. The move toward self-government was inextricably linked to full incorporation in the federal polity.[86] In 1796 Albert Gallatin of Pennsylvania reassured his fellow congressmen that the initiative taken by residents of the Southwest Territory in constituting themselves as the new state of Tennessee did not jeopardize the union. The new state could not sustain its independence— or look elsewhere for alliance or support—if Congress failed to seat its representatives. Gallatin's "opinion was that if they were a State, they were at the same time a member of the Union; that they could not exist as a State without being one of the United States."[87]

As Gallatin's paradoxical formulation made clear, statehood in America entailed the *renunciation* of sovereignty and independence. Freed from direct congressional rule, new states submitted to the authority of a federal union in which they now participated as equal members. By directing political energies *toward* membership in the union, congressional western policy succeeded in countering the centrifugal tendencies so feared by antiexpansionists. Congress asserted its "temporary" authority as long as there were legitimate grounds to question the political competence and loyalties of frontier settlers; relaxation of the territorial regime was then linked to the development of interdependent interests binding new settlements to the union and to a demonstrated capacity for responsible, truly "republican" self-government.

Political development in the national domain thus worked toward integration in the federal polity, not toward assertions of state sovereignty. The federal union offered extraordinary advantages to weak, lightly populated frontier states: membership meant protection against powerful neighbors, disproportionate influence in Congress through an equal vote in the Senate, and the opportunity to bargain for federal largesse while sharing generally in the further exploitation of the national domain. Statehood advocates were inspired as much by awareness of these advantages as by a determination to throw off the "galling yoke" of colonial subordination and enjoy the benefits of local self-government.[88]

The pace of political development in the territories was roughly synchronized with population growth. According to the schedule established by the Northwest Ordinance and extended, with modifications, across the national domain, territorial citizens would be entitled to elect a general assembly "so soon as there shall be five thousand free male inhabitants of full age"; once the free population reached 60,000, they "shall be at liberty to form a permanent constitution" and claim admission to the union. Congress could choose to admit a new state before that threshold had been crossed, however, if persuaded that the people of the territory were willing and able to assume the responsibilities of self-government.[89]

Partisan conflict in the Northwest Territory (Ohio) centered on the question of timing: when would a new state or states join the union, within what boundaries, and on what terms?[90] Republican statehood advocates sought to accelerate development through the final stage of territorial rule; Federalist opponents urged caution. According to an antistatehood meeting at Marietta in 1801, the organization of a new state should be delayed as long as the territory remained a "mixed mass of people, scattered over an immense wilderness, with scarcely a connecting principle."[91] Republicans retorted that the people of the territory were more than ready to govern themselves, and so "be re-instated into those rights and privileges which they formerly [before leaving their home states] enjoyed as citizens."[92] Significantly, however, statehood advocates did not challenge the Mariettans' developmental premise: instead, they argued, the very success of their efforts to mobilize opposition to Governor Arthur St. Clair's territorial regime demonstrated Ohio's readiness to participate in the affairs of the union.

Ohioans on both sides of the statehood issue accepted the principle that self-government was only feasible and safe after the territory had achieved a sufficient degree of political maturity. The ultimate test of the new state's political competence was the drafting of an acceptable state constitution and the negotiation of favorable terms of admission. Statehood advocates first had to persuade Congress to authorize an Ohio state constitutional convention. Congress's enabling act also included a set of propositions to the convention concerning federal property interests in the new state: in exchange for exempting federal lands from state taxes for five years after their sale, Congress offered to dedicate 5 percent of land sales revenue to roadbuilding, reserve one section in each township for schools, and grant Ohio control over the Scioto Salt Springs. These conditions were duly incorporated in the new state constitution. Once the constitution was reviewed and approved, Ohio's representative and senators could take their seats in Congress.[93]

Federalist resistance to the Ohio statehood movement illuminated the distinctive character of early American federalism. The same series of acts that constituted new states as political societies also bound them to the federal union. Federalist criticisms were premised on a *distinction* between these constitutional and federal functions: because of Congress's interference, the Ohio constitution was not the authentically self-constitutive act of a distinct political society; similarly, Congress had exploited the Republicans' eagerness for statehood to negotiate "an advantageous *treaty* . . . before we might demand admission."[94] Federalists thus urged the constitutional convention to declare the new state's independence of Congress, and the "degrading," "derogatory," "burthensome," and "oppressive" terms set forth in the enabling act.[95] In doing so, they made claims for the new state's independence and sovereignty *outside* the union. The Ohio Federalists' argument against immediate statehood in Ohio therefore was an argument against the possibility of union itself as the Jeffersonians defined it.[96]

The vast majority of delegates recognized, however, that Congress would not tolerate new state sovereignty pretensions that endangered federal property rights as well as the integrity of the union. If the Northwest Ordinance guaranteed statehood to the people of the Territory, it also stipulated that the new states "shall never interfere with the primary disposal of the Soil by the United States" and that they "shall forever remain a part of this Confederacy." Most crucially, statehood proponents understood that their political existence was a function of their membership in the union. To remain outside the union meant continuing submission to Congress's territorial government.

The admission of Ohio in 1803 set the pattern for the creation of new states in the national domain. Continuing federal control over the public lands after statehood secured the federal balance on the expanding periphery of the American union. With the completion of the Louisiana Purchase in the same year, the political and diplomatic options of would-be new states were still further circumscribed. Only by submitting to federal authority would the people of a territory complete their "apprenticeship to liberty" and, "by degrees . . . be raised to the enjoyment and practice of independence." Membership in the union made territories into states, perfecting the claims of imperfect, embryonic political communities. The genius of the system was encapsulated in Samuel Mitchill's definition of "territory; a word signifying a peculiar and mingled idea of a country and inhabitants in the inchoate or initial condition of a republic."[97]

The union was capable of expansion because new states were simultaneously "republicanized" and "federalized." Just as the original American states depended on the federal alliance to guarantee their survival as self-governing republics, frontier people linked their political aspirations to membership in the union. They became self-governing polities under approved republican constitutions at precisely the moment they were incorporated into the union and so renounced the conventional prerogatives of independent sovereignties. But the sacrifice of sovereign powers was more apparent than real. As defenders of the new federal Constitution asserted during the ratification controversy, pretensions to sovereignty exaggerated the states' distinctive corporate interests, fostered interstate conflict, and thus jeopardized the future of republican government in America. Union was the best guarantee of the rights legitimately retained by the states and therefore of their true interests.

The Republicans' conception of an expanding union did not command universal assent. Federalists naturally resisted further accessions to the administration party; easterners feared the shifting balance of power within the union. "Instead of these new States being annexed to us," Congressman Laban Wheaton of Massachusetts warned when Louisiana sought admission in 1811, "we shall be annexed to them, lose our independence, and become altogether subject to their control."[98] Federalists repeatedly questioned the motives of westerners as well as the ability of the federal system to absorb new members. Warnings that "a Southern and Western interest" would exploit its dominant power *in* the union thus alternated with predictions of the union's imminent demise.[99]

More dispassionate and disinterested observers endorsed the Federalist argument against an expanding union. A traveller in the Ohio Valley was convinced (in 1805) "that before many years the people of that great tract of country would separate themselves from the Atlantic States and establish an independent empire."[100] Englishman Gould Francis Lecky agreed. "A great federal republic, in extent equal to all Europe can never hold together," Lecky wrote in 1808. "The local interests of the states and the ambition of powerful individuals, will sow the seeds of division among them."[101] "The farther a state government is removed from the national centre," a Kentucky writer explained, "the less it hears, and sees, and feels, of that government, and the less interest it takes in its concerns."[102]

The common premise of all these predictions was that the states were proto-sovereignties, eager to pull away from the union in pursuit of their "local interest." Invoking conventional misgivings about the over-extended republic, Lecky identified America with Europe. Similarly, Federalist antiexpansionists invoked a European conception of the balance of power when they argued that the addition of new states would destroy "the political equipoise" of the union.[103] This obsession with balance was in turn predicated on an expansive conception of state sovereignty usually associated with the Jeffersonians, and apparently at odds with their centralizing tenets. But Federalists were "consolidationists" precisely because they continued to think in conventional, European terms: they feared the latent power of states and their inevitable tendency to promote their interests at each other's expense.[104] Robert Goodloe Harper set forth the guiding principles of the Federalist "system" in an 1801 letter to his constituents. A powerful central government that could protect the states against external threats was also essential for "maintaining our peace at home, by checking the ambition and repressing the passions of the several states, and balancing their forces so as to prevent the greater from overpowering and subduing the lesser."[105]

Jeffersonians insisted that they were the true "federalists," and not simply to gain rhetorical advantage over their partisan opponents. They were celebrating the triumph and progress of their conception of the union, which was now being realized in practice. Republicans welcomed the admission of new states, convinced that the expansion of the union—and the preservation of a balance of power among the states—did *not* depend on the corresponding expansion of federal power. Jeffersonian optimism reflected both a canny instinct for partisan advantage and a characteristically vaulting idealism. Most importantly, however, the Republican administrations that promoted expansion recognized that the tendency of new state political development was centripetal, not centrifugal.

The American states were not fully developed, "terminal" political communities. The state governments did not command the exclusive loyalties of a mobile, enterprising people who expected local governments to serve most of their immediate needs and who were equally prepared to look beyond the states toward the federal government when opportunities arose. This facility with manipulating multiple levels of government was particularly apparent in the public land states. Before admission, these states gained the political competence to govern themselves; they also gained practical experience in exploiting the federal government. Membership in the union enabled new state politicians to build on that experience. For them—and for their constituents—federalism was not simply or primarily a means of guaranteeing peace and stability in an expanding state system. It was above all a complex and rewarding structure of political and economic opportunity within which individual citizens could pursue their own advantage.

Federal politics offered extraordinary rewards and opportunities to ambitious politicians in the new states. New state representatives played a key role in distributing federal patronage in their home states; they could also serve the interests of their constituents by procuring federal charters, subsidies, and land grants. Far from seeking independence from the union, new state leaders were determined to exploit the federal connection for all it was worth. A strong federal military presence would not only secure vulnerable frontier regions but also pump up the local economy. The most important factor working to "federalize" new state politics, however, was the federal government's continuing ownership, administration, and sale of public lands. The route to individual success for most new state citizens was through the federal land office.[106]

≺ V ≻

The Expanding Union

The land office "federalized" private interest and initiative and helped foster an embryonic national citizenship in frontier regions prior to the attainment of statehood. As proprietor of the public domain, the federal government acted as trustee both for the present members of the union with their interest in land sales revenue and for future private purchasers. According to the terms of their admission, the new states pledged not to interfere in this primary relationship. Recognition of the federal government's continuing jurisdiction over the federal lands thus constituted a fundamental limitation on new state sovereignty, reenforcing the guarantes of limited, republican government in federal and state constitutions.

Expansion would not endanger the union by "multiplying the parts of the Machine" because new states did not have distinctive, potentially conflicting corporate interests.[107] The limited scope of state authority in turn reflected the primacy of constitutionally-guaranteed private rights. The American states were peaceful and harmonious not simply because they were republics, but also because they lacked the usual incentives—or the capacity—to make war on each other. By instituting a complex federal system, the American founders thus created the conditions for the "natural" harmony of interests optimistic Revolutionaries such as Thomas Paine believed would emerge spontaneously with the destruction of the old

order. Wars were inconceivable *not* because the states were republics, but rather because state governments did not represent their
citizens exclusively or authoritatively or promote distinct, fully articulated corporate interests. The American states were not "sovereignties" in the conventional, European sense of the word. Sovereignty instead remained with the people who delegated limited powers to various governments: the federal government would exercise
exclusive jurisdiction over interstate and foreign relations.

"Among the several states of America," Joel Barlow wrote in
1792, shortly after the new federal regime was inaugurated, "the governments are all equal in their force, and the people are all equal in
their rights." It was this equality, the foundation principle of the
larger, inclusive federal republic, which guaranteed a harmonious
union. "Were it possible for one state to conquer another state, without any expence of money, or of time, or of blood—neither of the
states, nor an individual in either of them, would be richer or poorer
for the event." Jurisdictional controversies that would have driven
European states into belligerent frenzies had already been decided
"in a few days, by amicable arbitration." The outcome of such disputes was, after all, "a matter of total indifference" to citizens whose
rights were secure "whether the territory in which they live were
called New-York or Massachusetts."[108] For this reason, the state governments might eschew violent sanctions in their contests with one
another. Just as republican state constitutions secured individual
rights, the federal constitution secured the rights of states; these
states—self-governing republics guaranteed against internal subversion and external assault—were much more comprehensively, substantially, and enduringly "equal" than the states of Europe could
ever hope to be.

Federal ownership of the public domain facilitated Congress's manipulation of the boundaries of embryonic new states before they
joined the union. Jurisdictional changes had no impact on private
titles derived from the federal government, and the corporate interests of future new states remained largely hypothetical. Once the
new states were formed, boundaries were definitively established in
order to preclude future controversy. At the same time, however,
these boundaries were permeable: citizens could move freely from
one state to another without jeopardizing their private rights.

Congressmen recognized that the careful management and distribution of federal property was crucial to the orderly expansion of the

union. The rapid distribution of federal lands or their cession to the new state governments could subvert the bonds of common interest while promoting a retrograde conception of state sovereignty dangerous to the peace of the union. The end of federal land ownership and the resulting diminution of federal influence had to be coordinated with the emergence of a class of orderly and enterprising citizens who identified statehood and self-government with the opportunity to participate in national government. The interests and loyalties of such citizens tended to be cosmopolitan. Originally deriving their private property rights from the federal land office, settlers in the national domain could only lay claim to political rights through the interposition of Congress and "the benign influences of the federal constitution."[109] Implicit in this development was a conception of a transcendent national citizenship: settlers could only exercise their full rights as American citizens *through* state governments recognized by Congress. But it was, as Joel Barlow suggested, "a matter of total indifference" which particular state this might be.[110]

In the American federal system, the rights of republican citizens were inviolable while the claims of states on their citizens were contingent and derivative. This was the relationship between governors and governed that liberal theorists believed would be secured under republican constitutions and that in turn would guarantee peace among states. American federalists recognized, however, that the protection of private rights and the limitation of republican states to their proper sphere depended on the existence of a "more perfect"— and, when necessary, a coercive—federal union. But it did not follow that states were mere ciphers under the new dispensation, Antifederalist warnings about the dangers of a despotic, consolidated regime notwithstanding. What is most remarkable about early American federalism is the extent of political decentralization. Emerging from their dependent, colonial condition, new states joined a union in which member states enjoyed extraordinary autonomy and exercised most governmental functions.

≺ VI ≻

Union and Disunion

In late 1791 James Madison contributed an essay on "Consolidation" to the *National Gazette* that described the kind of union he and his fellow founders hoped to perpetuate. "If a consolidation of the states into one government be an event so justly to be avoided," he wrote, "it is not less to be desired . . . that a consolidation should prevail in their interests and affections." The liberties of individuals and the rights of states were inextricably linked. But the states would only remain in their proper sphere if they were not drawn into conflict with each other by "local prejudices and mistaken rivalships." Madison thus concluded that it was the duty of all Americans "to consolidate the affairs of the states into one harmonious interest."[111]

For Madison and his Republican colleagues, the federal union provided the means of extending a liberal, republican regime across the American continent. The federal republic was a model world order that guaranteed that states would serve the interests of citizens, not citizens—or, more accurately, subjects—the interests of states. Antebellum Americans believed that their union protected them from the arbitrary exactions of all governments. Certainly frontier settlers cherished responsible local self-government and resented the continuing interference of territorial governments once law and order and private rights were well established. At the same time, however, they wanted unfettered access to national markets as well as the opportunity to move freely from state to state in pursuit of their private interests. These were the decisive advantages of the federal republic, a system that guaranteed the legitimate claims of its member states while eliminating artificial barriers to private interest and threats to private rights.

The rapid spread of settlement led to the formation of new states and the growing prosperity of the entire union, evidently fulfilling the most expansive visions of the Revolutionary generation. By constructing an alternative to the balance of power and its never-ending cycle of horrors, the framers of the Constitution had saved the American republics from a European fate. By 1815 the new nation had triumphantly surmounted what contemporaries saw as the clearest and most present danger to the union, foreign manipulation of the "clashing jurisdictions and jarring interests" of widely dispersed and doubtfully loyal frontier settlements.[112] American independence was secured by the union of old states and new states, East and West.

But Madison's "one harmonious interest," the necessary condition for an enduring union of free republics, could not be sustained. Suspicious of westerners' motives, Federalist antiexpansionists exaggerated the threat of new frontier states to the effectiveness of the federal regime and to the balance of power between East and West.[113] Increasingly, however, debate over western policy also prompted northeastern Federalists to express their growing concern about the distinct and potentially hostile interests of free and slave states. Of course, the original federal compact itself was predicated on a tenuous bundle of intersectional compromises and understandings that the growth of the union threatened to subvert. From the very beginning, therefore, the addition of new states was consciously linked to the preservation of balance between North and South.

The balance theme figured prominently in Federalist opposition to Louisiana statehood. With the admission of the new state, thundered Josiah Quincy, "the bonds of this Union are virtually dissolved." "The proportion of the political weight of each sovereign State," he insisted, "depends upon the number of the States which have a voice under the compact." Arguing from an old world conception of competing sovereignties, Quincy warned that if Congress should "throw the weight of Louisiana into the scale," the balance that the original states sought to sustain would be "destroyed." Quincy's famous speech can be read and dismissed, as it was by Republicans and even some Federalists, as a reactionary tirade. Quincy invoked outmoded European categories, "balance," "sovereignty," and "compact," to a set of problems, the addition of new states and the union of East and West, that the American federal system had already definitively resolved.[114]

Yet the implications of Quincy's speech would prove prophetic, for union finally depended on sustaining an intersectional balance and accommodating the fundamentally conflicting interests that his use of the language of state sovereignty so obviously assumed. Dismissing Federalist predictions and threats, optimistic Jeffersonians insisted that the threat of disunion had been forever banished: America would never be like Europe. But, of course, when the union did collapse, the "dogs of war" were finally unleashed and the powers of the new world reenacted the bloody struggle for dominance that had devastated the old world in the wake of the French Revolution.

The institution of slavery, some Jeffersonians were willing to concede, was "the darkest stain upon the American character, the eternal reproach of our boasted republicanism." But it would not, as they so fondly hoped, abolish itself in the fullness of time.[115] The durability and profitability of slavery instead fostered a growing awareness of distinctive corporate interests that was incompatible with the kind of union Republican orators celebrated at the time of the Louisiana Purchase. The conflict over slavery obstructed the free movement of people, property, and ideas; republican state constitutions could not guarantee the comity and compatibility that the Revolutionary generation assumed would preserve the federal republic.[116] Increasingly conscious that there was no true "union of interests," Jefferson's heirs would invoke states' rights ideas to protect their "peculiar institution" against "foreign" interference and influence, and ultimately to justify the destruction of the union itself.

In the first great surge of national expansion, Jeffersonian Republicans conceived and constructed an ever-expanding "empire of liberty."[117] Yet the same vast spaces that offered such scope to the American experiment also precipitated the final crisis of the union. The union may have been preserved and redeemed in the war between the states, but it was no more Jefferson's union than it was Calhoun's. Americans might still imagine themselves a peculiarly free and fortunate people, destined to lead the way toward progress and civilization. But, as a solution to the perennial problems of international politics, the federal union was a tragic failure. Americans could no longer offer their new world order as a model to the world.

Land and Liberty on the Post-Revolutionary Frontier

ALAN TAYLOR

T HE RELATIONSHIP BETWEEN frontier land and freedom in the early republic raises two questions: whose land, whose freedom? For Frederick Jackson Turner, writing at the close of the last century, the answers were easy because the story was simple. It began before the advent of white men with a rich but unpossessed land. Indians were a negligible presence in Turner's conception: a part of the wilderness backdrop, obstacles, like the wolves and bears, for the white settlers to conquer. The struggle to master the frontier remade Europeans into Americans: materialistic, individualistic, libertarian, and resourceful. Because no rulers could command such people, only a democracy, dependent on their support, could govern them. In sum, the occupation of a wilderness made America uniquely democratic. By obtaining the land, America's white settlers became free.[1]

Subsequent historians have challenged virtually every tenet of Turner's story. First, the land was not empty, but belonged to diverse Indian peoples with complex cultures and a tenacious determination to defend their homelands. Second, the values of Americans owed at least as much to their European cultural heritage as to their encounter with the wilderness. Determined to Europeanize the landscape to make it more familiar and profitable, the settlers changed the land more than it changed them. Third, countries without a legacy of frontier expansion have become democracies (for example, Western Europe) while some countries with such a legacy have been slow to do so (South Africa).[2]

This chapter attempts a more complicated story involving the struggle of three parties: natives, white settlers, and their national elite. Each group had a differing concept of freedom, each of which depended on possession of western land. Indians needed to retain their homelands to preserve their cultural and political freedom from white domination. Settlers sought the land to realize the ideal of household independence: freedom from direct economic control by a master. But white leaders insisted that Americans' freedom also depended on establishing an effective national republic, and they worried that the settlers' pursuit of independence in the West would undermine the construction of a viable national government. As warfare between settlers and Indians grew more widespread and uncontrolled during the later 1780s, the nation's leaders feared that the western settlers had become *too independent*, free not only from the dominion of private masters, but also from any public authority. To gain control over their own settlers, the nation's leaders had to take effective command of the war with the Indians. The critical moment in this tripartite competition for the land came during the 1780s and 1790s, in the immediate wake of the Revolutionary War, which established an independent American republic. After almost two centuries of slow, hard fighting to win the relatively infertile lands along the Atlantic seabord, the invading Americans surmounted the Appalachian mountains and entered the fabulously fertile and extensive interior drained by the Mississippi-Ohio-Missouri river system. Whoever won this extraordinary prize would realize their particular dream of freedom. In the 1780s and 1790s it was far from certain that the American republic would prevail, for circumstances on the frontier were fluid and uncertain. Retelling the story in this way preserves Turner's major insight: that the struggle for frontier land was critical to the particular shape of the American republic.[3]

≺ I ≻

Independence

White families went west driven by a compelling desire to minimize the control exercised over them by others. In 1796 an unusually sympathetic Congressman, Jeremiah Crabb of Maryland, told his colleagues, "Lands had become so high in most of the old States, that the hope of acquiring possession of the soil, and becoming independent, was lost; and the rents of lands had risen so high, that the tenants sorely felt the oppression of their landlords, and their last hope of releasement from this oppression was by emigration to this new country, which they looked on as common property. And will this House," he exclaimed, "blast this last remaining, this flattering hope, this natural and laudable desire of independence?"[4]

"Independence" was the key word at the heart of the republican persuasion of revolutionary America. The ideal of household independence did not mean complete self-sufficiency, for no one could live without some measure of neighborly assistance and market exchange. Rather, an independent man was free from economic dependence on a superior, free from domination by a landlord or employer or slave-master. The independent man was a master artisan or farmer who possessed enough productive property to employ himself and his family: a workshop or a modest farm.[5]

Poor men needed to acquire property to become truly free. In 1796 Congressman James Holland of North Carolina supported an amendment to sell the federal lands in relatively small lots of 160 acres to

accommodate, as much as possible, the poorer class of their citizens—a class of men who were the most valuable in a community, because it was upon them that they could chiefly rely in cases of emergency, for defence, and, therefore, they ought to be accommodated and made happy; to be put into a situation in which they might exercise their own will, which they would not be at liberty to do if they were obliged to become tenants to others. To live in that dependent way had a tendency to vitiate and debase their minds, instead of making them free, enlightened, and independent. By this amendment, this class of citizens would be enabled to become possessed of real property—a situation incident to freedom and desired by all.

Contrary to his more authoritarian colleagues, Holland felt that abetting the settlers' drive for independence was the only way to integrate frontier settlements into the nation.[6]

Not only was independence good for the aspiring poor, it was essential for the survival of the republic. Consequently, popular governance could not last unless property was widely distributed to maximize the number of independent households. Jeremiah Crabb explained, "The dividing of land into small lots would put it into the possession of real proprietors, and have a tendency to make good Republicans instead of servile tenants dependent upon tyrannical landlords."[7]

Settlers insisted that labor created property and that property made republican citizenship possible. Therefore, in a true republic, those who labored should own and benefit from the property they made: the crops, livestock, and buildings. Conversely, those who did not labor should not benefit from the property made by others. By the standards of their labor theory of value and their insistence on independence as the foundation of a true republic, American society in the East was less republican than the society of the frontier. In 1777 young Joseph Doddridge left western Pennsylvania to attend school in Maryland, where he found a land of dependence and mastery.

When I arrived there, I was in a new world. I had left the backwoods behind me. I had exchanged its rough manners and poor living for the buildings, plenty and polish of civilized life. Everything I saw and heard confounded me. I learnt, after some time, that there were rich and poor masters, slaves and convicts, and I discovered that the poor servants and convicts were under entire subordination to their masters. I saw that the slaves and convicts lived in filthy hovels called kitchens, and that they were poor, ragged and dirty, and kept at hard labor; while their masters and families lived in large houses, were well clothed and fed and did as they pleased . . . I thought it could be no otherwise than unjust, that some should have so little and others so much, and that one should work so hard and others perform no labor.

He added, "From this afflicting state of society, I returned to the backwoods, a republican . . . that is, with an utter detestation of an arbitrary power of one man over another." Doddridge hoped that the frontier would not replicate the systematic inequality, the perversion of independence, that he detected in much of the East.[8]

Historians of the ideological origins of the American Revolution tend to dwell on the conservative and exclusive implications of the stress on independence as a prerequisite for citizenship. To be sure, propertied men could cite the concept to deny political rights to the propertyless. But the ideal of independence could also be invoked by the poor to demand property as their *right*, to insist that the true republic would favor their claims to property when in conflict with those of the wealthy.[9]

An equality of condition in landholding neither existed nor seemed essential to most of the champions of an independent citizenry. In addition to vast domains of wilderness lands claimed by land speculators, there was a broad spectrum of improved landholdings, from plantations in excess of 1000 acres to small, marginal farms of 50 acres or less. But most white families did possess their own farms. By applying their labor to land they owned, they could

direct their own work and enjoy its fruits. Moreover, while the prevailing degree of inequality in the distribution of land was generally
accepted, there was a general antipathy toward the development of
greater inequality. It seemed that land was sufficiently well divided
to sustain popular government; but it also seemed that any further
concentration of landholding in the hands of the few would undermine the republic.[10]

Independence was so widespread among white men (despite the
inequality of landholdings) because of the relative abundance of land
available on the frontier margins of their society. Given the explosive
natural increase of white families, only sustained expansion westward maintained economic independence as the norm in eighteenth-
century America. Access to extensive frontier lands enabled white
Americans to marry relatively early (four to five years younger than
in Europe) and to bear additional children. Consequently, during the
eighteenth century, the American population grew about three percent annually, a doubling by natural increase every twenty-five years.
This explosive population growth fed a rapid expansion into the for-
ests of the interior. By 1776 emigrants from the Atlantic seaboard
had breached the Appalachian mountains to begin settlements in
Kentucky and Tennessee and along the upper Ohio in western Virginia and Pennsylvania. Most rural families responded to population
pressure by emigrating to the frontier because their heritage taught
them to dread the alternative: remaining at home and accepting dependency as wage laborers. Demographic conditions and the cultural
ideal of independence combined to drive the Americans deeper into
the continent to transform ever larger tracts of the forest into a landscape dedicated to agriculture. Independence was, simultaneously,
both the engine and the product of that expansion.[11]

Because almost every white family sought a farm and because the
white population doubled every twenty-five years, each new generation doubled the demand for land, putting increased pressure on the
beleaguered Indians of the interior. It was a bitter irony that, to obtain the property for independence, settlers violently dispossessed
the native tribes, destroying the independence of the Indians whom
they found in the supposed wilderness. One people's freedom came
at another's expense. Convinced of the superiority of their race, the
citizens of the early Republic felt that only white men warranted

independence. Whites saw Indians as inevitable, and probably deserving, victims of progress, by which they meant the American
conquest of the continent and its adaptation to their economic
purposes.[12]

≺ II ≻

Settlers

From 1774 into the 1790s, the endemic warfare between Indians and
settlers sustained a zone of pervasive danger and violence on the margins of the republic from the Gulf of Mexico to Lake Erie. "It is well
known," a Kentuckian remarked in 1786, that "every part of America
that has hitherto been settled, has flowed in blood for a long time."
This zone of horse-theft, cabin burnings, murders and revenge, of
raid and counter-raid, deterred emigration west by the sort of people
preferred as settlers by the nation's leaders: prosperous and orderly
folk committed to commercial agriculture and respectful of authority, people able and willing to purchase titles to their land and to pay
their taxes. Instead, the fertile but dangerous Ohio valley attracted
poorer and hardier families with few prospects of obtaining a substantial farm in the East. For example, in June 1789 in Pennsylvania
the surveyor Samuel Preston met "a large company of people moving
their horses and cattle," bound for the Ohio valley. Preston recognized them; he had been at their houses in the Delaware valley during the previous autumn. "They are a poor, indolent set of people,
and moving off because the country was like to be improved shows a
wild disposition to fly from society like the bears and wolves. They
were nearly out of provision, and I spared them a loaf of bread."[13]

   During the 1780s and early 1790s there were a few men of superior capital, connections, and ambitions sprinkled among the new
settlements, but by all contemporary accounts the overwhelming
majority of the frontier folk were poor. In 1785 settlers who had
crossed the Ohio to become squatters on Federal lands explained that
they came from

the Lowest Ebb of Poverty; the greatest part of us having no property in
Lands: our stocks Reduced almost to nothing: our Case seemed Desperate.
But viewing as it Appeared to us an Advantage Offering of Vacant Lands
which with the Alarming Nesesitys we were under Joined with the future

Prospect of Bettering our Circumstances: invited us to Enter on those Lands . . . Pregnant with hopes of Future Happiness we sat Content in the Enjoyment of our Scanty morsel.[14]

These settlers went west, driven as much by the inequities and inequalities of American society, as by the pressure of population growth. Most of Ohio's first settlers came from Pennsylvania and Kentucky, where complex land laws favored the claims of large-scale land speculators, who demanded rents or purchase payments from those who settled within their domains. During the 1780s those unable or unwilling to pay looked enviously across the Ohio to the rich lands held by the Indians and claimed by the federal government. In Ohio they sought the independence as freeholders that had eluded them in Kentucky and Pennsylvania. In a petition to Congress, 431 settlers explained that they needed lands in Ohio because Virginia's rule over Kentucky had blighted their hopes of free land there, "By which means almost the whole of the lands in the Country aforesaid are Engrossed into the hands of a few Interested men, the greater part of which live at ease in the internal parts of Virginia." The petitioners dreaded that they would "become Slaves to those Engrossers of Lands and to the Court of Virginia." By slavery, they meant dependence.[15]

Tax lists confirm that the emigrants had reason to dread dependence if they remained in Kentucky or Pennsylvania. In western Pennsylvania during the mid-1780s, over a third of the adult men did not own land, and the top decile of taxpayers owned a quarter of the real estate. Over the next decade, the proportion of landless men in western Pennsylvania increased to 41 percent while the concentration of land in the hands of the top decile increased to 35 percent. For poor white families, the prospects were even worse in Kentucky. In 1800 about 45 percent of Kentucky's adult white men owned no land, because title to so much of the state had been monopolized by the wealthiest: the 107 men who owned in excess of 10,000 acres represented only 1 percent of the taxpayers, but they owned one-third of all the taxable land in Kentucky. If liberty required independence, a surprising number of white men on the near frontier were not truly free by the standards of their day.[16]

Hard experience had taught the first settlers of the Ohio valley that to be landless was to be powerless and subject to the will of the powerful. Consequently, liberty meant the right to claim, use, develop, and, perhaps, ultimately sell, wilderness land. In 1785 the Ohio squatters petitioned Congress "to grant us Liberty: to Rest where we are and to grant us the Preference to our Actual Settlements." They insisted that titles should be created, not by state legislatures or the national congress, but by the families who first went on the land, marked blazes on boundary trees with a tomahawk, built a cabin, planted and reaped a crop of corn, and defended their homestead from Indian attack. Because settlers could not live in complete isolation, but needed one another for mutual defense and assistance in clearing land, building cabins, and harvesting crops, a local consensus tended to limit what any one family could claim. Joseph Doddridge, who grew up on the western Pennsylvania frontier, explained that most settlers regarded 400 acres, "as the allotment of divine providence for one family, and believed that any attempt to get more would be sinful." But there were other settlers, especially in Kentucky, who were possession speculators; they laid multiple claims for sale to later comers. According to Doddridge, the minority who made larger land grabs were "held in detestation." Because land brought freedom, the man who engrossed too much land denied others of their opportunity for the liberty of independence. Of course, even 400 acres was a generous grab that permitted the claimant to sell some land to latecomers as well as provide for his own family.[17]

Determined to cling to their new and tenuous independence, the settlers were, at best, ambivalent about legal and political authority. Settlers were willing to attach themselves to a larger polity or movement only to the degree that it served their local interests and tangible aspirations for land and for revenge on their enemies. They called for, and welcomed, state and federal assistance in fighting the Indians. But, in their experience, state and federal governments had been ineffective at defending the frontiers; indeed governments seemed much more effective at levying taxes and enacting laws and establishing courts to help wealthy and well-connected creditors and land speculators engross the money and lands of the common folk. One settler manifesto exhorted, "Petitions, Remonstrances, and decent Representations, have been disregarded. Your Bills of credit, your vacant Lands, your produce, and your all, has been iniquitously extorted from you, and disposed of, not for an equal and general good; but to depress you, and aggrandise a few."[18]

As government ignored their interests, settlers did their best to ignore the dictates of any authority located beyond their particular county. By crossing the Ohio to settle along the northwest shore, squatters defied a proclamation issued by Congress reserving that territory for those who would buy title from the United States. To justify their emigration, a defiant squatter spokesman named John Emerson issued a manifesto on 12 March 1785. "I do certify that all mankind, agreeable to every constitution formed in America, have an undoubted right to pass into every vacant country, and there to form their constitution, and that . . . Congress is not empowered to forbid them, neither is Congress empowered . . . to make any sale of the uninhabited lands to pay the public debts."[19]

To reassert control of the Ohio valley, Congress repeatedly sent federal troops to oust the squatters by burning down their settlements. On several occasions in 1785 armed bodies of squatters stared down patrols of federal troops. But it was more common for the squatters to bend to superior force, watch their cabins burn, remove back across the river to the Virginia-Kentucky shore, only to return and rebuild as soon as the soldiers moved on. After all, it took only a few days and almost no money for a squatter family to erect a log cabin. As federal troops put the torch to his cabin, Joseph Ross assured their officer, "Neither did he care from whom they came, for he was determined to hold possession, and if I destroyed his house he would build six more within a week." And the squatters kept coming "by forties and fifties" during the 1780s. Seeking the fertile bottom lands, they spread out for three hundred miles along the northwest shore of the Ohio and as far as thirty miles up the tributaries. In April 1785 one frustrated officer estimated that about 900 families of squatters had located on the northwest shore as far down as the mouth of the Scioto. To federal officials eager to restore peace with the Indians and to sell the lands to men who could and would pay, the frontier pursuit of independence had gone too far.[20]

The Indians saw that their freedom was imperilled by the independence of frontier whites, whom they called "Big Knives." In 1787 Half King and Captain Pipes, two Delaware chiefs, rebuked the American Congress for its inability to control the frontiersmen, who devastated the game, seized land, and murdered even peaceable Indians.

It seems very strange to us that such large bodys of men should slip off from you. It makes us doubt that you are carrying on a Confederacy with these people that strike us every now and then . . . We take it very hard that you allow us to be cut to pieces by your people. Call your people together and tell them not to do so any more.

In 1792 the Indians of the Ohio Valley complained, "If the United States could govern them, then the peace could stand sure. But the Big knifes are independent, and if we have peace with them, they would make slaves of us."[21]

≺ III ≻

Indians

Contrary to myth, the American frontier was not the boundary with an unsettled land, free for the taking. Instead, the frontier was where the expanding American population encountered native tribes who meant to preserve their homelands. The Indians who dwelled north of the Ohio and south of the Great Lakes possessed their own concept of freedom that also required abundant land. But the Indian concept of freedom stipulated a different relationship between people and the land than did the American concept. Where Americans believed that they needed to accumulate substantial amounts of property to become free from the control of domineering men, Indian men wished to be free, as well, from the systematic labor demanded by agricultural property. Both American and Indian concepts of freedom were male-centric; both saw women as adjuncts, subordinate but essential to the male pursuit of autonomy from control. But, where the quintessential free white man was the yeoman farmer privately possessed of at least 50 acres—fenced, cleared, and crowned with crops, livestock, and buildings—the free Indian man was a hunter able to roam at will in pursuit of mastery over free animals. In 1796 missionaries among the Oneida reported, "'Indians cannot work' is a saying frequently in their mouths. They have an idea that to labour in cultivating the Earth is degrading to the character of *Man* 'who (they say) was made for War & hunting & holding Councils & that Squaws & hedge-hogs are made to scratch the ground.'"[22]

In Indian cultures, women conducted the agriculture and most of the gathering, while men devoted themselves to hunting, war, and diplomacy. Women maintained the culture and economy of the village, while men roamed in search of game, enemies, or peace. A man became free by triumphing over wild (free) animals, or by mastering other free men in battle (it was far more satisfying and meaningful to defeat another Indian warrior, because he was freer than the ordinary white settler). The skills and attributes required for woodland hunting and warfare defined the ideal Indian man: loyal and generous to compatriots, patient and stoical under duress, ruthless and determined against enemies. By indulging their children—and especially their sons—Indian parents encouraged the development of a powerful sense of autonomy, an impatience with restraint. In 1799 Halliday Jackson, a Quaker missionary, observed of Indian boys, "Being indulged in most of their wishes, as they grow up, liberty in its fullest extent, becomes their ruling passion." Therefore, the loss of hunting and war imperilled the Indian man's sense of identity and self-worth. He became no better than a common white drudge. Determined to preserve the freedom of the hunter-warrior, Indians resisted the encroachment of the land-transforming and game-destroying settlers.[23]

Political cooperation and subordination were difficult in a culture that was so committed to the ideals of individual and community autonomy from any larger authority. Moreover the Indians who lived between the Great Lakes, the Ohio River, and the Mississippi River were a diverse lot of tribes with differing languages, customs, and kinship systems. The various tribes often found it easier to war on one another than to cooperate against the invading settlers. Moreover, tribes were loose congeries of small, dispersed, and virtually independent villages. A tribe was an ethnic group: a people who shared a language, myths, customs, and a kinship system. A tribe was not a centralized polity capable of coercing members, so Indian leaders had to rely almost exclusively on persuasion rather than command to influence their people. The people of a village, or a faction within a village, often ignored a decision they disliked.[24]

If freedom meant individual or community autonomy from political control, the Indians of the northeastern woodlands were the freest people on the North American continent. But Indians were subject to certain internalized restraints that exceeded those of white men. First, a pervasive ethos of mutuality and hospitality obliged the fortunate and the able to give away rather than accumulate any windfalls or surpluses. Security for an Indian lay, not in the accumulation of private property, but in the development of a respected place in the network of kinship and community obligations. Among Indians of the northeast there was virtually no accumulation of wealth and little inequality, but not much margin for times of prolonged hunger

or extended, systematic warfare. Second, the Indian conception of
the natural world as suffused with spiritual power obliged the individual to adjust his or her behavior to the demands or warnings of
dreams, omens, and sacred rituals. Compared to whites, Indians were
freer from political authority but less free from communal obligations and less free from the demands of spirits.[25]

Per capita, it required more land and less labor to sustain the Indian concept of freedom than that of the Americans. The Indian
economy consisted of a subsistence agriculture supplemented by extensive hunting and gathering. Because they sought bare subsistence
from their fields and reserved most of their territory for hunting,
gathering, and foraging, the Indians did not use the landscape as in-
tensively as white settlers, who sought a marketable surplus, as well
as family subsistence, from their farms. In their drive to create tangible property, settler families cleared and fenced much more land,
and built more and larger buildings, than did the Indians. Settlers
also killed the wild animals far faster than they could reproduce, destroying an essential part of the Indian economy and eliminating the
means to freedom for Indian men.[26]

The Indians could not understand the obsession of white men to
compete with one another to accumulate material possessions. Indians prized useful and attractive things, and could drive hard bargains
to obtain them, but they saw no purpose in acquiring more than a
family could readily carry as they moved with the seasons from farming to gathering to hunting and back again. And they saw no purpose
for a man to die owning more goods than he needed to be buried with
him. John Heckewelder, a Moravian missionary among the Indians
of the Ohio valley, explained,

> They wonder that the white people are striving so much to get rich, and to
> heap up treasures in this world which they cannot carry with them to the
> next. They ascribe this to pride and to the desire of being called rich and
> great. They say that there is enough in this world to live upon, without lay-
> ing anything by, and as to the next world, it contains plenty of everything,
> and they will find all their wants satisfied when they arrive there. They,
> therefore, do not lay up any stores, but merely take with them when they die
> as much as is necessary for their journey to the world of spirits.

As a consequence of this world view, the Indians were capable of sudden exertion and could endure severe privations, but they were loath
to undertake prolonged labor.[27]

As the Indians saw it, white men first enslaved themselves to a

hunger for things and then, in their craving for more, became menacing to their neighbors, particularly those of another color. In April
1781 Pachgantschihilas, a Delaware war-chief, warned the mission-
ized Indians at Gnadenhutten in the Ohio country to beware.

I admit that there are good white men, but they bear no proportion to the
bad; the bad must be the strongest, for they rule. They do what they please.
They enslave those who are not of their colour, although created by the same
Great Spirit who created them. They would make slaves of us if they could,
but as they cannot do it, they kill us! There is no faith to be placed in their
words. They are not like the Indians, who are only enemies, while at war,
and are friends in peace. They will say to an Indian, "my friend! my brother!"
They will take him by the hand, and at the same moment destroy him. And
so you will also be treated by them before long.

Eleven months later, most of those mission Indians were massa-
cred—men, women, and children—by frontier militiamen from western Pennsylvania.[28]

American leaders insisted that it was unjust and irrational for the
relatively small number of Indians to retain as a hunting ground so
many millions of acres suitable for farming. Americans were determined to remake the northeastern forest into a landscape dedicated
to the pursuit of freedom through private property. They demanded
that the Indians surrender most of their lands and forsake hunting for
agriculture, or they must (in General Benjamin Lincoln's words) "in
consequence of their stubbornness dwindle and moulder away." But
such a transformation struck Indians as a formula for their enslavement. As Indian men saw it, to become mere farmers was not only
demeaning but dehumanizing. In October 1792 Messquakenoe, a
Shawnee orator, counseled continued war because the American
president intended to give the Indians "Hoes in their hands to plant
corn for him & his people & make them labour like their beasts,
their oxen & their Packhorses." Consignment to agriculture would
tumble Indian men from the pinnacle of free life to the lowly station
of domesticated beasts.[29]

Both Indian and white men overdid their emphasis upon hunting
as the defining characteristic of Indian culture. For all of their differences from white society, the Indians of the Ohio valley were not the
wild men of the forest depicted by the Americans. They obtained
most of their diet, not from hunting and gathering, but from an agriculture that was more productive per acre than that of the white settlers. Most of the Indian domain remained a forest, but they cleared

and cultivated substantial fields along the major rivers. Their well-tended and flourishing crops of maize, beans, squash, and pumpkins were the envy of encroaching settlers. In August 1794 General Anthony Wayne invaded the Maumee and Au Glaize valleys to find crops that astonished him. "The very extensive and highly cultivated fields and gardens show the work of many hands. The margin of those beautiful rivers . . . appear like one continued village for a number of miles both above and below this place; nor have I ever before beheld such immense fields of corn in any part of America from Canada to Florida." Ordinarily, Americans would not credit the Indians with such agricultural accomplishment, because they defined a culture in terms of what men did and Indian men were warriors and hunters, so Indians were a savage people. White men dismissed what Indian women created as anomalous.[30]

Far from living in primitive isolation, the natives of the Ohio valley and Great Lakes had been in increasing contact with white explorers, traders, soldiers, and missionaries since the mid-seventeenth century. Adapting to that presence, the natives had developed an extensive and sophisticated diplomacy between their tribes and with the representatives of French, Spanish, and British colonists. The natives also bent their economic activities to obtain European trade goods that, by the eighteenth century, had become necessities. In the eighteenth century, Indian men hunted as much to secure pelts to sell to French and British traders, as to obtain meat for their families; the pelts procured guns, gunpowder, knives, axes, hatchets, clothing, jewelry, kettles, horses, and alcohol.[31]

By the 1780s prescient Indian leaders recognized that, to hang on to their homeland in the face of settler pressure, their peoples needed to develop a new sense of unity and a renewed confidence. In November 1792 an orator expressed their new sense of pan-Indian unity: "We are one people, of one color, on this island [that is, North America] and ought to be of one mind, and . . . become as one people in peace and friendship." The Revolutionary War afforded a measure of time as the British garrisons along the Great Lakes assisted the Indians in attacking the most advanced and exposed American settlements during the late 1770s, through the 1780s, and into the 1790s. The Indians used that time to begin to create a political confederacy that would counter the American strategy of divide-and-conquer. They insisted that the lands north and west of the Ohio were not so many parcels held by separate tribes but a common tract belonging to the confederacy which alone could control its dispensation. Consequently, the Indian Confederacy disavowed the treaties by which individual tribes had surrendered lands to the Americans during the 1780s. The confederation took shape with the advice of sympathetic British officials and of Iroquois leaders who were experienced in building inter-tribal cooperation, but the leadership belonged to chieftains from the Miami and Shawnee tribes. They tried, with varying success at different times, to include all of the Indian peoples of the Old Northwest: Delaware, Ottawa, Chippewa, Mingo, Pottawatomie, Wyandot, Kickapoo, Wea, Piankashaw, and various refugees who had come to the Wabash valley from the South and the East. Indeed, leaders of the Indian confederacy sought reenforcement and pan-Indian unity by offering a refuge to eastern Indians who had lost their lands, their wild animals, and, so, their standard of freedom. In 1792 a spokesman for the confederacy wooed the Mohicans, then confined to small reservations in western Massachusetts and central New York; he insisted, "they find themselves hampered among the white people and wanted to get into a place where they could be more at their liberty." The leaders of the confederacy believed that only in union could the Indians preserve the land they needed to be free from domination and exploitation.[32]

At the same time that the diverse American states were trying to craft an effective union, the Indians of the Ohio valley and Great Lakes were engaged in a parallel effort, albeit on a smaller scale. Both the American and the Indian confederacies rested their legitimacy and future prospects on the principle of common ownership of a public domain. But it was the same tract of land that the two confederacies relied upon, and they intended that domain for very different purposes. The Americans meant to reap a national revenue by selling farms to settlers seeking independence. The natives hoped to preserve their hunting ground and slow or halt the process by which the proliferating Americans sought household independence by consuming the western lands. Only one of the confederacies could succeed and endure.[33]

Just as the American effort to build a union was hampered during the 1780s by regional diversity, traditions of localism, political factionalism, and the competing ambitions of leading men, so too the Indian effort was difficult, halting, and incomplete. And the Indian

Confederacy-builders faced a far more difficult task because their peoples had never had institutionalized governance at any level. The Indian Confederacy had no taxes, no treasury, no laws, no courts, and no standing army. It only became manifest at periodic councils and when it was necessary to muster large numbers of warriors to repel an invading army. The various delegations of orators and bands of warriors came and went at will. The Indian Confederacy was an ideal, a goal, rather than a finished achievement. But the Indian proponents of confederation were strengthened by encouragement and supplies provided by the officials and officers of the British empire. Alarmed at American potential, but contemptuous of the republic's strength and coherence, the British hoped that the confederated Indians would hold the Americans at bay and contribute to the anticipated collapse of the United States. The Indians hoped that the British would quickly resume their warfare on the Americans and help to balance the odds facing the confederacy.[34]

During the later 1780s and early 1790s, the Indian Confederacy grew in confidence as it halted American expansion and inflicted heavy losses on American armies and settlements. In October 1790 the confederated warriors repelled an invading American army commanded by General Josiah Harmar. On 4 November 1791 the Indian confederation won an even greater victory by surprising a second American army, this time commanded by Arthur St. Clair. Led by Little Turtle, a Miami war chief, the Indians routed the Americans, capturing their encampment with its supplies and a train of artillery. The victorious Indians stuffed dirt into the mouths of the dead Americans that they might have some of the land they so hungered for. The Americans lost over half of their army: 630 dead and 283 wounded. In no single battle of the Revolutionary War had the Americans suffered so many casualties. Bolstered by victory, the Indian Confederacy secured the enthusiastic support of villages and tribes that had previously held aloof.[35]

Determined to roll back the American settlements, in November 1792 the Indian confederation sent an address to the Americans asserting that the boundary with the United States must revert to the Ohio River as established by the treaty of Fort Stanwix in 1768; the American settlers and soldiers who had crossed the river would have to withdraw. The council of the confederacy also expressed a new pride and confidence. No longer would they accept the rhetorical formulas of inferiority imposed upon them by the Americans at past treaty negotiations: of "younger brothers" or "children" who must defer to their "elder brothers" or "fathers," the Americans. Reversing the formula, they asserted, "We have been informed, the President of the United States thinks himself the greatest man on this Island. We had this country long in peace, before we saw any person of a white skin; we consider the people of a white skin the younger."[36]

≺ IV ≻

The United States

The Indian victories and the simultaneous development of a substantial frontier population of the poor and potentially disaffected jointly threatened to unravel the new American union. Even before St. Clair's catastrophic defeat, national leaders regarded the West as filled with menace for their fragile new republic. The West seemed more a problem than an asset in January 1791 when Secretary of War Henry Knox reported to the President: "The United States have come into existence as a nation, embarrassed with a frontier of immense extent." The vast frontier arc from Georgia to Maine seemed to dwarf and endanger the new union of states along the Atlantic seaboard. Belligerent foreign empires, the British to the north and the Spanish to the south, plotted to hem in the American union by wresting away the West. In the center of the frontier arc a growing population of settlers sought farms, decimated the game animals, and provoked the Indians into hostilities. Afflicted by Indian raids, the settlers clamored for military assistance from their national government. In its absence, settlers acted on their own. Their volunteer expeditions widened the war by indiscriminately attacking Indian villages—the previously neutral as well as the already hostile. Small wonder that Knox considered the frontier to be "critically circumstanced."[37]

At the very least, continued Indian victories threatened the fiscal solvency of the new American nation. The recent war for national independence from Great Britain had been successful but expensive, burdening the new republic with a national debt that the secretary of the Treasury, Alexander Hamilton, estimated at over 77 million dollars (including 25 million in state debts he expected the federal government to assume) in 1790. This was no small sum in a nation of about four million inhabitants, a nation whose gross national product had been cut almost in half by the war's devastation. Taxes alone were inadequate to fund the debt, partly because, as the New England Regulation (Shays's Rebellion) of 1786–87 and the Whiskey Rebellion of 1794 demonstrated, so many rural Americans were prepared to resist them violently. Ever since 1776 congressmen had hoped to reap a desperately needed revenue by selling the lands north and west of the Ohio River. Congress had begun to do so in 1787–88 by wholesaling six million acres to three speculative land companies: the Ohio Company, the Scioto Company, and the Associates of John Cleves Symmes. But after 1788 Congress had to postpone further land sales because the native tribes successfully defended their homelands against the encroachments of federal soldiers, surveyors, and settlers. During the years 1792–96 public land sales accounted for only one-tenth of one percent of all federal revenues; the nation earned three times as much from the sale of postage. Instead of providing lands to sell to diminish the national debt, the Northwest Territory had become a drain on the republic's resources as the sustained warfare with the Indians cost five million dollars and accounted for almost five-sixths of all federal expenditures in the years 1790–96.[38]

National leaders worried that without a revenue from land sales the federal republic would fail and the liberty of white men would be lost. Leading nationalists felt that liberty's survival depended on more than household independence among the citizenry; it also required a government potent enough to compel obedience from refractory minorities. Otherwise, they feared, unchecked liberty would dissolve all social bonds into an anarchy that would destroy once and for all the American experiment in republican government. Endowed by the federal constitution with new powers and with a substantial new revenue from customs duties, the national republic was, during the early 1790s, stronger than it had been during the preceding decade. Nonetheless, the nation's prospects remained clouded so long as its potential resources continued to bleed away on the frontier.[39]

Federal leaders feared that there was worse to come if they failed to gain control over the fighting in the West. The settlers might dispense with the national government as irrelevant, renounce their allegiance, secede from the Union, seize control of the fabulously fertile lands of the Ohio valley, and turn to the British or Spanish for assistance. Without the West, the federal government would be hard-pressed to pay its debts or fund its continued operations. Worse still, national leaders as different as Thomas Jefferson and John Jay expected that an independent West would remain hostile to the East, compounding the military expenses of the Union. Because the West was larger and more fertile, it would continue to attract migrants from the East, especially as the Union increased taxes in a desperate effort to finance its survival; every migrant to the hostile West would further weaken the eastern republic.[40]

Federal officials posted in the West found plenty of evidence to confirm the fears of their eastern superiors. A federal surveyor pronounced the Ohio squatters to be a "lawless set of fellows" who were "more our enemies than the most brutal savages of the country." In January 1786 General Richard Butler, a Congressional emissary, reported that the Ohio valley squatters were about to seize control of the Northwest Territory; he urged Congress to post additional troops in the West and rapidly to sell the land to loyal settlers.

This will not only sink the public debt, but interest every purchaser in supporting the authority of the United States in and over this country, which if neglected must ultimately end in the loss of both country and inhabitants, and fix them determined enemies to the government of the United States; and the good citizens of course [will] remain unpaid, and loaded with the debt and interest already due, as well as the expense of defending their frontier from the encroachments of these people, who are not only very strong, but rendered desperate by their situation and may take with them many good citizens, who rather than lose all, will favor them.[41]

The nation's leaders concluded that the pursuit of independence needed to be restrained and regulated. Federal leaders hoped to raise the threshold for access to independence in order to screen out those they deemed undeserving and so preserve the West for those they considered worthy: the industrious, moral, and orderly. To this end, settlers in the northwestern territory would have to purchase their lands, either directly from the federal government or, more commonly, from a speculator who had bought the nation's title to a large tract. To meet the payments, settlers would have to work hard to develop the commercial potential of their lands. The indolent would either be winnowed out or be re-educated by the necessity to work for the independence they wanted. Equally important, charging for access to independence would contribute to the national revenue and would advance the interests of the large-scale land speculators who were so well represented in Congress and in the executive branch.[42]

If the national leadership could gain the initiative, the West could become the republic's greatest asset rather than its worst menace. The key was to monopolize the use of force by obliging the settlers to accept federal control over the warfare with the Indians. On the one hand, the nation needed to demonstrate its ability to control its frontier folk in order to convince the Indians that it was in their interest to negotiate. Conversely, restraining the Indians would send a message to the disaffected settlers. Knox insisted that "Government must keep them both in awe by a strong hand, and compel them to be moderate and just." He explained, "it is essential to show all lawless adventurers that notwithstanding the distance, Government possesses the power of preserving peace and good order on the frontiers. It is true economy to regulate affairs instead of being regulated by them."[43]

If the Union could achieve military primacy along the frontier arc, the settlers would be inclined to accept national control of the western lands. They would have to buy their farms, generating the revenue the federal government so desperately needed. Arthur St. Clair, governor of the Northwest Territory, predicted, "The People would derive Security, at the same time that they saw and felt that the Government of the Union was not a mere shadow:—their progeny would grow up in habits of Obedience and Respect—they would learn to reverence the Government; and the Countless multitudes which will be produced in that vast Region would become the Nerves and Sinews of the Union." Properly guided, the settlers might assist the republic rather than turn upon it.[44]

The challenge confronting the federal leaders was to master and shape the relentless flow of westward migrants. The leaders of the early republic did not subscribe to the idea, now associated with Frederick Jackson Turner, that frontier conditions would automatically guarantee the development and perpetuation of democratic institutions. Instead, much depended on the policies projected onto the West by the federal government in advance of settlement. The new American republic needed to manage the process of frontier expansion so as to preserve the independence of American households yet integrate those households into a national republic. Thereby the West would be secured to the nation and the republic would be preserved. The first step was to undermine the independence of the Indian Confederacy: peaceably—if possible; with force, if necessary.[45]

≺ V ≻
Confrontation

The surprising strength of the Indian confederation and the depleted national treasury gradually convinced the Washington administration that it would be cheaper and more just to revise the nation's frontier policy in hopes of mollifying the Indians. The principal architect of the new policy, Secretary of War Henry Knox, described it as "a conciliatory system ... of managing the said Indians and attaching them to the United States." He insisted that "both policy and justice" united to urge the new approach because persisting in the old "system of coercion and oppression" would "amount to a much greater sum of money" while "the blood and injustice which would stain the character of the nation, would be beyond all pecuniary calculation."[46]

The Federalist administrators of the new policy—especially Washington, Knox, Benjamin Lincoln, and Timothy Pickering—sought to validate their self-image as exemplars of an enlightened and benevolent elite, the proper leaders at the pinnacle of a natural hierarchy of virtue and ability. Yet common white men, especially on the frontier, often disappointed the leading Federalists by denying them the deference they coveted. They found a delicious relief in negotiating with delegations and councils of Indians who had been rendered dependent: relatively small, exposed, and vulnerable tribes that needed protection from their settler neighbors (especially the Iroquois who had remained in New York). In such settings Federalists could play their coveted role as virtuous patrons dispensing justice and reaping gratitude from the dependent.[47]

Federal leaders hoped to separate settlers and Indians from one another, interpose federal forts, soldiers, and officials, and punish anyone who crossed the newly defined boundary to attack the other. Knox declared, "the sword of the republic only, is adequate to guard a due administration of justice and the preservation of the peace." He expected that "the Indians would be convinced of the justice and good intentions of the United States, and they would soon learn to venerate and obey that power from whom they derived security against the avarice and injustice of lawless frontier people." By holding the middle, federal officials hoped to preclude the expensive wars sparked by indiscriminate violence. By controlling the middle, federal officials meant to manage the pace at which the Indians receded and the settlers advanced. By maintaining a steady, rather than headlong, expansion, the federal leaders hoped to regulate the amount of land available to settlers and, thereby, maximize federal revenues and maintain a high threshold for independence. By treating the Indians with a new respect, Washington and Knox hoped to reduce the nation's military expenditures, enhance the national revenues, and tie the settlers to the national interest.[48]

The new policy spoke of coexistence and adaptation, at least in the short run. But the long run goals were essentially the same: to transfer control of the western lands from Indians to whites, and to transform their use from hunting to agriculture. After all, federal officials believed that time was on their side, as the American population would continue to surge and, by progressively decimating the wild animals, would ensure that the Indians continued to dwindle in numbers and recede westward and northward. "The lands being valuable to the Indians only as hunting grounds," Knox predicted, "they will be willing to sell further tracts for small considerations." Within fifty years the Indians would "be reduced to a very small number." Indeed, unless they adopted agriculture and Christianity, "The idea of an Indian on this side of the Mississippi will only be found in the page of the historian." Consequently, short-term patience and restraint would eventually reward Americans with the continent at a minimal expenditure of blood and treasure.[49]

For the moment, the federal government had to act with a new humility in hopes of procuring peace from the Indians of the Ohio valley and the Great Lakes. In the summer of 1793 the United States sent three commissioners—Benjamin Lincoln, Timothy Pickering, and Beverly Randolph—west to meet with the council of the confederated tribes. Previous treaties had been held under the guns of American forts, with predictable results; this time the American negotiators agreed to venture unarmed into the heart of the Indian Confederacy, to the villages at the Maumee rapids. In July of 1793 the commissioners reached Lake Erie to find that the council of the Indian Confederacy would not meet with them until they promised to concede the Ohio River as the boundary for white settlement. On 31 July the commissioners sent a plaintive letter begging the Confederacy to grant them a hearing. The commissioners promised

such a large sum, in money or goods, as was never given at one time, for any quantity of Indian lands, since the white people first set their foot on this island. And because those lands did every year furnish you with skins and furs, with which you bought clothing and other necessaries, the United States will now furnish the like constant supplies; and therefore, besides the great sum to be delivered at once, they will, every year, deliver you a large quantity of such goods as are best suited to the wants of yourselves, your women, and children.

In effect, the commissioners promised the Indians a comfortable support if they would surrender their hunting grounds and become wards of the United States government. Or, if the Indians preferred, the commissioners would concede most of the trans-Ohio lands obtained by the United States at the treaties of Fort Harmar. But, the commissioners insisted that, because settlers had begun to settle in southern and eastern Ohio on lands sold by Congress, it was "impossible" for the United States to retreat all the way to the Ohio River.

You are men of understanding, and if you consider the customs of white people, the great expenses which attend their settling in a new country, the nature of their improvements in building houses, and barns, and clearing and fencing their lands, how valuable the lands are thus rendered, and thence how dear they are to them, you will see that it is now impracticable to remove our people from the northern side of the Ohio.[50]

The American proposal did not impress the council of the Indian Confederacy. On 13 August the council replied,

Brothers: You have talked to us about concessions. It appears strange that you should expect any from us, who have only been defending our just rights against your invasions. We want peace. Restore to us our country, and we shall be enemies no longer . . . We desire you to consider, brothers, that our only demand is the peaceable possession of a small part of our once great country. Look back, and review the lands from whence we have been driven to this spot. We can retreat no farther, because the country behind hardly affords food for its present inhabitants; and we have therefore resolved to leave our bones in this small space to which we are now confined.

Instead, the council proposed an innovative and provocative alternative to accommodate the settlers.

Money, to us, is of no value and to most of us unknown: and as no consideration whatever can induce us to sell the lands on which we get sustenance for our women and children, we hope we may be allowed to point out a mode by which your settlers may be easily removed and peace thereby obtained. Brothers: We know that these settlers are poor, or they would never have ventured to live in a country which has been in continual trouble ever since they crossed the Ohio. Divide, therefore, this large sum of money, which you have offered to us, among these people: give to each, also a proportion of what you say you would give to us, annually, over and above this very large sum of money: and we are persuaded, they would most readily accept of it, in lieu of the lands you sold them. If you add, also the great sums you must expend in raising and paying armies, with a view to force us to yield you our country, you will certainly have more than sufficient for the purposes of re-paying these settlers for all their labor and their improvements.[51]

This proposal confounded the stereotype of the natives as naive primitives clinging to a lost world and unaware of the pressures driv-ing white settlement. The proposal suggested a radical new set of relationships both between the races, and between the social classes within the white race. The proposal declared Indian independence from debilitating dependence on treaty annuities bestowed by white authorities in paltry return for the natives' lands. Since the 1760s Indian tribal leaders had, time and again, when faced with military defeat, felt obliged immediately to ease the circumstances of their people by bartering away portions of their homelands for coveted stocks of food, tools, clothing, and alcohol. But in 1793 the Indian leaders united to reject the greatest amount ever proferred to them by the United States; they preferred to retain their entire homeland intact. The Indians also proposed breaking the dynamic by which American society transformed class conflict into westward expan-sion. The Indians recognized that the inequality of white society shunted the poorest and most alienated to the frontier margins to battle for resources with the native tribes. American culture insisted that it was more legitimate for poor white men to dispossess the natives than to demand a redistribution of the improved property in the East. The Indians demanded that the American government redistribute wealth by paying their society's rural poor to with-draw from the frontier. The Indian confederation challenged the American government to purchase yeomen independence out of the unevenly-distributed wealth of the nation, rather than from the In-dian domain.[52]

The Indian proposal was far too radical for the American commis-sioners to consider. Breaking off contact, the commissioners hastened home. They knew that their nation's prospects were predicated on continued expansion, on the continued multiplication of family farms, independent from any landlord, but integrated into the republic's economy and polity. Expansion would build the wealth and numbers the new nation needed to hold its own in the competition with the British and Spanish empires for mastery of North America. Continued expansion would invest the Union with the enhanced revenue needed to sustain its operations and fund its debt. And it would preserve social peace among whites by providing an outlet for poor families in search of property and the liberty it afforded. Without expansion the national republic would implode. In the consequent vacuum, the national elite foresaw a nightmare scenario of class conflict, civil war, and foreign intervention that would destroy the liberty of America's white men.[53]

Rather than concede to the Indian demands, the United States resumed military operations against the Indian Confederacy. In the summer of 1794 a formidable new American army led by the resourceful and vigilant General Anthony Wayne advanced relentlessly into the Maumee valley, the breadbasket and headquarters of the Indian Confederacy. At that critical moment the Indians lost the British support needed to counterbalance American power. In 1793 and early 1794 British officials had encouraged the Indians to expect that the hostility between the British and Americans would deepen into overt war within a year. Instead, as the American troops moved northwest into the Maumee country, British diplomats in London opened negotiations with the American envoy John Jay to clear up the sources of conflict between the two nations. The British garrisons on the Great Lakes received orders to hold their ground but to avoid interceding on behalf of the Indians so long as the negotiations in London continued. Demoralized by the new indifference of their British allies and by the prowess of the new American army, many Indians abandoned the confederacy and drifted away to their villages. The remnant suffered defeat and dispersion when they attacked Wayne's army at Fallen Timbers near the Maumee rapids on 20 August. The Indians were further disheartened when the British troops at a nearby fort declined to assist them. Wayne's victorious troops proceeded to systematically destroy the thriving villages and fields of the Indian heartland along the Maumee and Au Glaize rivers. In the spring of 1795 the Indians learned that in Jay's Treaty concluded the preceding November the British had agreed to withdraw from all of their posts south of the Great Lakes.[54]

Deprived of any hope of British assistance, the Indian confederation collapsed and the several Indian tribes sued for peace. Pointedly addressing Indian negotiators in August 1795 as "younger brothers," General Wayne compelled the Indians to agree to the Treaty of Greenville. The more independent Indian orators, principally Little Turtle, continued to address the Americans simply as "brothers," but most of the native speakers were sufficiently cowed to speak of "elder brothers." In the treaty, the Indians surrendered the southern two-thirds of Ohio and agreed to allow the Americans to build forts throughout their remaining domain. In return the United States paid $20,000 in goods and pledged annuities of $9500 in goods "every year, forever."[55]

The Treaty of Greenville did not mark a complete retrocession from the conciliatory policy adopted by the federal government in response to the earlier Indian victories. By a measure of restraint, the federal officials hoped to purchase a peaceful interlude for settlers to occupy southern Ohio and for the federal government to reap payments from them for land titles. The land acquired at Greenville was about the same as that conceded by some of the individual tribes by the treaties of Fort Harmar in 1789; the treaty recognized that the Indians retained title to their remaining lands until they saw fit to sell them to the United States; and the treaty stipulated that anyone who crossed the boundary to squat on Indian lands "shall be out of the protection of the United States" and the Indians could "punish him in such manner as they shall see fit."[56]

≺ VI ≻

Conclusion

During the years 1794–96 the federal government turned the corner in its long struggle to master its frontier. Both the British and the Spanish empires retreated from their efforts to hem in the American republic. By Jay's Treaty the British withdrew to the north side of the Great Lakes. By the Treaty of San Lorenzo (Pinckney's Treaty) concluded in October 1795, the Spanish retreated south to the 31st parallel and west across the Mississippi and opened the mouth of the

Mississippi to American trade. The profits of that trade brought prosperity to the western settlements and accelerated American emigration into the Ohio valley. Victory at Fallen Timbers and the peace made by the Treaty of Greenville secured once and for all the hegemony of the United States over the Indians on its borders. The American Union had prevailed by shattering the parallel effort by Indians to build an effective confederation. In 1794–95 the Indians lost their last and best chance to sustain a pan-tribal confederacy capable of dealing with the Americans as equals.[57]

The land and the freedom it endowed passed to the whites and the Indians gradually became their dependents—subject to all of the humiliations that an independent people felt were proper to those who had become dependent. In subsequent treaty negotiations, that steadily transferred the Indians' remaining lands to their conquerors, the natives reverted rhetorically to "children" of their American "fathers." Thereafter, Indian resistance could occasionally slow, but never stop, the relentless American expansion to the Pacific. After Thomas Jefferson and his party swept the Federalists from national power in 1800, Indian policy gradually became more overtly coercive and less solicitous of native sensibilities. More comfortable with the egalitarianism of common whites and more confident of basking in popular support, most of the leading Jeffersonians did not share the Federalists' need for, and delight in, acts of benevolent patronage to dependent Indians. In 1803 Thomas Jefferson remarked, "We presume that our strength and their weakness is now so visible, that they must see we have only to shut our hand to crush them." In the 1830s President Andrew Jackson openly renounced the federal policy of attempting to re-educate the Indians in American ways; at his direction, federal officials and soldiers systematically rounded up most of the Indians east of the Mississippi and removed them to reservations in the present-day states of Kansas and Oklahoma.[58]

By triumphing over its imperial and Indian rivals for control of the West, the federal government cemented its legitimacy among and control over the settlers. Settler independence had been rendered tributary to national integration. After 1795, federal officials continued to fret that squatters would pre-empt valuable lands and deprive the Union of needed revenue. But, in general, settlers bought the land. Indeed, land sales (in combination with customs receipts) helped retire the national debt by January 1835.[59]

As the settler population surged into the Northwest Territory, independence quickly proved as elusive there as it had been in the East. By 1810 the distribution of property in the new state of Ohio was about as unequal as that of Kentucky or western Pennsylvania during the previous two decades: 45 percent of the men did not own land while the top 1 percent of the taxpayers owned almost one quarter of the taxable real estate. The economic historian Lee Soltow concludes, "At the top of the land scale stood about a dozen great landowners who monopolized many thousands of acres, and not coincidentally held many of the reins of political power and social prestige in the new state." National land policy permitted the accumulation of wealth by large-scale land speculators, enhancing the unequal distribution of power in American society. In combination with continued population growth, that inequality propelled further expansion westward, continuing the destruction of the conditions that sustained the Indian concept of liberty.[60]

The Meaning of Freedom for Waterfront Workers

PAUL A. GILJE

IN THE STORY OF HOW Americans stumbled their way from resistance to rebellion to revolution, the waterfront looms large. It was
waterfront workers who served as the shock troops for the mobs that
made the Stamp Act unenforceable. It was on the waterfront that
Americans learned how to tar and feather opponents. It was on the
waterfront, too, that the Boston Tea Party took place. Once war broke
out, tens of thousands of Americans served on privateers, seeking
their fortunes and waging economic war on the enemies of the new
republic.

The waterfront remained central to the United States in the early
years of the republic. Although many sailors and dockside laborers
were excluded from elections, the waterfront emerged as a significant political symbol of the new nation. Nowhere was this more evident than in the great celebrations of ratification of the Constitution
in Philadelphia, Baltimore, and New York. In these cities leading
Federalists organized massive processions that included not only
many artisans—great numbers of whom worked in maritime trades—
but also a large model of a frigate representing the ship of state and
manned by Jack Tars. While processions with similar ships were an
old tradition in northern Europe, this ritual was novel in America
and testifies to the powerful associations between the new nation
and the waterfront. In New York this connection was most explicit,
uniting the state's political leadership, commerce, and the waterfront by the name of the model ship—*Alexander Hamilton*.[1]

This combination of nationhood and the waterfront was not co-
incidental. During the 1790s and early 1800s American prosperity
depended in large measure upon the carrying trade of the American
merchant marine. As Jefferson's yeoman farmers produced an agri-

cultural surplus devoured by a Europe at war, and as the United States assumed the role of the greatest neutral carrier in the world, waterfront workers became the lubricant that kept the American economic machine operating.[2]

Politicians recognized this development and appreciated how it was threatened by impressment. Such forced recruitment of sailors into the British navy challenged American definitions of citizenship and violated the integrity of American nationhood. Refusing to accept naturalization, the British held that anyone born in the United Kingdom remained his majesty's subject, liable to service in the royal navy. They also blatantly disregarded the nativity of American-born sailors. Thousands with documents attesting to a place of birth on American soil in hand were swept into the British navy. Moreover, impressment made commerce more expensive for it limited the labor pool and increased the risks of a sailor, thereby helping to increase wages.

While there is no denying the importance of sailors to American politics and economics, their position remained anomalous within society. Thomas Jefferson, for instance, viewed mariners as more "valuable citizens" than artisans, yet he considered both inferior to "cultivators of the earth" and condemned all urban denizens. Indeed, for Jefferson "the mobs of great cities," including sailors, were like a cancer that ate out the heart of the republic.[3] James Madison believed that the sailor was least likely to make a good republican citizen since "his virtue, at no time aided, is occasionally exposed to every scene that can poison it."[4] The sailor's behavior ashore often reenforced this impression. Mariners and other waterfront workers did not always exhibit "virtue," either in the republican sense of sacrificing for the greater good, or in the liberal sense of working hard and arduously pursuing their economic self-interest. Moreover, the sailor's "independence" fell far short of that ascribed to both the mythical yeoman farmer and the urban artisan.

Despite these misgivings, the role of the waterfront in the Revolution, and its economic and political significance during the early republic, elevated it to a special prominence. By the early 1800s sailors even came to symbolize the new nation in political iconography and rhetoric. The smart and swaggering tar defying John Bull appeared repeatedly in illustrations, and one of the great rallying cries in the years leading up to the War of 1812 was "Free Trade and Sailors' Rights."

If the waterfront was so important to the Revolution and the early republic, how important was the Revolution to those on the waterfront? How far down did republican ideas of liberty and freedom reach? How was the world of the waterfront changed by the experience of the Revolution? These questions have ramifications that go beyond the waterfront and offer an important test case for our understanding of the conditions of freedom in the new republic. Indeed the ambivalent attitude of men like Jefferson and Madison, exponents of the most democratic strain of republicanism in the 1790s and early 1800s, makes answering such queries more imperative. The odd combination of symbols associated with Jack Tar—part emblem of the nation and part remnant of a dependent and corrupt world—allows us to view the waterfront worker as one representative of the larger universe of the disenfranchised.

Approaching an understanding of the conditions of freedom on the waterfront entails more than studying abstractions and ideas; we need to examine life experiences and see how conceptions of freedom derived from actions. Few of those who lived and worked by the sea left a record of their life. All that we can do, therefore, is to rely on the handful of men who have somehow left us a sliver of their world to study. The analysis here centers upon the most visible of waterfront denizens—the sailor—but also includes some discussion of others whose lives were allied closely to these workers and of whom we have some glimpse.

Did the ideas of waterfront workers concerning liberty and freedom change as a result of the sacrifices they made in the creation of the American republic? Like the image of the sailor in the early republic, the answer to this question will be mixed. Republican ideas of liberty emphasized a concern for property and a mode of behavior that were alien to many sailors. Yet the ideas about equality that became a hallmark of the age of revolution—in part derived from the participation of the waterfront and other elements of the disenfranchised—added form and substance to the anti-authoritarianism and egalitarianism imbedded in waterfront culture. Thus waterfront workers were not entirely immune to the rage for freedom that swept the Atlantic world at the end of the eighteenth and beginning of the nineteenth century. This world, however, did not change that dramatically: the waterfront remained a scene for the exploitation of an underpaid and poorly treated work force. Most sailors clung tenaciously to their traditional concepts of freedom, and their lives remained bounded by an endless round of harsh living and working conditions aboard ship followed by liberty sprees ashore awash in alcoholic binges.

I

Liberty Ashore

Richard Henry Dana and Herman Melville knew a great deal about sailors, both experiencing life in the forecastle in the nineteenth century. Dana wrote that "a sailor's liberty is but for a day; yet while it lasts it is entire." The tar thus experienced an exuberance of liberty that was denied most others. Released from shipboard discipline, Dana asserted that he was "under no one's eye, and can do whatever and go wherever he pleases." Of his own initial "liberty" Dana exclaimed "this day, for the first time, I may truly say, in my whole life, I felt the meaning of a term which I had often heard—the sweets of liberty."[5] Melville reiterated this point and captured the spirit of a world turned upside when he declared that "all their lives lords may live in a listless state; but give the commoners a holiday, and they out-lord the Commodore himself."[6]

Liberty ashore meant more than mere license and included an ideological commitment to specific freedoms: freedom from shipboard discipline; freedom from shoreside attachments; freedom from material possessions; and freedom to control one's own life. Implicit here was a refutation of the bourgeois notion of accumulating property through saving. The sailor's liberty represented a counterculture that had special attraction to those on the margins of society; it included a strain of anti-authoritarianism that denied hierarchy ashore; and, in light of the emphasis on fraternity and brotherhood among shipmates, it contained a strong current of egalitarianism.

This ideal of sailor liberty, however, fell somewhat short of reality. There was a direct relationship between excesses of liberty on shore and the loss of liberty in economic and personal terms. Similarly, while many sailors shared in the intoxicating joys of their shore liberty, not every mariner fit the stereotype and imbibed so deeply of the same waters. Yet, despite these limitations, examination of sailors' liberty ashore reveals a core of ideas—a mentality—that persisted throughout the age of revolution and marked the world of those who lived and worked on the waterfront.

Sailors fully recognized and understood the unusual liberty they took while on shore and knew that it stood in contrast to the discipline and hardships of the ship. In his *Life on the Ocean* George Little provided a detailed explanation of the relationship between life ashore and afloat. After describing the cramped living quarters, meager rations, and perilous working conditions at sea, Little declared, "if to these are added hard living, hard usage, and hard words" it was no wonder that sailors were enticed to drink and misbehavior.[7]

Although Little blamed "landsharks" for leading the sailor astray, Jack Tar often consciously played up to his own stereotype.[8] The inculcation of the peculiar dockside values of the sailor began at an early age. Nothing could be more preposterous than ten-year-old Horace Lane and other young seamen on their first liberty in 1799 mimicking more seasoned sailors. Lane remembered that "monkey like, all that we heard or seen practiced by the sailors, we thought it becoming in us to say and do." Several of the older boys rented horses and a few carriages and took "each his fancy girl with him to recreate at a tavern about three miles in the country." Seeing this, Lane went to the captain and asked him for some money. Then, with six dollars jingling in his pocket—more than a week's wage for an adult worker—he hired a horse and carriage and toured the countryside. Stopping at a tavern, he and another boy started drinking milk punch. Lane became so drunk that he could not leave that night and his friend had to return the horse and carriage.[9]

The sailor's liberty enabled many seamen to avoid regular employment and encouraged disdain for the daily routine of land-based workers. At one point in his maritime career Samuel Leech agreed to an apprenticeship to a bootmaker in the hope of breaking from his "wicked mode of life." However, he dreaded "the confinement to the shoe-bench," which his "riotous fancy painted as being worse than a prison." This fear drove him from his purpose and he rejoined his shipmates to engage in a life of "dissipation and folly."[10]

Locked into a world of authority and deference at sea, Jack Tar enjoyed giving vent to his anti-authoritarianism by flaunting social barriers and relationships while at liberty on shore. The sailor's determination to rent a carriage as soon as he reached terra firma was indicative. Carriages were not only a mode of transportation, but also status symbols that everyone in the early republic understood. To the landlubber the sight of a carriage reeling by with a couple of tars and a prostitute on either side may have appeared totally absurd, but to

the sailor it was the epitome of style. Sailors, in other words, aped
their social betters by playing at being gentlemen. One seamen recalled an old story of two ladies sitting by a window who, upon sight-
ing a couple of tars in the street, proclaimed "There goes two sailors,
gentleman for a week." To which one sailor responded to the other,
"Yes . . . and there sits two strumpets for life."[11]

The apocryphal meeting between the ladies in the window and
the sailors in the street reveals a certain antagonism in gender relations along the waterfront. Perhaps the women mocked the pretensions of the seamen because they resented both the sailors' independence and their rejection of values that would have kept them closer
to hearth, home, and female companionship. The sailors, not surprisingly for men who had been out at sea in a largely male fraternity,
focussed on the sexuality of the "strumpets." The women are not
clearly identified; they may have been prostitutes, members of the
laboring class, or real ladies. To the sailor telling the story it almost
did not matter. From Jack's cynical perspective, all three types were
captives to their sexuality and whatever relationships that entailed.

Male attitudes toward women along the waterfront, however,
were not clear cut. Sailors cherished the image of mothers who represented the purity, nurturing, stability, and comfort that they had
surrendered upon turning to the sea. Yet the stereotypical sailor relished his independence from women and advised young tars against
wedlock. Mariners, like Nathaniel Ames in his *Nautical Reminiscences*, condemned marriage, in a strange twist of logic, citing the
"proverbial infidelity of sailors' wives."[12] The odd vision of woman
as a virgin Madonna and a temptress Eve came to haunt sailor William Widger as he slept in Old Mill Prison during the Revolutionary
War. His dream transported him from his bleak surroundings in England to the familiar wharves of Marblehead. There, he was told, his
wife had just given birth to a child. This news angered him because
he had been away for two years. Shortly thereafter he met his mother
on the Marblehead waterfront. Despite his great "pashan" she urged
him to go home and see his wife, insisting that the baby "was a honest begotten Child," that it was his, and "was Got before" Widger
went to sea. The push and pull of Widger's relationships with women
continued as he and his mother argued. Widger declared that he was
a fool for coming home and swore that he "would Never See hur" (it
is unclear if he meant his wife or mother) again. His mother persisted

and, according to Widger, "she intreated me to go home." On the one side of the argument stood his unfaithful wife driving him away and back to the sea that would free him from his attachment to women and offer him solace in the male brotherhood of the forecastle. On the other was his mother, whom he still trusted as she told him the unbelievable, and the sanctity of the familial fireside. The debate was never resolved. Widger reported that "before I was don talking With hur a bout it I awaked."[13]

There was less uncertainty among many sailors about material possessions. It was not that sailors shunned money. They did not. Instead it was the freewheeling way they spent money and displayed contempt for saving that marked this aspect of sailor liberty. Thomas Gerry, son of politician Elbridge Gerry, wrote home from aboard the U.S.S. *Constellation* that money was "the *life* and *wife* of a sailor," but was "so scarce, that when we receive it the sum affords us no advantage and is offered to the God of *Pleasure* for want of a better berth."[14] Further down the social scale the attitude was much the same. Captured from an American privateer in 1776, cabin boy Christopher Hawkins found himself forced to serve aboard an English man-of-war for over a year. Earning a full share of the prize money taken by the enemy of his country, Hawkins joined in the celebrating on a shore leave and quickly spent what he had earned. As Hawkins explained, the sailor's creed was "What I had I got, what I spent I saved, and what I kept I lost."[15] In a similar situation Joshua Penny, an American seaman pressed into the British navy, went on liberty in London sometime around 1800. Later he reminisced, "We went to London, with too much money not to loose a little. I had lived so long without the privilege of spending any thing, that I, too, was a gentleman while my money lasted." Penny concluded "No man spends his money more to his own notion than a sailor."[16] Indeed, superstitious old salts would toss coins they discovered in their pockets toward the dock as they left port in the belief that otherwise they were in for a streak of bad luck.[17]

Closely allied to this notion of freedom from both material goods and acquisitiveness was a belief that while ashore a sailor was in control of his own life. This sense of liberty assumed several different dimensions. Sailors donned flamboyant clothes, freely cursed and used their distinctive argot, bucked all authority, and engaged in brawls in every dockside neighborhood. The most important of all these characteristics of freedom was the use and abuse of alcohol. Samuel Leech declared that "to be drunk is considered by almost every sailor as the *acme* of sensual bliss." Indeed, once, when Leech returned sober from a liberty the officers and the crew made fun of him for not behaving like a true sailor.[18]

However, the sailor's liberty ashore was a two-edged sword. While it allowed the sailor to enjoy excesses of personal freedom, seamen frequently lost the reality of economic freedom. A sailor might enjoy a frolic, participate in rowdyism and consciously act out the stereotype of the jolly tar, yet he quickly spent the earnings of months and even years of labor. By using up his money the sailor left himself open to an economic exploitation that curtailed not only his own freedom in the marketplace, but also the freedom of all who lived and toiled on the waterfront. Moreover, the fast and loose lifestyle pursued by many while on liberty led to difficulties in maintaining relationships with family and friends. In all, life on the waterfront was often cruel and nasty.

Despite a belief that he dictated the terms of his own labor, the sailor often abdicated even this control over his life. Throughout the Revolutionary era the key agents in signing sailors aboard ships were the boardinghouse keepers. These individuals, including both males and females, were controversial figures of the waterfront. Some boardinghouse keepers ran large establishments that could accommodate twenty or thirty men, while others merely rented out space to two or three sailors from their sparse living quarters. Often they were ex-sailors themselves, or the wives of men at sea.

In the early nineteenth century reformers portrayed the boardinghouse keeper as the villain in the system of corrupting influences upon seamen. It was the boardinghouse keeper who greeted the sailor as he came ashore, took his baggage and offered him lodgings, drink, and whatever other services he required. But the boardinghouse keeper, for a price, was doing little more than providing what seamen wanted. When the sailor's money ran out, the boardinghouse keeper extended credit until he could arrange for the sailor to sign aboard his next voyage. When the sailor needed anything for his "kit," or sea chest, the boardinghouse keeper provided it. When the sailor found himself in trouble with the law, the boardinghouse keeper offered bail. While groggily getting his sea legs on his next voyage, many a sailor cursed his boardinghouse keeper as a landshark for taking him for all he was worth; but that same sailor eagerly sought the boardinghouse keeper when he returned to port.[19] Yet despite a large amount of money apparently passing through their hands, few boardinghouse keepers seemed ever to get very rich.

Because of their devotion to extreme freedom, sailors found it difficult to maintain personal relationships. By its very nature, working the oceans was a mobile occupation, casting its labor force literally across the seven seas. American sailors were notorious for jumping ship and signing on another if the wages were right. Nathaniel Ames believed that it was as "impossible to calculate" the movements of a sailor "as it would be to predict the direction and extent of the next skip of the most eccentric of all animals, a flea."[20] Men sometimes were absent from their families for years, if not decades. Francisco dos Santos was a Portuguese sailor who worked out of New York City for two years in the opening decade of the nineteenth century. He had a wife and children back in Portugal, but after a shipwreck that left him upon the American shore, he made little effort to return to his native land. Between voyages he caroused, drank, visited loose women, and brawled until one day in 1805 he stabbed a rigger with a knife. Unbeknownst to his family Dos Santos ended his life on the gallows, a confessed murderer.[21]

The tragedy of Dos Santos, while not necessarily typical, highlights some of the difficulties experienced by women and families who lived on the waterfront. Liberty for the sailor reenforced the marginality of their families. Ironically, women on the waterfront often discovered an independence born of necessity. Some women seized upon the impermanence of male relationships and, acting as barmaids, prostitutes, and dockside entrepreneurs, took advantage of tars while they were ashore. Some were driven by despair to the same occupations. Many women, however, strove for respectability and maintained their households by washing, renting space to boarders, and somehow eking out an existence while their sons and husbands were at sea. Moreover, just as men turned to one another in the special fraternal bonding of sailors, women found solace and an identity in the community of other women who were in the same situation. When the Reverend Henry Chase made the rounds of waterfront homes on Henry Street in New York City in 1822 he came upon a despondent wife who had just heard that her husband was probably lost at sea. Consoling her was a widow from the neighborhood whose husband had drowned off Cape Cod the year before.[22]

Not every sailor conformed to the jolly tar stereotype. Sailors with strong shoreside attachment were often more careful with their money. Some went to sea only to build up a bankroll that could be used to establish themselves in an occupation on shore. During wartime men expected and sometimes achieved quick rewards through privateering. In peacetime the process consumed more time. Whaling offered an opportunity to accumulate capital. A successful whaling cruise might last two or three years, but the sailor's lay—his share in the profits—could amount to a small fortune of several hundred dollars. Even aboard regular merchant vessels wages that ordinarily ranged between ten and eighteen dollars a month could add up if properly managed and saved. Many men also hoped to make their careers at sea. Captains and other officers aboard ship came largely from the ranks of common sailors; at sea, knowledge and ability counted above all else.[23]

Yet it was the image of the jolly tar that remained most vivid in popular minds and dictated the definition of liberty that dominated the waterfront. This notion of liberty stood in contrast to and in conflict with mainstream ideas. Liberty on the waterfront revolved around a freedom of action that was almost antithetical to the property-bound definitions that preoccupied the age. While sailors worked to acquire money—an aim that would meet the approval of their land-bound critics—the tars' concern with immediate gratification and their rapid disposal of money implied a lack of respect for property that frightened those more interested in the accumulation of wealth. For men who were disenfranchised and whose grasp on property was fleeting and tentative, the sailor's liberty ashore had a distinct appeal.

≺ II ≻

Freedom at Sea

Life at sea was a study in contrasts. Set against the openness of the ocean and the exhilaration of seeing wind and sail driving a great vessel toward far away places were the limits of board and plank and the frequent helplessness of a sailor to set his course for home. In contrast to the universal brotherhood of the sea and the male bonding that occurred between shipmates were the petty conflicts and hatred built up between human beings forced to live on top of one another. Finally there stood the contrast between the almighty power of the quarter deck and the many means of resistance and assertion of independence exerted from the forecastle. The sea simultaneously represented a passport to freedom and a life akin to slavery.

On the waterfront a sailor might act out his fantasies and enjoy excesses of liberty, but at sea he experienced a different kind of freedom—the freedom that came from the vast expanses of the ocean and the fact that he had the whole wide world to explore. We must be careful not to romanticize the sailor's life. Aboard ship, life was incredibly hard, and often miserable. Yet there was an attraction. Herman Melville opened *Moby Dick* with Ishmael on the waterfront drawn to the sea as an escape from "a damp, drizzly November" in his soul. Richard Henry Dana could be almost lyrical in describing a ship in a light breeze under full sail. "Notwithstanding all that has been said about the beauty of a ship under full sail, there are very few who have ever seen a ship, literally, under all her sail . . . with all her sails, light and heavy, and studding sails, on alow and aloft, she is the most glorious moving object in the world." The more prosaic Benjamin Morrell summed up this feeling succinctly when he recalled how going to sea for the first time in 1812 excited him and "My soul seemed to have escaped from a prison cage—I could now breathe more freely."[24]

For many sailors the camaraderie of the sea offered some compensation and solace in the face of adversity. Dana relished the life of the forecastle and viewed it as a release from the supervision of the officers. He believed that "No man can be a sailor, or know what sailors are, unless he has lived in the forecastle with them—turned in and out with them, and eaten from the common kid."[25] The sense of community and shared experiences was very important to sailors and fostered equality before the mast. Each tar knew the dangers he confronted from the elements as well as the depredations of pirates and foreign predators. Special bonds developed between men who ate together, stood frozen watch together, reefed sail together, listened to one another's yarns, and lived within and opposed the same authoritarian structure.

The forecastle, however, was not always united. In Herman Melville's fictionalized account of his own first experience at sea, Redburn found himself repeatedly abused by a mean spirited sailor named Jackson.[26] Tensions between different nationalities in a crew added to the misery of some sailors. J. Ross Browne described the forecastle of a whaler as "black and slimy with filth . . . It was filled with a compound of foul air, smoke, sea chests, soap-kegs, greasy pans, tainted meat, Portuguese ruffians, and sea-sick Americans." While he found much to admire in his American shipmates, he thought the foreigners were intolerable and objected to the idea of sharing living quarters with blacks. When he did not join a work stoppage protesting the captain's refusal to grant the men liberty in port, the Portuguese sailors wanted to drive him out of the forecastle. Isolated and hated by both captain and crew, Browne had to leave the ship.[27]

Technically the power of the captain at sea was supreme. Signing the articles of a ship—the contract that established pay scale and regulations during the voyage—theoretically dictated complete abdication over one's own person. The sailor not only agreed to work the ship but also consented to the discipline established by the captain and his officers. Nathaniel Ames described the captain as a "discretionary bashaw" who "enjoys the reality of power of punishing, after which all having authority so greedily aspire."[28] More than one observer compared the sailors' lot to that of black slaves.[29] William McNally explained "I know of no situation in which men can be placed where they can be rendered so completely miserable as on board ship, if the officers are disposed to make them so." If the captain does not want to redress grievances, the "vessel becomes a perfect hell, and the law has left no alternative for the crew but to suffer his caprice, whims, tyranny in silence for a long voyage, or else do a deed that will bring them to the scaffold, or haunt them to their grave."[30] As one old salt explained to a novice sailor, there was no ground between duty and mutiny. You either did your duty—regardless whether the captain was wrong or right—or you mutinied.

Yet life aboard ships was more complex than this simple dichotomy between mutiny and duty suggests. A closer examination of several limitations on the captain's authority indicates that the relationship between quarterdeck and forecastle was in a state of constant negotiation and reveals sailor ideas about liberty and freedom at sea. Seamen utilized a variety of tactics to prevent the captain from pushing the crew too hard. On the most basic levels this behavior included running away, work slow downs, and grumbling and disrespect. In extreme cases, of course, there was mutiny and piracy. The mere ideal and image of these violent acts, which were practiced less frequently than the more innocuous forms of resistance, affected shipboard behavior.[31]

Countless sailors, in this and other periods, jumped ship. Indeed, there were probably few vessels that ever stopped in a port that did not lose a sailor or two. Sometimes, it was merely a matter of a pet peeve on the part of the tar. Perhaps the captain and a particular sailor did not get along. Often there was a specific confrontation that convinced the sailor to exert his independence. When in 1807 a midshipman had James Durand flogged for not responding to his call, Durand became very angry. He later wrote that "I considered myself my own man, as the term of my enlistment had been up these eight or nine months. Therefore I put on what clothing I could wear that belonged to me and quitted the ship."[32] Sometimes the decision to run away was a function of more general discontent. In 1781 almost every one aboard the *South Carolina* was unhappy. When the ship stopped in Bilboa, several seamen did not return from their liberty ashore.[33] Other times, motivation was economic. In certain ports the going wage was higher, and many a sailor chose to leave one vessel simply because he would make a few dollars more a month on another. Before independence, colonial ports were notorious for luring seamen off ships with higher wages. The same situation pertained to the new republic and partially explains the large number of British sailors leaving his majesty's navy to join the American merchant marine. By 1815, regional differences within the United States began to have some impact on seamen's wages. In the port of New Orleans many ship captains lost their entire crews to higher paying vessels.[34]

Sailors relied upon a variety of subtle means to resist the will of the captain. Dana noted that "Jack may be a slave; but still he has many opportunities of thwarting and balking his master." When the crew of the *Pilgrim* was denied some liberty in port on a Sunday and told to do some work, they resorted to "*Sogering*." The men honed foot dragging to an art: "Send a man below deck to get a block, and he would capsize everything before finding it, then not bring it up till an officer had called him twice, and take as much time to put things

in order again." Tools were not to be found and "knives needed a pro-
digious deal of sharping, and generally three or four were waiting
round the grindstone at a time." If a man was sent aloft, he would
soon come slowly down again for something he had forgotten.
"When the mate was out of sight, nothing was done. It was all uphill
work: and at eight o'clock, when we went to breakfast, things were
nearly where they were when we began."[35]

Similarly, the ability to grumble, talk back, and swear also gave
the sailors some powers and limited the captain's ability to command. Captain John Manly, a noted Revolutionary War naval officer,
complained in 1777 of the mutinous crew of the *Hancock*, wanted
to court martial Philip Bass, Jr., for "abusing the commanding officer" with "ill language and seditious speeches," and singled out several other men "for treating the Officers with bad language."[36]

Resistance from the "people" of a ship occurred aboard privateers
and regular navy ships in the eighteenth and early nineteenth century. During the Revolutionary War the renowned Gustavus Conyngham claimed that the crew of his privateer cutter *Revenge* had
insisted, against his wishes, that they seize some neutral shipping
because it carried English goods.[37] Insubordination plagued the U.S.S.
Constitution in 1812. When William Bainbridge replaced Isaac Hull
as captain of the *Constitution* many of the crew were very unhappy
and expressed this discontent to the captain. Fresh from their victory
over the *Guerriere* the men remained personally attached to Hull,
while several sailors claimed that their previous experience with
Bainbridge was unpleasant. Two months later, off the coast of Brazil,
"the men came on deck in a mutinous manner & complained to the
commd. that the allowance of bread and water was not sufficient."
After stern words and an explanation the men relented and went
back to duty.[38]

The shrewd captain recognized that there was a point beyond
which he dare not push the crew. He might use brute strength—his
own or others, sweet words and promises, or merely good treatment.
But the aim was always the same; maintenance of authority and
the continued smooth functioning of the ship. Otherwise, a mutiny
might be successful. During a voyage in the West Indies in January
1777, the crew of the *Tyrannicide* gathered outside their captain's
door and demanded to know if he planned to return to Massachusetts. He ordered them away, and when they insulted him, he struck

two of them. The crew returned to the forecastle and drew up a round robin—a circular document traditionally used by sailors to pledge mutual loyalty during a mutiny—and refused duty. Properly cowed, the captain apparently relented, ignored further "ill Language," and sailed for Boston.[39]

Even more important than the number of mutinies or near mutinies was the image of freedom cast by a few of the most famous cases of shipboard rebellion. Almost every sailor, for example, had heard of the story of the mutiny on the *Bounty*. Although some of the earliest published versions of this mutiny stressed how eventually the long arm of the law caught up with most of these mutineers, rumors persisted of the exotic life and complete freedom experienced by some. When George Little visited Hawaii in 1809, just as the Pacific was being opened to western shipping, it was whispered aboard ship that the English adviser to the ruler of the islands was one of the crew of the *Bounty*. Whether true or not, the point was that the men aboard Little's ship, and others, believed that it was true and spoke of the man with a reverence and awe as a result.[40]

Connected to the image of rebellion and mutiny, of course, was the issue of piracy. Most sailors rejected the brutality, illegality, and abnormality of piracy. Yet the counter-culture represented by pirates held some attraction; pirates stood as symbols of men who freed themselves from authority and economic dependency.[41] Thus, the image of the pirate played upon the sailors' sympathies and lay deeply imbedded in their folklore. George Little reported that one Saturday night aboard the *Dromo*, a sailor sang over twenty verses of the famous pirate song, "My name is Captain Kidd," much to the delight of the whole forecastle.[42]

Despite this sympathy, not every sailor jumped at the chance to join a mutiny or to become a pirate when the opportunity offered. While the image of piracy and mutiny appealed to the sailor's antiauthoritarianism and sense of personal freedom at sea, the reality remained something different. William McNally might quote the dying words of mutineer Cornelius Wilhelms explaining that "the master treated them so badly" that the crew of the *Braganza* "were obliged" to murder the captain and mate as an object lesson for others. Yet McNally was fully aware that some of that crew refused to join in the crime. Likewise, during the vicious murder and mutiny aboard the whale ship *Globe* in 1824, many of the crew stood in total fear of the mutiny leaders, abandoning them at the first opportunity to return to legitimate society.[43]

To help deal with the tensions and limitations aboard ship certain freedoms were granted sailors, suggesting that even captains recognized that their authority at sea had to be tempered by some liberty. Foremost of these was the grog ration—the daily doses of liquor that helped sailors through the hardships of the day. George Jones believed that nothing "would sooner stir up a mutiny in the ship, than a refusal to serve out grog."[44] In response to reformer efforts to do away with alcohol aboard ships, Richard Henry Dana echoed these sentiments. Indeed, Dana confessed that although he did not particularly like rum, while he served his two years before the mast he took his ration eagerly and praised "The momentary warmth and glow from drinking it; the break and change which it makes in a long and dreary watch by the mere calling all hands aft and serving it out." Dana also believed that its value lay in just "simply having an event to look forward to and to talk about."[45] Aboard some ships an extra grog ration was issued on holidays or after some arduous task like reefing the topsails. Most war vessels served a helping as they prepared for action to inure the men to the blood and violence of combat at sea. In all of these cases the idea was to offer a taste of freedom—even though it was limited to a mere jolt of alcohol pumping through the veins—amidst the toil and surroundings of confinement aboard ship.[46]

There were also some specific moments of license that occurred aboard ships. A captured ship usually became complete bedlam between the time of surrender and the moment of occupation by the victorious enemy. Once the colors had been hauled down, sailors stopped obeying officers and quickly began to ransack their own ship. In a last bout of liberty before imprisonment, men broke into the liquor cabinets and drank themselves to oblivion. Others ran for the food chests and feasted on whatever they could stuff in their mouths, secreting leftovers that they hoped to hide from the occupying marines. Others stripped the ship of canvas and moveable objects that they planned to trade once imprisoned. The victors behaved no better. Sometimes they would join the captives in the orgy of food and drink; other times, they simply robbed them. More than one captured merchantman was recaptured a few days later with a prize crew that was too drunk to manage the ship properly.[47]

At least two rituals also allowed for moments of misrule. On long voyages the captain would occasionally "pipe the men to mischief," allowing the men to dance, frolic, and enjoy a break from work. George Little, on an illegal trading venture to the Spanish Pacific, reported how on 18 February 1809, when the crew of the *Dromo* was piped to mischief "the forecastle and main deck" were given up to the men to enact scenes which "were truly ludicrous." For a couple of hours "the crew were tripping away the merry dance to the sweet sounds of our ravishing band" while "The utmost good humor and harmony prevailed throughout."[48] Edward Cutbush, who served as a medical doctor in the navy in the opening decade of the nineteenth century, believed that these amusements broke up the monotony of the voyage and cemented relations between the officers and the crew.[49]

The other ritual also occurred on long voyages and signaled the crossing of a major geographical line such as the equator. On these occasions there would be a visit from King Neptune—a sailor in disguise—who would initiate novices with a special shave, filling their mouths full of lather, or subject them to some other form of public humiliation. Like piping to mischief, the ritual was intended to ease tension and boredom on a long voyage; and similar to rituals of misrule on land, the idea was to temporarily suspend the normal rules of behavior as a means of insuring the traditional lines of authority the rest of the voyage.[50]

Thus while life at sea confined the sailor, he was not as restricted as might at first appear. The crosscurrents of the physical setting, the psychological bonds and enmities, and the authority and resistance aboard ship all contributed to the sailor's appreciation for his peculiar brand of liberty. Wind and wave promised to release the sailor from any sense of permanence on land; his shipmates confirmed and solidified the tar's identity; and a seaman could always proclaim himself his own man through acts of resistance ranging from a smattering of profanity to mutiny and piracy. Similarly, sight of shore promised a release from close quarters, an escape from despised crew members, and an end to the dictatorship of the quarterdeck.

The broad outlines of the sailor's image of liberty both upon the ocean and along the waterfront retained a certain timeless quality. The sudden elevation of the common man that accompanied the age of revolution, however, offered an infusion of new and sometimes

competing ideas that threatened to alter the sailor's world. Through
the experience of living in the age of revolution, through the heightened identity of Jack Tar with the new nation, through participation
in politics out-of-doors, and through evangelical religion, revolutionary ideas of equality seeped into the forecastle.

≺ III ≻

Surviving the Age of Revolution

The wars of revolution robbed many sailors of their freedom. Probably as many as ten thousand Americans were impressed into British
service between 1793 and 1812. During the Revolutionary War ap-
proximately that number died aboard the British prison ships in New
York harbor. Many others lived through that ordeal or were held as
captives in prisons in England, Halifax, and the West Indies. Still
others joined or were coerced into royal service during that conflict.
Thousands of American seamen, likewise, were captured during the
War of 1812 and held aboard prison ships throughout the Atlantic
world; many ended the war in the dismal penal compound in southwest England known as Dartmoor. Sailors had long been survivors;
the ordeal of revolution put that trait to test.

Paradoxically, this experience with the loss of freedom during the
age of revolution had important implications for the sailor's concept
of freedom. Emerging out of the turmoil of the age of revolution was
a new sense of nationalism for many sailors, that, given the rhetoric
of the day, began to transform the conditions of freedom along the
waterfront and challenged traditional notions of sailor liberty. Republican ideology included a complex of ideas that underwent rapid
development during the late eighteenth and early nineteenth centuries. One component of this ideology was the need to sacrifice one's
own self interest for the greater good of society. Compelled to make
extreme personal sacrifices, sailors began to assert they had a special
place in the annals of American liberty as representing this republican value.

Impressment of American seamen merely marked a continuation
of British practice during the colonial period. Despite the belief that
laws prohibited warships from seizing American seamen, impressment occurred frequently before 1776. Indeed, during the French and

Indian Wars several incidents sparked disturbances in colonial ports, the most famous of which was the Knowles riot of 1747 in Boston.[51] After independence, of course, the British could no longer sweep the waterfront in the same manner, but they could lay off port, search ships entering and leaving, and take what men they wanted. American seamen were also vulnerable to impressment in England and the West Indies, two of the most frequent destinations for merchant vessels. During times of intense demand for manpower in the royal navy, British cargo ships had a difficult time hiring a crew for fear of the press gangs in England. Captains therefore offered a premium wage to anyone who would sail with them. Although American vessels ordinarily paid higher wages than the British, the doubling and even trebling of normal British salaries had a way of enticing the enterprising American tar to sign aboard British merchantmen. These Americans hoped that their protection—an easily forged statement of United States citizenship—would save them from the press gang. They had misplaced their hopes. His majesty's press gangs had little qualms about seizing these seamen sailing under a British ensign.[52]

From the British perspective, impressment made great sense. Any time a British vessel came into an American port it seemed to disgorge men. British sailors jumped ship and for a few dollars could buy themselves a forged protection. The American merchant marine was expanding rapidly and American commercial opportunities thrived as a function of the neutrality of the United States. Short of manpower as it fought a war against France, Britain needed to ensure the fighting readiness of its vessels.[53] One British captain informed an American tar about to be impressed that he did not want to see or hear about his protection; the captain's job was to sail his vessel, and he could not do so without the requisite manpower.[54] What this meant for American sailors was that every time they took to the sea they were liable to be impressed. Once in the British navy, if they survived the ravages of disease and battle, they could look forward to years of hard service and potential abuse.

Many American seamen suffered great hardships as a result of impressment, but despite these constraints on their freedom, and despite the denial of their citizenship, these men continued to live as sailors much as they had before. In August 1809 James Durand found himself impressed off an English merchantman in Plymouth, England. The officers ignored his protection and he lost all of his possessions and cash left aboard the brig he was taken from. At first he refused duty and did not eat for 12 days. Fearing a flogging, he began to do as he was told. Durand claimed he soon showed an ability and willingness to fight in combat, and he even became a member of the captain's band. Denied shore leave for three years, when he was finally granted liberty he enjoyed "every kind of diversion" he thought proper. In other words he drank and lived it up. Durand did not receive his discharge until 21 September 1815.[55]

Although Durand accommodated himself to his situation, he retained some patriotism. He had previously sailed on the U.S.S. *Constitution*, and he refused to serve while his ship was cruising off Long Island in 1814.[56] Similarly, thousands of impressed American seamen aboard British ships applied for prisoner of war status during the War of 1812. They did so in an effort to escape the bondage of the British navy, but in the process they merely exchanged one form of unfreedom for another.[57]

As prisoners of war, American sailors again demonstrated their ability to survive, despite extreme deprivation and loss of freedom. There can be no doubt that the worst of all such experiences was to be confined aboard one of the prison ships in New York harbor during the Revolutionary War, the most notorious of which was the *Jersey* in Wallabout Bay. To be placed aboard that ship as a prisoner of war was almost tantamount to receiving a death sentence. Captain Thomas Dring reported that as soon as he entered the ship he was coated with vermin. Surrounded by men suffering smallpox and in overcrowded conditions, he thought his only hope for survival was to inoculate himself with a pin, using pus from a sore from someone who already had the disease. Short rations that were poorly prepared also added to the death toll. The prisoners, like those elsewhere, attempted to organize a form of self-government to enforce cleanliness and restrictions, but they had little success. Everyone was so desperate that it was impossible to leave any item unguarded and filth was everywhere.[58]

Luckier prisoners during the Revolutionary War were those held in England. The British sent these Americans to Mill or Forton Prison where the mortality rates were far lower and the chances of exchange greater. In these prisons the efforts at self-government were more successful and the total number of escapes incredibly high. The porous walls of these English prisons seemed to drip prisoners by the dozens. Yet the personal narratives of the prisoners can be deceptive. The most successful escapees were officers who could afford to buy their way out of the prison and out of England. Many of the common sailors who escaped were quickly recaptured. Indeed, some of these allowed themselves to be retaken so that the reward could be split between some local contact, who footed the bill for a short spree while the prisoner was outside the walls, and the prisoner himself.[59]

For many prisoners during the Revolutionary War the issue of loyalty was very clouded. Within the prisons a spirit of camaraderie developed and a sense of common cause prevailed among many of the captured sailors. Holidays like the fourth of July, Washington's birthday, and even some of the victories at arms were celebrated with relish and often in confrontation with those who guarded them. Yet there were also a great number of sailors who found captivity unbearable and who sought escape by joining the British armed forces. Like those who were impressed after the Revolution, these Jack Tars were exhibiting their special survival skills developed from their arduous and difficult lifestyle. Indeed, many prisoners of war never made it to the prison compounds. Any seaman serving aboard a merchant ship was automatically put into the British navy when his vessel was seized. Likewise many younger seamen and cabin boys found themselves forced to serve the king. Sometimes, when captured by a privateer, a crew might eagerly join their captives in the hope of earning prize money under the British flag. On at least one occasion some prisoners of war escaped from Mill Prison only to go to the nearest port and sign aboard a British privateer. Needless to say, the same confused loyalties existed on the part of Englishmen, and almost every American warship and privateer, as well as many French ones, had captured British sailors serving aboard them.

Yet American sailors took pride in their participation and their sacrifices during the American Revolution. Successes like those of John Paul Jones—though his crew was less than half American born—stood as examples of American prowess at sea. Equally important, the sordid stories of imprisonment, especially of the nightmare of the *Jersey*, became an important symbol of Jack Tar's suffering and commitment in the years of the early republic. Indeed, when American sailors again found themselves imprisoned in the War of 1812, they repeatedly referred to that earlier experience.

The American sailors at Dartmoor developed their own little

copy of the larger society. Various types of workshops, gambling establishments, and other businesses appeared, giving new meaning to the slogan, as one sailor jokingly put it, "free trade and sailor's rights."[60] Black sailors, in a segregated building, joined this endeavor and even organized theatrical entertainments and pugilist schools to which the whites flocked. The American prisoners also organized a government of elected committees to regulate behavior among themselves. Once again, American sailors demonstrated their penchant for surviving, even under the most severe of conditions.[61]

Dartmoor, however, like the prison hulk *Jersey* was destined to a special infamy in the hearts of American sailors. For a long time, American prisoners there felt abandoned by their government since the agent assigned to protect their welfare, Reuben Beasley, appeared to ignore them. Eventually he began to pay them more attention and see that they were given a daily allowance of a few pennies. But the grievances mounted. After French prisoners started to leave in 1814, many of the Americans became even more despondent. That despair briefly turned to elation when news of the Treaty of Ghent arrived. The excitement did not last because there were many delays in releasing the prisoners. Knowing that they ought to be freed in early 1815, by March many prisoners started to lose patience. Indeed, they demonstrated their dissatisfaction with Beasley by parading him in effigy. They also resisted the British authorities, rioting over rancid bread in early April. Finally, on 6 April 1815, another riot erupted and a frenzied commandant ordered his men to fire upon the unarmed prisoners, six of whom were killed and many more wounded.[62]

Taken together, the experiences with impressment and imprisonment greatly affected sailors' freedom and acted as an entering wedge for revolutionary republican ideas. On the most fundamental level both experiences deprived thousands of Americans of their freedom and thereby dramatically altered their lives and the lives of their families. Beyond this immediate impact, however, lay political developments. Because impressment became such an important issue during the 1790s and early 1800s—Jack Tars believed that it was the reason for the War of 1812—many sailors began to believe that their personal freedom was intimately connected to the nation's political freedom. In a similar fashion, although many prisoners of war concentrated on their own immediate survival—either by joining the enemy or making do in a difficult situation—the memory of the living hell of the prison hulk *Jersey* and the outrage of the Dartmoor Massacre stood as persistent reminders to sailors, and to all dockside workers, of the sacrifices they made for the new American republic. Reenforcing these developments were events along the American waterfront.

≺ IV ≻

Politics on the Waterfront

The involvement of sailors and other waterfront workers in the political process remained limited throughout the age of revolution. Because of their mobility and because of their poverty, few sailors and waterfront workers voted either at the beginning or the end of this period. Yet, despite this disenfranchisement the people of the waterfront had an active role in politics. Their participation in politics centered on three crucial areas: public demonstrations in the street, the commitment in battle on the seas, and the use of egalitarian rhetoric. The first area was important in the colonial period, became crucial in the resistance to British imperial measures in the 1760s and 1770s, but declined in significance thereafter. The second area came to the fore only during war and varied from the Revolutionary War to the War of 1812. The third area represented a gradual development that can be seen in the language utilized by some sailors and in the emergence of a literature about, and sometimes by, common seamen in the first half of the nineteenth century.

In the colonial period sailors and the waterfront were central to politics out-of-doors. Any time a crowd gathered in one of the major cities—all of which were ports—the waterfront was sure to be well represented. In part this presence was a function of the sailor's penchant for rowdiness and reflected his own conception of liberty ashore. But more importantly, it represented the crucial place the waterfront held in colonial American society. Any issue that called upon a clamorous crowd to act was an issue that some way or another also affected the waterfront. This connection of interests was obvious in the many demonstrations and disturbances against impressment and in crowd actions against customs enforcement. But it was also true in other instances as well. For example, sailors and waterfront workers took an active part in the Philadelphia "bloody election riot" of 1742. In that disturbance about 70 sailors, armed with clubs and angered by the colony's pacifist policies, assaulted Germans and Quakers at a polling place in an effort to disrupt the appointment of pro-Quaker election officials.[63]

Such conjunctions of interests increased in the resistance movement of the 1760s and 1770s. This experience placed sailors in the forefront of political change. There is no sure way to identify all of the faces in the crowds of the 1760s and 1770s. Recent studies, however, have emphasized the participation of artisans from a variety of socio-economic backgrounds. While these individuals appeared in the riots of the resistance movement, many sailors and other waterfront workers were there as well. In New York City, for instance, before there were Sons of Liberty, the Stamp Act rioters were called the Sons of Neptune. When local Whig leaders wanted to calm the crowds they asked sea captains and ex-privateersmen, who had sailed with many of the people in the street, to help. Seamen participated in these crowds for several reasons; quite a few sailors were out of work because of an economic recession, they resented the new imperial regulations, and they retained an animosity toward British officials because of impressment.[64]

In the years after the Stamp Act crisis, seamen and waterfront workers remained active in crowds. In April 1769 a Philadelphia mob of sailors drove a customs collector off a wharf as he tried to insure that requisite duties were paid on recently imported wine.[65] Nearly every crowd that behaved this way contained some waterfront people. In both New York City and Boston confrontations with British soldiers involved the waterfront. In the January 1770 riot in New York City known as the Battle of Golden Hill, sailors took a prominent part. In Boston, the so-called massacre of 5 March 1770 had its roots in a brawl between soldiers and workers at a ropewalk—a waterfront-related trade—a few days before. Moreover, Crispus Attucks, the famed mulatto who was among those killed in front of the Customs House, was a seaman.[66]

The participation of waterfront workers, along with others of the lower classes, helped radicalize the revolution. Resentment of wealth surfaced repeatedly in riots, such as that destroying Thomas Hutchinson's house in August 1765, and other acts of extremism. Equally important was the sense of equality fostered by crowd action. The people in the street knew the Whig leaders depended upon them to sustain the revolutionary movement and believed that this political activity placed them on the same level as those they had once considered their social betters.[67] When George Robert Twelves Hewes, a Boston shoemaker who had more than one stint at sea, reported that he and John Hancock had worked together to dump tea into Boston harbor, he was making a political statement that testified to a new and increasingly egalitarian landscape.[68]

Oddly enough, the success of the American Revolution led to a decline in the direct political input of the waterfront through crowd action. In the years after the Revolutionary War, as representative government took on both substance and form, the political leaders came to believe the "people out-of-doors" threatened the new republic. Waterfront workers still participated in crowd actions, but important distinctions emerged between peaceful political demonstrations and any behavior that threatened the public peace. For example, throughout the 1790s and early 1800s Jeffersonian Republicans organized parades and public meetings that no doubt included waterfront workers, but if the waterfront workers attempted to act on their own, they were bound to wind up in trouble. In New York City government officials broke up strikes by sailors in 1802 and by all waterfront workers in 1825 and 1828. Similarly, city officials greeted a public demonstration for relief during the embargo of 1808 with suspicion and fear. Indeed, they wanted to prevent the meeting from taking place.[69]

Ironically, this loss of political influence occurred at the same time that Jack Tar's commitment to the United States appeared to be increasing. Whereas loyalties often shifted and were mixed during the Revolutionary War, by the War of 1812 many sailors fully identified with their country. There were, of course, some very patriotic seamen in 1776. When the British captured young Christopher Hawkins, he sported pewter buttons on his jacket with the words "Liberty and Property" emblazoned on them.[70] Moreover, the various narratives and first person accounts from the early nineteenth century are full of protestations of loyalty to the republican cause. Yet, the record shows that far more Americans switched sides in the earlier contest than they did in the later. No doubt more than three decades of independence, the quasi-war with France, the battles with the Bar-

bary pirates, the expansion of the American merchant marine, the threat of impressment, and the trumpeting of sailor's rights as a political cause all contributed to increased nationalism.

Despite a diminished political role in influencing and guiding policy that might be interpreted as a decrease in political freedom, men from the waterfront began to express a greater awareness not only of American nationalism, but also of republican and egalitarian ideals that they identified with the government of the United States. Central to this development was a belief that the American tar, born free, could exhibit great sacrifice for his country but could not endure slavish treatment from a would-be tyrant. Joshua Penny, for instance, related how American sailors could not suffer flogging in the British navy without fainting and quoted one shipmate explaining to the captain, sometime around 1800, that "we Americans can't bear flogging like you Englishmen, we are not used to it."[71] Moses Smith recited a similar story from his experience aboard the U.S.S. *Constitution* right before the beginning of the War of 1812. When one American sailor was about to be flogged he delivered a short patriotic speech in which he proclaimed that "I thought it was a free country; but I was mistaken. My father was American born, and my mother too. I expected to be treated as an American myself; but I find I am not." The lieutenant suspended the flogging.[72]

Although the evidence is inconclusive, relations between officers and crew might have been affected by egalitarian and revolutionary ideals. Samuel Leech, born in England, served in both navies. Soon after being captured aboard the *Macedonian* he joined an American warship and immediately noticed a difference in the officers. When a petty officer threatened Leech, he reported him to the lieutenant, who then reprimanded the petty officer. Another time a midshipman ordered Leech to wash his clothes, and Leech, claiming that this was not part of his duty, resisted this "sprig of American aristocracy." To his surprise, no one forced him to change his mind. This type of relationship with officers was unheard of in British service. So, too, was the injection of democratic procedure. When the captain died aboard Leech's ship, the lieutenant asked the crew if they wanted to continue the voyage.[73]

On occasion, just as in the rioting of the 1760s and 1770s, revolutionary ideals and the traditional sailor notions of liberty could merge. This conjunction occurred in the prison ships and yards during the wars against Great Britain. In Dartmoor, for example, prisoners applied republican principles of representative government to create an elaborate committee system for most of the prison blocks. Organized along stridently egalitarian lines, with a rapid rotation of representatives and judges, the prisoners passed legislation and held courts that ordered punishment for minor as well as more major infractions. This type of organization also appeared in prisons in Capetown, in the West Indies, and on the Thames River.[74] Prisoners held by the British during the War of 1812 also persistently defended their "rights," whether it be for provisions or in the mere expression of patriotism. Controversies concerning the proper bread to be served the prisoners arose in Dartmoor shortly before the massacre, as well as aboard a prison ship a year earlier. In both instances—and here the infusion of more traditional ideas of sailor liberty came in—the American sailors confronted overwhelming firepower head-on in an effort to defend what they believed to be rightfully theirs. Such controversies, however, often assumed game-like characteristics that resembled the "spirit of *fun* and frolic" of the sailor spree.[75] Benjamin Waterhouse, a doctor who would later become a leading republican ideologue, had been captured while serving aboard a privateer and carefully observed the conduct of his fellow prisoners. He believed that American tars indulged in acts of resistance "beyond all others in the world" and claimed that this misbehavior "ought to be considered as one of the luxuriant shoots of our *tree of liberty* . . . It shows the strength, depth and extent of its roots, and the richness of the soil."[76]

There were other times when revolutionary ideals and traditional notions of sailors' liberty appeared in stark conflict. Many republicans, for instance, hoped to extend their notions of virtue and correct behavior through reform. These men and women strove to limit what they saw as the evil consequences of the excesses of liberty practiced by many sailors—especially the drinking of alcohol—and wanted to teach waterfront workers increased self-discipline. By the early nineteenth century reformers believed that they offered sailors a means to liberate themselves through temperance from the economic bondage under which they toiled and hoped thereby not only to elevate the common tar, but also to create a more efficient work force. Often led by evangelical merchants and sea captains, reflecting the middle class origins of reform, this activity paralleled efforts to transform society in other areas of American society centered around religious revival.[77]

There had always been a few religious sailors; but during the early nineteenth century, with revivals sweeping the United States, more and more sailors began to turn seriously toward religion. Men like Simeon Crowell, who during his youth in the 1790s revelled in "wicked conversation" and the "many carnal songs with which" he "diverted the crew at times," became serious Christians and with conversion altered their work and leisure habits.[78] Moreover, reformers established a series of chapels and special non-alcohol-serving boarding houses for seamen. The reformers also called for the end of grog rations, and some vessels sailed as temperance ships without any alcohol on board.[79] These changes threatened to alter dramatically the waterfront world and end personal freedom as it had been understood by sailors for generations. However, they never entirely succeeded. The activity of the reformers, while adding to the diversity of waterfront culture and increasing the number of religious tars, barely scratched the surface of that world.

Also important in politicizing the waterfront was the emergence of books and articles by and about the common seaman. One basis for this literature was the call for reform aboard ships and along the waterfront. Efforts to bring the gospel to the waterfront led to the development of pamphlets and special magazines devoted to seamen that not only carried stories about religion, but also included pieces of general interest to sailors. This same reform impulse also lay behind many of the personal reminiscences that have been cited in this chapter. Horace Lane wrote the sordid account of his life as a part of the effort to encourage sailors to avoid the evils that befell his speckled career at sea and on shore.[80]

Many of these first-person accounts were part of the growing fascination with the American Revolution during the early nineteenth century. With the men who participated in the Revolutionary War passing away, second-generation Americans searched feverishly for remaining founding fathers—even of humble birth—who could parade before the public on the fourth of July. This interest became so all-consuming that there was a rush to write down the stories of the aging revolutionaries. Ebenezer Fox explained that he published the tale of his adventures in the Revolutionary War because his grandchildren wanted to hear them and he was unable to talk due to a cough. He then went on to apologize for his "simple narrative," which he recounted in the "belief that any circumstances relating to the most interesting period of our history, would prove entertaining to the young."[81]

Although Fox's protestations may have been a matter of literary form, they reveal another key aspect in the political visibility of the waterfront. "Simple narratives" about ordinary men gained in popularity in the early nineteenth century as the rising tide of the ideal of the common man swept the nation toward Jacksonian America. Indeed, such tales became important morality lessons whether they dealt explicitly with religion or not. The good men stayed true to their country, while Great Britain was cast in evil hues. This story line extended to the literature on impressment in the 1790s and early 1800s, and imprisonment during the War of 1812.[82]

Sailors were not the only common men to relate their experiences in print, yet their efforts may have had a special appeal. The image of Jack Tar continued as an important symbol representing the United States. Part of the appeal of these stories, however, also derived from the centuries-old tradition of spinning sailor yarns in the forecastle or during a long night watch. Seamen, in other words, were great story tellers who suddenly found a means to reach a larger audience that, because of the egalitarian tenor of the politics of the early nineteenth century, was especially receptive. Cheaper printing costs allowed for more prolific publication, while widespread education among both the sailors and their readers enabled some seamen to translate an oral tradition to written form.

Ultimately American authors of note brought this development of a sea literature focused on the common sailor to its most artistic form. In his *Two Years Before the Mast*, Dana not only addressed reform, but placed the life of the sailor at the heart of the American romantic movement. This celebration of the common man recognized the sailor's hardship, while leaving the reader breathless over the exhilaration Dana gained from the forecastle. James Fenimore Cooper, who always remained more comfortable on the quarterdeck than in the forecastle, at first etched his common sailors out of stone or portrayed them in stereotype. But in his chronicle of the life of Ned Myers he purposefully focused his attention on the men before the mast. Nathaniel Hawthorne merely edited the yarn of a friend to relate the tragic story of the prisoners of war at Dartmoor. In his *Is-*

rael Potter Melville used an account by a sailor prisoner of war as the basis of his story, and many of his other works are dependent on either his own career at sea or chapbooks and other publications about common seamen. Moreover, Melville's *White Jacket* helped to influence reform efforts in Congress.[83]

The people on the waterfront became aware of all of this attention. J. Ross Browne wrote to Dana that he first ran into a copy of Dana's book in the hut of a trader in Madagascar and that many sailors had spoken favorably of it.[84] Another correspondent reported a quarrel he had with a captain and a mate on a voyage to Cuba concerning Dana's efforts to help seamen. Both the captain and the mate swore that the word "on the wharves" of Boston was that Dana "kept a man employed to board vessels that came in for the purpose of instigating the hands to make law [sue] out of any quarrels that might have occurred with the officers."[85]

Fueled by this interest in their lives, and infused with over a generation of national identity, some sailors began to pick up on the call for reform and place it within a democratic context. For example Joseph G. Clark declared in his *Lights and Shadows of Sailor Life* that "When seamen shall feel their relative importance in the great operations of the country, and indeed of the world, when they recover in a measure from the effects of their former degradation, it will be clearly seen that there are freemen alike in the forecastle and the cabin, each having their appropriate duties and spheres of action."[86] Samuel Leech declared that "A man should be secured the rights of a citizen on the planks as on the soil of his country." William McNally attacked flogging using similar egalitarian rhetoric and asserted that "Seamen know that they are born free, and freemen will never submit to the lash of slavery." McNally also conjured up the legacy of the American Revolution when he pointedly lambasted some officers in the American navy, asserting that "You must have forgotten the principle features in the declaration of independence and constitution of our country: 'All men are born equal.' "[87]

≺ V ≻

Freedom and the Waterfront

How did the age of revolution affect the waterfront? Despite the waterfront's continuing symbolic centrality to American society and politics, its people remained largely on the periphery. Throughout the period sailors retained their own timeless definition of liberty that set them apart from mainstream America. When a sailor was at his liberty he drank, caroused, spent freely, and could, indeed, play the gentleman while his money lasted. This behavior was more than mere license and represented a set of ideas that reflected the realities of life on the waterfront and at sea. Crucial to this way of thinking was the belief that the sailor, though operating within a world of hierarchy and deference, and despite his low social status, enjoyed the independence and freedom of being his own man. Reality, of course, often refuted this ideal; this excess of freedom frequently entailed the abdication of both economic and personal freedom. Yet, as long as waves lapped against the nearby shore, and as long as wooden ships powered by the mysteries of the wind stood ready and in need of good hands to work the sails, the masts, and the rigging, then the sailor believed that he always had his passport to new rounds of freedom in another locale and far from any attachments that might have developed.

The ideals of the age of revolution offered a set of definitions for liberty and freedom that sometimes competed and sometimes coincided with the beliefs of Jack Tar. The American Revolution, for instance, began with a concern for the protection of property that the sailor had difficulty understanding. Yet, when it came to restraints on his personal freedom, through impressment, through restrictions on trade that limited employment, and, once war broke out, through imprisonment, the sailor eagerly joined the fray. This participation, in turn, affected both ends of the spectrum. Utilizing the tar to symbolize the nation added a note of egalitarianism that many revolutionary leaders may not have anticipated, while the sailor found himself increasingly politicized and pulled away from his traditional notions of liberty.

The transformation, however, was never complete. While the leaders of the nation and the people of the waterfront sometimes utilized the same rhetoric of freedom, they remained worlds apart. Men like Jefferson and Madison might recognize the value of Jack Tar to the American republic, yet they still viewed him with suspicion. For his part Jack may have helped to propel the resistance movement of the 1760s and 1770s toward revolution. He may also have become an important representative of the ideal of the common man in iconography and literature. At times he may even have taken the democratic rhetoric to heart and wanted to apply it to life aboard ships. Yet he remained an outsider. His impact on formal and electoral politics was minimal. More important, despite efforts by reformers from above and from within the forecastle, the essential outlines of his labor system remained exploitative. As long as Jack was left on the fringe of society, his only real alternative was to cling to his own definition of liberty.

The Idea of an Informed Citizenry
in the Early Republic

RICHARD D. BROWN

IN THE MINDS OF DIVERSE American leaders, both during the Revolutionary War and later when they were creating the republic and putting it to work, there was unanimous agreement on several basic political principles. Foremost was the necessity for governments of laws, sheltered from the arbitrary tendencies of rulers as well as the capricious impulses of the people. To secure such governments, whether at the state or national level, written constitutions must be crafted that would establish their design and the parameters of their powers. Although Americans argued passionately over the actual provisions of the constitutions they drafted, no one doubted that written compacts were necessary to secure liberty.

At the same time, however, none of America's leaders supposed that written constitutions alone could guarantee freedom. When he attacked the British constitution in 1776 Thomas Paine had written that "*it is wholly owing to the constitution of the people, and not to the constitution of the government,* that the crown is not as oppressive in England as in Turkey"; and although few Americans would have gone that far in disparaging constitutional forms, there was agreement that what Paine called "the constitution of the people" was vital to the survival of free republics.[1] Virtue, it was believed, was a necessary characteristic for the people as well as their leaders, among families and individuals and collectively within communities. Only an honest, sober, industrious people, one committed to duty, service, and the public good, would be capable of sustaining republican government in the face of threats from foreign powers and the hazards of domestic faction. Yet a virtuous citizenry was the most problematic challenge a republic faced. Neither the wisdom of the most enlightened political science nor the heroic sacrifices of great leaders could supply a virtuous citizenry. No mechanism, however brilliantly contrived, and no array of public-spirited gentlemen could insure that the people would be virtuous.

How, then, could the American republic create and sustain a virtuous citizenry? According to people of all persuasions, from the most enlightened rationalists to the most evangelical Calvinists, one answer was institutions: political, religious, economic, and cultural. Even those whose temperament verged on fatalism believed that however vicious men might be, institutions such as free government, independent land-holding, churches and schools, and a free press would promote virtue. These institutions could not guarantee the realization of a republican heavenly city, nor could they erase the most fundamental enemies to public and private virtue—pride, covetousness, lust, anger, gluttony, envy, and sloth—but they were agents of progress and signs of a political new birth.

The survival of free institutions, it was generally believed, required an informed citizenry. All history proved that virtue would languish in a society where ignorance and superstition prevailed. As Thomas Jefferson warned, "if a nation expects to be ignorant and free in a state of civilization, it expects what never was and never will be."[2] Freedom, virtue, and knowledge were understood to be interrelated and mutually supporting. Viewing the American republic from the vantage point of long experience, the retired President James Madison wrote in 1822 that "a popular Government, without popular information, or the means of acquiring it, is but a prologue to a farce or a tragedy; or, perhaps both."[3] Madison and Jefferson could not be certain that an informed public would make wise judgments and so assure the success of the republic, but they and their contemporaries were convinced that an ignorant public could not long maintain liberty. An informed citizenry was not sufficient to assure a bright future for the American experiment, but it was necessary.

In a general way this set of beliefs is familiar to scholars, who have located its origins in Enlightenment philosophy and in the political doctrines of the Radical Whigs of eighteenth-century Britain.[4] But the precise contours of these ideas and the ways that they became embedded in the national ideology of the new republic have not been examined closely. To understand the reasoning that persuaded Jefferson and Madison, John Adams, Benjamin Franklin, George Washington, and many others to formulate the ideal of an informed citizenry, and the methods they adopted to implement it, enlarges our comprehension of the meanings of republican citizenship. For the American vision of an informed people was new in the Revolutionary era, and Americans elaborated on it in distinctive ways and supplied it with unique institutional support. To the Revolutionary War generation the ideal of an informed citizenry was not yet a truism canonized by decades of rhetoric; it was a vision aimed at creating a popular civic culture such as the world had never seen. The creators of this vision did not, of course, start from scratch. They drew first from English traditions and, as with most of their ideas, called on broader Enlightenment ideas as well. But what they came to propose in the 1780s, and to elaborate fully thereafter, embodied an innovative challenge to conventional beliefs in the transatlantic context.

≺ I ≻

The English Heritage

Because England was among the first Protestant kingdoms that emerged after the Reformation, it might be assumed that the English church and state were generally committed to popular literacy so as to promote Bible reading and personal salvation. Church and state records, however, indicate no such general commitment. In 1537 Parliament passed a law for "abolishing diversity in opinions"; and in the 1540s the autocratic Henry VIII signed yet another act of Parliament "for the Advancement of true Religion and for the Abolishment of the Contrary," which not only prohibited the reading of the Bible in English in every church, but also forbade most commoners from reading it at all. According to the 1543 law, no artificers, apprentices, journeymen, yeomen, or lesser serving men, no laborers or husbandmen—and no women whatsoever—were to read the New Testament in English, in virtually all cases the only language in which they might possibly be literate.[5] Bible reading was reserved for men of high rank such as merchants, lawyers, and gentlemen, in addition to the clergy, who alone were permitted to inform themselves firsthand of the facts and teachings of Christianity. Church and state authorities believed that conformity and public order were linked necessities. Information and opinion must be orthodox and unitary,

they maintained, or else men would tear society apart. A literate, in-
quiring population was dangerous. After the civil and religious broils
that culminated in the Marian executions of hundreds of Protestants
in the 1550s, public policy asserted the powers and rights of rulers,
not subjects; and obedience was promoted as the supreme civic virtue. Contrary voices were heard only intermittently.

But as Arthur B. Ferguson has shown, other ideals were circulating within England's educated elite. In 1548, for example, the
preacher and printer Robert Crowley published a pamphlet called *An
Information and Petition against the Oppressors of the Poor Commons of this Realm*, in which he argued that because good government depends on information, men who were literate and learned
should speak out publicly. It was all very well, he said, for members
of the Parliament and Privy Council to supply information to the
king, but so should other subjects. Some Tudor clergymen even saw
themselves as social and moral critics, duty-bound to "speak against
the faults of all degrees without exception."[6] Here, surely, was the
germ of the idea of the informed citizen who spoke freely so as to
assure good government.

It is important to recognize, however, that such expressions by
learned clergymen and humanists did not embrace all subjects. The
Renaissance concept of citizenship was limited to men of high birth,
large property, and classical learning. Inspired by the Athens of Pericles and the Rome of Cicero, learned gentlemen and clergy regarded
citizenship as a select status from which the many were properly excluded. This was the humanist tradition, as modified by later experience, that was carried forward from the Tudor into the Stuart and
Hanoverian eras.

While there was some latitude within this framework for unrestricted religious and philosophic inquiry, the idea of free political
speech was contested. Political criticism was printed and circulated
clandestinely during the reigns of Elizabeth I and James I, but not
until the era of John Milton and the Civil War was the ideal of free
speech fully articulated. Moreover, in the seventeenth-century British colonies the older ideal of a closed ruling elite who could maintain political and religious orthodoxy prevailed. In Massachusetts-
Bay, the most populous North American colony, Puritan authorities
were friendly to the revolution that executed Charles I and elevated
Oliver Cromwell, and they extended citizenship privileges more

broadly among inhabitants than had ever been done in England; but their idea of an informed citizenry remained narrow. For salvation's sake they advocated universal literacy and used the force of law to support schooling, but the objective for common people was piety, not political engagement. Only at the level of training their elite at Harvard College did they join civic to religious purpose. The kind of free speech or inquiry associated with John Milton was as alien to their political tenets as the idea of a "speaking democracy." A religious tract written by the Springfield, Massachusetts, settler and Puritan magistrate William Pynchon, published in London and brought back to Boston, was officially burned in the Boston marketplace by the common executioner in 1650 because the legislature deemed it "erronyous and hereticale."[7]

To the south, in the Virginia colony, the degree of central control was less perhaps, but the ethos of the ruling elite was, if anything, more restrictive than in Massachusetts. Here government had no interest whatever in promoting literacy, and the attitudes of ruling officials were reminiscent of the Tudor repudiation of the idea that "every subject should busily intermeddle with" public affairs.[8] In 1672, a few years before rebels seized his capital, the long-time Virginia governor William Berkeley passionately trumpeted the authoritarian battle cry: "I thank God, there are no *free schools* nor *printing*, and I hope we shall not have these [for a] hundred years; for learning has brought disobedience, and heresy, and sects into the world, and printing has divulged them, and libels against the best government. God keep us from both!"[9] This was reactionary doctrine, but it was well within the boundaries of political discourse. Less than a decade earlier an English printer had been hanged, drawn, and quartered for a single unlicensed publication that had run afoul of the Licensing Act of 1662, which sought to curb disorder, sedition, and treason. Moreover the proceedings of Parliament, which had long been kept secret to protect against undue royal influence, would not be published regularly until 1689.[10]

Whether people should be informed or not—and which people and on what subjects—remained controversial throughout the Restoration era and even after the Glorious Revolution had laid the foundation for the Whig establishment of the eighteenth century. The issues were of such complexity that the politics of public information were often disordered and unpredictable. Thomas Hobbes, for example, warned against the dangers of "the Night of our naturall Ignorance," claiming that ignorance and superstition would tyrannize unless knowledge and reason were marshalled by the state. Even common people, he maintained, must be enlightened in order to allow rational self-interest to operate.[11]

And yet the pro-parliamentary government of William and Mary continued to be wary of public discussion and in 1693 won parliamentary renewal of the Licensing Act.[12] The fact that this censorship law was allowed to lapse in 1695 was not due to any positive desire to liberate public information and the press, but rather to Parliament's inability to agree on a specific system of press regulation. Thereafter, and for more than a decade, there were repeated calls for a new licensing act. Tories, especially, were convinced that the surviving restrictions on publication, imposed after publication through ordinary prosecutions in the judicial system according to standing laws of treasonable, blasphemous, or seditious libel and breach of parliamentary privilege, were inadequate.[13] By 1715 it is doubtful that any major public official would have denounced free schools and printing in the manner of Governor Berkeley in 1672, but both the degree of press freedom and the appropriateness of education for common people were vigorously debated.

In the next generation, however, free speech of a limited sort triumphed conclusively. Proposals for prior censorship and licensing acts faded away, and Whig theorists came to differentiate their own superior brand of political liberty from the "tyranny" of the French monarchy on precisely those grounds. By 1775 the Genevan philosophe Jean Louis DeLolme could summarize the prevailing view by noting that "the liberty of the press, that great advantage enjoyed by the English nation, does not exist in any of the other monarchies of Europe." In the American colonies such as Massachusetts, where the first newspaper began publication with government authorization in 1704, prior censorship lapsed and in the 1720s the requirement that all newspapers be "published by authority" following the scrutiny of the province secretary or its governor was dropped.[14] Now, only the laws of libel and breach of parliamentary privilege limited press freedom. Although print or speech which might be construed as potentially subversive remained risky and legislatures suppressed publications they found threatening, Englishmen on both sides of the Atlantic congratulated themselves on having secured freedom of speech and of the press because prior censorship was dead.

The foundation for this broad consensus lay in the final victory of the Renaissance ideal of the informed citizen, a gentleman, more or less, to whom affairs of state were entrusted and who must, for the sake of the public good, enjoy free access to knowledge. Government's role in this process was fundamentally negative—that is, it must not actively restrict the circulation of information among gentlemen. The idea that either the Crown or Parliament must somehow promote actively the information and education of Britain's inhabitants was alien. Indeed because there was no place for common men in public affairs, no useful purpose was served by informing or educating them.

Worse, in the view of some of Britain's political and cultural leaders, the idea that common people should be informed was absurd. The press was disparaged in 1719 for "prating to all qualities, ages, sexes, constitutions and parties," or because with general access to information "in Politics, every man is an adept, and the lowest mechanic delivers his opinion, at his club, upon the deepest public measures," as Henry Fielding remarked ironically in 1746.[15] To popularize learning was ridiculous. It was no more proper for a common man to be informed or to speak on public matters than for a fishmonger to dress in silks.

At one level, perhaps, these attitudes merely expressed the routine snobbery that was integral to Britain's competitive, stratified social order. But sometimes these criticisms cut deeper. In 1757 Soame Jenyns, an essayist who also sat in Parliament, directly attacked the whole notion of an informed public as misguided. Ignorance, Jenyns wrote, was properly "the appointed lot of all born to poverty and the drudgeries of life." It was, he declared, "the only opiate capable of infusing that sensibility, which can enable them to endure the miseries" of their lot. "Never," he said, should they be "deprived" of their God-given ignorance "by an ill-judged and improper education," since it would ruin them for their appointed roles in life and upset what Daniel Defoe called "the great law of subordination."[16] This was a political vision often shared by Tories and high Churchmen that went beyond mere snobbery. By the second half of the eighteenth century it became increasingly difficult to promote ignorance publicly as Jenyns did; but opposition to the charity school movement as well as tax-supported schooling usually rested on assumptions similar to those of Jenyns.[17]

Bernard Mandeville's widely-read *The Fable of the Bees*, first published in 1714, was perhaps the most influential work which openly attacked charity schools, declaring that "ignorance is . . . the Mother of Devotion, and it is certain that we shall find Innocence and Honesty no where more general than among the most illiterate, the poor silly Country people."[18] Dismissing all pious reveries, Mandeville bluntly pointed out that:

> Abundance of hard and dirty Labour is to be done, and coarse Living is to be complied with: Where shall we find a better Nursery for these Necessities than the Children of the Poor? None certainly are nearer to it or fitter for it. Besides that, the things I called Hardships, neither seem nor are such to those who have been brought up to 'em, and know not better. There is not a more contented People among us, than those who work the hardest and are the least acquainted with the Pomp and Delicacies of the World.[19]

According to this caustic conservatism, informing common people was not amusing or harmless, but positively dangerous, because it would breed discontent among the hewers of wood and the drawers of water, the vast majority of the population.

Mandeville delighted in his unsentimental vision, as did many readers for decades throughout most of the eighteenth century. But his were not the dominant social and political principles. At the time that he wrote he noted sarcastically that he would be called "an Uncharitable, Hard-hearted and Inhuman, if not a Wicked, Profane, and Atheistical Wretch"; and in the second half of the century his views came to be seen as reactionary.[20] For the charity school ideology triumphed as most of Britain's religious and political leaders, as well as Augustan England's social theorists, came to believe that literacy, virtue, and salvation were linked. A sinner could be brought around by education, and a good Christian would be made even better through the power of learning. So, too, would the productivity of workers be enhanced and the incentives to criminality reduced. Education, in the view of its advocates, could supply an all-purpose remedy for the nation's social and religious ills. Mandeville lost the battle with Christian reformers, who helped to make Britain an unusually literate nation, especially in Scotland and the north of England.[21]

But it is important to recognize that the particular idea of an informed population that triumphed emphasized Christian knowledge and the common practical skills of reading, writing, and arithmetic. Charity schools, which were said to be "the greatest Instances of publick Spirit the age has produced," were never intended to create politically-informed citizens, but to put children "into Methods of Industry" and to encourage the "honest Artificer [and] . . . a Race of good and useful Servants," who would be obedient, loyal, and pious. Productivity, godliness, and social control, rather than political education, were the objectives of the secular and religious leaders whose programs spread through British parishes. Training in subjects that were regarded as essential to political education such as history and geography—not to mention law or the Constitution—had no place in the common man's curriculum. Anglican reformers endorsed education for a deference that would sustain the *status quo*.[22]

There was yet another set of voices that entered the discussion, coming particularly from other reformers, like James Burgh, who were associated with the Dissenting academies and the Dissenter interest more broadly.[23] Although they, too, were committed to social stratification and the privileges of wealth, pious celebrations of the *status quo* stank in their nostrils. Together with Radical Whigs, they built upon the teachings of John Locke and Robert Molesworth a more comprehensive idea of an informed citizenry.[24] At its core were what they believed to be the necessary connections between free inquiry, a free press, and political criticism and liberty. Reaching back to ideas that had been voiced in the Renaissance by authors such as Robert Crowley, defender of the right to "speak against the faults of all degrees without exception," and John Milton, whose *Areopagitica* (1644) had called on governments to refrain from censorship, they asserted the necessity of an informed citizenry. "Let her [Truth] and Falsehood grapple," Milton had written; "who ever knew Truth put to the worse in a free and open encounter."[25] Just as critical inquiry was vital for establishing scientific truth, from this perspective a politically-informed citizenry, one that was ready to evaluate public policy critically, was vital for the wellbeing of the commonwealth.

By 1750 a Radical Whig position that emphasized a politically-informed citizenry, rather than a realm composed of subjects indoctrinated in religious and social orthodoxy, was well established and could even be found in the pages of widely-read periodicals like Addison and Steele's often-reprinted *Spectator*, the *Craftsman*, and the *Gentleman's Magazine*. In the American colonies, the New Yorker William Livingston and a few colleagues produced a fully elaborated statement of this position as early as 1753 in the *Independent Reflector*, a magazine inspired by the *Spectator*. Here, in an article on "The Advantages of Education, with the Necessity of instituting Grammar schools for the Instruction of Youth, preparatory to their admission into our intended College," they asserted the civic necessity of an informed citizenry: "Knowledge among a People makes them free, enterprising and dauntless; but Ignorance enslaves, emasculates and depresses them." Here, it was asserted, lay the only sure security for the preservation of British liberties: "When Men know their Rights, they will at all Hazards defend them, as well against the insidious Designs of domestic Politicians, as the undisguised Attacks of a foreign enemy." The natural ignorance that Mandeville and Jenyns had praised as a necessary bastion of social peace was here said to open the way to tyranny: "While the Mind remains involved in its native Obscurity, it becomes pliable, abject, dastardly, and tame: It swallows the grossest Absurdities, submits to the vilest Impositions, and follows wherever it is led." To any who dared to contemplate a contrary view there was the irrefutable evidence of world history, all confirming the necessity of an informed citizenry: "He must be a Stranger to History and the World"—an ignorant provincial—"who has not observed, that the Prosperity, Happiness, Grandeur, and even the Strength of a People, have always been the Consequences of the Improvement and Cultivation of their Minds." In menacing, even apocalyptic tones, Livingston and his colleagues warned that wherever the improvement and cultivation of a people's minds were neglected, there "triumphant Ignorance has opened its Sluices, and the Country been overflowed with Tyranny, Barbarism, ecclesiastical Domination, Superstition, Enthusiasm, corrupt Manners, and an irresistible confederate Host of Evils, to its utter Ruin and Destruction."[26] Given the paucity of educational institutions in the New York colony and its absolute lack of a college, New York was imperilled.

This full-blown polemic on behalf of an informed citizenry was not precisely a rebuttal to conservative voices like Jenyns and Mandeville, since both sides agreed with the notion that "gentlemen" should be politically informed. After all, Livingston and his associates never specified that yeomen and journeymen, let alone laborers or women, should be informed. Nor were they prepared to level all ranks and abolish deference. Radical Whigs like others closer to the center of the political spectrum endorsed the idea of an informed citizenry that included men of property and leisure. Tories, and conservatives generally, were more apt to emphasize the limited objectives of popular instruction, aiming for a level of information that remained consistent with due subordination. The tendency and thrust of the two viewpoints diverged, but they were not yet wholly incompatible.

The Livingston argument did, however, anticipate the innovative path along which American ideas were moving. Livingston and his associates were advocating a college so as to produce generations of genteel, cosmopolitan leaders; but at the same time they expected that the new institution would "make a vast Alteration in our Affairs and Condition, civil and religious." For the fruits of learning and of enlightened, liberal values would not be confined within college or council-chamber walls: "It will, more or less, influence every Individual amongst us, and diffuse its Spirit thro' all Ranks, Parties and Denominations."[27] This suggestion of an inclusive, even comprehensive conception of the citizenry was unusual in the 1750s, and it is all the more remarkable because it was expressed in one of America's most heterogeneous colonies. What was crucial in this viewpoint was not the belief that elite education supplied benefits to the whole society—that was commonplace. What was new, and potentially radical, was the idea that the very same values, ideas, and information might penetrate and permeate the entire social order, if only in attenuated form; and that the minds as well as the manners of the lower ranks mattered.

The voice of William Livingston in the *Independent Reflector* did not, obviously, represent the mainstream of the British heritage regarding an educated, politically-informed citizenry. Certainly the Society for the Propagation of Christian Knowledge, an Anglican evangelical organization which focussed on producing quiet, deferential Christian subjects, rather than captious, politically-informed citizens, more fully represented the broad consensus within Britain's ruling classes. But Livingston's ideas also grew out of the British heritage and are traceable in writers like Burgh, Addison, John Trenchard, and Thomas Gordon, as well as Molesworth and Locke. Tradition included a variety of ideas; and in the generation after 1760, Ameri-

can revolutionaries would carry some older lines of thought in new
directions, drawing out their logical consequences so as to promote
radical results.

≺ II ≻

Revolutionary Combinations

With very few exceptions, the men who led the colonies into the
Revolution did not see themselves as social or political innovators
before 1775. Almost all were wealthy planters and men of affairs who
enjoyed the privileges of gentility and had no wish to disturb the social order. From their perspective, the British Ministry and Parliament were the sources of innovation in taxing and administration
that they aimed to block. When they began to protest against British
measures in the early 1760s, they mostly followed procedures that
confined discussion to legislative chambers and the occasional newspaper essay or pamphlet, which were extensions of legislative debate
and intended to reach a limited audience of gentlemen. One significant exception, however, was the Boston Town Meeting in May
1764, at which the assembled voters and other inhabitants—a socially inclusive gathering of men—discussed and then adopted a remonstrance against the Revenue Act of 1764.[28] Conscious that their
protest would find more support there than in the General Court,
the "gentlemen" merchants who felt most aggrieved brought the
issue before this town meeting. What was unusual here, though
not unprecedented, was that a New England town meeting, a long-
established agency that was normally occupied with matters of local
administration and finance, was employed in such a way as to engage
a broad collection of citizens in rendering a judgment on an imperial
political question.

It is unlikely that any of those who supported this tactical
move—even Samuel Adams—was completely conscious of its full
implications. By bringing the issue out of the closed, exclusive forum
of the legislature and into the open, inclusive town meeting, they
were doing more than merely gaining adoption of their resolution.
Indirectly and without specific intention, they were resorting to the
model of political action that would soon come to dominate the resistance movement—that is, an appeal beyond the regular circles of

political gentlemen, outward so as to comprehend the whole gamut of men who owned property and even many who did not. The gentlemen who led Boston politics were discovering in 1764 what leaders in other colonies would come to recognize the following year: that by engaging the citizenry-at-large in their protests, they became formidable to the Royal administrations in their colonies, and perhaps even to the Ministry and Parliament.²⁹ It was the recognition of this political reality, more than any other single factor, that convinced Revolutionary leaders, who had not previously devoted much thought to the subject, that an informed citizenry was vital as a matter of practical politics.

In a sense it was the structure of the political conflict that dictated the Revolutionaries' mobilization of the general citizenry. Royal officials, who already possessed substantial political authority, worked to strengthen their position through lobbying in Britain, a strategy that was both practical and congruent with the ideology of parliamentary and Crown supremacy over the colonies. Their opponents outside the administration, who held local offices and legislative seats, also tried lobbying; but increasingly they looked to their constituents, who mobilized on their behalf. Though few contemporaries fully recognized the long-term implications of this alteration in the structure of politics, the active engagement of common farmers and tradesmen profoundly affected the character of public life. Suddenly, what common people believed was starting to influence events, sometimes decisively. The concept of public opinion was being redefined more broadly than ever before; and because public opinion was becoming a more powerful and unruly force, shaping it became crucial. Public information, which had always been important, assumed a new significance.³⁰

The Revolutionaries came to appreciate the importance of an informed citizenry at two levels, practical and theoretical. Most immediately, practical politics required that citizens be properly informed, that is, instructed in the right facts and the correct interpretation so that they would support resistance measures. More generally, they should be informed concerning Whig theory in the manner that Livingston's *Independent Reflector* had prescribed so that they would always know their rights and not fall prey to the machinations of tyrants. This consciousness was evident among patriots in the most explicit terms. As Thomas Young, one of the founders of the

Boston Committee of Correspondence, wrote to a New York member of the Sons of Liberty in 1772: "You complain of the ignorance of the common people, you may as well complain of the roughness of a desart! Our people would have known as little as yours had we taken as little pains to instruct them."[31]

Boston, indeed, was among the chief centers of political education and had been since the Stamp Act resistance of 1765. Several of its newspapers as well as its town meetings operated as open forums for critical analysis of British measures. Indeed even the lower house of the legislature had been opened up by the construction of public galleries in 1766, two years after the Virginia House of Burgesses had acted to admit spectators.[32] By thus creating "so Noble a School of Political Learning," as John Adams put it, the "spirit of virtue" would be encouraged.[33] Five years later, following the Boston Massacre of 1770, the town created America's first political lecture series, with annual memorial orations that laid out Radical Whig political doctrines. Through such measures to build a broad political base, efforts that were analogous to the New Light mobilization of Christians during the Great Awakening, Boston patriots created a new, inclusive kind of informed citizenry in which men of small property and large—or even of no property—were tutored in Radical Whig ideas so as to become actively engaged in public affairs.[34]

So active and so successful did the patriot information and indoctrination onslaught appear to its adversaries in Massachusetts, that Lieutenant-Governor Thomas Hutchinson and his brother-in-law covertly published a newspaper in hopes of redressing the public information balance.[35] It was, however, a losing proposition; after less than a year a discouraged Hutchinson gave it up. There was some irony attached to Hutchinson's effort because the Royal government generally opposed the idea of mobilizing colonial public opinion. Two years later Lord Dartmouth, the secretary of state, would actually reprimand Governor Hutchinson for debating the imperial constitution with the legislature.[36] Hutchinson himself rejected the idea of popular engagement in imperial affairs, and his paper had only aimed to stiffen administration support within the commercial and political elite. What Governor Hutchinson and most Royal officials failed to recognize was that the concept of an informed citizenry was expanding to embrace the very men whom they believed should be

deferential to British authority. These officials understood that artisans and yeomen were not simply hewers of wood and drawers of
water—they did own modest amounts of property—but such people
had no business challenging Acts of Parliament and Royal administration. Samuel Adams and his ilk, officials claimed, were nothing
but rabble-rousers.

In every colony the pressure of events pointed in the same direction, toward a more and more inclusive politics and hence an ever
broadening conception of the citizenry that should be politically informed. Informing the public had begun in the 1760s with instruction largely; but by 1774 instruction, information, and consultation
all figured in the process of creating an informed citizenry. Mechanisms varied, from huge, open air "meetings of the people" to newly-
formed committees and conventions.[37] In Philadelphia, where as far
back as the 1720s a Pennsylvania governor had solicited popular support in city taverns, the crisis of independence led to first one, then
another, and finally a third political steering committee with a membership numbering over one hundred representatives.[38] Radical Whig
ideas concerning an informed citizenry were reenforced by practical
political requirements. In order to succeed the Revolution became a
broad popular movement; and in order that it be sustained, both politically and militarily, an informed and engaged citizenry, rather
than the occasional mob, was a necessity.

When Thomas Paine's *Common Sense* appeared in January 1776,
a vast audience believed that the issues he took up lay within their
compass; they were awaiting the information, interpretation, and exhortation he advanced.[39] Paine's *Common Sense* was, of course, a
truly remarkable publication, appealing as it did to hundreds of thousands of common people as well as to many thousands who stood
higher in the social spectrum. It is, in fact, a great landmark in the
history of an informed citizenry in America: it demonstrates that in
advance of the broad citizenship doctrine announced by the Declaration of Independence, the great mass of colonial men no longer considered themselves deferential subjects for whom public information
was superfluous. Rather, they were citizens who should be informed
and active. Generations of literate, dissenting Protestants had been
activated politically by the results of the previous decade of opposition to British measures. The fact that the United States began its

existence with a broad recognition of the importance of an informed citizenry would foster this ideal's further development and shape debates as to what it meant and how it should be achieved.

Common Sense is also significant because at this earliest moment of the American republic, Paine's pamphlet aroused fears regarding a *properly* informed citizenry. Not everyone who agreed with Paine's central conclusion—independence—supported the arguments he had used to reach it. One early and ardent advocate of independence, the learned John Adams, was not only chagrined to hear that he was rumored to be the author of *Common Sense*, he was even more deeply troubled by the wide dissemination of Paine's attack on balanced government and the British constitution, as well as Paine's support for unicameralism. Adams was well aware that after declaring independence the states, individually and collectively, would have to form new governments; and he regarded the principles Paine had so dramatically asserted as dangerous to the future of American liberty.[40]

In 1776 few other friends of independence were equally troubled by Paine's arguments, but in the 1780s and 1790s, when it became clear that broad citizen participation was a permanent feature of American government, Adams's concern for a correctly informed and educated citizenry was widely shared. Indeed at the Federal Convention in 1787, Roger Sherman of Connecticut, one of Adams's fellow drafters of the Declaration of Independence, spoke against popular election of the national legislature because he was convinced that "the people . . . want information and are constantly liable to be misled."[41] The events of 1776, it was clear, had redefined politics and government so as to elevate public opinion and the citizenry to a crucial role, whether citizens were virtuous and informed or vicious and ignorant. Now, with virtually all free white men enjoying citizenship status, and a high proportion exercising voting rights, the modern discussion of an informed citizenry could begin.

At the outset two questions were paramount: who, precisely, should be informed; and what, exactly, should they know? Clearly, the old British charity-school ideal of simple literacy for a pious and docile work force was not a Revolutionary goal. Being informed, it was understood, meant a knowledge of public affairs; but whether it involved only a knowledge of one's rights so that they could be defended, or meant more comprehensive and positive information so that the people could identify and pursue their interests generally, would be matters of contention for two generations. In the colonial era the people "out-of-doors" engaging in political demonstrations had included propertyless artisans, laborers, boys, Africans, even women; and now that the people were being recognized and brought "indoors" as enfranchised members of the body politic, expectations about the identity and responsibilities of citizenship needed adjustments.[42] Controversies over inclusiveness as to who should be informed—according to property, gender, and race—would become heated and intractable.

These tensions were exposed in discussions of free speech, education policy, and the notion of public opinion. The British rhetorical heritage of constitutional and political liberty was glorious and elevated, but it was also so broad and various that it was often invoked indiscriminately. In 1766, for example, a Connecticut newspaper had reprinted a passage from the London press that declared that "every good Englishman will at all times be an advocate for liberty of the Press" because "public knowledge and public Freedom depend alike on its preservation." But who was to say exactly what "public knowledge" meant? Ribaldry, falsehood, scurrility, and invective should not be protected. For such licentiousness "there can be no liberty, either in speaking, writing, or printing."[43] Revolutionaries generally shared these views, grandly proclaiming their belief in free speech so long as it remained within the boundaries of decency and truth.

Deciding the limits of free speech became especially difficult because the new republican principles elevated the role and importance of the people and "public opinion" in government. It was easy enough to assert that "the PEOPLE are the Basis on which all power and authority rest," and that "the extent of their knowledge and information" determines public security; but it was harder to agree on the proper "extent of their knowledge and information" in practical terms.[44] Early in President Washington's administration his secretary of state, Thomas Jefferson, advised him that appropriate "knowledge and information" should include criticism of the government, even the present government, because "No government ought to be without censors: & where the press is free, no one ever will."[45] Within a few years, however, Jefferson qualified his support of a free press with words that looked back to 1766 and forward to the Federalists' Sedition Act of 1798. "Printing presses shall be free," Jefferson proclaimed, "except as to false facts published maliciously."[46] The necessity of distinguishing liberty from license, and protecting the one while prohibiting the other, seemed inescapable.

At the most fundamental, abstract level American leaders agreed with Jefferson on the necessity of a free press and an informed citizenry. But when it came to actual cases their perspectives differed. Often the differences were partisan and depended on whether their own policies were being attacked. But as the 1790 debate between Vice-President John Adams and his cousin Samuel Adams, the Massachusetts lieutenant-governor, revealed, disagreements could also be based on different assessments of human nature and institutions. Both Adamses believed "that knowledge and benevolence ought to be promoted"; but even so, John declared that they would never be "sufficiently general for the security of the society." The problem was "human appetites, passions, prejudices, and self-love," which were so powerful that they could "never be conquered by benevolence and knowledge alone."[47] To this, Samuel Adams replied with an historical argument: "Wisdom, Knowledge, and Virtue have been generally diffused among the body of the people" in Massachusetts, enabling them to preserve "their rights and liberties." And if knowledge and virtue could be so effective in Massachusetts, they could work elsewhere as well. "The present age is more enlightened than former ones," he reminded the Vice-President, and reeled off a litany of advances: "Freedom of enquiry is certainly more encouraged: The feelings of humanity have softned [sic] the heart. The true principles of civil, and religious liberty are better understood: Tyranny in all its shapes, is more detested, and bigotry . . . is despised." Now, with the victory of American liberty and the promise of a republican revolution in Catholic France, Samuel Adams clinched his point by declaring what most American leaders, including John Adams, believed— that "future Ages will probably be more enlightned [sic] than this."

Where John Adams emphasized human "appetites, passions, prejudices," his cousin declared that "The Love of Liberty is interwoven in the Soul of Man."[48] This debate had its ironies, because the professed religion of Samuel was orthodox Calvinism and John was a rational Deist. Yet their views were alike on many political issues; and they were agreed as well on the fundamental human potential for good and evil, and on the necessity of promoting the former and discouraging the latter through human institutions like governments, churches, and schools. But even among leaders whose origins, beliefs, and constituencies were so close, policies concerning free speech and an informed citizenry could provoke debate.

Much of the sensitivity surrounding these subjects grew out of a new-found appreciation of the importance of what James Madison called "public opinion." In a brief, unsigned newspaper commentary of December 1791, Madison declared that rules and constitutions notwithstanding, "public opinion sets bounds to every government, and is the real sovereign in every free one."[49] At the time, Madison's words did not evoke much discussion, but by the end of the 1790s the control of public opinion became a leading theme of partisan politics. The first amendment to the Constitution, drafted by Madison and prohibiting Congress from "abridging the freedom of speech, or of the press," was challenged by the Sedition Act, which President John Adams signed into law on 14 July 1798. This law and its denunciation by Jeffersonian partisans as a violation of the First Amendment illustrated just how hard it was to reach consensus on the line between liberty and license where public opinion was at stake.

The Sedition Act forbade "writing, uttering or publishing any false, scandalous and malicious writing" with the intent to "defame" or excite "contempt" or "hatred" toward the government of the United States, the President, and the Congress, or to stir up opposition to laws. Contrary to English jurisprudence, the law followed the libertarian principles of New York's Zenger case of 1735: that is, defendants could present "the truth of the matter" as evidence, and juries would "determine the law" and not just the fact.[50] Therefore the authors of the Sedition Act could claim with some justification that their law was preserving free speech by establishing its limits, with Jefferson, at the "false, scandalous and malicious" boundary. Such restraints, it was said, were necessary to preserve "the purity of public opinion."[51] Public opinion must not only be informed; it must be rightly, truthfully informed. An informed citizenry must not be left to chance.

In Massachusetts, where the Puritan concern to maintain a literate population was joined to the Radical Whig ideal of a politically-informed citizenry, the state constitution of 1780, drafted by John Adams, emphasized the fundamental importance of the Whig ideal, and supplied institutional means for its support. In the opening section of the constitution the "Declaration of the Rights of the Inhabi-

tants" called for "the public worship of God" because public happiness and civil order required "public instructions in piety, religion
and morality." Significantly, this religious establishment was justified in secular rather than sacred terms; the state was not interested
in salvation, but in order and ethics. Religious instruction was said
to supply social benefits, and for that reason "the support and maintenance of public protestant teachers of piety, religion and morality"
were required in every locality within the state. "Attendance upon
the instructions of the public teachers" was also enjoined unless
such attendance violated an individual's religious scruples.[52] The
first objective of all these institutional arrangements was not to assure entrance into heaven, but to create a citizenry sufficiently informed in Christian principles to embrace morality and so to maintain civic virtue. Being morally informed was part of the prescription
for republican citizenship.

Political information, however, was equally important; and the
same declaration of rights also guaranteed the "liberty of the press,"
which the constitution declared to be "essential to the security of
freedom in a state."[53] In addition to a free press, all of the other
means that had been employed by patriots to inform the people from
1765 onward would be protected in perpetuity: "to assemble to consult upon the common good; give instructions to their representatives; and to request of the legislative body, by the way of addresses,
petitions, or remonstrances, redress of the wrongs done them, and of
the grievances they suffer."[54] These general guarantees of free press
and assembly were widely adopted by the states in the 1770s and
1780s, drawn as they were from the Radical Whig repertoire of requirements for the preservation of a free state.

In Massachusetts these passages in the declaration of rights recalled the English heritage of the very recent past; whereas the provision for a religious establishment, which had referred to citizens as
"subjects of the commonwealth," blended elements of the Puritan
legacy with the Anglican conservatism that linked piety and order.
To combine these different, even contradictory traditions—Radical
Whig, Puritan, and Anglican—to promote a coherent political order
was problematic, and would later generate conflict. In the short term,
however, the combination was creative. The fifth chapter of the Massachusetts constitution, devoted to "The University at Cambridge,
and Encouragement of Literature &c," was even more innovative. It

expressed a whole new republican vision of an informed and cultivated citizenry that would be elaborated by leaders throughout the
United States for two generations, and which would have major institutional consequences. Here John Adams drew on cosmopolitan
Enlightenment ideas so as to shape a new mission for government.

The constitutional provisions for Harvard were in themselves ordinary. Chiefly, the constitution guaranteed Harvard's property and
its system of governance. In addition, however, the state extended
the purpose of the university far beyond its original mission of training the leaders of church and state. "The encouragement of arts
and sciences, and all good literature," the constitution proclaimed,
"tends to the honour of God, the advantage of the christian religion, and the great benefit of this and the other United States of
America."[55] Here Massachusetts was assigning a broad range of secular objectives to the university, objectives whose fulfillment would
enrich the state and the nation.

What was remarkable, however, was not the portion dealing with
the university: the ideal of an informed elite, after all, reached back
to the Renaissance. It was the next paragraph, titled "The Encouragement of Literature," which concerned the information and education
of common people—presumably common men—that was revolutionary. Here earlier Puritan and Radical Whig traditions were transformed into an Enlightenment ideal of comprehensive education
that would ensure a society that was not only Christian and free, but
also just, humane, and progressive. According to the commonwealth
constitution:

Wisdom, and knowledge, as well as virtue, diffused generally among the
body of the people, being necessary for the preservation of their rights and
liberties; and as these depend on spreading the opportunities and advantages
of education in the various parts of the country, and among the different orders of the people, it shall be the duty of legislatures and magistrates, in all
future periods of this Commonwealth, to cherish the interests of literature
and the sciences, and all seminaries of them; especially the university at
Cambridge, public schools, and grammar schools in the towns; to encourage
private societies and public institutions, rewards and immunities, for the
promotion of agriculture, arts, sciences, commerce, trades, manufactures,
and a natural history of the country; to countenance and inculcate the principles of humanity and general benevolence, public and private charity, industry and frugality, honesty and punctuality in their dealings; sincerity,
good humor, and all social affections, and generous sentiments among the
people.[56]

Adams's tribute to universal education, embracing all productive and illuminating fields of endeavor, was ratified by the voters of Massachusetts narrowly, only after some 350 towns in Massachusetts and Maine, communities where the narrowest localism often prevailed, had met to consider it. Indeed in light of the actual policies and appropriations of state and local governments in New England and beyond, this section in the Massachusetts constitution of 1780 represents a climax of enlightened elite influence in the early republic. In reality the vision that was proclaimed here could be realized in only a piecemeal, fragmentary way during succeeding generations.

The vision, while cosmopolitan in its origin, appealed to all classes of free men and came to include women as well. But who was so committed to the scheme as to be willing to pay for it? The struggle in Virginia over Thomas Jefferson's 1778 "Bill for the More General Diffusion of Knowledge" reveals how many political obstacles stood between ideal declarations of principle and their actual implementation.[57]

Jefferson's bill possessed the same Radical Whig and Enlightenment origins as Adams's constitutional provision. The first objective was to block the rise of tyranny; and the bill asserted that an informed citizenry was ultimately the only effective barrier. The bill proposed "to illuminate . . . the minds of the people at large, and more especially to give them knowledge of those facts, which history exhibiteth, that, possessed thereby of the experience of other ages and countries, they may be enabled to know ambition under all its shapes." Thus informed, common people would be "prompt to exert their natural powers" so as to repel tyranny. A further objective was to secure "publick happiness," a goal requiring laws that were "wisely formed and honestly administered." Since the people could not make and implement laws on their own, they needed the guidance of men possessing natural "genius and virtue," whose "liberal education" rendered them worthy to rule. For that reason the bill called for a two-tier school system leading to college, whereby the ablest and most virtuous youths might be brought forward "without regard to wealth, birth or other accidental condition."

The whole system was to be maintained financially by a combination of local taxes and private tuitions. At the lowest level "all the free children, male and female," were to receive three years of schooling at public expense. And though the subjects of instruction were reading, writing, and arithmetic, the textbooks should also "make them acquainted with Graecian, Roman, English and American history."[58] A secular education both practical and political, including both boys and girls, would provide the foundation for the free commonwealth Jefferson envisaged. The scheme was frankly elitist: Jefferson later explained that "twenty of the best geniuses will be raked from the rubbish annually," thereby gaining for the state "those talents which nature has sown as liberally among the poor as the rich, but which perish without use, if not sought for and cultivated." As for those possessed of ordinary abilities, the system would cultivate political perspective: "it will avail them of the experience of other times and other nations; it will qualify them as judges of the actions and designs of men; it will enable them to know ambition under every disguise it may assume; and knowing it, to defeat its views."[59]

It was a grand scheme that promised benefits for a broad range of political constituents. To the poor and middling farmers and artisans it offered unprecedented access to education at all levels, including as it did free primary schools and an elite-sponsored, competitive mobility upward into the grammar schools and college of Virginia's ruling class. To prosperous planters, who had hitherto hired tutors to educate their children, the system assured primary and grammar schools located conveniently throughout the state. And in the view of Virginia's most cosmopolitan leaders, men like Peyton Randolph and George Wythe, who were often frustrated by the cramped parochialism of Virginia politics, the Bill for the More General Diffusion of Knowledge would elevate their fellow citizens of whatever rank to a higher plane of enlightenment. Even those great planters who felt most comfortable with the *status quo* could like Jefferson's plan, since it would send only a single scholarship boy to college annually and thus preserve Virginia's social and political pyramid intact. The plan was so shrewdly conceived that when it was presented to the House of Burgesses no one proposed an alternative program. As James Madison later wrote to Jefferson, "the necessity of a systematic provision on the subject was admitted on all hands."[60] In principle almost everyone supported it.

But after being kicked around in the legislature from December 1778 until December 1786, the plan died. Because of its expense, the difficulty of its implementation in sparsely-settled counties, and western complaints about inequalities in the size of districts—all complaints with a parochial flavor—the much admired Bill for the More General Diffusion of Knowledge became a victim of the very political ills it aimed to remedy.[61] Existing county officials were jealous of sharing power with new boards of aldermen, and the wealthy resisted financing schools for their neighbors' children. Anglicans disliked the generally secular character of the system at a time when state support for religion was being terminated; Presbyterians disliked giving support to the Anglican College of William and Mary; and Baptists and Methodists resented all tax-supported establishments. The goal of achieving an informed citizenry would have to be primarily a private endeavor.[62]

The fate of Jefferson's plan, which James Madison had championed in the Virginia legislature, though disappointing to cosmopolitan republicans, was actually characteristic of state policies in the United States generally. Now that every free man was a citizen, the idea that every free man should be informed concerning public affairs was widely accepted. But, as in Virginia, there was no consensus as to who bore responsibility for achieving such a goal. Except in Connecticut and Massachusetts, where an attenuated version of a religious establishment survived, legislatures ended the state's role in supporting religious instruction; and except for these two states, access to secular information and education had always been chiefly private and voluntary. Parents paid for as much schooling for their children as they would or could. Adults sought out opportunities to enlarge their understanding of public affairs to the extent that their occupation, social standing, resources, and temperament dictated. The English heritage concerning public policy focussed on a free press and free public assembly; that is, restraints against government interference rather than a positive government role. And with a few significant exceptions, it would be this negative conception of the state that would prevail for generations in America. Schools and libraries, debating clubs and lyceums, political parties and religious sects—as well as the newspapers and periodicals that flourished in every region: all these expansive, innovative agencies of public instruction were private and voluntary.

Ironically, the leaders of the early republic who were most concerned to assure that the United States would have an informed citizenry directed most of their attention to government policy, rather than private initiatives. In the United States Land Ordinance of 1785

Congress set aside one square mile in every thirty-six-square-mile western township so as to endow "the maintenance of public schools within the said township." Two years later Congress reenforced its intentions in the Northwest Land Ordinance, declaring that "religion, morality, and knowledge, being necessary to good government and the happiness of mankind, schools and the means of education shall forever be encouraged."[63] Evidently national leaders viewed the defeat of Jefferson's bill as only a temporary setback, for they used his plan as a point of departure for carefully designed programs to erect multi-tiered public school systems. The American Philosophical Society, the club that included most of the nation's leading thinkers, even sponsored a contest in 1795 aimed at selecting the best "plan for instituting and conducting public schools in this country."[64]

Both Republicans like Benjamin Rush and Federalists such as Noah Webster were deeply engaged in the attempt to design rational mechanisms that would mold a perpetual supply of virtuous citizens to maintain the republic and raise it to ever higher levels of production and civilization. The prevailing orientation of these learned, cosmopolitan republicans is suggested by the fact that one of the prize-winning plans affirmed that "it is proper to remind parents that their children belong to the state," and that it was the duty of the nation "to superintend and even coerce the education of children," while the other advocated a "uniform system of national education."[65] So steeped were these learned men in classical models that they expressed a most un-British, indeed positively Roman, confidence in the state, modelling their notions of citizenship on their readings in Cicero and on the history of the Roman Republic.[66]

They departed from tradition, British and Roman, however, in the attention they gave to women's education. To be sure, women would not be among those citizens who possessed political responsibility directly. But the Roman matron, who raised virtuous citizens and managed a civilized and productive household, was vital to the well-being of the state indirectly. This was one of the reasons that the Virginia Bill for a More General Diffusion of Knowledge had provided for public education for girls; and this was why Benjamin Rush argued that in addition to their "usual training," women should be taught "the principles of liberty and government, and the obligations of patriotism." They would not serve in the Senate or lay down their lives on the battlefield, but as mothers and wives they influenced

men from the cradle to the grave. Indeed, Rush said, women's approval was often "the principal reward of the hero's dangers and the
patriot's toils."[67] Consequently, Rush maintained, women's education, like men's, must not be left to private discretion; it was a public
responsibility.

Such arguments for extensive public education, articulated by
members of the American Philosophical Society and other elite cos-
mopolitans up and down the Atlantic seaboard, were rarely challenged directly. In fact, to judge by public discussion one would almost suppose that these cosmopolitan republicans were merely expressing a broad, nonpartisan American consensus. But the history
of their bills in the state legislatures indicates that even though their
ideas commanded support and there were victories for public education—sometimes at the primary level and sometimes on higher levels—that support was always limited and qualified, so that the overall results were inconsistent and piecemeal. One legislature after another repudiated both a national system and the idea that children
belonged to the state rather than their parents.[68]

The precise character of resistance to a multi-tier national system
varied from one state to another, but the overall pattern of responses
was much like Virginia's in the 1780s. Tax resistance, sectarian jealousies over who would control the system and for whose benefit, as
well as a multitude of regional and jurisdictional differences all combined to make education mostly a local and voluntary affair operating within flexible state guidelines.[69] Indeed some believed that this
was the best solution. They opposed public school establishments
just as they resisted church establishments. Both, it was asserted,
were founded on the unduly gloomy belief that common people were
naturally vicious and thus required compulsory indoctrination. But
just as men and women could find religious truth freely, so it was said
that humanity's natural, inquisitive spirit would lead Americans to
inform themselves through voluntary means.[70] As a result, when a
descendant of Jefferson's 1778 bill was finally adopted by Virginia in
1796, it was in a drastically cut form. It provided for primary schools
only; and even these were not required. Instead, local officials were
given discretion over whether to create such schools and to tax inhabitants accordingly.[71] Local volition triumphed. The formation of
the state university would have to wait another whole generation;
and then it would be formed in the wake of the Missouri crisis, in

response more to anxious sectional concerns than to confident national and cosmopolitan impulses.[72]

≺ III ≻

The Idea of the Informed Citizen in the Cultural Marketplace

As it turned out, during the two generations from 1776 through 1826 the idea of a nationally-defined and generated program for the formation of an informed citizenry never flourished in the United States. There were elements of positive government support nationally both in the 1785 United States Land Ordinance's provision for a square mile set aside to finance schooling in every thirty-six-square-mile township and in the creation of an extensive postal system whose rate schedule subsidized the distribution of newspapers; there were also many state provisions for public education. But at the national level the ruling principle was usually a policy of empowerment for states and localities, rather than direct United States government support. Though early national leaders were sometimes reluctant to accept it, releasing the energies of groups and individuals, and encouraging their initiatives to engage in all sorts of political, economic, and cultural activities, was more popular politically than any national, centralized, tax-supported program.[73]

In New York the antifederalist governor, George Clinton, urged the 1792 legislature to promote "seminaries of learning" because "the diffusion of knowledge is essential to the promotion of virtue and the preservation of liberty." Ten years later he sought "encouragement of common schools" inasmuch as "the advantages to morals, religion, liberty and good government arising from the general diffusion of knowledge" were "universally admitted."[74] What was not universally accepted, Clinton had learned, was any particular scheme to supply the state with common schools. Only in 1812, after another decade's worth of political maneuvers, did the New York legislature adopt a durable arrangement. This plan, significantly, drew on programs that had been set up in the 1790s, whereby the state shared up to one-half of school costs with localities. In every case, New York required local communities to take the initiative in 1812 and thereafter. The community would supply a school building within which a state-reimbursed teacher would instruct children in

"reading, writing, arithmetic, and the principles of morality," prefer-
ably to include the reading of chapters from the Bible at the opening
and closing of the school day.[75]

Except for Bible reading, the public consensus regarding the curriculum was confined narrowly to skills rather than substance. As
the legislative report of 1812 explained:

Reading, writing, arithmetic, and the principles of morality, are essential to
every person, however humble his situation in life. Without the first, it is
impossible to receive those lessons of morality, which are inculcated in the
writings of the learned and pious; nor is it possible to become acquainted
with our political constitutions and laws; nor to decide those great political
questions, which ultimately are referred to the intelligence of the people.
Writing and arithmetic are indispensable in the management of one's private
affairs, and to facilitate one's commerce with the world. Morality and religion are the foundation of all that is truly great and good, and are consequently of primary importance. A person provided with these acquisitions,
is enabled to pass through the world respectably and successfully.[76]

In the North, at least, providing the basic means for citizens to educate themselves was politically appealing, because it was relatively
inexpensive and did not demand that a divided, heterogeneous elec-
torate reach agreement as to the specific information the public
ought to command. Within states such as New York or Virginia, as
in the nation as a whole, representative politics precluded uniform,
centralized, European-style systems to inform or indoctrinate the
citizenry with some particular body of knowledge. Even within communities as small and homogeneous as a Connecticut school dis-
trict, each family selected the textbooks their own children would
read; nothing of substance was centrally prescribed. Broadly speaking, responsibility for shaping the specific characteristics of America's informed citizenry was left to families, individuals, and the cultural marketplace.

This is why the most dramatic, far-reaching developments in the
elaboration of ideas concerning an informed citizenry occurred in the
private sector. Here decentralized, private, voluntary movements
sprang up and multiplied on an unprecedented scale. The great
statesmen, John Adams, Thomas Jefferson, and James Madison, who
advocated the idea of an informed citizenry for primarily defensive
reasons—to safeguard liberty from tyrants and demagogues—never
saw all of their favorite public information schemes enacted into law.
Still, they all witnessed the emergence of a great voluntary move-

ment to acquire information so as to empower citizens socially, culturally, and politically, thus enabling them to enrich and improve their lives.

The foundation of this movement—which was carried forward in the press, in public speaking, and in a wide array of voluntary associations—was the ideal that they had articulated and promoted so assiduously. It was true that people were reluctant to employ state power to require people to be informed; but it was also true, as the response to *Common Sense* had suggested in 1776, that many Americans believed that being informed was a necessary part of their citizenship. So long as being informed did not demand deference, and so long as it was voluntary, they demonstrated a huge appetite for information. Moreover, because Americans were a diverse people without centralized institutions, with no one orthodoxy prescribed in religion or politics, their appetite for information promoted a self-intensifying competition among messages and media for public attention.[77]

Such competition was manifest even within particular genres of printed goods in addition to competition between such information media as print, oratory, and voluntary organizations.[78] Almanacs, for example, had been a fairly standard item in the eighteenth century. Designed to sell within a particular regional market as defined by latitude and commercial networks, almanacs varied mostly because of the personal tastes or idiosyncracies of their publishers. But in the early republic, and especially after 1800, they lost their generic identity. Almanacs carrying the neutral name of their printers were widely supplanted by almanacs identified as Christian, temperance, farmers, mechanics, and anti-slavery, among others. Information as innocuous-seeming as that contained in an almanac was packaged according to cultural preferences in a segmented market.[79]

The same kind of development was characteristic among periodicals, which were increasingly tailored to specific audiences. By 1830 every movement and every denomination, and almost every trade and occupation, seemed to have its own monthly journal. Technical and scientific information, sometimes called "useful knowledge," was also conveyed to various audiences by specialized magazines. A process of specialization was underway that served the needs of efficiency and of personal identity simultaneously. In actual fact, the contents of many publications with specialized labels, such as *The*

Christian Herald and Seaman's Magazine, which was published in
New York City from 1816 to 1824, overlapped with more general
publications. At the same time, however, they possessed a distinct
character and appeal.[80]

American culture exhibited some unexpected paradoxes. Many of
the same citizens who adamantly rejected deference when it was
compulsory embraced a kind of cultural deference voluntarily. No
Adams, Jefferson, or Madison, they thought, should prescribe their
behavior; but many aspiring common men hastened to emulate the
cultural preferences of their betters. This "democratization of gentility" comprehended a wide range of tastes in personal fashion, fur-
niture, architecture, and manners.[81] It also included learning and the
idea of being politically informed. Books, newspapers, reading, and
education generally became fashionable. Tax support for public secondary schools could seldom be found, but private academies and social libraries flourished. The informed citizen was in vogue in republican America.

The public goal of universal education was extensively and variously pursued as a private, voluntary enterprise. In 1789, for example, a New Jersey printer founded *The Christian's, Scholar's, and
Farmer's Magazine*, which he hoped would sell widely by providing
instruction in the liberal arts to traders and shopkeepers as well as
farmers and mechanics. Because all kinds of citizens "should possess
considerable degrees of Literature," the publisher aimed to provide
his subscribers with college training at home, without demanding
that readers know Latin.[82] To judge by the polite magazines of the
early republic, all sorts of information, from the culture of turnips
and the management of bees to the meanings of Hebrew and Anglo-
Saxon words, were desirable to master.[83]

Newspapers, too, became repositories for information about the
natural world, history, politics, and culture. The Reverend William
Bentley, a celebrated Massachusetts polymath, spent much of his career preparing news digests so as to provide the public with a comprehensive stream of information on public affairs, natural and ecclesiastical history, and scientific advances. Enlightenment-bred optimism led Bentley, like other Jeffersonian intellectuals, to hope that
the challenge of creating the informed citizenry the republic needed
could be fulfilled by making knowledge broadly available. If people
were given access to the refreshing streams of information, they
would drink.[84]

Although this optimism was not universal, in the half-century following the Revolutionary War the expansion of American printing and publishing, the rise of American learned societies, and the spread of voluntary associations rendered it plausible. It was, after all, a matter of established fact that private initiatives for promoting an informed citizenry were flourishing as never before, and on a comprehensive scale that overshadowed government-sponsored schooling. One emblem of the realization of this vision was the lyceum movement that began in the late 1820s. Begun in Boston by the immigrant mechanic Timothy Claxton, who joined with the Yale-educated Yankee Josiah Holbrook, the lyceum had roots in the British movement to spread useful technical information via mechanics' institutes. At first the lyceums emphasized popular scientific subjects, including physics, chemistry, and geology. But after Holbrook turned the orientation of the lyceum movement towards families in the 1830s, their content became more eclectic. General adult education, including geography, history, and literature in addition to science, broadened the movement to include clerks and farmers, women, and youth of both sexes. In the 1830s and 1840s, as lyceums sought and achieved ever greater popularity across the nation, the uncertain balance between useful and entertaining knowledge shifted toward the latter. Judgments about which topics were useful and which were merely entertaining, such as the hugely popular subject phrenology, were bound to be subjective.[85]

The concept of "useful knowledge," which from the time of Francis Bacon had joined the material and practical to the speculative and cultural, came to be all-encompassing. Care of the body as well as the soul could be served by advances in information, as could care of the farm, the shop, and the store. Attention to the practical advantages to be gained from the circulation of information was not new—Benjamin Franklin had published a "Proposal for Promoting Useful Knowledge among the British Plantations in America" in 1743—but now, in contrast to 1743, Americans responded through their reading preferences and their associational activity.[86] The enlightenment of practical improvements that Franklin championed, as well as the cultural enrichment and social elevation his own career embodied, possessed a broad appeal in a society where both the means of production and the ambition to advance were widely distributed.

The predominant concerns of the cosmopolitan leaders who most assiduously promoted an informed citizenry, Adams, Jefferson, Madison, and Franklin, were secular. To the degree that such republican leaders recognized the importance of religious information it was, as the Massachusetts constitution stated, so as to secure social and political benefits in this world. But there were other voices in the early republic for whom an informed citizenry meant being informed regarding the vital facts of damnation and salvation. Largely separated from the Radical Whig preoccupation with political liberty or from any social aspiration toward republican gentility, tens of thousands of people who viewed republican civic culture with a skeptical eye expressed a powerful demand for information focussed on the next world.[87] As the Second Great Awakening unfolded, those who were engaged in this movement seldom contributed directly to public discussions of the idea of an informed citizen; but their interest in freely developing evangelical information, production, and distribution networks worked to buttress politically as well as economically the whole private and voluntary information marketplace. And like their secular counterparts, evangelicals were ready to innovate and to employ the whole panoply of publications and associational activities. The same enabling legislation and preferential postal rates that fostered secular information activities applied equally to the efforts of religious groups.

These several kinds of commitment to an informed citizenry— political, social, practical, and religious—supplied the impetus that led Americans to make print, which had long been a scarce commodity, into one of the ubiquitous necessities of life.[88] These commitments led Americans to merge their drive for information with their sociability, what Tocqueville called the "natural social principle," so as to form and patronize thousands of voluntary associations in the decades between 1780 and 1830.[89] To be sure, there were regional variations. In the North, where a more densely-settled, egalitarian social system operated, and where economic development and transportation networks stimulated each other, the movement for an informed citizenry was more pronounced and reached a greater portion of the free population than in the South. But in the South, too, the same interest in reading and the same penchant for voluntary associations was growing.[90] One evocative manifestation of the several cultural tendencies that were coming together was the 1833 resolution of the Petersburg, Virginia chapter of the American Bible Society. Quoting an injunction of Isaiah that "the earth shall be full of the knowledge of the Lord," the Virginians resolved "that the world shall be supplied with the Holy Scriptures in twenty years." Because there was a "responsibility resting upon Christians for the universal diffusion of the sacred Scriptures," the national organization went on to prepare a plan that would furnish Bibles "to all the inhabitants of the earth accessible to Bible agents, and who may be willing to receive, and able to read, that sacred book."[91]

Such a resolution could never have passed a state legislature or won tax support; and originating as it did in a region where one-third of the inhabitants, being slaves, were often forbidden access to literacy by statute, it expressed a peculiar irony. Still, the goals expressed by the American Bible Society resolutions describe one of the many variant forms that the ideal of an informed citizenry took in the early republic. Enlightened and romantic at the same time, and blending the Christian idealism of encompassing all the peoples of the world with the practical recognition that Bibles were only useful to those who could read, the project indicates the kinds of motives that were operating freely in the competitive environment of early republican political culture.

Education promoted both secular and religious objectives. Good Christians would be good citizens. As a Massachusetts Unitarian clergyman explained in an 1806 Independence Day oration, "the elementary plan of education, which is extended to the rich and the poor, which embraces the whole mass of our citizens," will provide "the ability to understand our religion, in its evidence, its spirit and design; by which men are guarded against . . . superstition . . . the delusions of enthusiasm, and are enabled to direct their religious observances to real attainments in moral life."[92] Christianity itself was "above everything else adapted to the preservation of our freedom."[93] Now its advocates proclaimed that the idea of an informed citizenry, which had first been shaped by the political needs of Renaissance gentlemen, could be extended not only to every free boy and girl in the United States, but to virtually every living soul on earth and need have nothing whatever to do with the state.

In its universalism the Bible Society scheme to place Holy Scriptures in every hand represents the almost boundless reach of the idea of an informed citizenry in the early republic. In practice, however, the idea's reach was far more restricted. The slave system, for example, barred the realization of a universal ideal because slave preaching was carefully monitored and literacy was often forbidden to slaves by state statutes and informal prohibitions among masters that were extended and strengthened in the 1830s and 1840s.[94] The core tradition, after all, had never been universal; it was national, secular, and political, and its focus was enfranchised citizens. Liberty and just government joined with enlightened inquiry and progress were the ideals that were emphasized as connected to an informed citizenry in thousands of Independence Day orations, political speeches, and newspaper commentaries, as well as in the charters of schools, colleges, libraries, debating societies, and lyceums. The political benefits of a broad diffusion of information among citizens, regarded as critical for repelling the greedy march of ambition and tyranny, remained central to American beliefs.

Nevertheless the ideal of an informed citizenry shifted significantly during the early decades of the nineteenth century. The acute anxiety which the Revolutionary War generation of leaders expressed over tyranny and the survival of the United States had led Adams and Jefferson to advocate a major role for the state in education. To them it appeared that the republican state must require its citizens to be informed in order to assure its own permanency. In the wake of the French Revolution and the election of Thomas Jefferson, Federalists especially worried over the direction that education would take. "By education the tender youth may be fitted for treason, stratagem, and death," a Federalist orator warned in 1802, "or they may be trained up for order, peace, and happiness. Much depends on the systems of education." Such dangers were not merely hypothetical since "the disorganizers of the present day" were indeed "infusing into the minds of the young the principles of disorder, and training them up for anarchists." Early in the century such hysterical reactions— which in this case included anathemas against atheism, skepticism, and "sending abroad the fairer part of creation in the attire of a female Greek"—could be voiced by advocates of public education.[95]

But by the 1820s these anxieties had eased; and elite American leaders had witnessed several decades of dramatic improvements in the dissemination of information, wherein private, commercial, and voluntary efforts were paramount, and the state had only played an enabling role. Moreover, in contrast to Adams and Jefferson's generation, the leaders of the 1820s had been touched by romanticism. And although they paid an almost obsequious homage to the Revolutionary War generation, they confidently extended the ideal of the informed citizen to include a comprehensive vision of knowledge broadly diffused and ever expanding. Among old Federalists and Whigs especially, the old worries persisted and acted as a continuing spur to action. But publicly, at least, the glass was decidedly half full, not half empty; and the new generation of leaders answered the dire fears of the Revolutionary War leaders optimistically in the celebratory eulogies of 1825 and 1826.

Daniel Webster's nationally-celebrated speech at Bunker Hill on the fiftieth anniversary of the battle was so widely reprinted in the next generation that it became, quite literally, a textbook example of American oratory.[96] In it Webster rang numerous changes on the heroism of Revolutionary soldiers and the glories of American liberty. It is significant, therefore, that his patriotic exhortation included a panegyric to the expansion and diffusion of knowledge that reached toward infinity. Webster did, of course, affirm the basic political point, maintaining that "the popular form of government is practicable, and that, with wisdom and knowledge, men may govern themselves."[97] But he elaborated on a truly transcendental scale with the declaration that "knowledge, in truth, is the great sun in the firmament," giving life and power to men.[98] As a demonstration of this assertion Webster proclaimed that "knowledge has, in our time, triumphed, and is triumphing, over distance, over differences of languages, over diversity of habits, over prejudice, and over bigotry." What was emerging around the globe was a "vast commerce of ideas" that enabled "innumerable minds, variously gifted by nature, competent to be competitors, or fellow-workers, on the theatre of intellectual operation."[99] From this historic development, he was sure, political and material progress would flow, giving to mankind a genuine hope of peace and prosperity. The concern for the purity of public opinion that had animated Webster's Federalist forbears was supplanted by confidence in commerce and the competition of a free marketplace of ideas. As Webster painted the scene, ignorance, not purity, was the issue. To remain ignorant deliberately in such an era was worse than unpatriotic, it was atavistic. To be informed, he implied, was not just a duty of citizens, it was the duty of everyone who was not forcibly restrained by tyranny or bondage.

According to United States Supreme Court Justice Joseph Story, the foundation for such bold declarations lay in the growing realiza-

tion that, notwithstanding the shortcomings of popular politics and
the inadequacies of public education policies, the United States was
enjoying a "general diffusion of knowledge" among all social classes,
including "the peasant and the artisan." In another classic oration of
the period, Story, the one-time Federalist turned Republican, whom
Madison had appointed to the high court, underlined Webster's arguments and elaborated on them. Owing to the freedom of the press
and its "cheapness," the "universal love and power of reading" had
come to fruition in the present era, what Story called "the age of
reading."[100] As Story viewed it, the republic was secure because here,
as "wherever knowledge circulates unrestrained, it is no longer safe
to oppress; wherever public opinion is enlightened, it nourishes an
independent, masculine and healthful spirit."[101] Story's confident
tone, like Webster's, was new. The connections between ignorance
and dependence, knowledge and independence were embedded in the
Revolutionary tradition. Usually, however, these ideas had been expressed as warnings, admonitions against a chronic peril. "Ignorance
and slavery, knowledge and freedom are inseparably connected," a
clergyman had proclaimed at the Massachusetts ratifying convention
nearly 40 years before Webster's and Story's orations; and 20 years earlier a Vermont Jeffersonian had tersely explained that "knowledge is
the standing army of Republics."[102] But now the tone was celebratory.
A literate public with access to a free market of ideas and information was secure; the public good would be realized through the private pursuit of individual aspirations in a free, competitive society.
Clearly, the ideal of an informed citizenry had attained a fulfillment.

The richness and scope of this fulfillment was much broader and
more comprehensive than leaders of the Revolutionary generation
anticipated. Their own ideas had been drawn from secular British and
Enlightenment traditions so as to link free speech and a vigilant, politically-informed citizenry with free scientific inquiry and the conquest of tyranny and superstition. Now, however, Jefferson's former
protégé, Story, in the same speech in which he extolled knowledge as
the bulwark of liberty, went on to declare that it was "the peculiar
pride of our age, [that] the Bible may now circulate its consolations
and instructions among the poor and forlorn of every land in their
native dialect."[103] Although this Christian universalism overlooked
American slavery, it gave the idea of an informed citizenry an almost unlimited appeal. The American Philosophical Society and the

American Bible Society, like political, religious, and reform movements of all stripes, were invited to shelter under the capacious tent of the informed citizenry.

The triumphant spirit of orators in the 1820s and later was based largely on their perceptions of improvement. Statistics on post offices, newspapers, books, schools, lyceums, and the like mounted, and it became evident that public information, once scarce, was now circulating extensively and that institutions to promote learning in all of its branches were more and more part of the cultural landscape. Orators' own experience and their hopeful intuition encouraged the belief that with the demise of practical impediments to the circulation of information, in time virtually everyone would become sufficiently informed so that enlightened knowledge would vanquish superstition. Paradoxically, Americans had adopted a policy that relied primarily on private, voluntary means to achieve the public goal of an informed citizenry.

Owing to their own diversity and their widespread resistance to tax-supported public institutions, Americans embraced a system that was driven by competing, voluntary efforts to inform the public. What was overlooked, however, was the sheer multiplicity of popular concerns and interests, among which civic consciousness was not necessarily a high priority. Every white man might be a citizen, but partly because that status no longer conferred prestige, citizenship was not the primary conscious identity of many men. Identifying themselves in terms of family, occupation, sect, and community, they often displayed only haphazard or superficial interest in mastering information connected to citizenship. It was important surely that public information was available; but being informed required time, energy, and, most important, motivation. During the Jacksonian era it would be recognition of this factor—the primary importance of motivation—that would drive politics. Then, a principal objective for all concerned with promoting an informed citizenry became persuading men that partisan rallies and parades were not enough; they should take the time and trouble to be correctly informed.

Jurisprudence and Social Policy
in the New Republic

DAVID THOMAS KONIG

IN 1790 JAMES WILSON inaugurated his appointment to the first chair of law at the College of Philadelphia with a public lecture. Wilson, a Pennsylvanian, had played a prominent role in the Federal Convention of 1787 and had recently begun serving as an associate justice of the new United States Supreme Court. His lecture attracted "[t]he President of the United States, with his lady—also the Vice-President, and both houses of Congress [t]he President and both houses of the Legislature of Pennsylvania, together with a great number of ladies and gentlemen."[1]

The attendance of this "most brilliant and respectable audience"[2] testified more to the importance placed on law as the foundation of a free republic than it did to the stature of the speaker. Indeed, three years later in New York a distinguished assemblage of local dignitaries turned out to hear an obscure former assemblyman, barely thirty years old and only recently admitted to the bar of the Mayor's Court in that city, deliver his introductory lecture for the newly created law professorship at Columbia College. Aware of his own obscurity, James Kent knew why the event drew such interest. The establishment of a law professorship, he admitted, was "peculiarly proper at this day, when the general attention of mankind is strongly engaged in speculations on the Principles of Public Policy."[3] The attention paid to law professors in the new American republic attested to the fact that "The Theory of Government, and the Elements of Law" were now being "examined with a Liberal spirit, and the profoundest discernment."[4] The intense interest of Americans in law reform began almost immediately upon independence. Wilson, Kent, and others were continuing the effort that Thomas Jefferson had begun in the autumn of 1776 when he had resigned from Congress to return to Virginia, motivated by "his persuasion that our whole code must be reviewed, adapted to our republican form of government."[5]

Unconvinced that public law (which governed the state's relations with ordinary individuals) sufficed as the solution to their dilemma, they undertook to reevaluate and revise private law jurisprudence—the principles and rules regulating citizens' relations with each other.[6] In the first years of the federal republic, therefore, the founders worked at devising systems of laws that would encourage vigorous social institutions and harmonious relationships. A virtuous *society* encouraged by laws and protected by the courts—"the least dangerous branch" of government[7]—became a great interest of legal reform. Resistant to corruption, a "people free, contented and united" would stand between liberty and the encroaching power of internal tyrants or external foes.[8]

Such a goal—creating a social policy appropriate to the preservation of a free republic—would not be served by the conventions of metropolitan English jurisprudence. Despite its general usefulness, English law included "many vicious points which urgently required reformation," and which endangered American liberty by perpetuating the evils of English society.[9] Like the political inventiveness that culminated in the federal Constitution, the creation of an American jurisprudence drew upon an eclectic body of sources widely discussed by provincial reformers on both sides of the Atlantic but never before possible of implementation. Drawn from the rich and diverse—even contradictory—legal cultures of Great Britain, these ideas had never before been combined to create the coherent body of jurisprudential thought that Americans would devise in founding the republic. Selecting those ideas that confirmed their experiences and suited their needs, they would attempt to create a jurisprudential trinity of "policy, utility, and justice."[10]

≺ I ≻

A "system of jurisprudence purely American"

In beginning his law lectures at Glasgow University in 1766, Adam Smith had defined jurisprudence as "that science which inquires into the general principles which ought to be the foundation of the laws of all nations."[11] To Jesse Root of Connecticut, introducing one of the first published law reports in the United States in 1798, Americans were confronting a more specialized task—that of "forming a system of jurisprudence congenial to the spirit and principles of our own government."[12] Root, Kent, Jefferson, and others recognized that doing so was more easily stated than accomplished, however. As James Wilson posed the problem to his students in 1791,

> Let us . . . suppose, that, notwithstanding all the efforts of opposition, the principles and doctrines of freedom are successfully propagated and established; yet how many and how formidable are the barriers that remain to be surmounted, before those principles and doctrines can be successfully carried into practice? The friends of freedom, we shall suppose, are unanimous in their sentiments; does the same unanimity prevail with regard to their measures?[13]

Chief Justice John Jay, on circuit addressing a federal grand jury, also recognized the practical problem and agreed that no unanimity existed: "The expediency of carrying justice as it were to every man's door, was obvious," he observed in 1790; "but how to do it in an expedient manner was far from being apparent."[14]

Practical implementation defied whatever models Americans had before them. Published law reports, which Root correctly saw as necessary, were virtually nonexistent. The notes and opinions that Kent tried to draw upon, he complained, were cursory and contradictory, and few court records survived for consultation in local courthouses. "In short," Kent recalled when he described his early years of practice, "our jurisprudence was a blank."[15]

The easy accessibility of conventional English jurisprudence in Sir William Blackstone's *Commentaries on the Laws of England* posed a more insidious problem. Popular as a textbook for aspiring lawyers, the *Commentaries* insinuated into their education imperial legal principles dangerous to American concepts of liberty. Wilson, who considered Blackstone no "zealous friend of republicanism," assailed his fundamental "notion of a superiour . . . a notion unnecessary, unfounded, and dangerous; a notion inconsistent with the genuine system of human authority" based on "the consent of those whose obedience the law requires."[16] To St. George Tucker, the glib superficiality of Blackstone's jurisprudence threatened to restore the monarchical "union of the sovereignty with the government, [which]

constitutes a state of absolute monarchy." Tucker thus set out to produce for his law students at the College of William and Mary his own
edition of the *Commentaries*, with appropriate appendices pointing
out the wisdom of Virginia's rejection of Blackstone's antirepublican
tendencies.[17] Jefferson complained that Blackstone's "honeyed Mans-
fieldism" had led the legal profession ("the nursery of our Congress")
to "slide into toryism" by rendering law "more uncertain under pre-
tence of rendering it more reasonable." In a "free country," he wrote
in 1785, "every power is dangerous which is not bound up by general
rules."[18] While the common law might serve as the basis from which
to begin an American jurisprudence, it was essential that reformers
purge it of corruption and "accommodate it to our new principles and
circumstances."[19]

English common law, like systems of jurisprudence devised for
other societies, was inappropriate for the unique social circumstances and political imperatives of the new republic. "We have
passed the Red Sea in safety," wrote Wilson of the Revolutionary War
years; "we have survived a tedious journey through the wilderness:
we are now in full and peaceable possession of the promised land:
must we, after all, return to the flesh pots of Egypt?" "Is there not
danger," he asked, that when one nation teaches, it may, in some
instances, give the law to another?"[20] Had Americans "declared the
Common law to be in force," James Madison wrote to George Washington, it "would have brought over from G[reat] B[ritain] a thousand
heterogeneous & antirepublican doctrines, and even the *ecclesiastical Hierarchy itself*, for that is part of the common law."[21] The new
states therefore did not rush to receive the common law, or adopted
only those portions appropriate to their needs. In its 1780 constitution Massachusetts carefully avoided the term "common law" and
instead retained only those "laws which have heretofore been
adopted, used and approved in the Province, Colony or State of Massachusetts Bay, and usually practiced on in the Courts of law."[22] Root
therefore reflected a widespread sentiment when he prefaced his law
reports with the opinion that "I think we ought to resort, and not to
foreign systems, to lay a foundation, to establish a character upon,
and to rear a system of jurisprudence purely American, without any
marks of servility to foreign powers or states."[23]

≺ II ≻

*"[C]ivil liberty is capable of still greater
improvement and extension"*

American law reformers nonetheless faced their task in the confident expectation that "civil liberty is capable of still greater improvement and extension than is known even in its present cultivated state."[24] In part, they did so because they had the uncommon opportunity of framing a legal system by selective adoption using only those principles and practices that would advance their goals. The nation's jurisprudential moment was propitious, Chief Justice Jay noted, because other legal systems "had [been] organized in force or in fraud," unlike the new American republic, whose deliberations would be "unawed and uninfluenced by power or corruption."[25] Like other jurists at the founding, Wilson recognized the advantage of being able to jettison the irrelevant accretions of a legal system designed for and by another society, and to erect in its place a system designed to foster a free society. "'How happy would mankind be,' says the eloquent and benevolent Beccaria, 'if laws were now to be formed!'" Wilson quoted. "The United States enjoy this singular happiness. Their laws are now first formed."[26] Even the hesitant and shortlived efforts of the wartime confederation, Jay conceded, had left a legacy as "useful experiments" whose failings would remain cautionary.[27] Such was the opportunity for the new republic to join the other "great eras" of history, Wilson told his law students. "Why should not the present age in America," he asked rhetorically, "form one of those happy eras?"[28] Sharing in this widespread confidence that hitherto "visionary speculations of theoretical writers" might now be implemented, St. George Tucker in his republicanized version of Blackstone noted, "The world, for the first time since the annals of its inhabitants began, saw an original written compact formed by the free and deliberate voices of individuals disposed to unite in the same social bonds."[29]

More significantly, many Americans like Wilson shared in the confident assessment of their efforts as taking place in an advanced chapter in the history of human progress. "The works of human invention were progressive," he wrote, and American legal reform was being undertaken at a refined stage of human development far beyond the rude and barbaric period when English jurisprudence had been "founded on improper principles and directed to improper objects."[30] Reflecting on this opportunity as he compiled his law reports and his thoughts on jurisprudence in 1793, Nathaniel Chipman thankfully acknowledged the opportunity to reject archaic facets of the English common law that had been made "at a time, when the state of society, and of property, were very different, from what they are at present; in an age, when the minds of men were fettered in forms." By contrast, he observed, "Society was now in a state of melioration . . . The clouds, which had long hung over the reasoning faculties, began to be dispersed; the principles were examined, and better established."[31]

In the first years of the Revolution, many Americans possessed an overweening confidence in the opportunities presented at "this moment in perfection."[32] But confidence in "perfection" did not bespeak an expectation of achieving a state of finality—that is, of completeness beyond which no alteration would be necessary. In the English-speaking Enlightenment, the term "perfection" referred to a continuing process, not to a static creation. "Though unable in this world to attain final perfection," explains David Spadafora, "man is *perfectible*."[33] He cites Richard Price to describe the widely shared British belief in mankind's "natural improveableness," a capacity for gradual progress.[34]

Adam Smith put this hope and caution in terms welcome to American Whigs. "The idea of the perfection of policy and law," he wrote, was a necessary theoretical basis for action, because the more "improved" a society became, the more laws it needed to effect "[t]he first chief design of every system of government," which was "to maintain justice."[35] But Smith, in a manner typical of the Scottish Enlightenment, cautioned against "establishing all at once . . . every thing which that idea may seem to require." Such a hope, to Smith no less than to the American Founders, reflected the "arrogance" of "sovereign princes" who "consider the state as made for themselves, not themselves for the state."[36] Two generations after independence had been won, this concept still recurred in American thinking about government and law. The Constitution's framers, wrote Joseph Story, "were not so bold or rash enough to believe, or to pronounce it to be perfect. They desired, that it might be open to improvement . . . to be perpetually approaching nearer and nearer to perfection."[37]

≺ III ≻
"[L]iberty and sociability"

"[I]n the beginning," wrote John Locke, "all the world was *America*."[38] From that prelapsarian jurisprudential beginning, it might be expected that "the laws of nature, and of nature's God," to which Jefferson referred in the Declaration of Independence, would serve as the basic conceptual foundation upon which the American quest to perfect its legal order rested. And, indeed, this notion enjoyed widespread currency in the colonies and new nation. According to conventional legal and political thought, mankind secured its rights in two separate stages, each of which was marked by a contract among the members of a society. At first, explained the Boston minister Simeon Howard in a formulation of the theory repeated countless times, "men are under no civil government, God has given to every one liberty to pursue his own happiness in whatever way, and by whatever means he pleases." This condition, though prepolitical, was "not a state of licentiousness" because mankind had entered a compact to obey "the law of nature which bounds this liberty, forbids all injustice and wickedness, allows no man to injure another in his person or property, or to destroy his own life." In a typical description of the next stage, Howard told the Ancient and Honorable Artillery Company in 1773,

experience soon taught that, either thro' ignorance of this law, or the influence of unruly passions, some were disposed to violate it, but encroaching upon the liberty of others; so that the *weak* were liable to be greatly injured by the superior power of bad men, without any means of security or redress. This gave birth to civil society.[39]

This second, or political, contract was conventionally termed the "original contract"[40] and allowed individuals to exercise their natural rights, provided they "keep within those restrictions which they have consented to come under."[41]

Yet natural rights—those rights possessing a validity and authority independent of human enactment or custom—did not offer much practical guidance in the formation of new legal systems. Despite its undoubted value as a means of contravening Britain's constitutional rejection of America's demands, and despite its near-ritualistic incantation in the writings of the Revolutionary era, natural law was too vague and too vulnerable to competing interpretations to serve as a basis for a clearly articulated American jurisprudence. While it may go too far to speak categorically of the "[i]rrelevancy of natural rights" in eighteenth-century America, it is surely true that they were "fantasized and void of any practical application."[42] Thomas Paine believed that any statement of natural rights should be limited to those

as are either consistent with, or absolutely necessary toward our happiness in a state of civil government; for were all *great natural* rights, or principles . . . to be admitted, it would be impossible that any government could be formed thereon, and instead of being a Bill of Rights fitted to a state of civil government, it would be a Bill of Rights fitted to man in a state of nature without any government at all. It would be an Indian Bill of Rights.[43]

By the end of the eighteenth century natural law had little or no practical force in American jurisprudence, despite the claims of some "speculative jurists." Rejecting, in *Calder v. Bull* (1798), Justice Samuel Chase's argument voiding any law "contrary to the *great first principles* of the *social compact*," Justice James Iredell noted that "the Court cannot pronounce it void merely because it is, in their judgment, contrary to the principles of natural justice." Recognizing the unstable and subjective nature of the concept, Iredell continued,

The ideas of natural justice are regulated by no fixed standard: the ablest and the purest men have differed upon the subject; and all that the Court could properly say, in such an event, would be, that the legislature (possessed of an equal right of opinion) had passed an act which, in the opinion of the judges, was inconsistent with the abstract principles of natural justice.[44]

To the extent that it survived, natural justice did so as but one element of the social contract and the original political contract, where American jurisprudence could unite its long tradition of community with the liberating potential for individuals in the new nation. The fusion of group and individual rights was a linkage perfectly compatible—indeed necessary—within eighteenth-century social and political thought. Each was necessary as a qualification of the other; alone, either would have been unacceptable.

Simultaneously liberating and cohesive, contract theory provided a compellingly attractive paradigm for the reconciliation of collective and individual needs. In addition, it reconciled the American quest for a return to uncorrupted natural forms with the acknowledgement that increasing social complexity required laws to recapture and ensure that state of affairs. Like any paradigm of great explanatory power, it led Americans of the Revolutionary and early national period to redefine their history and to construct their national identity in its terms. The first description of the agreement among the Pilgrims in 1620, for instance, had referred simply to their "association and agreement," while William Bradford had described only the "combination made by them before they came ashore." In the eighteenth century, by contrast, this act came to be known as a "contract" or "compact,"[45] and when James Wilson used it in his law lectures he, too, called it a "compact."[46] While natural rights lay at the basis of Revolutionary belief, then, they could only be realized and protected collectively within the formulation of the original contract as understood in the post-Lockean world of legal and political theory.

The political dimension of the original contract ideal gained popular force from its consonance with a more mundane, though practically meaningful, analogy drawn from a widespread experience of early American life—the commercial contract. Theophilus Parsons, later a justice of the Massachusetts Supreme Judicial Court, carefully spelled out the manner and extent to which natural rights were preserved when he explained why his county had rejected the proposed commonwealth constitution of 1778. For the purposes of enjoying the benefits of law when "the good of the whole requires it," Parsons wrote, mankind surrenders certain rights—but, significantly, only a certain type of rights, which Parsons described as "alienable." Such rights, he noted, "may be parted with for an equivalent." If no "consideration" was received in return, this contract (or "bargain"), like any other, would be "void."[47] Such argument was little different from standard contract theory and practice in the courts of colonial and Revolutionary America. Without equivalent consideration, no contract was valid. Indeed, as has been amply demonstrated in careful examinations of the way in which contract law operated in eighteenth-century Massachusetts, the community imposed a sense of fairness upon transactions and allowed wide discretion to juries to set aside arrangements they regarded as contrary to it.[48]

Alexander Hamilton also emphasized that the original contract ("the origin of all government") "must be a voluntary contract, be-tween the rulers and the ruled; and must be liable to such limita-tions, as are necessary for the security of the *absolute rights* of the latter; for what original title can any man or set of men have, to gov-ern others, except their own consent?"[49] No contract was valid with-out consent. Early Americans were quite familiar with the concept of the alienability of certain forms of property only with freely given consent—dower rights are an obvious example, requiring an exami-nation of a wife in private to demonstrate that no duress was being used, and that consent was offered. But some rights simply could not be alienated under any circumstances. All persons receive equal rights at birth, some of which are "alienable," while "[o]thers are un-alienable and inherent, and of that importance, that no equivalent can be received in exchange." Parsons had no difficulty—theoreti-cally, at least—in reconciling the organic, corporate unity of repub-licanism with the natural rights of individuals. "When men form themselves into society, and erect a body politic or State, they are said to be considered as one moral whole, which is in possession of the supreme power of the State." Nevertheless, he added as a neces-sary corollary, "This supreme power is composed of the powers of each individual collected together, and VOLUNTARILY parted with by him. No individual, in this case, parts with his unalienable rights, the supreme power therefore cannot controul them."[50]

Basing the state in its origination via compact of freely consent-ing individuals drew the discussion onto the ground of recapturing a lost natural order of human sociability. It was natural, wrote innu-merable writers of the Revolutionary era, that people should com-bine, but not out of a need to restrain the Hobbesian impulses of a predatory nature. Explicitly rejecting the view that "society is not natural, but is only adventitious to us," James Wilson emphasized the inseparability of "liberty and sociability."[51]

Wilson's linkage of "liberty and sociability" reflected his deep familiarity, from his student days at the University of St. Andrews, with this staple of the Scottish Enlightenment. The idea that human rights are guarded in and by society—rather than by individual as-sertion—had a powerful influence not only on Wilson but on many other Americans of the founding generation. Jefferson copied into his legal commonplace book that passage from Kames's *Historical Law*

Tracts that argued: "Man, by his nature, is fitted for society, and society by its conveniences, is fitted for man. The perfection of human
society, consists in that just degree of union among individuals,
which to each reserves freedom and independency, as far as is consistent with peace and good order."[52] Like Kames, Jefferson and other
Americans saw society as undergoing a process of refinement and
progress in which association via contract advanced individual wellbeing. Again quoting Kames, Jefferson wrote: "Moral duties, originally weak and feeble, acquire great strength by refinement of manners. Promises and covenants particularly, have seldom among bar-
barians weight sufficient to counterbalance appetite or passion. In
the progress of social life the use of a covenant becomes visible."[53]

Many Americans looked back proudly upon the period between
the collapse of royal government and the Declaration of Independence, when newly independent republics established themselves
formally, as an example of mankind's naturally sociable nature. Contrary to the dire predictions of those who mistook the Lockean repudiation of England as a return to some savage state—and who thus
misunderstood the continued validity of the prepolitical social contract—it was clear that Americans had endured their "unsettled
state" with "honour." An anonymous Pennsylvanian in 1776 hoped
that posterity would remember "that by the common consent of
Citizens, the public peace was preserved inviolate, for nearly three
years, *without law.*" He knew that although the political contract
had been dissolved, the social one had not been, and that a new original political contract appropriate to the nation's advanced stage of
freedom might be established. With independence, he proudly announced, "We are now arrived at a period from which we are to look
forward as a *legal people.*"[54]

≺ IV ≻

*Property, Utility, and "the equalizing
genius of the laws"*

The American Whig concept of the contract of government began
with the legal equality of those establishing the compact. Their first
usage of this idea was, admittedly, not to emphasize individual
equality, but rather the corporate equality of groups within the Em-

pire. Each colony, this argument asserted, deserved equal rights with any political unit in the British Isles or, for that matter, in England itself.[55] Despite this emphasis—or, in at least one case, because of it—many Americans refused to separate the two notions.[56]

The legal equality of individuals, unimpaired by artificial distinctions, was a foundation of American thought at the founding, but no corollary of material equality followed. Timothy Ford, writing as "Americanus" in 1794, argued "from the laws of nature" to assert "that *equality of rights* and *equality of conditions* are matters entirely distinct."[57] Madison, expressing the widely shared orthodoxy of the time, noted the inevitably "unequal faculties of acquiring property" that derived from inequalities of talent and fortune, accepted it as a given in *Federalist X*, and opposed any scheme "for an equal division of property."[58]

The ideal of impartiality must not, however, suggest that the founders envisioned the state as merely a neutral arbiter in a laissez-faire economic order, blind to outcome and unconcerned with the possibility that legal equality might exaggerate social inequality. American opposition to government partiality was as much the product of colonial experience with mercantilism as it was a canon of Enlightenment political economy, and drew upon a legacy of resentment toward the imperial government's siding with the powerful to exaggerate inequality via special privilege and monopolistic powers.[59] This ideal of evenhandedness in government, which challenged Britain's mercantilist policy of bestowing favors on special groups to maximize national wealth and power, struck Joseph Priestley as a vital condition of assuring a free government. It was "a *maxim of policy*" in the United States, he wrote in approving contrast to British commercial supports, "not to favour one class of citizens more than another by any measure of government, especially the merchant more than the farmer."[60]

Even John Locke and Adam Smith saw morality, at least, as condemning the excessive aggrandizement of property. Although Locke admitted that labor would "begin a title of property," he added that "it was useless as well as dishonest" for even the most diligent laborer "to carve himself too much, or to take more than he needed," and that God had "given his needy Brother a Right to the Surplusage of his Goods."[61] Smith, too, disdained selfishness in the accumulation of property, and denounced Mandeville for grounding

acquisitiveness in base motives rather than the mutuality of benefits received; that "wholly pernicious" Mandevillian philosophy, he
warned, produced only "licentious societies."[62]

Although the laws of nature did not command equality of property, sound policy dictated that the laws work against excessive inequality, and natural law did not stand in the way. For many Americans a useful and accessible body of English radical thought joined
this policy to jurisprudence. Richard Price, a friend of Jefferson and
Franklin, and correspondent of Rush and Adams, condemned "an unequal distribution of property" as a threat to freedom.[63]

In addition, a powerful tradition in Scottish legal writing, which
reached a peak in its "classical period" in the second half of the eighteenth century, placed greater restrictions on property for the public
interest than did English common law. Beginning with the *Institutions of the Laws of Scotland* (1681) by Sir John Dalrymple, Viscount
Stair, Scots law embraced a jurisprudence grounded as much in social
utility as in natural rights.[64] The product, as it developed more fully
in the eighteenth century, became the foundation of jurisprudence
for many writers who had wide influence among Americans of the
Revolutionary generation. It was this impulse, derived from his
struggle with reconciling rights and ethics while professor of moral
philosophy at Glasgow University, that drove Francis Hutcheson to
formulate his famous utilitarian axiom, "That Action is best, which
procures the greatest Happiness for the greatest Numbers."[65] For
Adam Ferguson, the result was that "[l]aws, whether civil or political, are expedients of policy to adjust the pretensions of parties, and
to secure the peace of society."[66] Kames, whose influence was so
strong in America, thus crafted a jurisprudence that balanced natural
justice with utility, refusing to rely exclusively on either, in dealing
with the social demands that might be placed upon property rights.[67]

The Scots' modifications of natural law theory, which might be
termed "natural jurisprudence," must be seen as "neither a set of
eternally valid, substantial laws," explains Knud Haakonssen; "nor
is it a deliberate human construction. It is, rather, a few universal
test-principles, which necessarily refer to the existing value-system
in a society."[68] By emphasizing human nature and needs, natural jurisprudence served the purposes of Americans seeking to give force
to the theoretical goals of natural law within the practical context of
the new republic's effort to secure liberty without the coercive instruments of the state that so troubled them.[69]

Americans such as Wilson, Madison, and Jefferson, all heavily influenced by Scottish Enlightenment jurisprudence, could draw upon
this conceptualization and apply it to their thinking about property
rights and their utility in society. "Property, highly deserving security," wrote Wilson, "is, however, not an end, but a means. How miserable, and how contemptible is that man, who inverts the order of
nature, and makes his property, not a means, but an end!"[70] Madison,
whose education at Princeton was deeply influenced by its Scots
president John Witherspoon, also carefully specified the relationship
among property, individual rights, and the social good. "The personal
right to acquire property," he continued to maintain late in life, was
"a natural right," but "property, when acquired" has "a right to protection, which is a social right."[71] "It is agreed by those who have
seriously considered the subject," remarked Jefferson, whose thinking was shaped by the Scots he read and studied with at the College
of William and Mary, "that no individual has, of natural right, a separate property in an acre of land . . . Stable ownership is the gift of
society."[72]

Considerations of social policy led many to the conclusion that
the more equal the distribution of property, the more stable and vigorous were both government and society. It was clear from history,
wrote the Delaware Antifederalist Robert Coram, "that the unequal
distribution of property was the parent of almost all the disorders of
government."[73] Poverty, which accompanied inequality, also had ter-
rible social effects. Coram, an autodidact who read widely enough to
open his own school, quoted an obscure Yorkshire physician to make
his point:

Poverty makes mankind unnatural in their affections and behavior. The
child secretly wishes the death of the parent, and the parent thinks his children an incumbrance and has sometimes robbed their bellies to fill his own.
Many yield themselves up to the unnatural lusts of others for a trifling gra-
tuity, and the most scandalous practices are often the effects of necessitous
poverty.[74]

Few agreed with the American economist Samuel Blodget that
the rich must "accept a *sufficient tax on their income*," although
Jefferson, shocked by the gross inequality he observed in France, once
suggested to Madison that one "means of silently lessening the inequality of property is to exempt all from taxation below a certain
point, & and to tax the higher portions of property in geometrical
progression as they rise."[75] Instead, for most reformers (including Jef-

ferson) the professed solution took the form of equalizing property
through an equal division among heirs. St. George Tucker listed the
"abolition of *entails*" and "of the right of *primogeniture*" at the head
of his list of the most important legal changes effected by the Revolution.[76] In his list of how government must cope with the inherent
dangers that attended the necessity of parties in a free government,
Madison listed "political equality" but then placed the need for government to act by "withholding *unnecessary* opportunities from a
few, to increase the inequality of property, by an immoderate, and
especially an unmerited, accumulation of riches." Eschewing redistribution, Madison instead called for "the silent operation of the
laws, which, without violating the rights of property, reduce extreme
wealth towards a state of mediocrity, and raise extreme indigence towards a state of comfort."[77] To Nathaniel Chipman, any effort to
achieve the ultimate goal of equality in propertyholding was a "Pro-
crustean exercise," but an equal division of property among heirs
would suffice. "The operation of the equal laws of nature," he emphasized, "tend to exclude, or correct every dangerous excess."[78]
   Noah Webster regarded such partibility as more important than
any other fundamental of law, owing to its equalizing potential. "An
equality of property, with a necessity of alienation, constantly operating to destroy combinations of powerful families, is the very *soul
of a republic.*" The social effect of equalized property was more important than even the legal protections of a free press, habeas corpus, or Magna Carta, Webster believed, "all inferior considerations,
when compared with a general distribution of real property among
every class of people." Linking property with political participation,
he concluded, "Let the people have property, and they *will* have
power—a power that will for ever be exerted to prevent a restriction
of the press, and abolition of trial by jury, or the abridgement of any
other privilege."[79]
   The attack on encumbered estates attracted many reformers. Although Massachusetts, for example, had abolished primogeniture in
the seventeenth century, it had done so only for estates held in fee
simple; those held in fee tail might still descend to a single heir.[80] In
1791 the commonwealth finally abolished primogeniture for estates
held in fee tail.[81] Virginia, of course, abolished the fee tail in 1776,
and in 1785 enacted that equal partitioning would replace primogeniture in intestacy.[82] Other states applied constitutional bans on
both primogeniture and entail.[83]

More than bans on primogeniture and entail would be needed to assure the broader distribution of property, however. Indeed, it was the function of law to aid and foster what Henry Chipman had referred to as the "equal operation of the laws of nature." It was a truism, according to Scottish Enlightenment theories of a society's increasing complexity, that more human laws were needed to restore those "laws of nature" that tended to be overwhelmed by the progress of social refinement. For much the same reason that Adam Smith advocated some governmental attention to economic activity, Henry Chipman in 1806 cited the need for "*artificial* laws, resulting from new and increased relations," to advance the natural order and adapt it "[a]s a nation advances in refinement and increases in population." "Nature forms the diamond," he explained, "and art gives it the polish."[84]

Accordingly, it was necessary to employ both those laws "which are founded on the principles of human nature in society, which are permanent and universal," explained Nathaniel Chipman, "and those which are dictated by the circumstances, policy, manners, morals and religion of the age."[85] Among the changes dictated by the latter, St. George Tucker lauded Virginia's abolition of primogeniture and entail, as well as its ending

of the preference given to the *male* line, in respect to real estates of inheritance; and of the *jus accrescendi*, or right of survivorship between *joint-tenants*; the *ascending* quality communicated to real estates; the *heritability* of the *half-blood*; and of *bastards*; the *legitimation* of the latter, in certain cases; and many other instances in which the rules of the COMMON LAW, or the provisions of a statute, are totally changed.[86]

Such laws, in common with others, attempted to free property from encumbrances or concentration, and to facilitate its circulation and make it more accessible. "It is not so much the quantity of wealth," explained Thomas Paine, "as the quantity that circulates."[87] Adam Smith had emphasized the advantages of small parcels left equally to children, in that it tended to place a greater amount of property on the market, driving down the price generally and acting to reduce monopoly prices in particular.[88] James Kent, an avowed disciple of Smith, approvingly cited *Wealth of Nations* when he noted that "property should have a free circulation, and free employment, without any of the fetters of entailments and perpetuities." Regardless of the inegalitarian purposes to which Kent's defense of property might be put later in the nineteenth century, his progressive purpose was clear in the post-Revolutionary years: he opposed laws that would "foster excessive inequalities of property" because they would "invite to indolence, damp enterprize, facilitate corruption, unduly widen distinctions, and humble the poor under the proud superiority of the rich."[89]

Those wary of the effects of economic inequality reflected a distrust of unrestrained acquisitiveness, and in 1776 Pennsylvania almost adopted a constitutional provision committing the new commonwealth to restrain excessive accumulation of property. "An enormous Proportion of Property rested in a few Individuals," reported a draft committee, "is dangerous to the Rights, and destructive of the Common Happiness of Mankind; and therefore every free State hath a Right by its Laws to discourage the Possession of such property."[90] Though rejected, this proposal reflected a widespread unease that people might use the liberating impulses of the Revolution to pursue personal gain for its own sake, without regard for its social impact or political effects. Worried by the potential that unrestrained acquisitiveness held for the republic, many observers agreed with Hamilton that the "name of liberty" was being employed as an excuse for greed.[91] "I know there are Mandevilles among you," wrote Richard Henry Lee in 1779, condemning by association those who adhered to the English philosopher who argued that "private vices" actually produced "public virtue." These Americans, Lee complained, "laugh at virtue, and with vain ostentatious display of words will deduce from vice, public good! But such men are much fitter to be Slaves in the corrupt, rotten despotisms of Europe, than to remain citizens of young and rising republics."[92] One need not have been an orthodox republican, such as Lee, committed to the primacy of the group and the suppression of self-interest, to doubt that a multiplicity of evils could ever produce an aggregate good. Wrote Associate Supreme Court Justice James Iredell in *Calder v. Bull*, "Providence never can intend to promote the prosperity of any country by bad means."[93]

A philosophy celebrating self-interest bothered James Madison, too, and it informed his conceptualization of clashing social groups. Despite the great fame of *Federalist X* in which he set out his classic formulation of interest group politics, Madison had misgivings about rampant partisan activity. In 1792 he reassessed his understanding of parties and published his remarks in the *National Gazette*. Seeing the political party as essentially evil, he refused to accept the Mandevillian corollary that such vices, taken in the aggregate, had a positive effect. He explicitly rejected Mandeville's principle, seeing in the multiplication of individual evils only an aggregate evil. Nevertheless, he recognized, parties were "unavoidable," owing to "difference of interests, real or supposed." "The great object," he wrote, "should be to combat the evil," for which he had proposed efforts toward the "mediocrity" of propertyholding. His formulation ought to be quoted in full: "From the expediency, in politics, of making natural parties, mutual checks on each other, to infer the propriety of creating artificial parties, in order to form them into mutual checks, is not less absurd, than it would be in ethics, to say, that new vices ought to be promoted, where they would counteract each other, because this use may be made of existing vices."[94]

The use of the laws to meliorate or retard the process of inequality, then, appeared to many a necessary condition of freedom. In 1774, for example, the Continental Congress used this impulse as an inducement to the Quebecois to join their movement. Quoting "the celebrated Marquis *Beccaria*," it established as a principle that "In every human society there is an *effort, continually tending* to confer on one part the heighth of power and happiness, and to reduce the other to the extreme of weakness and misery. The intent of good laws is to *oppose this effort*, and to diffuse their influence *universally* and *equally*."[95] Noah Webster called this process "the equalizing genius of the laws."[96]

Madison appreciated that groups, like individuals, were not equal, and the rich seemed to be increasing the inequality that existed naturally. Responding to Jefferson's request for comments on his proposed Virginia constitution in 1788, Madison ruefully observed of what had transpired in the new states of the Confederation, "In all the Governments which were considered as beacons to republican patriots and lawgivers, the rights of persons were subjected to those of property. The poor were sacrificed to the rich."[97]

Inequality troubled Madison as more than a moral matter: it was poor social policy that threatened political liberty. Creating the conditions of freedom required some attention to at least preventing a further erosion of the position of the poor, as well as to stopping the impoverishment of others. Madison feared the exploitative legislation that favored one group over another, and that tended to favor the rich. Looking back on the progress of society in 1821 and arguing that suffrage be extended to the propertyless, Madison reminded his listeners "that there are various ways in which the rich may oppress the poor; in which property may oppress liberty . . . It is necessary that the poor should have a defence against the danger."[98]

Providing that defense was beyond the capacity of classical republicanism, which posited a homogeneity of interests within the community, and not a concern for other and variant communities that might coexist in a complex, modern society. Madison's theory of group differences, which accepted the inevitability of ranks, also contained within it an assumption that even supposedly neutral acts might have unequal impact.[99] "We cannot," he reminded the Philadelphia convention in 1787, "be regarded even at this time, as one homogeneous mass, in which every thing that affects a part will affect in the same manner the whole." Madison feared the poor and their emergence as a dangerous interest group that might threaten social peace and the security of property. Becoming ever more numerous, they would eventually "outnumber those who are placed above the feelings of indigence. According to the equal laws of suffrage, the power will slide into the hands of the former." The product, he feared, would be "a levelling spirit" and the loss of liberty.[100]

≺ V ≻

Justice in the Uncertain Marketplace of Life

The experiences of the 1780s had demonstrated precisely this threat of a government responsive to the will of people bent on destroying the liberties of others. The great danger in a republic, according to Madison, came from "the majority of the Community" pursuing its special interests and abusing individuals and minorities under the color of law, and "not from the acts of Government contrary to the sense of its constituents."[101]

Madison had grounded his formulation in years of experience while serving as a delegate to the Virginia Assembly during the tumultuous 1780s. But he did not regard his insight as one limited to the years of crisis. Rather, Madison shared a widespread perception that American society was unpredictably changeable. The majority coalitions he described in the *Federalist* might have difficulty forming (a positive factor, he believed, to be aided by establishing an "extended republic"), but form they would, and rights would inevitably become endangered by a majority.[102]

What troubled Madison, however, was not merely the spectre of a simple majority of the poor overwhelming the rich; the problem was that the dynamic quality of the American experiment left uncertain who might gain or lose by the process of change. Those with property had as much to fear from *others* with property who might win what Adam Smith in *Wealth of Nations* called "the race for wealth and honours."[103] Already since 1776 the nation had seen Crown supporters, once prominent and wealthy, consigned to poverty for their support of the wrong political position.[104] It had seen regions gain and then lose by the fortunes of economic change. Rich farm areas had fallen into depression, as newer lands came under the plow. Merchants trading to the West Indies failed, while others opening new ports thrived. Success bred not always more success, but possibly overextension and collapse.[105]

In this unstable situation no one could be certain that he would not avoid the fate of the losers. Because traditional political theory did not account for such a turnabout of fortune, it allowed those with power and rights, comfortable in the expectation that they and their children would never fall from their comfortable status, safely to exclude others and to deny them equality. "It is always to be taken for granted, that those who oppose an equality of rights never mean the exclusion should take place on themselves," wrote Paine in 1795. Such people "conceive they are playing a safe game, in which there is a chance to gain and none to lose."[106] But people inevitably did lose, even if it took generations; the descendants of today's rich might easily become the poor of the future.

Concerns about the future drove the logic of rights onto the ground of equal protection of the laws. "In framing a system which we wish to last for ages," Madison told the Federal Convention, "we sh[oul]d not lose sight of the changes which ages will produce."[107] George Mason, working from the same assumption, also told the Convention that all interests and groups needed legislative representation to assure their rights under changing circumstances. Mason, according to Madison,

had often wondered at the indifference of the superior classes of society to this dictate of humanity & policy, considering that however affluent their circumstances, or elevated their situations, might be, the course of a few years, not only might but certainly would, distribute their posterity throughout the lowest classes of Society. Every selfish motive therefore, every family attachment, ought to recommend such a system of policy as would provide no less carefully for the rights—and happiness of the lowest than of the highest orders of Citizens.[108]

The uncertainties of life chances in a fluid American society gave a powerful impetus to the drafting of laws that would guarantee, as closely as possible, the equality of rights once possessed in the social equality of the imagined era before the original contract. Describing the process by which "natural Equality is lost," Thomas Gordon as "Cato" in 1721 had attributed inequality to "the use [people] make of their faculties, and of the Opportunities that they find." But "Fortune" was less kind. Gordon described how "she acts wantonly and capriciously, often cruelly; and counterplotting Justice as well as nature, frequently sets the Fool above the wise Man, and the Best below the worst."[109]

Democracy could only worsen this situation encouraging individuals to compete for the power of becoming tyrants themselves. As Priestley gloomily concluded,

the government of the temporary magistrates of a democracy, or even the laws themselves, may be as tyrannical as the maxims of the most despotic monarchy, and the administration of the government may be as destructive of private happiness. The only consolation that a democracy suggests in those circumstances is, that every member of the state has a chance of arriving at a share in the chief magistracy, and consequently of playing the tyrant in his turn.[110]

More sinister, in the minds of men such as Gouverneur Morris, was the expectation that after losers wrought vengeance on those who had once oppressed them they would be the next to suffer in a vicious cycle of recrimination. "In the madness of Victory are they free from Apprehension?" he asked. "What happens this day to the Victim of their rage may it not happen tomorrow to his Persecutors?"[111] Aware of this process, Jefferson explicitly forswore vengeance against the Federalists when he took office as President in 1801. "All . . . will bear in mind this sacred principle, that though the will of the majority is in all cases to prevail, that will to be rightful must be reasonable; that the minority possess their equal rights, which equal law must protect, and to violate would be oppression."[112]

Blind to what the future might bring, the Founders entered their original compact with a strong sense that any power they gave themselves, any potential for abuse they established, might be turned against them or their descendants. "Rights are permanent things, fortune not so," Thomas Paine warned the people of Pennsylvania. "Freedom and fortune have no natural relation. They are as distinct things as rest and motion. To make freedom follow fortune is to suppose her the shadow of an image on a wheel—a shade of passage—an unfixable nothing."[113]

Although the founders were well aware of their own special interests, they recognized the need for rules of equal justice that would assure fairness even in the distant and unpredictable future. Already, the children of the founders were setting off westward, into lands where their place in society was anything but assured. Instability, if not chaos and degeneracy, loomed ahead of them.[114] If the populations of these new regions of America, as well as those of older ones, were to maintain their liberties, provision had to be made to assure a political system based on constant recourse to justice. Hamilton urged this on the people of New York in *Federalist LXXVIII*, when he noted that "no man can be sure that he may not be tomorrow the victim of a spirit of injustice, by which he may be a gainer today. And every man must now feel that the inevitable tendency of such a spirit is to sap the foundations of public and private confidence, and to introduce in its stead, universal distrust and distress."[115]

≺ VI ≻

*Sociability and the "operations of
social virtue"*

The threatening specter of "universal distrust," buried as it is among the larger questions of federal jurisdiction in *Federalist LXXVIII*, has been ignored by historians reading that document from the vantage point of the twentieth century. In the eighteenth, however, Hamilton's reference to "distrust" in a society spoke to a concern that his readers would have readily recognized. The idea was so commonplace in the discourse of the early republic that it seems, in retrospect, to have been merely rhetorical convention, high-minded window dressing on the more important structure of material concerns.

James Madison was not invoking an empty abstraction in his attack on religious assessments, however, when he warned that forced religion threatens the "bands of society."[116] Rather, he was addressing the same impulse that led John Adams in the Massachusetts constitution of 1780 to enjoin "sincerity, good humor, and all social affections, and generous sentiments, among the people."[117] For Jefferson, a polity of free citizens required "that harmony and affection without which liberty and even life itself are but dreary things."[118]

Hamilton, Madison, Adams, and Jefferson were all emphasizing a concept that enabled Americans to reinterpret their communitarian and organic traditions with the dynamic and centrifugal tendencies released by an expanding economy. Unwilling to embrace the spartan simplicity required by republicanism, yet still restrained by traditional fears of self-interest and material acquisitiveness, many Americans in the years after 1783 found the unifying concept they needed in the Enlightenment principle of mankind's inclination to society and sociable relations. Distrusting government—even as bounded by the confines of the original political contract—and looking instead to the pre-political *social* contract foundations of human organization, many writers located their hopes not in individual vigilance or personal virtue, but in "Society." "Unless . . . some vigilant, powerful, and independent corrective is retained by Society," wrote Tunis Wortman in 1800, "nothing can prevent its becoming the devoted victim of Despotism."[119]

This reliance on the vigor of social institutions reflected the Enlightenment's heightened interest in mankind's social nature and its material needs in an increasingly complex and relentlessly advancing society. A staple of natural jurisprudence, the manner in which Americans united refinement and liberty was not, therefore, purely a product of post-Revolutionary disillusionment with the classical republican concept of spartan self-denial. As early as 1776 Carter Braxton had deplored the excesses of "elegance and refinement," but he acknowledged that "sumptuary laws" that "restrained men to plainness and similarity in dress and diet" were ill-suited to America:

Schemes like these may be practicable in countries so sterile by nature as to afford a scanty supply of the necessaries, and none of the conveniences of life; but they can never meet with a favourable reception from people who inhabit a country to which Providence has been more bountiful. They will always claim a right of using and enjoying the fruits of their honest industry, unrestrained by any ideal principles of government, and will gather estates for themselves and children without regarding the whimsical impropriety of being richer than their neighbours. These are rights which freemen will never consent to relinquish, and after fighting for deliverance from one species of tyranny, it would be unreasonable to expect they should tamely acquiesce under another.[120]

While still a law student, Jefferson had been deeply impressed by Kames's historical contextualizing of law. Jurisprudence, he learned, became "only a rational study, when it is traced historically, from its first rudiments among savages, through successive ages, to its highest improvements in a civilized society."[121] As society reached its commercial (and highest) stage, law adapted to its needs. America could not escape this process, and even Jefferson was forced to recognize it. "All the world is becoming commercial," Jefferson admitted to George Washington in 1784. "Our citizens have had too full a taste of the comforts furnished by the arts and manufactures to be debarred the use of them."[122]

The unattainable self-denying *individual* virtues of classical republicanism, then, had to be refashioned as the "social virtues" that would produce the "internal strength and beauty of the state," said the Reverend Phillips Payson in his election sermon of 1778. "We should take mankind as they are, and not as they ought to be or would be if they were perfect in wisdom and virtue." Social policy (such as a "general distribution of property") and legal protections ("full liberty of the press") must therefore be established to allow such enjoyment yet prevent the slide into tyranny.[123] These provisions would serve as a *"preventive jurisprudence"* that would "make government easy."[124]

In the Scottish Enlightenment Americans had an appealing model for such thinking.[125] Owing to the energy of its disciples in North America, who brought with them a coherent philosophy of moral and civic improvement, and perhaps as well to the way that the incorporation of Scotland into the United Kingdom had overwhelmed the northern kingdom's independence, many ideas prevalent in eighteenth-century Scotland possessed a strong attractiveness.[126] Like their provincial cousins in America, the Scots had to deal with the ambivalent meaning of their legal and constitutional status within the empire. On the one hand, both cultures celebrated those English liberties that reached beyond a border or an ocean. Like the

Americans after the Declaratory Act, however, Scots were acutely
aware of their limited role in government after their absorption by
the Act of Union, and they strove to preserve their identity and autonomy.[127] John Witherspoon brought to Princeton his own resent-
ments about English encroachments on Scottish culture, and at the
Continental Congress railed against the "incorporating Union, and
not a federal" one, that reduced Scotland to subordinate status in the
United Kingdom.[128] Jefferson learned of this struggle (undoubtedly
from his Scots teachers) and noted how "Scotland had suffered by
that Union,"[129] and Adams witnessed it from a closer perspective
while abroad in 1783. "There are discontents in Scotland, as well as
in Ireland," he noted in his diary.[130] Like the Scots, the Americans
suffered from the limitations imposed by the metropolis on its distant dominions. "It is paradoxical," notes John Brewer in his study of
how the juggernaut English state weighed upon the provinces, that
"[t]he heavy-handedness of British rule increased the farther it extended beyond the metropolis."[131] Madison acknowledged this fact
axiomatically when he noted the perils of distance as they had operated in the power exerted by "G.B. towards America."[132] Operating
within a shared context of historical contingencies, Americans and
Scots thus shared many of the same premises and drew many similar
conclusions.

Conscious of this history at a time when they were establishing
a distant central government, Americans needed ways to limit its
power. Two of the amendments in the Bill of Rights, in fact, may
have derived from American awareness of Scotland's military vulnerability to central power after 1745, when England reacted to the Jacobite rising by ensuring that the northern kingdom be unable to resist
armed force. The Second Amendment reflected the long American
hostility to standing armies, and it also spoke to their colonial experience of British attempts to disarm provincial militias in 1775.[133] In
addition, however, it might also reflect the outright ban on militias
in Scotland after the Jacobite rebellion, and English rejection of Scottish efforts to reestablish them between the 1750s and 1780s.[134] Another aspect of this tyranny—the billeting of troops in homes—may
have contributed to thinking about the Third Amendment. Sir William Blackstone wrote proudly of the English freedom from un-
wanted quartering of troops, but it was a freedom that had no constitutional protection in Scotland.[135]

For the American founders, the struggle against centralized power gave them common cause with the Scots' reliance on society and the "science of man" as a guide to developing a natural jurisprudence of liberty. Not only would public law promote the rights of the individual, but private law would also define his moral responsibilities toward the creation of an orderly society capable of resisting corruption and tyranny. Though scarcely all Scots theorists were Whigs, and after 1775 Scots in general gave little support to the American cause,[136] their efforts to identify the social factors contributing to liberty were well known and influential in America.[137]

James Wilson drew upon this identification of a vigorous society as guarantor of liberty when he joined rights and obligations as the Scots did. After explaining in his law lectures how utility must inform morality, he continued with another linkage: "Congenial with this principle, is another, which has received the sanction of some writers—that sociability, or the care of maintaining society properly, is the fountain of obligation and right: for every right there must be a correspondent obligation."[138] Wilson's emphasis on "obligation" did not presage a call for the self-suppressing virtues of classical republicanism. Rather, the concept of sociability—or "the law of sociality," as the Aberdonian George Turnbull called it[139]—pointed to an idea which, while consistent with republicanism, was simultaneously capable of nurturing individual enterprise and accommodating the ever more apparent diversity and pursuit of self-interest in American society. It also served a role badly needed in an era when people had been repelled by the corruption of politics. Fearful of the dangers faced in the creation of a new political system, especially a national one potentially more powerful than any they ever had experienced, Americans were seeking a way to use government to promote public order and protect liberty, yet simultaneously enable society to resist corruption by the state. Sociability provided a persuasive and readily acceptable way of answering this problem.[140]

The concern with frustrating a powerful state preoccupied opposition political thought and activity among British reformers on both sides of the Atlantic and the Tweed in the eighteenth century, but the private law principles undergirding the idea of sociability served these purposes in ways that other methods did not. Institutional restraints such as checks and balances focussed on the state and failed to confront the Revolutionary effort to separate the concepts of state

and society—or, in the words of Gordon S. Wood, to effect "the dis-
embodiment of government." Owing to a "breakdown of confidence"
in government[141] it was necessary to recognize the distinction between society and government and to nourish the former as a counterweight to the latter. "We should be cautious how we unite the
words *society* and *government*," wrote Robert Coram, "they being
essentially different."[142] Thomas Paine made this distinction clear
in *Common Sense*: "it is wholly owing to the constitution of the
people, and not to the constitution of the government that the crown
is not as oppressive in England as in Turkey."[143] Turning their attention and hopes to the pre-political and sociable nature of man before
the necessary compromises of the original contract of government,
many Americans also turned their attention to society and its wellbeing, for they understood that "the evils which happen in a state are
not always to be charged upon its government."[144] To Tunis Wortman, this distinction must be recognized. "The existence and perpetuity of freedom depends upon the people themselves," he urged.
"Never, O never forget this important lesson—That the only sure
foundation of public liberty is social virtue."[145]

The quest for "social virtue" reveals that American society in the
early republican years was neither the organic community of classical republicanism nor the atomistic collection of discrete, self-
seeking individuals of classical liberalism. Simultaneously drawing
on the appealing aspects of both traditions while never having committed themselves unreservedly to either, Americans also found in
sociability an attractive and persuasive additional fund of concepts,
terms, and goals. Amid the particular exigencies of the postwar era,
sociability presented the model of a diverse entity whose interacting
units produced a society united by mutual benefit. People choose different professions and employment, noted James Wilson; "these va-
rieties render mankind mutually beneficial to each other, and prevent too violent opposing of interest in the same pursuit." Although
the inevitable result would be inequality, he conceded, "diversity
forms an important part of beauty; and as of beauty, so of utility likewise." Wilson thus saw diversity as a virtue that ought to be encouraged; indeed, it was as much a "necessity" as a virtue. Variety generated "commerce and friendly intercourse," thus promoting "the operations of social virtue."[146] Directly contrary to the homogeneous,
monolithic state of undifferentiated citizens called for at this time by

Rousseau, this formulation saw society ideally as composed by different social units and institutions.[147]

< VII >

"The aggregate of liberty"

Americans had many sources and traditions from which to draw in creating an ideology of sociable relations in society. Eighteenth-century Americans well understood that the "common good" of society was not opposed to individual goals. "Public good, is not a term opposed to the good of individuals," explained Thomas Paine; "on the contrary, it is the good of every individual collected . . . for as the public body is every individual collected, so the public good is the collected good of those individuals."[148] The public good was not served if individual wellbeing was overlooked, and citizens must enlarge their outlooks to acknowledge the needs and wants—and, of course, the material self-interests—of others. Jesse Root, introducing his published law reports, stressed that in the new American society happiness must involve "a conscious enjoyment of freedom, health, peace, and competence." He continued: "The great end of civil government is social happiness; to induce us to respect the rights, interests, and feelings of others as our own, conformable to that great command of the law, which is the foundation of all relative duties from man to man: to love our neighbour as ourselves, and to do to all as we would they should do to us."[149] Root's version of the Golden Rule reflected more than a religious veneer to traditional secular ideas. More was involved than the good wishes of a benevolent heart or the elevation of sentiments to refined habits and good manners.[150] Adam Smith's dictum was too well understood in Federal America: namely, that "man has almost constant occasion for help of his brethren, and it is vain for him to expect it from their benevolence only."[151]

Rather, those attempting to craft an ideology of individual self-interest and the common good had a real and tangible example to illustrate their goal. From the experience of commercial development as well as from the world of public finance, the concept of the growing common stock had a powerful attraction. To many it had become clear that the pooling of funds enabled its greater circulation, an increased traffic in goods, and thus the increase of wealth. By the end of the Revolutionary War it was commonly accepted that debts and future expenses might be paid from small initial amounts of money combined for investment growth. Samuel Blodget explained this "national arithmetic" in 1801, pointing out how more funded capital stock would reduce interest rates and raise the value of land for all Americans.[152] James Wilson argued similarly in his support of banking, comparing the circulation of specie to "a sort of wagon-way through the air," which unites individuals, promotes development of unused land, and multiplies national wealth.[153]

This metaphor—of an increasing common stock benefitting the individuals who subscribed to it—had powerful persuasive force in the confident early republic, when growth and expansion stood as a national credo. What makes it so significant is that it exerted a potent influence on jurisprudence, too: rights, like funds, grew when pooled and when they advanced interaction. As Paine had observed, "civil government necessarily implies a surrender of something into a common stock, constituting a common purpose, and to be used for the mutual good of all the proprietors."[154] The state, wrote Levi Hart in 1775, was like a "trading company, possessed of a common stock, into which every one hath given his proportion."[155]

Rights, like money, increased when used. They did not rest, in a zero-sum balance, whereby citizens gave up some rights in order to protect only what they retained. Rather—and this point was crucial to them—those rights they retained actually increased. As James Wilson told the Pennsylvania ratifying convention,

in entering into the social compact, tho' the individual parts with a portion of his natural rights, yet it is evident that he gains more by the limitation of the liberty of others, than he loses by the limitation of his own; so that in truth, the aggregate of liberty is more in society, than it is in a state of nature.[156]

Activities in the aggregate offered Americans the opportunity to pool their resources and expand them. Acting together, they might also create the kind of intermediary private associations and organizations that protected them from the state just as they advanced their interests. As a new form of community, specialized as to purpose and membership, intermediary institutions offered a formula for reshaping a received tradition of group effort and common commitment. Although the pursuit of interests apparently at odds with that of the larger society once bore the taint of faction, the new acceptance of diversity and its benefits made such pursuits an asset. Jefferson and Madison saw this clearly with regard to religious diversity. "Would the world be more beautiful were all our faces alike?" asked Jefferson when he spoke to religious heterodoxy. Would American society be better, "were our tempers, our talents, our tastes, our forms, our wishes, aversions and pursuits cast exactly in the same mould?"[157] Madison recognized the balance between private and public loyalties well when he observed in his defense of religious liberty that "a member of Civil Society, who enters into any subordinate Association, must always do it with the reservation of his duty to the general authority."[158]

The business corporation embodied these ideas in a sharply secularized context. In an age when private enterprise seemed far less threatening than government, the business corporation offered a formula for the creation of intermediate institutions capable of advancing both individual and collective goals, and of creating bulwarks against the state.[159] Americans rushed to embrace the corporate form, aided by laws of general incorporation that stripped it of its hated monopolistic quality and protected by case law that shielded it from unwarranted government interference. Almost no private business corporations existed in the confederated states in 1782; by 1800 more than three hundred had been organized. By 1832 the law of "corporations aggregate" would need its own treatise.[160]

≺ VIII ≻
Promoting the Conflict and Circulation of Ideas

The First Amendment rights of freedom of speech and press were a legacy of a long colonial struggle,[161] although it is worth noting that once the Stamp Act was repealed little imperial threat to the press existed, and fears for freedom of speech played no role in precipitating the Revolutionary crisis.[162] As the "right of the people to enquire into, censure, approve, punish or reward their magistrates,"[163] however, freedom of speech and press represented a necessary vehicle for mobilizing the people to defend their liberties against government encroachments, especially in the years of superheated political conflict that produced the federal Sedition Act and numerous prosecutions of criminal libel under state law.[164]

But these freedoms meant more than this essentially Whig Zengerian public law ideal. Rather, they represented the very modern concept that a diversity of ideas was the symptom not of vice and degeneracy but of virtue and growth. To Tunis Wortman, "diversity of sentiment . . . is far from being unfavorable to the eventual reception of Truth."[165] Indeed, the acceptance of oppositional politics paved the way not merely for tolerating contrary opinions as necessary evils or censorial checks, but also for justifying them as positive and creative social forces. Richard Price illustrated this distinction when he identified "Liberty of Discussion" rather than liberty of speech as embodying the promise of the American Revolution.[166] Though speech might be important for persuasion, it was equally vital to the transfer of ideas, Adam Smith observed.[167] James Otis, sounding more like an advocate of polite sociability than of impassioned revolutionary persuasion, wrote his first publication on this subject in 1760. Speakers ought to aspire to appear "like a kind and sincere friend," he wrote. Seeking the "affection of his hearers," a speaker must "inspire us with fine ideas of sentiments and things, of beauty and of order, qualities of the same date and existence with our souls."[168] Language, to James Wilson, was "fitted to express the social as well as the solitary operations of the mind. To express the former is indeed the primary and direct intention of language."[169] In the paradigm of sociability, such freedoms fostered the circulation of ideas that, in contact and debate with each other, would help perfect knowledge.

For those looking to the advance of society in an age of progress, therefore, free speech had an importance reaching beyond its "censorial" Whig political purpose. Tunis Wortman described how the conflict of opinions "produces collision, engenders Argument, and affords exercise and energy to the intellectual powers; it corrects our errors, removes our prejudice, and strengthens our perceptions; it compels us to seek for evidences of our knowledge, and habituates us to a frequent revisal of our sentiments . . . It cannot surely be visionary to predict the ultimate triumph of truth."[170] Wortman's praise for the clashing of diverse ideas in an open and pluralistic society revealed his faith in the potential for growth of properly exercised liberty. "One truth will infallibly lead to another, and the laws of percipient causation will inevitably operate in perpetual geometric progression."[171] Drawing on the wellknown metaphor of the ever-growing investment, he explained how society "has united the powers of individual intellect into a common bank, and multiplied the *peculium* of each by a general combination of the whole."[172] Returning to this useful metaphor, he continued: "Knowledge is a general fund, of which all have a right to participate: it is a capital which has the peculiar property of increasing its stores in proportion as they are used."[173]

The same idea held true for Benjamin Rush, though he preferred scientific metaphors. "*Conversation* connects ideas, multiplies apprehension, elicits ideas by collision." The interchange of ideas had a much more salutary effect than solitary reading, he noted, which was "chyle only to the mind."[174] It was partly for this reason, along with his aversion to priestcraft, that Jefferson supported the multiplicity of religions at his new university; "by bringing the sects together . . . we shall soften their asperities, liberalize and neutralize their prejudices, and make the general religion a religion of peace, reason, and morality."[175]

Jesse Root chose yet another metaphor, though to the same purpose. "True knowledge in the soul is like light and heat in the sun," he wrote in describing this stimulus to growth. "It awakens, enlightens, and invigorates every noble and social passion."[176] Madison realized that the free exchange of ideas was not just a matter of speech and the press, and that the circulation and collision of information must be a staple of public policy in the United States. Four years after *The Federalist* and still concerned with disabusing Americans of their reservations about the survivability of freedom in a vast extended republic, he cited the importance of artificially achieving the equivalent of "a contraction of territorial limits" by way of increasing "general intercourse of sentiments."[177] "Whatever facilitates a general intercommunication of sentiments and ideas among the body of the people," he wrote, "as a free press, compact situation, good roads, interior commerce &c, is equivalent to a contraction of the orbit in w[hi]ch the Gov[ernmen]t is to act: and may favor liberty in a nation too large for free Gov[ernmen]t or hasten its violent death in one too small & vice versa."[178] For Joel Barlow, the conventional list of roads, water communication, postage, and travel served simultaneously to promote and cope with change, "inspiring that confidence and friendship so necessary to the political union of men who feel themselves able at all times to change their connexions at pleasure."[179]

Those who considered systems of local justice also took these notions of sociability into account. Benjamin Rush suggested that by "multiplying villages and towns, we increase the means of diffusing knowledge." Public officials who had to travel to the state capital would return with valuable information. Even judges and lawyers would contribute to the process, as "those who attend the courts that are held in these towns seldom fail of leaving a large portion of knowledge behind them."[180] Rush's idea was based on mundane considerations compared to the epistemological puzzle solved by James Wilson. In his law lectures Wilson acknowledged the problematical nature of truth itself and confessed that the courts had great difficulty in arriving at just verdicts. Indeed, because litigation involved the clash of disputed facts, it might be necessary, in the quest for truth, for a jury to acknowledge both opinions and award "what may be called their average result."[181]

Wilson's extraordinary idea received little, if any, support; but it testified to the widespread concern for the purpose behind it. Addressing the governor and legislature of Vermont in 1801, Jeremiah Atwater praised the fact that in Vermont men could "freely associate with their less informed fellow-citizens, for diffusing among them useful information." Travelers, who brought ideas with them, would invariably meet "with the marks of civility and cordial welcome, from the cheerful sons of toil."[182] A national postal service had been a goal since before the Revolution, advocated by Daniel Dulany as well as by James Otis.[183] When an anonymous South Carolinian attempted to deduce the "Rudiments of Law and Government" from natural law in 1783, he, too, cited "the postage of letters" that promoted mankind's sociable nature. Additionally, he called for large public squares, with "walks and gardens," and streets that were "airy and convenient," "wide and regular," as well as public carriages and stages, and canals.[184] The solitary ideal had little appeal. Robinson Crusoe, noted James Wilson, could have achieved nothing without his knowledge of tools, which were "the productions of society."[185]

The benefits gained from the circulation of ideas argued strongly for the protection, and thus the encouragement, of ideas. Patent protection, it was widely believed, was necessary if inventors were to

exert the effort needed to develop useful products, including vital necessities, "the want of which would convert the human race into hordes of wandering, naked, and houseless savages, much more miserable and defenceless than the brute inhabitants of the wilderness."[186]
The improvement of mankind was integral to the Enlightenment
ideas that underlay much of the new republic's jurisprudence, and
William Fessenden's treatise on patents shared the language of sociability and the concept of the multiplication of benefits. The public's
contribution of protective laws, he wrote, induces the inventor to be
creative. "In return for such disbursements from the common stock,
the personal convenience and profit of every member of the community are more than proportionately increased." Patent protection,
he added, was particularly well suited to American society, where no
great patrons existed—or ought to exist.[187] James Wilson saw patents
as little different from other forms of property acquired through hard
work, and which would be "used or imitated" for public benefit.[188]
Thus Madison could confidently write in *Federalist XLIV*, "The
utility of this power [to patent] will scarcely be questioned."[189] The
Constitution, therefore, protected inventors by authorizing Congress
to grant patents and copyrights and thereby extend the security that
twelve states already had given to literary works.[190]

Madison's confidence was not universally shared, however, because others saw such protections as an evil reminiscent of monopolies. If ideas could be monopolized, either through copyright or
patent, they would be no different than any variety of property with-
held from public utility for the benefit of a few. Paine therefore had
proudly announced with *The Rights of Man*, "I gave the copy-right
to every State in the Union."[191] Jefferson reasoned this way, too, and
when serving on the Patent Board while secretary of state he did all
he could to narrow the range of patentable ideas. The revised act of
1793 made it harder for inventors to obtain patents and easier for rivals to circumvent existing ones. Inventors in the early republic thus
worked at severe disadvantage, lacking protection for their ideas,
which spread by appropriation and imitation.[192]

Sociability required not only the circulation of ideas, but a preference for truth, since falsehood threatened to erode the confidence
that citizens must hold for each other. "It would, methinks, become all Men to maintain *Peace*, and the common Offices of Humanity, and *Friendship in the diversity of Opinions*," wrote John

Locke, presaging the eighteenth-century emphasis that Tunis Wortman called for when he noted, "There is not a virtue more useful
than Sincerity."[193]

For this reason, the suppression of fraud and misrepresentation
assumed a new urgency and attracted the attention of law reformers.
St. George Tucker assailed the Virginia land policy that contributed
to fraudulent real estate transactions,[194] for the same reason that Nathaniel Chipman lauded Vermont's new statute of conveyances requiring greater "notoriety" so that creditors and purchasers might
not be misled and harmed.[195]

Truth was not, however, an inviolable ideal, and the manner in
which jurists limited its applicability is highly instructive. As a public law matter, truth was admitted as a plea to be presented to the
jury by the federal Sedition Act of 1798. The corruption of this rule
by Federalist judges plunged that law into deserved obloquy, but succeeding statutes on the state level weakened the rule by making
truth only a partial defense. As articulated in the famous *Croswell*
case of 1804 and then framed as a statute by the New York legislature
the next year, a defendant in an action of libel brought by a public
official must not only prove the factual truth of the statement but
also demonstrate that it had been made with good motives and jus-
tifiable ends.[196] Because the people were now the sovereign, their
peace must not be disturbed. Chancellor Kent, who played roles in
the defense brought by Croswell and in the drafting of the New York
statute,[197] summarized the purpose of such doctrine when he explained the reasoning behind a similar requirement made by the
Massachusetts Supreme Judicial Court in 1808; this rule, he explained in his *Commentaries*, "was held to be founded on sound
principles, indispensable to restrain all tendencies to breaches of the
peace, and to private animosity and revenge."[198]

The *Croswell* decision, as limited as it was, had no effect on private actions for defamation. Indeed, it is a fact little remarked upon
in the history of free speech that two of the officials criticized in
Croswell brought private actions against the publishers of *The Wasp*,
which had printed the offending articles; one of them, Attorney General Ambrose Spencer, won a considerable damage award.[199] Ironically, Croswell's defense attorney, Alexander Hamilton, had specifically distinguished the manner in which civil actions were tried from
the way he was arguing for criminal ones: the former allowed truth

as a justification, but it had to be pleaded specially. That is, the judge would first decide if the nature of the statement was actionable at law, and only then would the jury be allowed to decide on its truthfulness.[200]

Truth had long been a defense in civil actions, but in practice it remained a very limited one. As politics in the early republic grew ever more unstable and less deferential,[201] political debate grew all the more nasty and led jurists—as well as aggrieved politicians— to see the wisdom in allowing legal remedies to punish licentious words. As Kent set forth the reasoning,

> it is easy to be perceived, that in the case of libels upon private character, greater strictness as to allowing the truth in evidence, by way of justification, ought to be observed, than in the case of public prosecutions; for the public have no interest in the detail of private vices and defects, when the individual charged is not a candidate for any public trust; and publications of that kind are apt to be infected with malice, and to be very injurious to the peace and happiness of families.[202]

James Wilson explained the basic principles of the doctrine to his law students: "Without mutual confidence between its members, society, it is evident, could not exist. This mutual and pervading confidence may well be considered the attractive principle of the associating contract. To place that confidence in all the others is the social right, to deserve that confidence from others is the social duty, of every member."[203] Accordingly, he gave special attention to "prosecutions for libels and actions of slander: both of which suppose an unjustifiable aggression of character."[204] Reputation, like property, was a socially useful right that must be protected by law. Accordingly, constitutional provisions protected reputation in several states; Delaware, for example, established the natural right of "enjoying and defending life and liberty, of acquiring and protecting reputation and property."[205]

≺ IX ≻

The Power of Contracts

Contract law offered a clear focus for the amalgamation of notions of sociability into jurisprudence. Wilson made this explicit in his law lectures, when he praised "Veracity, and its corresponding quality,

confidence." These, he said, indicate mankind's "designation for society," from which it was axiomatic that "confidence in promises"
was vital. "The conclusion is," he said, "that the performance of
promises is essential to society," because contracts were "social
acts."[206]

No one needs reminding of the struggle over sanctity of contract
in the 1780s, when financial reversals made the repayment of obligations impossible for countless debtors and provoked a deep crisis
for every state government.[207] Nonetheless, the attempts to enshrine
contractual obligations should not be seen purely as an effort to secure property rights to those who possessed capital. Rather, it must
also be recognized that the breaking or impairing of contracts also
destroyed social trust—the "necessary confidence between man and
man" that gave coherence to a society.[208] Contractual obligations,
Francis Hutcheson had written, served a social utility and not merely
as a protection of an individual's inviolate rights.[209]

This sense of social obligation existed long before the crisis of the
1780s. In 1774 Nathaniel Niles had phrased the issue in precisely the
terms appropriate to the need for sociable virtue. Honoring contracts,
he wrote, gives individuals "credit with our neighbours" and lays "a
foundation for public confidence." Later a Vermont Supreme Court
judge, the Reverend Mr. Niles combined a variety of themes when he
preached, "Contracts are sacred things. The man that doth not feel
himself bound by them, is totally incapacitated for political intercourse with mankind."[210] If commerce were to provide the social cohesion so vital to the vigorous society of a free republic, confidence
must be maintained. Thirteen years later, when the fulfillment of
contracts took on a greater urgency, the Reverend James Madison
wrote to his brother Thomas, an attorney and brother-in-law of Patrick Henry, that the federal Constitution would "prevent most of
those iniquitous Interferings in private Contracts, w[hi]ch destroy
all Confidence among Individuals."[211]

The Constitution's contract clause (Article 1, Section 10, Clause 1)
must be seen in this context. All debtor relief laws, wrote the *Maryland Gazette*, harmed "justice and good faith."[212] Instead, the parties
ought to seek composition, with assurances of payment and protection of the obligation. In distant retrospect, such language seems
transparently exploitative of the debtor. And, in practical fact, it had
that effect, although it would take more than a generation before this

language lost its element of sociability and public confidence and in the conservative Antebellum period became an instrumental tool for predatory actions at law.[213]

So, too, the Constitution's bankruptcy clause (Article 1, Section 8, Clause 4) bore in its origination a rationale different from its later evolution. To James Madison, bankruptcy law retained the anti-absconding purpose it had served in colonial times—to "prevent so many frauds where the parties or their property may lie or be removed into different States." The "expediency" of a federal bankruptcy jurisdiction, he wrote in the *Federalist*, was so obvious that "it seems not likely to be drawn into question."[214] Nevertheless, the problematical effects of such a law did produce considerable debate. Despite financial panics in 1792 and 1797, a federal bankruptcy act was not passed until 1800, but its goal—to protect creditors from fraud—was undone when crafty debtors succeeded in evading provisions of the act intended to prevent fraudulent collusive actions with friendly "creditors." The law, whose failure had "inflicted a deep wound upon the confidence of man with man in the ordinary transactions of life," was quickly repealed in 1803.[215] Decades later, in a changed political and economic climate, an entirely new body of bankruptcy law emerged.[216] As in so many other areas of American life in the Antebellum era, confidence had been replaced by competitiveness, and a new jurisprudence would emerge to serve it.

This new jurisprudence would draw on Revolutionary notions of the sanctity of private property, but it was put into operation by men who lacked the lived memory of the Revolution. The Founding generation venerated private property, but they could do so only because they attached to it as an inseparable corollary the notion that private property was a social right whose ultimate purpose was the public welfare of a republic. This equilibrium between private interest and public purpose the founding generation had hoped to preserve through an impartial judiciary. The political leaders that came of age in the years after the second President Adams, however, were too young to recall that balance, and they were influenced by economic forces inconceivable at the founding. When partisan popular assemblies elected in a period of rapid change and intense political rivalry asserted that they embodied the public interest, it seemed to the Revolutionary generation that politicians were now usurping law and allowing private interests to define the community welfare to their own advantage. So felt Chancellor Kent in 1837, when he expressed his "disgust" at the *Charles River Bridge* decision to an equally discouraged Joseph Story. The decision, wrote Kent, "injures the moral Sense of the Community & destroys the *Sanctity of Contracts.*"[217] Private property remained, but it lacked its Revolutionary partners.

From the Bonds of Empire to the Bonds of Matrimony

NORMA BASCH

IN 1787, SARAH EVERITT petitioned the New York Court of Chancery for a divorce from her husband William, a New York City butcher to whom she had been married for twenty-two years. The uncontested suit was a simple one with regard to the circumstances of her marriage, which had come to an informal end well before the suit began. The couple's two sons, one a fifteen-year-old apprenticed to a butcher and no longer living at home, the other a thirteen-year-old about to follow in his brother's footsteps, were not a factor in the case, and William, who had previously "absented himself," in the words of the court, from Sarah's "bed and society," was propertyless and insolvent.[1] As a result, the sole purpose in undertaking the action was to bring a legal end to a marriage that was long since over.

The adjudication of the case was swift. Custody, support, and property were not at issue, and neither was the proof of William's adultery. Among the witnesses who came to court was a woman named Mary Moncrief, who not only admitted to living with William in an ongoing state of adultery, but who also testified to having a son with him. William, it seems, had embarked on a second union with Mary and was raising a second family while he was bound by law to his first union with Sarah and to the obligations of his first family. In October of 1787, not long after the Federal Convention had concluded its affairs in Philadelphia, the court brought his union with Sarah to an official and unequivocal end. Given the redundancy of the decree, there could be no mistaking its finality. The marriage was "entirely and absolutely dissolved and declared to be null and void."[2]

The Everitt case provides a vivid point of departure for reflecting on the recognition of divorce in the aftermath of the American Revolution. Adjudicated in the year the state of New York passed its first divorce statute and the federal constitution was drafted, it not only highlights a chronological convergence between the legal reordering of marriage as a social institution and the political reordering of the society at large, but suggests the possibility of deeper connections.[3] Furthermore, because the case embodied both legal and extralegal forms of marital dissolution, it alerts us to the diverse ways in which Americans of the Revolutionary era both conceived of and acted on divorce.[4] At the same time, the roles played by the parties in this classic but untidy human triangle exemplify the transition that was underway. Cast by the law into a sharply adversarial configuration, with Mary set off to the side as a witness, husband and wife were presented in the end with an orderly legal resolution.

Other resolutions were possible. As William's apparently unilateral arrangements indicate, putting an end to a marriage in the early republic did not hinge on the statutory recognition of divorce. Extralegal and customary alternatives filled the void in divorceless jurisdictions, and they continued to flourish alongside the law in jurisdictions providing for divorce.[5] But if William's simple strategy of self-divorce and pseudo remarriage was undoubtedly familiar to his contemporaries, the remedy now available to Sarah was something of a novelty. Moreover, if we use William's occupation as the measure of Sarah's social standing, we are bound to be struck by the broadly democratic thrust of the state's earliest divorce provisions. One of the first plaintiffs in the state to sue under the terms of the new statute was the wife of an obscure and impoverished tradesman.

The Everitt divorce serves as a fitting frame, then, for the questions that animate this chapter. How did the state come to legitimate the dissolution of Sarah Everitt's marriage? And how did Sarah Everitt, in turn, come to submit her marital difficulties to the disposition of the state?[6] Although these open-ended and interrelated questions about political motivation and individual agency do not lend themselves to conclusive answers, they are, nonetheless, worth raising, not so much because of the quantitative place divorce would assume in the long run as because of its qualitative place in the context of the late eighteenth century. Moreover, linked as they are to the interplay of the social contract and the marriage contract, such questions invite an exploration of the striking convergence of revolution and divorce in the last quarter of the eighteenth century.

≺ I ≻

The Legitimation of Divorce

The symbolic association of government and marriage was a familiar motif in Western political theory, and the United States was not alone in legitimizing divorce in the age of revolution. The first French republic, which went from upholding the complete indissolubility of marriage to instituting the most permissive divorce code in the western world, provides a stellar example of the late eighteenth-century confluence of revolution and divorce. In France even more conclusively than in the United States, the right to put an end to an unsatisfactory union was an integral part of the revolutionary order. As the deputy Pierre-Francois Gossin argued in the National Constituent Assembly, "After having made man again free and happy in public life, it remains for you to assure his liberty and happiness in private life."[7]

In light of Gossin's distinctions, we can safely assume that the word *man* in his reference to private life encompassed *woman* as well and therefore recast marriage into a far more egalitarian union than it had been under the Old Regime. The same cannot be said for his reference to public life. Nevertheless, if as Joan Landes has argued, the transition from French absolutism to a bourgeois, secular state entailed the silencing of women in the public sphere, endowing them with the right of divorce empowered them at least symbolically in the private sphere. Petitions to legislatures in the early years of the Revolution indicate that divorce was routinely construed as a wife's legal counterweight to her husband's conjugal authority. Furthermore, the notion that the right of divorce for both husbands and wives was a fundamental freedom that flowed from the new political order was evidently widespread. Relying on the fact that the French constitution of 1791 designated the institution of marriage as a civil contract and thus freed it from the grip of the church, numerous public officials granted divorces to disaffected spouses even before the passage of the divorce law of 1792. Not only did that remarkable but shortlived law provide for divorce with the mutual consent of both spouses—a provision akin to the no-fault statutes of our own day, but one spouse could petition unilaterally on the ground of incompatibility and receive a decree without producing either affidavits or witnesses.[8]

The terms on which Americans recognized divorce were rather
more modest and, as a result of state-by-state variations, somewhat
eclectic. Still, the impress of the Revolution was unmistakable. No
sooner, it seems, did Americans create a rationale for dissolving the
bonds of empire, than they set about creating rules for dissolving the
bonds of matrimony. To be sure, a few caveats are in order regarding
the novelty of American divorce. Not only did Puritan jurisdictions
provide for divorce in early America, but Connecticut did so on such
liberal terms that it granted almost 1,000 decrees between 1670 and
1799.[9] By comparison, those states that relegated divorce to a legislative decision after the Revolution instituted a highly restrictive
divorce policy. Nonetheless, even in such restrictive jurisdictions, a
complete divorce with the concomitant right to remarry became a
legal possibility for the first time. Thus, although American divorce
policy may have paled before the robust liberality of its French counterpart, in an Anglo-American context it assumed more radical dimensions. By 1800 fault divorce, as we have come to call it in our era
of no-fault, was a legal concept that departed significantly from the
parliamentary and ecclesiastical precedents on which it was based.
In its gender-neutral approach to fault, in the completeness of its dissolutions, and in the access it afforded litigants, American divorce
already diverged dramatically from its principal English roots.

The timing of this development was as telling as its substance.
Concern with providing for formal divorce arose simultaneously
with the political turmoil of the 1770s. With the notable exception
of the Puritan jurisdictions, Britain's North American colonies did
not challenge English divorce policy in any collective or sustained
way until that time, nor did England attend to the few challenges
that were in fact made. Indeed, throughout the colonial period, the
balance of the colonies passed no more than a handful of provincial
divorce bills, and these together with the wholesale disregard of the
English rules by both Connecticut and Massachusetts were largely
ignored in the affairs of empire. As Linda Kerber has observed, the
Privy Council exhibited an almost studied ignorance on the subject
of colonial divorces.[10] As late as 1769, the Board of Trade and Plantations declared the Pennsylvania legislative divorce of Curtis and
Anne Grubb to be "not repugnant to the Laws of England." Yet confronted by a similar Pennsylvania decree three years later, the board
found that it represented a dangerous power "rarely and recently as-

sumed in your Majesty's colonies in America." An extended ruling by the board in 1773 designated "Acts of Divorce in the Plantations" as "either Improper or Unconstitutional." Subsequent divorce bills from New Hampshire and New Jersey were also disallowed and reported to the Privy Council, which instructed colonial governors to void all future provincial divorces.[11]

Thomas Jefferson, who advocated legalizing divorce, may very well have had this prohibition in mind when he drafted the section of the Declaration of Independence denouncing the British monarchy's refusal to "Assent to Laws, the most wholesome and necessary for the public good." More important, his notes supporting divorce anticipated the rationale he employed to justify independence. "No partnership," he declared, "can oblige continuance in contradiction to its end and design."[12] In a sense, the right to end an adverse marital partnership was a direct byproduct of the frustration experienced under an adverse political partnership, for in the wake of independence, those colonies that were overruled by the Privy Council provided for divorce in new state statutes. Other states followed suit. By 1795 a disaffected spouse could put an end to a marriage in a local circuit court even in the Northwest Territory. Entitled "A Law respecting Divorce, Adopted from the Massachusetts code," the simple territorial statute providing for that right highlights the flow of divorce westward with the settlers who spilled over the Appalachians. "Divorces shall be decreed," it declared, "where either of the parties had a former wife or husband alive, at the time of solemnizing the second marriage; or impotency or adultery in either of the parties."[13]

Although the states carved out of the Northwest Territory would eventually expand their statutory grounds to encompass both desertion and cruelty, New York continued to adhere to terms very close to those in the territorial statute. Clearly, statutory provisions could vary widely. If the South tended to lag behind the North both in recognizing divorce and in placing it within the jurisdiction of the civil courts, east-west distinctions became even more pronounced, with "western" states tending to render divorce more readily accessible to their restless new inhabitants. This was true even for the post-Revolutionary South. Whereas South Carolina eschewed divorce altogether, the first Tennessee divorce statute provided for adjudication in the state's superior courts, and in addition to adultery and the traditional grounds for annulment, recognized willful desertion or

two years absence without a reasonable cause.[14] However, far more
significant than the divergent terms that were being spelled out in
state statutes was the wholesale legitimation of divorce itself, especially in those areas that had been officially divorceless. By 1799
twelve states in addition to the Northwest Territory had recognized
the legal right of divorce.[15]

The stunning nature of this legal departure is best appreciated
when balanced against late eighteenth-century English practices. In
England female plaintiffs, who were required to prove aggravated
adultery (adultery compounded with some other marital offense
such as physical cruelty), were all but shut out of the divorce process except for formal separations. Of the 325 complete divorces that
Parliament granted between 1670 and the legal reforms of 1857, only
four went to women. Inasmuch as a decree permitting the complain-
ant to remarry, as opposed to a divorce from bed and board, depended
upon securing a private bill from Parliament, men hardly fared much
better. In order to secure such a decree a male plaintiff would need to
begin with a suit for damages against his wife's paramour in the civil
courts, follow it with a suit for separation in the ecclesiastical courts,
and then pursue it to completion in Parliament. In contrast to the
speedy decree issued to Sarah Everitt, the New York butcher's wife
with whom we began, a complete divorce in England was an option
for very privileged, very determined, and very patient men who still
had to be prepared for failure at any point in the process.[16]

From both a substantive and procedural perspective, then, divorce
law in the early republic was light years beyond its English equivalent. Moreover, despite striking variations in the particularities of
early divorce provisions, there were broad commonalities in the fundamentals, and it is the fundamentals that concern us here. Shared
notions about divorce were embedded in three dominant strands of
early national culture: an essentially Protestant view of the moral
order, a distinctly English legal heritage, and the indigenous political
culture of the American Revolution. These three great currents of
thought—three discrete ways of looking at the world in general and
the conjugal in particular—were by no means prerequisites for the
mounting of divorce as a legal institution, nor did they always flow
together in harmonious confluence. But their convergence in the
United States in the last quarter of the eighteenth century not only
determined the course of American divorce but also shaped its un-

derlying tensions. That particular historical conjunction ensured that the moral premises for divorce would emanate from the New Testament, the forms for its implementation from the English ecclesiastical courts, and the political foundations for its legitimation from the singular experience of independence itself. Because independence was the catalyst in the process, the event separating English legal traditions from American innovations, it merits special attention.

≺ II ≻

Contract and Consent

At a tangible political level, independence freed the states to depart from English law, which had channeled divorce along a path so costly and tortuous as to render England virtually divorceless. But that account still begs the question of why states departed from English law in the first place. Viewed at a symbolic level, however, independence looms as a compelling prototype for divorce, and nowhere more than in its most celebrated text. Consider that in letting the "Facts" be submitted to a candid world, the Declaration of Independence at once explained, decreed, and sanctified a divorce from the bonds of empire, and from the bonds of empire to the bonds of matrimony, it was but a short conceptual step.

The principle of comparability that structured eighteenth-century concepts of knowledge only served to enhance the time-honored association of family with state and vice versa. As Natalie Davis observed of early modern France, all the weighty and contentious issues in the larger political order could invariably be symbolized "in the little world of the family." Reversing the order of the analogy in *The Social Contract*, Rousseau asserted that families are the first models of political societies.[17] This common maxim of Western political theory, however, acquired new and expansive meaning in the Anglo-American context. Jefferson's use of words such as *bretheren, consanguinity*, and *kindred* in the Declaration not only exemplifies the easy interchangability of family and state in Enlightenment thinking, but also encompasses its transfiguration. His language intimates that severing the bonds of empire entailed the radical and complete separation of two peoples who were as intimately related as the members of one family. That family, to paraphrase the end of the

Declaration, was no more; and the two peoples, once knitted together as one, were to regard each other now as enemies in the war
that was already underway. As this imagery suggests, the Revolution predisposed Americans to think of themselves as dissolving one
family by declaring their independence and, at the same time, as constituting another. The import of that image is even greater than has
been generally recognized. The Revolution not only killed the king,
metaphorically speaking; it separated the family.

Admittedly, Jefferson's allusion seems to conjure up a schism between male kinfolk. Still, for Americans of the Revolutionary era,
the image of the severed family could extend beyond filial and fraternal bonds to embrace marital bonds as well. As a legacy from
the English Civil War, the political exploitation of conjugal symbols
was readily familiar to Jefferson and his contemporaries. As Carole
Pateman has observed, the relation of a husband to his wife was as
central to seventeenth-century English debate over the political order as was the relation of the king to his subjects. Her observation is
instructive for the eighteenth century as well. Framing the schism
between Great Britain and its North American colonies as a divorce
not only highlights the interplay between the social contract and the
marriage contract; it accents the role of gender in Revolutionary discourse. As Pateman has cautioned, to consider social contract theory
without considering the marriage contract, or what she calls "the
sexual contract," is to suppress the gendered part of the story of contract.[18] In keeping with her caveat, the Revolutionary deployment of
the familial paradigm merits a reading in conjugal terms.

Although a host of scholars have elaborated on the antipatriarchal
dimensions of Revolutionary culture, they have focussed largely on
the filial ramifications of killing the king. Historians have noted that
whereas a tyrannical parent-child relationship supported the logic of
American rebellion, the bonds of filial affection came to exemplify
the post-Revolutionary ideal of union. To be sure, apart from the apparent Freudian appeal of the killing-the-king paradigm, there is a
good deal of cultural evidence to support it, and there are flesh-and-
blood figures who embody it. It is not difficult to envision George
Washington as a humane and virtuous post-Revolutionary father who
came to replace the despotic figure of George III. But recent scholarship exploring the centrality of consent in antipatriarchal representations of the republic has projected a more gendered reading of the

post-Revolutionary transition by demonstrating that conjugal ties came to supplant filial ties in popular representations of the state. As Jan Lewis has shown, both the hopes and fears for the nation's political order were consistently dramatized in relations between the sexes. Hence the popular seduction tales of the early national era, she advises, should be read as political tracts that probed the problem of sustaining virtue in an all too corrupt world. Clearly, if virtue stood any kind of chance, it was in a loving and legitimate union where conflict would be assuaged by the warm bonds of affection. As Lewis suggests, the happy and harmonious conjugal union of the brave husband and his chaste wife came to represent nothing less than the happy and harmonious political union of the young American republic.[19]

That the success of both unions hinged on the element of consent provides important clues to the legitimation of divorce because it underscores its contractarian underpinnings. In a legal as well as a moral context, marriage derived its primary legitimacy from the principle of consent. In the prevailing legal construction of marriage, there could be no contract without consent, and if consent were absent or compromised, the contract could be deemed null and void.[20] Of course in traditional legal terms, once the marriage was validly contracted, the contract was indissoluble, consent ceased to be a factor, and the equality that prevailed at the time the contract was made was effaced by the requirements of coverture. To put it in political terms, one could say that having contracted for her ruler, a wife was consigned to his rule for life. As will become evident, Americans of the post-Revolutionary era were not altogether comfortable with such an image, but neither were they prepared to abandon it completely. Both their discomfort with the traditional legal model of marriage and their reluctance to adopt a thoroughly contractual alternative illuminate the degree to which social contract theory intertwined with their perceptions of marriage and divorce.

Their dilemma was hardly new. It is precisely because marriage in its consensual-but-indissoluble form stood as a far-reaching metaphor for the existing political order that it served as a convenient hedge against incipient political upheavals. A common analogy for the relationship between rulers and the ruled, it was exploited by Royalist defenders of Charles I to equate Parliament's rebellion with the ludicrous prospect of a wife divorcing her husband.[21] Gender, of

course, was central to the effectiveness of the analogy. The figurative
use of a divorce by a woman to signify the anarchic breaking of a
sacred contract and thereby subject the action to ridicule intimates
that domestic rebellion enjoyed less credibility than political rebellion. But it also reveals parallels between the two rebellions in the
very grain of Anglo-American political thinking. The advent of the
American Revolution turned the thrust of the analogy on its head,
for just as divorce could serve to discountenance revolution, revolution, in turn, especially a successful one, could serve to legitimate
divorce.

Clearly, the act of legitimating divorce is not the same as the act
of legitimating revolution, and to assert metaphorically that it is,
is inherently reductive and demonstrably wrong. And yet because
the very effectiveness of a metaphor emanates, in a sense, from its
wrongness, from its capacity to conflate widely disparate actions
into a simple, unitary framework, the correspondences between revolution and divorce could be manipulated into remarkably powerful
analogies. As ethnographers have long known, charting patterns in
such analogies in a specific time and place can help to expose a culture's fundamental premises and underlying tensions.[22]

With a caveat on the blatant reductiveness of such analogies,
then, it is useful for a moment to pursue the correspondences between revolution and divorce in the context of Revolutionary culture. The framework for a just divorce code, like the juristic rationale
for independence outlined in the Declaration, would need to stipu-
late under what extraordinary circumstances and for what grievous
offenses a dissolution of the contract might take place. Still, it would
pivot on an agonizing dilemma: how to dissolve those contracts that
had been so seriously violated as to destroy the ends of marriage (the
Everitts' marriage presents a good example) without at the same time
destroying marriage itself. For Jefferson's contemporaries, the Revolution posed a comparable dilemma: how to dissolve their connections to a legitimate but despotic government without at the same
time putting "the axe to the root of all government," to cite an English critic.[23]

One solution, as Gordon Wood has observed, was derived from
the notion of breach of contract. It consisted of delegitimizing the
contract with the duly constituted government by documenting the
nature, intensity, and duration of its despotism. But breach of con-

tract was not the only legal construction that suggests striking parallels between declaring political independence and justifying divorce. Equity was another, and it supplied an important modification to the relatively crude concept of breach of contract. Following J. W. Gough's analysis of Locke, Peter Hoffer has argued that both the sequential pattern and the conceptual structures on which the Declaration is modeled were derived from a bill in equity, a form which Jefferson as a Virginia lawyer would have drawn on with some regularity. All the complaints at the core of the Declaration, Hoffer insists, "showed their equitable origins, fitting categories familiar in chancery." Because Hoffer, like Gough, depicts the relationship between the governed and their governors more as a trusteeship that has been violated than as a contract that has been breached, he locates the Declaration's appeal squarely within the purview of the protective and discretionary sorts of justice meted out by a court of chancery.

Marriage, by analogy, could assume the same hierarchical characteristics of a trusteeship in which the husband acted as the wife's trustee but could be held accountable for his actions in a court of equity. It is worth noting that given the absence of ecclesiastical courts, divorce in America began as a proceeding in equity in those jurisdictions that maintained a distinction between law and equity. Of course, equity was itself an integral part of the inherited legal system with its own long-established procedures and precedents, but it was distinguished, as Hoffer points out, by its distinctly remedial dimensions. Thus divorce entered American jurisprudence with a set of procedures that translated a suit to dissolve a marriage into a quest for a remedy that was not ordinarily available. Accordingly, after spelling out a list of harrowing abuses suffered at the hands of the allegedly guilty spouse, a divorce petitioner typically concluded with a prayer for relief, an appeal, if you will, to a higher and more flexible form of justice not unlike that invoked in the Declaration.[24]

In a variety of ways, then, the Declaration of Independence endowed the women and men of the Revolutionary era with an elegant and eloquent example of how to dissolve a sacred contract. Resting as it did on its purported proof of English despotism counterpoised against colonial innocence, its argument unfolded very much like that of a petitioner in a divorce suit who, in the absence of printed forms, piled up and compounded the alleged causes regardless of the statutory grounds. Sacred contracts are not dissolved casually, and the long and arduous route to the decisive stage of separation, ran the argument in the Declaration, was determined by the respondent's cumulative and unremitting guilt. In unmistakably Lockean language, the Declaration averred that severing the bonds of empire was not undertaken for light and transient causes, but only in the wake of a long train of abuses and usurpations to which the petitioner had submitted patiently. So intense and sustained were these abuses, went the narrative, that it was not only the right but also the duty of the petitioner to seek a formal dissolution of the union.

The juristic language, the familiar truths, the judicious caveats, the assembled facts—none of these could obviate fully the unbounded possibilities that lay at the heart of the Declaration, which was shaped, after all, so as to justify the right to begin all over again. As Carl Becker long ago observed, the classic philosophy in the Declaration would lose ground in the nineteenth century precisely because it was used with such stunning success in the eighteenth and might be so used again in ever more radical causes.[25] Yet if fear of endless dissolutions and countless reconstitutions ran below the surface of post-Revolutionary culture, thereby posing a potential threat to the legal recognition of divorce, it was assuaged by an abiding faith in the justness of the Revolution. The very same intellectual premises that supported independence predisposed Americans to support the right of divorce.

The connections between the political ideology of a just revolution and the liberating potential of a just divorce code were strong, durable, and deeply rooted; the American Revolution only served to strengthen them further. It is no mere accident that John Milton wrote his divorce tracts in the midst of the English Civil War, tying the freedom to divorce to "all hope of true Reformation of the state." Nor should we be surprised that reference to the incompatibility between a contractarian theory of government and the principle of indissoluble marriage can be found in John Locke's *Second Treatise of Government*.[26] In the wake of American independence, moreover, at least one wife expressed the belief that the Revolution had directly empowered her to reject a despotic husband. When Abigail Strong petitioned for a divorce in Connecticut in 1788, she reasoned that she was no longer under any obligation to submit to her husband's authority, since "even Kings may forfeit or discharge the allegiance of their Subjects."²⁷ And when the nineteenth-century spiritualist leader Andrew Jackson Davis advocated greater equality in marriage, he linked his vision of an ideal union to the freedom from tyranny delineated in the "covenant . . . signed by the brave Fathers of our republic and sealed by the heart's blood of Patriots and Heroes." The Declaration of Independence, he insisted, was as "sacred still as the testament of a new-born savior."²⁸

Nonetheless, because legal sources were rarely as explicit as Abigail Strong's politically-charged petition, it is far easier to chart the connections between revolution and divorce at a high level of abstraction than it is to understand their influence on ordinary people. It is not clear how the collective experience of revolution reshaped individual attitudes toward either law or marriage to create support for formal divorce. The persistence of customary alternatives to formal divorce may very well indicate that for countless Americans it did not. Yet while we should not assume that divorcelessness in the pre-Revolutionary era meant that marriages stayed intact, neither should we deny that in complex ways that continue to elude us, independence set the stage for the acceptance of new forms of divorce. Old arrangements were rendered unsatisfactory, if not, in fact, obsolete, and this was true for litigants like Sarah Everitt as well as for jurists and legislators, although not necessarily for the same reasons.

≺ III ≻

Reshaping the Social Order

Glimpses of how Revolutionary ideology opened out to recast understandings about the social order in general and marriage in particular can be found in the burgeoning popular literature of the Revolutionary era.²⁹ Parables and limericks, essays and advice columns, novels and dramas—all expressly and self-consciously didactic—redefined the ends of marriage, and in so doing, tentatively approached the appropriate bases for divorce. As *The Emigrants*, a 1793 epistolary novel championing the right of divorce, put the case for proselytizing through fiction, "perhaps it is the most effectual way of communicating moral instruction, for when the vices and follies of the world are held up to us so connected with incidents which are interesting, it is most likely they will leave a more lasting impression than when given in a dull narrative."[30] Such prefatory remarks, which represented an effort to counter criticism against the sexual seductiveness of novel-reading, were designed to bolster the author's prescriptive authority.[31]

Prescriptions, of course, are not descriptions, but the range of moral instruction that informs this literature illuminates the connections between government and marriage at a popular anecdotal level. This is precisely the level where analogies between the social contract and the marriage contract were commonly deployed, where the issues of conjugal power and female subordination were directly confronted, and where the problems of how to place constraints on sexual unions into a democratic context were regularly addressed. Admittedly, since much of this literature concentrated on distinguishing the true foundations for a harmonious union from those that were spurious, uncaring, despotic, and mercenary, it was focussed in both a social and political sense on securing a more perfect union. Union, as Jay Fliegelman has observed, was the critical word in the Revolution and after, and liberty was equated regularly with the freedom to choose one's bond.[32] Still, allusions to marriage invariably contrasted the hollow forms that chained an incompatible couple together with the silken bonds of mutual affection. Given the prevailing political assumption that some bonds could be legitimately dissolved, support for divorce was at least implicit and sometimes even explicit in the sharpness of the distinctions.

Few writers were as ardent in extolling the right to end an unhappy marriage as Tom Paine. Paine, who was separated from his wife in England, dramatized the contrast between a loving and loveless union in a little fable about Cupid and Hymen in the *Pennsylvania Magazine.* In his tale, Cupid, the god of love, prevents Hymen, the clerk of matrimony, from legitimating a wedding of convenience in Arcadia, where marriages were clearly made of better stuff. Although Paine does not use the fable to advocate dispensing with Hymen's formal services, he wants them to be regarded as subordinate to the affective contributions of Cupid. "'Tis my province to form the union, and yours to witness it," asserts Cupid, hero of the tale and Paine's avatar of marital values, and "besides you are such a dull fellow when I am not with you, that you poison the felicities of life." The message is clear. Hymen might "chain couples together like criminals," but the only laws that ought to be binding on them were the universal "laws of affection."[33] A few months later, assuming the persona of an American savage considering all the follies in a typical Christian marriage, Paine carried his theme to its logical conclusion. He alleged that not one in a hundred unions bore any relationship "to happiness or common sense," and without the freedom to end their unions, spouses simply doubled each other's misery "by way of revenge." Concluding with an innovative gloss on the union of Adam and Eve, Paine used it to develop the claim that since God made us all in perfectly matched pairs, it was our duty to find the partner we were destined to have and to consummate the perfect partnership, presumably even if it took more than one try.[34]

In view of the fact that Adam and Eve were traditionally offered up as the embodiment of the one-flesh doctrine and hence as corroboration for God's support of indissoluble marriage, Paine's reading of Genesis was uncommonly bold. But although few contemporaries would venture as far as he did in advocating an open-ended quest for Edenic happiness, the theme of the perfect partnership was a popular one when it assumed more secular dimensions. "On Marriage," for example, presented a handy neoclassical version in which Jupiter broke Androgyne, the perfect whole person, into two incomplete and unsatisfactory halves, leaving every man and woman thereafter with the need to find their other half.[35]

Finding one's very own other half augured a richly rewarding life, for in the loving and completed circle of a harmonious conjugal union, as in a harmonious political union, the whole was always greater than the sum of its parts. True love, defined as an abiding friendship between a man and a woman, was a union of "congenial souls," an affair of the head and the heart, a matter of intellect and affection. Cautioned against the subtle tyranny of imprudent passion, suitors were advised to value inner resources in a woman over outer appearances. Conversation with a woman endowed with beauty but bereft of intellect could be exhausted after a few words on the weather, whereas marriage to a woman with "an elegant intellect" would be elevated by "the sweet touches of sympathy in the converse of a chosen friend." Marriage at its best was an elevated and enduring form of companionship that eased life's inevitable trials. Who could be more interesting, asked a "Panegyric on Marriage," than the friend "we have selected from the whole world to be our

steady companion in every vicissitude of season or life?" Where
other friendships might languish over time or disintegrate under
pressure, the friendship of true love lasted over a lifetime.[36]

As for those who had already chosen their partners, practical advice on sustaining the partnership could be rendered in a distinctly
political idiom which imbued men with a potential for tyranny and
women with a penchant for rebellion. Men, declared an essayist for
the *Boston Magazine*, should not be tyrants to women, because tyrants produce rebels, and rebels when they prevail become tyrants
themselves. No one was better positioned to appreciate those sentiments than the members of the Revolutionary generation, who were
preoccupied, if not obsessed, with redefining the relationship between the rulers and the ruled. But contract was the basis for obedience as well as dissent, and men remained the rulers in the marriage
contract, albeit with telling limitations. Men should rule women,
conceded a writer for the *Columbian*, but not with a "rod of iron."
Another essayist counseled the husband, be not "a barbarian" to your
wife just because you know that she is your property, and the wife,
"to let thy gentle bosom be the pillow where all . . . cares may be
forgot."[37] In the face of unremitting despotism, however, dissolution
of the union remained an option. As the cautious advice of The Matron, a columnist with a persona like that of Dear Abby, indicates,
within the still hierarchical relation of marriage, certain kinds of behavior went beyond the pale. Considering the problem of an innocent
young bride who had contracted a venereal disease from her worldly
husband, The Matron held out hope for the union only if he would
confess and agree to be treated. But if he failed to accept blame for his
wife's condition, or even worse, accused her of infidelity, she advised
the young woman to "summon up all her fortitude and leave him."[38]

Advice on appropriate conjugal behavior, however, had its limits,
for the ultimate fate of a marriage, according to popular counsel, was
determined more by the choice of a mate than any other single factor.
It was the key to the perfect partnership and its most egalitarian component. Both sexes exercised freedom of choice here, and both staked
their futures on making the right choice.[39] Both, moreover, were
susceptible to making tragic mistakes. Examples of those who had
chosen foolishly, who married for the wrong reasons, or who simply
misread the true character of a prospective partner punctuated the
literature on marriage. "The Bad Effects of an Imprudent Matrimo-

nial Connection" chronicled the fate of a woman who fell victim to a money-seeking libertine. The consequences of her mistake were devastating. Her profligate partner, who "had a taste for social company," expensive diversions, and the pleasures of the alehouse, and very little inclination to hard work, squandered away all her money and was never to be seen at her side.[40]

Profligacy and licentiousness, adultery and seduction, bigamy and desertion—these were the misbegotten fruits of the wrong choice, and popular advice readily acknowledged that they could not always be avoided. One could enter into a union with a pure heart and with the best intentions only to be foiled by a deceitful spouse. And while the deceitful spouse went on his (only rarely her) merry way, the innocent spouse remained bound by law to the original union. The element of free choice that was so vital to a contractarian reading of marriage seemed to place an extraordinary burden on a potential female partner. Of course, men too could be deceived, cuckolded, and deserted by a faulty partner, but the consequences were never quite the same. Addressing "The Directory of Love" in the *Royal American*, for example, John Jealous complained that after living for some time in wedded bliss, he found his wife with a gentleman in the most private part of the house. Although "a thousand methods for getting rid of this problem" occurred to him, he wanted to know which option to pursue.[41] As his query suggests, men do not appear in this literature as desperate victims without tangible options. Women do, in part because of their subordination to men, and in part because marriage is the principal context in which they work out their destinies.[42]

Justice required a remedy for the wronged spouse, and the remedy was consistently construed as benefitting women as the victims of the double standard. As the author of *The Emigrants* averred in a long aside on the double standard, "I have no doubt but that the many misfortunes which daily happen in domestic life, and which too often precipitate women of the most virtuous inclinations into the gulf of ruin, proceed from the great difficulty there is in England, of obtaining a divorce." A man, by contrast, had ways of escaping the confines of a miserable marriage. He was free to look "abroad for those amusements which alone can compensate for domestic feuds," and should he transgress his marriage vows, no one would call him to account. But a woman seeking "some mitigation of sufferings" was destined to be "branded with contempt, and condemned to live in poverty, unnoticed and unpitied."[43]

Queries about how to proceed in untenable marriages flourished in the advice columns of popular periodicals, and although many undoubtedly came from the pens of creative editors, they demonstrate contemporary concern with the problem of failed marriages. "I am one of those unhappy young women," averred A.B., "whom fortune favoured with a husband; but not long after the conjugal rites were ended, he void to all humanity, left me and went and married a second wife." The balance of the column focussed on her right to remarry. She wanted to know: "As my husband married *first*, whether or no I can by law, marry afterwards during his life? . . . Or if it is a felony in the wife, then, was it not a felony in the husband first?"[44]

Court records exhibit no lack of real-life counterparts for A. B., nor is it difficult to understand their readiness to remarry without resorting to the law.[45] When Elizabeth De Franqueen's husband left Pennsylvania for Europe and wrote that he would never return, she married Joseph LeClerc, believing herself to be "at liberty to form a new matrimonial connexion."[46] A private bill passed by the territorial legislature of Indiana embodied a similar dilemma, but in this case, the legislature validated the wife's second union. Sympathy for the deserted wife is evident from the language in the official record. It has "been represented, that the said Catherine Moore, then Catherine Prince, feeling herself deserted by her said husband, and being in a forlorn and distressed situation, and being informed of the said John Prince, having contracted a second marriage, she was induced to contract on her part a marriage with one Robert K. Moore."[47] Bigamy, which is what the second marriage of A. B.'s husband, as well as those of both John Prince and Catherine Prince was, and pseudomarriage, a union not properly solemnized—like that of our old friend, William Everitt—were generally portrayed as tools employed by wicked men against innocent women. Indeed, they were denounced as the seedbed of seduction, the devices whereby men deceived women and ultimately destroyed them. In *Amelia; or the Faithless Briton*, pseudo-marriage was the source of a hoax perpetrated by a British officer who seduced and impregnated a young American girl by enticing her into a feigned marriage ceremony.[48]

The solution to these outrages lay in sharpening the boundaries around marriage. Blurred boundaries, commentators insisted, nourished the dangerous practice of self-divorce and illicit remarriage because they supported the deceptively simple notion that marriage was a private arrangement to be made and unmade at the will of the two parties. Traditional customs like the reading of the banns were encouraged not only because they buttressed the public character of marriage but because they embodied the look-before-you-leap approach so popular in advice columns. Thus "A Friend to the Fair Sex" praised the Quakers, whose practice of announcing marital intent before the assembled meeting was followed by the congregation's investigation of the character of the prospective spouses and was capped off by a waiting period before the celebration of the ceremony. The waiting period, which underscored the seriousness of entering into marriage, was viewed as a deterrent to marrying as a whim perhaps after a long night of drinking or as a result of runaway passion. And although settlements and antenuptial contracts were denounced as European refinements that reduced marriage to a crass business deal, premarital considerations that revolved around character rather than money supported both the affective and reciprocal aspects of the post-Revolutionary marital ideal.[49]

Post-Revolutionary critiques on blurred boundaries are particularly revealing, for in a government of laws, rules providing for exit from the marriage contract are even more important to the social order than those that control entry. In the wake of revolution, the American legal system did, in fact, move both toward redefining marriage and defining divorce. Yet the terms on which these parallel movements evolved could not have been more different. If American courts came to recognize a so-called common law marriage, a consummated union to which the parties had agreed, they were not about to recognize a comparable form of divorce.[50] Whereas the former put the best face on an existing arrangement, legitimized children from the union, and brought the husband under the obligation of support, the latter undermined the whole institution of marriage.

Supported as it was by the concept of breach of contract, divorce was construed far more strictly than marriage. Contemporaries could not advocate statutory divorce by mutual consent, much less by unilateral decision, because the underlying justification for rescinding an innocent spouse's marriage promise hinged on the assumption that the reciprocal promise had been broken first by the guilty spouse.[51] It is not that eighteenth-century moralists and jurists could not envision a world of no-fault; they could and they did, and it caused them no end of consternation. Fault, so crucial in popular accounts of failed marriages, was no less crucial in creating the rules for their dissolution. It was an integral part of a mental universe that pivoted on causative reasoning. Even the so-called omnibus clauses in early divorce statutes, catch-all phrases providing broad judicial discretion in decreeing divorces, assumed a fault that was too unique or elusive to be defined by statute, but that could be readily apprehended in the courts by the judiciary.[52]

This fundamental reliance on causative reasoning not only informed both the legal and moral contours of divorce in the early national era; it provided the rationale for legitimating it in the first place. As a 1788 pamphlet alleged in ardently anticlerical terms, attention to causality would permit formal divorce to assume a reasonable middle ground between religious fanaticism on the one hand and runaway anarchy on the other. On the one extreme, argued the anonymous pamphleteer, there was the example of India, where burning the widow alive fulfilled the biblical admonition that what God has joined together should not be put asunder. Here was ample proof that in matters of great importance to the general welfare, a too-literal adherence to scripture was folly. But at the other extreme, he conceded, there was need to address the danger that "one separation would make way for another like beasts, and their families and kindred would be unknown and unprovided for and their names and distinctions lost." The way to counter the anarchic tendencies in divorce, ran this argument, was to require formal complaints, institute careful inquiry into the causes, and demand adequate provision for children. Such precautions would alleviate untold amounts of individual suffering while maintaining the boundaries around marriage.[53]

Casual dissolutions were to be avoided at all costs. In the prescriptive literature of the period, sentiment for causeless divorce, as it was called, was likely to come from the lips of a libertine like Major Sanford, a character in Hannah Foster's popular novel, *The Coquette*.[54] "As we lived together without love," he reasoned, "we parted without regret." Although his account of a marriage coming apart through no one's fault has a remarkably modern ring, it emanates here from a man who, as Foster avers on every other page, was devoid of any semblance of virtue. Indeed, Sanford embodied all the perils in causeless divorce. Only "a professed Libertine," practiced "in the art of seduction" would treat the boundaries of marriage so cavalierly or entertain its dissolution so casually. A virtuous society, by implication, would mandate strict rules for marriage, strong sanctions against the spouses who broke them, and effective remedies for their innocent victims, including the legal right to remarry.[55] Following the English model of formal separations, one essayist noted, would not do, because without the capacity to remarry, the innocent spouse might very well suffer more than the guilty, or be tempted into an illicit union.[56] Concern with licit versus illicit unions even made its way into the lyrics of a song entitled "The Married Man," where the case for marital legitimacy was made with signal clarity.

> The Joys which from lawless connections arise
> Are fugitive—never sincere,
> Oft stolen with haste, and oft snatch'd by
> surprise
> Interupted [sic] by doubt and by fear;
> But those which in legal attachments we find,
> When the heart is with innocence pure,
> Is from every imbit'ring reflection refine'd
> And while life can taste joy can endure.[57]

The contrast drawn here between lawless and lawful connections suggests that divorce was, among other things, part of a larger effort to delineate the married from the unmarried. That is not to infer a consensus on what constituted a legitimate marital dissolution, much less on what were the proper substantive terms, but considering the problem of marital legitimacy helps to account for the wholesale recognition of divorce in the post-Revolutionary era. In retrospect we can see that it was the decision to accept formal rules for divorce in the first place and not so much the rules themselves that constituted the true legal revolution in marriage. Yet the initial acceptance of divorce proved far less controversial than the subsequent working out of the particularities. On the threshold of the nineteenth century, not only had the notion that divorces could be decreed for gross violations of the marriage contract already acquired statutory legitimacy, but it had done so with remarkably little opposition.

≺ IV ≻

The Limits of Liberation

By the middle decades of the nineteenth century, as litigants tested the limits of statutory provisions in ever increasing numbers, virtually every legal, social, and moral facet of divorce would become the object of critical scrutiny. The contrast with the late eighteenth century is striking. It seems as if in legitimating divorce in spare and simple statutes, eighteenth-century legislators embraced a solution without fully comprehending the problem. Not only did they neglect to address some thorny substantive and procedural issues, but they failed to anticipate the sheer numbers of men and women who would come to rely on the divorce process. Yet given the novelty of formal divorce in the early republic, it could hardly have been otherwise. While it was understood that an innocent spouse might sever her or his conjugal ties to a guilty partner, the available prototypes were still spare and lacking texture. There was often little clarity about precisely what behavior constituted the violations designated by statute, or what was required as proof, or even what was the proper tribunal to determine its validity. Legal fairness to spouses engaged in the divorce process was assumed rather than defined or contested. And in a legal innovation that could deeply affect both the lives of individuals and the welfare of the society, the relation between the right of divorce and its collective impact was only dimly imagined.

Post-Revolutionary legislators, however, were addressing a specifically post-Revolutionary problem: the persistence of extralegal marital dissolutions. If independence provided both the intellectual and symbolic resources for accepting the concept of divorce, concern for marital legitimacy supplied the catalyst for legalizing it. In this context divorce can be construed as a legal fiction designed to bring extralegal dissolutions under the aegis of state government. Couples were ending their unions anyway, and it remained for legislators to provide ways to end them legally. In every country among "the lowest ranks," noted an observer of wifesale, "men part with their wives, and wives with their husbands, with as little delay or remorse as they would move from one boarding house to another." Since law was "not to be had for nothing" in either England or the United States, since there was no property in question, and with "the object being only a wife," wifesale, he concluded, was not even deemed worthy of formal prosecution.[58] For a variation on wifesale in the marketplace, consider the tale of the runaway American wife who arrived in Chatauqua, New York, with her lover, only to be followed by her enraged husband. When the lover offered the husband fifty dollars to relinquish his wife, he accepted it and "returned home apparently satisfied, leaving the happy couple . . . exulting in their triumph."[59]

Since there is little evidence that wifesale enjoyed as much prominence in North America as it did in England, such stories need to be taken with a grain of salt. Still, Americans "of the lower ranks" devised their own extralegal forms for divorce which exhibited very little reverence for fault. As a consequence, potential litigants carried an image of divorce that was far less stringent than the statutes that provided for it. In contrast to the trickle-down theory of cultural diffusion, then, the persistence with which such potential litigants implicitly challenged the prevailing legal system suggests the validity of a bottom-up alternative. For those spouses who wanted the terms for marital dissolution to be as easy as possible, mutual consent proved a highly appealing justification not only because it was swift and inexpensive but because it comported nicely with the pursuit of happiness. Moreover, the active support of friends and neighbors was an index to the weight that was customarily accorded to both the approval and disapproval of the community. There was a compelling logic to the communal support of divorce by mutual consent, for if a proper marriage hinged on the mutual consent of the couple made public before witnesses, why not divorce as well?

It was an idea that died hard and perhaps never completely. Well into the nineteenth century, state legislatures were besieged with crude divorce petitions, signed with an "X," and often accompanied by vague depositions that affirmed the consent of both parties together with broad community approval.[60] Indeed, consent was often the basis on which legislative decrees were denied. And yet petitioners evinced an enduring faith that the sheer number of friends and neighbors who supported the dissolution would sway the minds of legislators. Tennessee legislative divorce petitions, for example, could carry up to seventy or eighty signatures.[61] One Pennsylvania community even used its members to arbitrate the division of marital property. The designated arbitrators decreed that "Fry and his wife should separate, and either should be at liberty to marry who they pleased."[62] Although it is not clear if the members of this informal tribunal were ignorant of the state divorce statute or unwilling to abide by its relatively liberal terms, their willingness to create generous terms of their own speaks volumes to their belief in the legitimacy of a community-sanctioned dissolution. Moreover, in contrast to the custom of wifesale in the marketplace, this form of community approval exhibited an undeniably juristic dimension. If there was conflict over divorce in the post-Revolutionary era, it turned not so much on whether divorce should be legitimated—the Revolution seems to have provided a measure of consensus on that question—as on whose terms.[63]

As for the motives of "the state," a question that animated this chapter from its inception, to some extent they can be discerned in the language of its statutes. The 1787 New York statute, which enabled the Everitt divorce to take place, carried the message that divorce was to be avoided at all costs and was to be granted only for the most egregious breach of the marriage contract, the sin of adultery. Reading more like a criminal statute on adultery than a civil statute on divorce, its preamble averred that "the laws at present in being within this State respecting adultery are very defective."[64] Yet the law was a good deal more than a statute on adultery. It seems likely that extralegal marital dissolutions followed by long-term second unions were occurring just often enough to warrant legislation that rendered both the dissolutions and the unions more clearly illegal than ever before. To put the proposition another way, to make divorce legitimate was to make all other dissolutions illegitimate. That adultery was to be punished by the prohibition against the remarriage of the guilty spouse exemplifies the punitive thrust of the New York statute. Instead of a scarlet "A," an adulterous spouse like William Everitt was to carry the burden of an invisible "D."

The ensuing debate over the 1787 law reveals that at stake in these early statutes in New York and other jurisdictions were the terms for closing the gap between formal law expressed as divorcelessness and various customary divorce practices. In the process of balancing the punitive advantages of the New York statute against the undesirable consequences of its restrictiveness, the Council of Revision vetoed it, asserting that unless it were possible to lock up adulterous spouses in a cloister, the prohibition on remarriage was an invitation to immoral and illegal unions.

What is more, because a guilty spouse might remarry out of state, or, given the level of recordkeeping, even within the state, there was the practical problem of enforcement. At issue here was nothing less than calculating the long-term, collective influence of divorce law on day-to-day marital behavior. Because legal rules had the power to influence moral choices in an area that had traditionally belonged to the church, even the invisible "D" was not without purpose. As

Benjamin Trumbull argued in his assault on easy divorce in Connecticut, statutory failure to provide punishment for the guilty spouse could serve to undermine deeply-rooted religious convictions. Referring to the citizens of Connecticut, he warned: "The silence and sanction of law in a special manner are such soothing cordials, such effectual opiates, that no flashes or thunder from the divine world would alarm their conscience."[65]

Passing the original statute over the veto of the Council, New York legislators presumably wagered that in providing for divorce on highly restrictive terms, they were taking some sort of middle ground between easy divorce and complete divorcelessness; they were discouraging casual legal dissolutions while making some dents in the extralegal ones. Similar constraints were evident in statutes with broader grounds. The preamble to the Pennsylvania divorce statute of 1785 averred that it was "the design of marriage, and the wish of the parties entering into that state that it should continue during their joint lives."[66]

To see the legitimation of divorce as an effort at social control in which statutory recognition was deemed the lesser of two evils goes a long way toward explaining why divorce assumed the shapes that it did.[67] Indeed, the very marginality of our defendant, William Everitt, intimates he was precisely the sort of person legislators had in mind when they fashioned the New York statute. Yet a top-down model of social control requires considerable qualification because it slights the degree to which interest in the stability of marriage cut across both gender and class lines. Given the extensive interdependence of men and women in the political economy of post-Revolutionary marriages, we can understand the willingness of many couples to live out their lives in decidedly uncompanionate relationships, despite the possibility of extralegal or legal dissolutions. Most men and probably women to an even greater degree did not want countless dissolutions and reconstitutions.

Another important consideration is the adversarial role played by female litigants. Legal development, after all, owes as much to the actions of ordinary litigants as it does to the pronouncements of legislators and jurists. It is becoming evident that in numerous jurisdictions over a variety of time spans women constituted the majority of divorce plaintiffs. To be sure, as economic dependents confronting an all-male legal system that embraced the double standard, they suffered structural disadvantages as plaintiffs that are all too apparent. Nonetheless, to the extent that suing for divorce was a legal option that depended on the voluntary, active, and even tenacious participation of female plaintiffs, it represented a conceptual reordering of the marriage contract. The old common law fiction that husband and wife were one and the husband was the one no longer held quite the same authority. In fact, in this context, divorce presented women with a form of liberation because it challenged the male-dominated corporatism of the marriage contract.

That brings us at last to Sarah Everitt, whose liberation seems so highly qualified as to create doubts about who was being liberated from whom.[68] We cannot be sure of what lay beneath the simple chancery record, but on its face, it appears that William was the one who liberated himself from Sarah, and she legitimated the deed by coming to court. Perhaps there were property considerations, such as earnings or an inheritance, that impelled her to separate her legal identity from his, or perhaps there was a suitor waiting in the wings. Or perhaps she simply wanted to be free to remarry sometime in the future, and presented with an option to put her life in legal order, she pursued it in the courts. Beyond all these practical considerations, however, there was surely a powerful symbolic component to her legal appearance. In a world where the repudiation of a spouse had been a husband's prerogative, we should not dismiss the import of her right as a woman to repudiate her husband in a court of law. One thing is certain; divorce by a woman no longer represented the anarchic breaking of sacred contract.[69] Indeed, since it was William who was defined as the anarchist who broke the contract here, perhaps we should read Sarah's determination to divorce him as a declaration of independence.

The Second Great Awakening and the Market Revolution

NATHAN O. HATCH

AMIDST THE FLURRY OF recent studies on the early American Republic, no question has been so riveting as the attempt to understand the origins of liberal capitalism, the market revolution. How did the United States become a liberal, competitive, market-driven society—instead of a hierarchical society like Britain or a republican society envisioned by the founders? How did the small-scale eighteenth-century world of individual artisans and farmers, of patriarchy and inheritance, become transformed into a society characterized by commercial advancement, individual pursuit of self-interest, and legitimation of competing factions? While historians agree that liberal mores came to dominate American society, debate rages about when this transition occurred, who opposed it, and what were its implications for issues of class, gender, race, and ethnicity.[1]

Historians charting the rise of a liberal society have given scant attention to one important line of inquiry, the links between commerce and religious culture. As Michael Zuckerman has recently noted, scholars have largely severed the study of the rise of a commercial society from its animating moral and religious structures.[2] Unlike earlier scholarship which accorded Max Weber and the Protestant Ethic a central place in the consideration of American economic development, today religion has become irrelevant to prevailing understandings of economic and social history.[3] The most authoritative contemporary studies of early American economic development do not include even a single index entry that pertains to religion.[4] In assessing the rise of American capitalism, historians have seen religious beliefs and practices as peripheral to the real motors of change: issues such as demography, land availability, household strategies, capital accumulation, and the rise of a cash economy. Those most inclined to speak of the moral economy of common people have done little to explicate the religious mentality by which these people increasingly ordered their world.[5]

This is a puzzling omission given a wealth of recent studies that point to the Republic's first decades as the period of greatest religious ferment and originality in American history. The wave of popular religious movements that broke upon America in the generation after independence decisively changed the center of gravity of American religion, worked powerfully to Christianize popular culture, splintered American Christianity beyond recognition, divorced religious leadership from social position, and above all, proclaimed the moral responsibility of everyone to think and act for himself. Christendom had probably not witnessed a comparable period of religious upheaval since the Reformation—and never such an upsurge of private initiative. Whatever the exact connection between the Second Great Awakening and the market revolution, what cannot be ignored is that they transpired simultaneously and that both involved a comparable upsurge in voluntary activity, in popular mobilization and competition, and in outsiders struggling to get ahead.[6]

Both the economic and the religious restructuring of the early Republic were linked to the political earthquake that was the American Revolution. The last quarter of the eighteenth century was dominated by a cultural ferment over the meaning of freedom. Three times during these years Americans deliberated on fundamental propositions about government. Each time—during the Revolution, during the debate over the Constitution, and during the political passion of the 1790s—the issue of popular participation in government flared up with greater intensity. Pressing issues about liberty, authority, and popular sovereignty became serious business for everyone.[7] Above all, the Revolutionary era dramatically expanded the circle of people who considered themselves capable of thinking about issues of freedom, equality, and representation. Respect for authority, tradition, station, and education eroded. And ordinary people increasingly expressed their right as republican citizens to take charge of their own fate, the labor of their hands as well as the devotion of their hearts.

Why have historians so easily missed the transparent connections between the religious upsurge of this era, the Second Great Awakening, and the origins of liberal America? What insights do the dynamics of popular religion suggest about the advent of capitalism and about the extent to which common people aided, resisted, or even recognized the new reality? This chapter suggests that the Second Great Awakening reflected and accelerated forces that were shaping an open society of free individuals: in its marketing of faith through innovative mass communications, in its radical and competitive pluralism, and in its focus on conversion and individual choice—the elevation of the volitional conscience. Exploring these facets of the Awakening will enhance our understanding of a decisive moment of change in American history: a sudden bursting forth of entrepreneurial energy, of religious passion, and of pecuniary desire.[8]

≺ I ≻

Methodism and the Market: The Interpretive Landscape

The explosive growth of the Methodist Episcopal Church was the most surprising religious development in a republic that turned its back on state-sponsored religion. The American followers of John Wesley, who could boast no more than four ministers and 300 laypeople in 1771, were threatened with extinction during the Revolution. All their leaders save Francis Asbury returned to England, leaving the Methodist faithful to struggle with the stigma of disloyalty throughout the war.

Under the tireless direction of Asbury, the Methodists advanced from Canada to Georgia emphasizing three themes that Americans found captivating: God's free grace, the liberty of people to accept or reject that grace, and the power and validity of popular religious expression—even among servants, women, and African-Americans. Led by unlearned preachers committed to sacrifice and to travel, the Methodists organized local classes or cells and preaching circuits at a rate that alarmed more respectable denominations. When Asbury died in 1816, the Methodists claimed over 2,000 ministers and 200,000 church members.

This dynamic growth and its social implications has lately intrigued sociologists more than historians. Comparing denominational statistics for 1776 and 1850, Roger Finke and Rodney Stark noted how decisively the leading denominations of colonial America—Anglican, Presbyterian, Congregational—crumbled in a free market religious economy. It was the mobilization of outsiders and upstarts that won the heart of America. In 1776 only 17 percent of Americans were church members. This percentage doubled by 1850 with more aggressive groups operating in an unregulated religious market. By 1850, also, Methodists and Baptists could claim almost two-thirds of the country's religious adherents. And the influence of once-dominant churches had declined precipitously: Congregationalists from 20.4 percent to 4 percent of adherents, Episcopalians from 15.7 percent to 3.5 percent, and Presbyterians from 19 percent to 11.6 percent. The Congregationalists, who had twice the clergy of any other church in 1776, could not muster one-tenth the preaching force of the Methodists in 1845.[9]

Taking into account such popular mobilization, George Thomas has recently posited an isomorphic relationship between revivalism and the organization of everyday life within an expanding market. Unlike Calvinism, which emphasized human corruption, divine initiative, and the authority of educated clergymen and inherited ecclesiastical structures, the Methodists proclaimed the breathtaking message of individual freedom, autonomy, responsibility, and achievement. If nothing else, the revivalism of the Second Great Awakening insisted that common people were responsible for themselves in religious matters and had to act accordingly. Thomas concludes that this dominant message converged with and reenforced the individualism of petty capitalism.[10]

Another sociologist, David Martin, has argued similarly that American Methodism resonated with the logic of liberalism. Methodism, he suggests, grew out of the collapse of the monopolistic relationship between religion and the state and between religion and the local community. Successful as a counterculture in England, the Methodists succeeded in America in defining the core of a democratic culture: "Arminian evangelical Protestantism provided the *differentia specifica* of the American religious and cultural ethos."[11]

For at least three reasons historians have not been drawn towards these lines of inquiry. In the first place, religious historians have generally told the story of the Second Great Awakening from the perspective of those elite churches which were declining rather than from those insurgent groups which were prospering and making dramatic inroads into popular culture. Most interpretations of the Second Great Awakening have seen it as a profoundly conservative force, an attempt by traditional religious elites to re-impose social order upon a disordered and secularized society. In this view revivalism reflected the attempt of fearful churchmen to salvage Protestant solidarity. In Perry Miller's words, the Second Great Awakening served as the churches' attempt to assert "the unity of culture in pressing danger of fragmentation." According to Richard Hofstadter, "Revivalism succeeded where traditionalism had failed. Emotional upheavals took the place of the coercive sanctions of religious establishments."[12] In a similar vein, scholars such as Clifford S. Griffin, John R. Bodo, Charles I. Foster, and Charles C. Cole, Jr., understood the Second Great Awakening as a conservative assertion of authority by ministers fearful of losing their traditional roles.[13] While the theme of social control has waned in recent years, newer studies of the ministerial profession in the early republic have focussed almost exclusively on clerical elites.[14] Even the study of women and religion too easily accepts the main story line as the "clerical disestablishment" of the New England Standing Order.[15]

Our understanding of religion and the market is also impeded by a related pattern: the curious lack of attention given to the rise to prominence of American Methodism. The Methodist Episcopal Church grew from 14,000 members and forty-two circuits in 1784, to over a million members, served by 3,988 itinerants and 7,730 local preachers, in 1844. As a denomination it was nearly half again as large as any other Protestant body.[16] Interpreting such a movement is a daunting task, but American religious historians have devoted surprisingly little attention to the subject. Their British counterparts, however, in the wake of historians Elie Halévy and E. P. Thompson, continue to wrestle with the broad social and political significance of British Methodism.[17]

Historians of American religion have posed few questions for which Methodist sources might provide clues or answers. For the generation of Perry Miller, Henry May, and Sidney Mead the Methodists represented the banal residue in America of what had been the noble and intellectually rich tradition of Puritanism, Edwardian Calvinism, and enlightened Unitarianism. More recently, historians have turned to study outsiders, and fresh studies have poured forth on Shakers, Adventists, Mormons, spiritualists, and occultists. With few notable exceptions, these studies omit the Methodists as too respectable and bland, and too much a part of the mainstream, to merit inclusion among real outsiders.[18] The most basic features of the Methodist terrain remain uncharted, with few arresting biographies, compelling local studies, renditions of Methodist ideology, or studies of Methodism and print communications. One result is difficulty in bringing larger economic questions into focus.

A third reason that popular religious movements remain unexplored is a surprising one given the deep commitment of a new generation of social historians to understand common people's lives in the age of capitalist transformation. While considerable attention is focussed on the changing nature of markets, on the decline of independent artisans and farmers and the rise of the American working class, surprisingly little energy is spent in exploring the dynamics of insurgent religious movements.[19] This neglect stems both from the neo-Marxist preoccupation with the formation of social classes and the assumption that religion is generally a conservative and pernicious force.[20] These studies fail to take into account that, for better or worse, the most dynamic popular movements in the United States were expressly religious. However powerful secular working class organizations became in cities such as New York and Baltimore, their presence cannot compare with the phenomenal growth and collective élan of the Methodists.[21]

It is curious that so many social historians have focussed their attention on the urban working class at a time when America was so profoundly rural. Between 1800 and 1820 the percentage of the American labor force in agriculture had increased from 75 to 80 percent—in sharp contrast with England where only about one-third of its workers engaged in agriculture. Only 7 percent of Americans lived in cities with populations over 2,500. Well over a third of the English population was urban, with 20 percent in cities larger than 20,000. The Methodists, under Bishop Francis Asbury, crafted an organization ideally suited to pursue an expanding agrarian and rural society. While Methodism retained a stronghold in the seaports of the middle states, Asbury hammered its organization into one that had a distinct rural orientation adept at expanding into thinly populated areas. "We must draw resources from the centre to the circumference," he wrote in 1797.[22]

Religious leaders from the rank and file were phenomenally successful in reaching out to marginal people, in promoting self-education and sheltering participants from the indoctrination of elite orthodoxies, in binding people together in supportive community, and in identifying the aspirations of common people with the will of God. While the hierarchical structure of the Methodist Episcopal Church may have seemed out of accord with the democratic stirrings of the times, the vital spring of Methodism under Francis Asbury was to make Christianity profoundly a faith of the people. From preachers like themselves, people received an invitation to join a movement promising dignity of choice and beckoning them to involvement as class leader, exhorter, local preacher, and circuit rider. Lay preaching, the hallmark of American Methodism, served as a powerful symbol that the wall between gentleman and commoner had been shattered.

Unfortunately, social historians interpreting American revivals have followed the interpretive framework of E. P. Thompson as faithfully as hounds to the horn. Religion is accorded little autonomous causal efficacy and revivals are seen as one more tool of elites to discipline the vagrant and unruly impulses of the working class. Bruce Laurie has examined the role of evangelical churches in instilling new norms of sobriety, industry, and economy among workers in Philadelphia. Similarly, Paul Johnson has described Charles G. Finney's revivalism in Rochester as "order-inducing, repressive, and quintessentially bourgeois." To Johnson, it was a middle-class solution to the problem of order in a manufacturing economy, a means by which entrepreneurs imposed discipline upon themselves and their workers.[23] In a similar vein, Charles Sellers has focussed his interpretation of religion in the Jacksonian era upon Calvinists and Charles Finney and has virtually ignored the importance of Methodists. Sellers's interpretation follows the assumption that a society's dominant strata determines its religion. Thus he concludes: "Sanctifying entrepreneurial visions of a disciplined capitalist society, the mainline clergy channeled the Moderate Light's gradualist millennialism into a cultural imperialism that would create a Christian capitalist republic." He interprets a popular religious movement such as the Mormons as a "precapitalist cultural revitalization" at war with the emerging market economy—"the magical spirituality of a parochial and fatalist countryside against the self-reliant effort of a cosmopolitan and activist market."[24]

In a similar vein, Johnson has also argued that popular faiths of the early republic were expressions of resistance to bourgeois individualism. He interprets prophets like New York's Robert Mathews or the Mormon leader Joseph Smith as rejecting the encroaching market and retrieving an eighteenth-century world of agrarian, familial patriarchalism.[25] This interpretation comports with E. P. Thompson's views on the moral economy of plebeian culture and the penchant of artisans and laborers to cling to eighteenth-century ways.[26] With neat ideological consistency, it portrays a transformation in which those who had the most to lose from market capitalism foresaw with all the accuracy of hindsight the movement of history and resisted it at all costs, inspired by a restorationist vision of a simple agrarian world. In these interpretations, the Second Great Awakening is seen either as a means by which capitalists hoped to control workers or a means by which workers resisted capitalism by retreating to the eighteenth century.

These interpretations fail to recognize the mainspring of the Second Great Awakening: that religion in America became dominated by the interests and aspirations of ordinary people. In the generation after the Revolution, American Christianity became a mass enterprise—and not as a predictable outgrowth of religious conditions in the British colonies. The eighteen hundred Christian ministers serving in 1775 swelled to nearly forty thousand by 1845. While the American population expanded tenfold, the number of preachers per capita more than tripled; the colonial legacy of one minister per fifteen hundred people became one per five hundred. This dramatic mobilization indicated a profound religious upsurge—religious organizations taking on market form—and resulted in a vastly altered religious landscape. Religious activists pitched their messages to the unschooled and unsophisticated. Their movements offered the humble a marvelous sense of individual potential and of collective aspiration.

While Methodism was a complex phenomenon and incapable of reduction to any single economic or political orientation, the movement eroded patterns of deference to established authority and tradition and dignified the convictions of ordinary people on important matters—whether religious, political, or economic. It elicited choice and participation by people long ignored, and bound them together in disciplined and supportive bands. Methodist culture also instilled habits of industry, sobriety, and mutual accountability. This kind of popular mobilization did not immediately transform yeoman-artisans who distrusted market society into individualists and petty entrepreneurs. But it did call them emphatically into a new life, an orientation whose latent capacity for effecting economic and political behavior awaits exploration. It is not surprising that Methodist artisans in Philadelphia in the 1830s were more successful than their peers, more likely to end up master craftsmen and small retailers.[27]

≺ II ≻
Religion as Private Enterprise

Since the time of George Whitefield, evangelicals in the Anglo-American world had adeptly exported religion into the marketplace. Harry Stout has recently depicted Whitefield's dramatic success in transferring preaching from church sanctuaries into the profane space of the market to compete with merchants, hawkers, and stage players. Whitefield's greatness, Stout suggests, lay in integrating religious discourse into the emerging language of consumption.[28] Yet the Great Awakening in America did not overthrow the pattern of state-controlled churches or parishes that sought to regulate worldly matters along godly lines. Jonathan Edwards, for instance, never divorced religion from public affairs, implicitly justifying an economic order that ran by its own principles. Edwards denied the possibility of a virtuous market economy and railed against economic individualism.[29]

The real divorce of religion from public affairs came in the wake of religious disestablishment, as insurgent leaders reconstructed evangelical life as part and parcel of the market. A whole range of rootless and visionary young persons, spurning conventional religious establishments and genteel social routines, championed religious movements intent on vast mobilization of people. Characteristically bold, self-educated, self-confident, and inventive, this dedicated corps of charismatic leaders developed an array of religious movements which differed radically in theological outlook and organizational intent. Yet, whether they came to fix their identity as Methodist or Baptist, Universalist or Disciple, Mormon or Millerite, these unusually strong personalities all shared a passion for expansion, a hostility to orthodox belief and style, and a zeal for religious reconstruction.

These preachers were marginal men, like the new breed of roving peddlers of books and pamphlets, who managed to carve out identities for themselves as mobile cultural entrepreneurs. They had the same hunger for achievement, and both facilitated the emergence of a market society by enlarging for mass consumption the weighty issues that had been the monopoly of gentlemen.[30]

In the era of the Second Great Awakening, the most distinctive feature of American Christianity was not the surge of an impersonal force called revivalism, descending like manna from heaven, but a remarkable set of popular leaders who proclaimed compelling visions of individual self-respect and collective action. This story is not one of established clergy fretting about loss of social authority, but rather the aptitude of religious entrepreneurs for mobilizing people.

This drive to reconstruct the church along voluntary lines set these dissidents apart from the generation of George Whitefield and Gilbert Tennant, who labored to revive lukewarm establishments, but who left the creation of new institutional forms to the will of providence and the discretion of those who pursued a New Light call. In the main, eighteenth-century church people stumbled at the threshold of founding new institutional churches because they had not fully shed the conviction that the deterioration of religious consensus and community cohesion was a sign of God's anger. In contrast, the collapse of religious conformity stirred no pangs of conscience in Francis Asbury, who welcomed the unfolding opportunity to mobilize people for the Methodist cause.[31]

Dissent in America after the Revolution was characterized by a shift from seeking converts for existing denominations to movement-building from the ground up. A battery of young leaders without elite pedigree constructed fresh religious ideologies around which new religious movements coalesced—Methodist, Christian, Disciple, Freewill Baptist, Cumberland Presbyterian, African-Episcopal Methodist, Latter-day Saint. W. R. Ward has noted that Francis Asbury was an entrepreneur in religion, a man who perceived a market to be exploited. The itinerant-based machine which he set in motion was less a church in any traditional sense than "a military mission of short term agents."[32] Similarly, the founder of the Churches of Christ, Barton W. Stone, eschewed normal pastoral duties and dedicated himself utterly to the pursuit of "causes" in religion. Elias Smith went so far as to define religious liberty as the right to build a movement by itinerating without constraint.[33] Another superb example of this type of visionary leader bent on movement formation is Sidney Rigdon, whose own dynamic presence led him to forceful roles first as chief lieutenant in the Disciples of Christ under Alexander Campbell and then in the Mormons under Joseph Smith. Smith said of Rigdon's willingness to abandon all for the sake of a cause: "Truth was his pursuit, and for truth he was prepared to make every sacrifice in his power."[34]

All of these leaders eventually defined success by the number of converts who identified themselves with a fledgling movement. This quest for organization lay at the heart of Methodism's success. One unfriendly critic observed that the movement produced such great results "because it took hold of the doctrines which lay in the minds of all men here, and wrought them with the steam, levers, and pulleys of a new engine."[35] These religious organizations thrived by breaking the mold of traditional church organizations and offering new models premised on voluntary allegiance.

Above all, these upstarts were radically innovative as mass communicators, their movements crusades for broadcasting the truth. Without any traditional parish constituency, an insurgent preacher had only one hope of success: fresh strategies to capture public attention. Drawing communication skills more from popular culture than from the organized church, preachers continued to refashion the sermon as a popular medium, inviting even the most unlearned and inexperienced to respond to a call to preach. These initiates were charged to proclaim the gospel anywhere and every day of the week—even to the limit of their physical endurance. The resulting creation, the colloquial sermon, employed daring pulpit storytelling, no-holds-barred appeals, overt humor, strident attack, graphic application, and intimate personal experience. These young framers of religious movements also became the most effective purveyors of mass literature in the early republic, confronting people in every section of the new nation with the combined force of the written and spoken word. In addition, this generation launched bold experiments with new forms of religious music, new techniques of protracted meetings, and new Christian ideologies that denied the mediations of religious elite and promised to exalt those of low estate.[36]

At the turn of the century, the commercialization of rural life in America involved an explosion of print and written communications in rural society. At the critical juncture when local newspapers promoted commercial exchange and weakened opposition to it, religious entrepreneurs flooded the market with an array of accessible religious literature.[37] These populist religious leaders were intoxicated with the potential of print. Exploiting a golden age of cheap and regional printing, obscure prophets like Elias Smith, Lorenzo Dow, and Theophilus Gates, or black preachers like Richard Allen or Daniel Coker, rose to an equal footing with a Jonathan Edwards or a Timothy Dwight. And they measured results according to standards of the market rather than the established church: success in multiplying the audience. A New England clergyman, who resented uneducated and unrefined greenhorns presuming to speak in the Lord's name, put it this way: "They measure the progress of religion by the numbers who flock to their standards, not by the prevalence of faith and piety, justice and charity and the public virtues in society in general."[38]

≺ III ≻

A Sea of Sectarian Rivalries

In the United States success marked those religious movements willing to market their religion to the people. With few restraints upon them nationally or locally, religious upstarts multiplied apace, catering to the interests of specific market segments—a proliferation that Adam Smith had predicted would result upon government deregulation of religion.[39] The net effect was the splintering of American Protestantism. In the eighteenth century the creation of new churches had been as rare and difficult to conceive as the granting of a corporate charter for business—only a half dozen of which had been made during the entire colonial period. The drive to invent new churches and religious organizations paralleled the explosion of charters for corporations which were rapidly becoming seen as popular entitlements. Between 1800 and 1817, states granted nearly eighteen hundred corporate charters.[40]

The comparable privatization of religion during these years wrought a period of religious ferment and originality unmatched in American history. Few traditional claims to religious authority could weather such a relentless beating. There were competing claims of old denominations and a host of new ones. Whereas in 1790 there had been only one non-Calvinist church in the Connecticut River valley of Vermont, by 1815 there were fifty two.[41] Wandering prophets appeared dramatically, and supremely heterodox religious movements gained followings. People veered from one church to another amidst the unbridled wrangling of competitors in a "war of words."[42] Religious competitors wrangled unceasingly, traditional clergy and self-appointed preachers foremost in the fray. And new and passionate causes sprang up within the church's walls around the issues of freemasonry, temperance, slavery, women's rights, and health reform. Julian Sturtevant, a Yale graduate and Congregational missionary to Illinois, found a "realm of confusion and religious anarchy" when he arrived in Jacksonville in 1829:

In Illinois I met for the first time a divided Christian community, and was plunged without warning or preparation into a sea of sectarian rivalries which was kept in constant agitation, not only by real differences of opinion, but by ill-judged discussions and unfortunate personalities among ambitious men.[43]

Whatever common spirit bound Protestants together in this period, it came to rest in few stable institutions. Recurring dissent blasted any semblance of organizational coherence. The array of denominations, mission boards, reform agencies, newspapers and journals, revivalists, and colleges is at best an amorphous collectivity, an organizational smorgasbord. Power, influence, and authority were radically dispersed, and the most successful came by way of popular appeal.

The democratic winnowing of the church produced not just pluralism but also striking diversity. The flexibility and innovation of religious organizations made it possible for an American to find an amenable group no matter what his or her preference in belief, practice, or institutional structure. Churches ranged from egalitarian to autocratic and included all degrees of organizational complexity. One could be a Presbyterian who favored or opposed the freedom of the will, a Methodist who promoted or denounced democracy in the church, a Baptist who advocated or condemned foreign missions, and a member of virtually any denomination who upheld or opposed slavery. One could revel in Christian history with John W. Nevin or wipe the slate clean with Alexander Campbell. One could opt for traditional piety or join a perfectionist sect. Religious options in the

new nation seemed unlimited: one could worship on Saturday, practice foot washing, ordain women, advocate pacifism, prohibit alcohol, or toy with spiritualism, phrenology, and health reform.

The nature of extreme dissent in the United States gives the most
telling evidence of these churning centrifugal forces. The Mormons,
the Shakers, and the Oneida community, for instance, did not lash
out at some imagined combination of Protestant churches and voluntary societies that had gained hegemony of the nation's spiritual
destiny. Instead, their passion for a new order grew out of the perception that there was no authoritative center. The entire religious
world, they believed, perched upon shifting sand, cried out for prophets who could recover the missing bedrock. Lawrence Foster has suggested that the acute crisis of authority that haunted each of these
groups motivated them to reconstitute sexual and family life. John
Humphrey Noyes was particularly jarred by the cacophony of ideas
and causes surrounding him. He feared an unraveling of the entire
social order and concluded that he was uniquely responsible for
achieving a new social and religious synthesis. He declared in a letter in 1837: "God has set me to cast up a highway across this chaos,
and I am gathering out the stones and grading the track as fast as
possible."[44]

The fragmentation of Christianity into 150 different Protestant
groups meant that none could exercise oversight of the entire society.
While Presbyterians and Congregationalists did sustain a valiant effort to preserve their role as moral arbiters, insurgent churches like
the Methodist, Christian, and Baptist were obsessed with fears of
Calvinist designs for social control. They resented the ongoing attempts of Calvinists to hold sway over all of society and its behav-
ioral norms. In Albany, New York, for instance, Methodist and mechanic ideologies appealed to the same constituency of less affluent
journeymen, petty shopkeepers, and laborers; and both accelerated
the collapse of any overall cultural system.[45] The whole impetus of
evangelical movements was towards a less tightly structured political, economic, and religious order.

The quest for gospel liberty that animated so much of popular religion in the new nation depicted politics, religion, and the
economy as different facets of a common reality. Just as tyranny had
gripped church, state, and society, so the advance of freedom and
equality would transform a full range of human institutions. The dis-

sident Methodist Lorenzo Dow refused to obtain a preaching license in England because it involved an oath of loyalty to the king. He linked the swiftly approaching termination of history to the downfall of privilege and the rise of equality. In two pamphlets first published in 1811 and 1813, Dow spelled out an interpretation of history built on the rise of inalienable rights of life, liberty, property, and private judgment.[46] Dow did not long to preserve an eighteenth-century world of patriachy and inheritance. On the contrary, he struggled to sever ties with the past and he revered Thomas Jefferson whose election in 1800 seemed to sound the death knell for corporate and hierarchic conceptions of the social order.

Dow resented monopoly, hierachy, and entrenched interests wherever they might be found. In a biting attack on "privileged orders" in 1829, Dow called for Americans to remember the principles of 1776 and resist the accumulating and interlocking power of merchants, clergy, gentlemen of the bar, and physicians. He was particularly incensed about a recent court decision in Connecticut that limited the ability of common people to divert water that ran through their own property, "whereby it becomes a trespass to make a dam for a hog wallow." Behind such decisions, Dow detected the "abounded influence and ascendency of mammouth manufacturing establishments." Dow hated capitalism of this form, just as he did any special interest that tried to monopolize honor and profit. But he himself became an active speculator in western lands, worked actively to market "Lorenso Dow's Family Medicine," and encouraged young people to imbibe a spirit of inquiry and to think and act for themselves. Dow loved the market because it opened new opportunity for outsiders like himself; what he despised was the hypocrisy of dominant interests who justified their actions in the market as if they were disinterested.[47]

Calvinists had long assumed that the clergy could play the role of objective umpire standing above the play of private interests. They could define for everyone the nature of greed, charity, civic virtue, and just commercial exchange. Insurgent movements scorned this notion of disinterested virtue and defined their own point of view against that of the privileged churches and their presumed oversight of society. Unknowingly, and even as they yearned for new forms of social unity, the upstarts were admitting that society was not an organic unity but a welter of contending interests. This revolutionary assumption was essential to the development of a market economy and of a democratic polity.[48] No gentlemenly elite would be taken seriously in their claim to understand and act in the best interests of everyone. All had the right to put forward their own best interest in religion, politics, and economic life. Although insurgent churches invoked the name of God to overturn patriarchal society, they were embodying the same calls for change that animated democratic reform from the Antifederalists to the Jacksonians.

These religious movements endorsed the market by default, by narrowing their scope of responsibility to spiritual matters, and by diagnosing society's ills as centered in elite domination rather than popular excess. Inverting the assumption that truth was more likely to be found at the upper rather than at the lower reaches of society, insurgent churches inveighed against all the patterns of deference by which gentlemen had kept common folk in their place. Jonathan Edwards, for example, worried about the greed of average folk and their emulation of the elite and urban rich: "The land is becoming exceeding extravagant . . . Common people show an affection to be like those of high rank."[49] The populist preachers early in the nineteenth century fingered a different culprit: the self-interested gentlemen who exalted the few at the expense of the many.

In an early edition of the *Herald of Gospel Liberty*, Elias Smith sketched a most revealing dialogue between the people and the privileged class. "The picture, is this: two companies standing in sight of each other, one large, the other small. The large containing every profession useful to society, the other small, wearing marks of distinction, appearing as though they did no labour, yet in rich attire, glittering with gold and silver, while their plump and ruddy countenances, prove them persons of leisure and riches." Seething with resentment, the people of Smith's dialogue happened to overhear what the privileged were saying to each other: "To mix and place ourselves on a level with the *common people,* would be beyond all measure degrading and vilifying. What! are they not born to serve us? and are we not men of a totally distinct blood and superior pedigree?" In response, the people insisted that they were going "to take the management of our affairs into our own hands . . . When the people declare themselves free, such *privileged classes* will be as useles[s] as candles at noonday."[50] Smith projected that the overthrow of hierarchical social order would, in and of itself, cleanse the moral defects of society.

This explicit faith in the virtue of common people characterized the movements of the Second Great Awakening. If a free market of exchange existed in every area of life, a world without dominating interests, then harmony and justice would prevail. Few preachers openly advocated laissez-faire economic arrangements, but their messages were replete with the themes of freedom, autonomy, and individual initiative. If capitalism is defined as the avid pursuit of improved circumstances through market exchange, then these evangelical preachers were eager capitalists—like so many of their constituents throughout rural America.[51] A society of contractual individualism was not merely foisted on the country by great merchants and aristocrats. A liberal social order percolated up from the convictions of ordinary people who were convinced that gospel liberty was the very meaning of America.[52]

Rather than looking backward and clinging to an older moral economy, insurgent religious leaders espoused convictions that were essentially modern and individualistic. They assumed that the leveling of aristocracy, root and branch, would bring prosperity and independence to American citizens. In this way, religious movements eager to preserve the supernatural in everyday life had the ironic effect of accelerating the break-up of traditional society and the advent of a social order of competition, self-expression, and free enterprise. In this moment of democratic aspiration, religious leaders could not foresee that their assault upon traditional churches, professions, and political statesmen would produce a society in which grasping entrepreneurs could erect new forms of tyranny in religious, political, and economic institutions.

≺ IV ≻

Elevating the Voluntary Conscience

American religion in all its diversity pushed families and individuals beyond the safe haven of custom and tradition into the heavy seas of deliberation and choice. Lucy Mack Smith, mother of Joseph Smith, the founder of the Mormons, wrestled interminably with the problems of competing denominations, each of which seemed to invalidate the claims of the others. "If I remain a member of no church," she confessed, "all religious people will say I am of the world; and if

I join some one of the different denominations, all the rest will say I am in error."[53] The Mormon elder Parley Parker Pratt, born in Burlington, New York, in 1807, recalled that his father was an equally devout but unattached believer: "He taught us to venerate our Father in Heaven, Jesus Christ, His prophets and Apostles, as well as the Scriptures written by them; while at the same time he belonged to no religious sect, and was careful to preserve his children free from all prejudice in favor or against any particular denomination, into which the so-called Christian world was then unhappily divided."[54] Americans were forced to think for themselves about religious matters, to weigh competing claims, and to take a stand. Voluntarism was a necessary hallmark of the Second Great Awakening.

The contagion of choice also swept far beyond religious boundaries. The democratic religious movements of the new nation all championed the free will of the individual as the only bedrock on which to build church and society. They advocated the right of people to think for themselves and to take as certain nothing that was not self-authenticating and convincing within the limits of their own observation and experience. A Methodist convert from Calvinism recounted in 1812 that in Methodist teaching "he found a system that seemed to harmonize with itself, with the Scriptures, with common sense, and with experience."[55] Methodists, Universalists, Freewill Baptists, and Christians all described conversion as finding gospel liberty. The renegade Presbyterian Barton W. Stone recounted that an elevated sense of choice was the distinguishing doctrine of the fledgling Christian Church:

> We urged upon the sinner to believe *now,* and receive salvation—that in vain they looked for the Spirit to be given them, while they remained in unbelief . . . that no previous qualification was required, or necessary in order to believe in Jesus, and come to him . . . When we began first to preach these things, the people appeared as just awakened from the sleep of ages—they seemed to see for the first time that they were responsible beings.[56]

The Baptist preacher and itinerant evangelist John Leland hammered out his views of conscience as he battled the state-church tradition of Virginia during the 1780s and of New England thereafter. In over thirty pamphlets and regular contributions to Phinehas Allen's Jeffersonian *Pittsfield Sun,* Leland spelled out a vision of personal autonomy that colored his personal life, his theological views, and his conception of society.

As early as 1790, John Leland began to sound his clarion call that conscience should be "free from human control." His passion was to protect the "empire of conscience," the court of judgment in every human soul, from the inevitable encroachments of state-church traditions, oppressive creeds, ambitious and greedy clergymen, and even family tradition. "For a man to contend for religious liberty on the court-house green, and deny his wife, children and servants, the liberty of conscience at home, is a paradox not easily reconciled . . . each one must give an account of himself to God."[57] Upon returning to New England in 1791, Leland assailed the Standing Order in a pamphlet *The Rights of Conscience Inalienable . . . or, The High-flying Churchman, Stripped of his Legal Robe, Appears a Yaho.* With language borrowed directly from Jefferson's *Notes on the State of Virginia,* he argued that truth can stand on its own without the props of legal or creedal defense. He reiterated the theme that "religion is a matter between God and individuals." Elsewhere Leland argued explicitly that truth would prevail in a free market of ideas: "Truth is in the least danger of being lost, when free examination is allowed."[58]

Leland is important in that he turned a quest for self-reliance—the very basis of church and republic—into a godly crusade. He believed that individuals had to make a studied effort to free themselves of natural authorities: church, state, college, seminary, even family. Leland's message carried the combined ideological leverage of evangelical urgency and Jeffersonian promise. Using plain language and avoiding doctrinal refinements, he proclaimed a divine economy that was atomistic and competitive rather than wholistic and hierarchical. The triumph of liberal individualism of this sort was not something imposed upon the people of America from above. They gladly championed the promise of personal autonomy as a message they could understand and a cause to which they could subscribe—in God's name no less.

The Second Great Awakening bequeathed to America two notable legacies: revivalistic Christianity that riveted attention on the conversion experience of the individual and an intellectual self-reliance that questioned any authority save the Bible alone. Francis Asbury, the architect of American Methodism, took great delight in the rousing success of the American camp meeting even as he jettisoned much of the churchly and liturgical elements of Wesleyanism—such as Wesley's prescribed liturgy and formal clerical attire.

Asbury preferred the roaring extemporaneous ethos of the camp meeting because of its success as an instrument of conversion. Describing the "overwhelming power" of a four-day meeting twenty miles northeast of New York, he estimated that 3000 persons and 100 preachers attended the sessions four times a day. Asbury found the level of activity so intense, with "weeping on all sides," that he was unable to sleep for the duration of the meeting. He also wrote approvingly of the presiding elder in Delaware who had scheduled for the summer of 1806 "100 days and nights to be in the woods." Asbury was a bold advocate of the camp meeting, boasting five years later that these occasions brought together three to four million Americans annually—an estimated one third of the total population. "Campmeetings! Campmeetings!" he exclaimed. "The Battle axe and weapon of war, it will brake down walls of wickedness, part of hell, superstition, [and] false doctrine."[59]

At the same time, British Methodists moved decisively to suppress camp meetings. They perceived a manifest subversiveness in the form and structure of the camp meeting itself which openly defied the proper structure of society. As Deborah Valenze has suggested, the camp meeting "elevated the debased to the realm of the sacred and upset the hierarchy of the experience essential to conventional social order."[60] Camp meetings moved beyond the once-radical field preaching that Wesley and Whitefield had instituted, shifting attention from conspicuous preaching performances to congregational participation. Those who led the meeting made overt attempts to have the power of God "strike fire" over a mass audience; they encouraged uncensored testimonials by persons without respect to age, gender, or race; the public sharing of private ecstasy; overt physical display and emotional release; loud and spontaneous response to preaching; and the use of folk music that would have chilled the marrow of Charles Wesley.

Methodist reliance on the camp meeting indicates the movement's commitment to allow common people to trust their own religious impulses. People were encouraged to express their faith with fervent emotion and bold testimony. In the most democratic gesture of all, some preachers took their cues from evidence of divine power in the audience. During a camp meeting on an island in the Chesapeake Bay, Lorenzo Dow was interrupted by a woman who began clapping her hands with delight and shouting "Glory! Glory!" In a response that was the opposite of condescension, Dow proclaimed to the audience: "The Lord is here! *He is with that sister.*"[61]

Two of the most thoughtful analysts of American revivalistic Christianity were John W. Nevin and Philip Schaff, reformed theologians and critics of the atomistic environment of which they were a part. Nevin and Schaff identified certain common intellectual patterns and reflexes beneath the rampant pluralism of American Protestantism. The most common of these was an exaggerated reliance upon the Bible. After surveying the statements of belief of fifty-three American denominations, Nevin surmised that the principle "No Creed but the Bible" was the distinctive feature of American religion. Nevin surmised that this emphasis grew out of a popular demand for "private judgment" and was "tacitly if not openly conditioned always by the assumption that every man is authorized and bound to get at this authority in a direct way for himself, through the medium simply of his own single mind."[62] Experience-centered and Bible-centered faith had great appeal for self-educated Americans with a thirst for knowledge and a hunger for improvement. It gave them little reason to cling to the past and firm confidence that the voluntary conscience was the watchword of the future.

Between the Revolution and the Civil War, American Methodists as a people enjoyed less material prosperity than any other major evangelical group.[63] Methodism had great appeal for the outsider and the dispossessed and its greatest age of expansion was driven by local amateur clergy. Methodist growth began to slump when the popular leadership of the circuit rider gave way to clerical professionals.[64] Methodism prospered as a genuine grass-roots movement.

It was also a movement with great appeal to upstarts who hungered for respect and opportunity. In the founding of Dayton, Ohio, for instance, the initial elite of the town, Federalist and Presbyterian, were challenged economically and politically by ambitious new arrivals who had a base in the Methodist church.[65] Methodists came to represent the petty bourgeois, rising groups, people on the make. Their story has not appealed to religious historians who want to study powerful ideas and theologies. Nor has it appealed to social historians intent on studying the disenfranchised—scholars who have real trouble coming to terms with the bourgeoisie.[66] Yet Wesleyans were quintessentially American and their story abounds with people who began as outsiders and struggled for respectability and self-improvement. It is not a fashionable tale, but it is central to the American experience and its democratic politics, pervasive materialism, and evangelical Christianity.[67]

In the early Republic, American society became engrossed in commerce and evangelical religion at the same time. Alexis de Tocqueville took note of this striking intermingling of God and mammon within the nation's soul: "I know of no country, indeed, where the love of money has taken stronger hold on the affections of men . . . there is no country in the world where the Christian religion retains a greater influence over the souls of men than in America."[68] To understand this conflation of materialism and spirituality, we must alter the traditional terms of the debate. In the first generation of the Republic, it is not so much the fate of Calvinism and its heirs that sheds light on the American economy. Instead, it is the meteoric rise of American Methodism that offers insight into a society that was awash in religion and in making money—and confident of divine favor upon both endeavors.

American Methodism and the spirit of capitalism is a question that invites sustained exploration. Methodism in its message and structure embodied a liberal conception of reality that broke decisively with the pre-Revolutionary pursuit of homogeneous community. As a movement of self-conscious outsiders, Methodism embraced the virtue of pluralism, of competition, and of marketing religion in every sphere of life—far beyond the narrow confines of ecclesiastical space. The Methodist regime of voluntarism and of disciplined collective action did not automatically translate into political or economic action, but it did become for thousands of Americans a profound shaper of behavior, a way of life, culturally atuned to the politics of self-professed interest groups and the economics of unabashed enterprise.[69] Philip Schaff recoiled from the competitive, entrepreneurial, uncontrolled methods of the revival: "Every theological vagabond and peddler may drive here his bungling trade, without passport or license, and sell his false ware at pleasure."[70] Yet it was the revival and the Methodists who gathered ordinary people in its name who most decisively shaped the moral economy of a nation that welcomed, even if it did not understand, the market revolution.

The Problem of Slavery in Southern Political Discourse

JAN LEWIS

IN 1835 GOVERNOR GEORGE MCDUFFIE addressed the South Carolina legislature on the question of slavery. Outraged by the attacks of abolitionists and somewhat chagrined by his state's inability to seek out and punish "these foreign incendiaries," he pleaded his case before the court of public opinion, hoping "to disabuse" his countrymen's "minds of false opinions and pernicious prejudices." Slavery, he explained, was justified by Scripture and the "physical, moral, and political" inferiority of the Africans themselves. The importation of African slaves into the United States had improved their condition, making them "cheerful, contented and happy, much beyond the general condition of the human race."

American liberty, McDuffie explained, was secured by the institution of slavery. When those who performed menial labor were admitted into the political community, "a dangerous element is introduced into the body politic," one that threatened always to undermine the rights of property. In the South, "where the menial offices and dependent employments of society are performed by domestic slaves, a class well defined by their color and entirely separated from the political body, the rights of property are perfectly secure, without the establishment of artificial barriers." Slavery, then, rendered unnecessary "an order of nobility, and all the other appendages of a hereditary system of government." "Domestic slavery," the governor concluded, "instead of being a political evil, is the cornerstone of our republican edifice."[1]

Governor McDuffie's message to the South Carolina legislature demonstrates how easy it was to construct a republican defense of slavery.[2] In the decades just before the Civil War, the logic that linked liberty and slavery seemed compelling, and the South's most ardent defenders of the institution, such as Alexander Stephens and James Henry Hammond, would repeat McDuffie's words almost verbatim.[3] More recently the historian Edmund S. Morgan has suggested that the analysis of these apologists of slavery was correct and that in fact slavery in colonial Virginia had functioned as "a flying buttress to freedom."[4] Nonetheless, whatever the logic of enslavement might suggest or its antebellum defenders insist, there is little evidence that slaveholders in the Revolutionary era were aware of this connection.

If indeed slavery served as liberty's essential support, it is remarkable that Americans of the Revolutionary generation apparently were neither willing nor able to perceive this relationship and explain it in republican terms. The closest one comes to a republican justification of slavery in the Revolutionary period is Charles Pinckney's observation in the Federal Convention that "the blacks are the labourers, the peasants of the Southern States,"[5] but he was talking about the slaves' economic position—as producers of wealth—and not their political standing. Several years later James Madison seemed to recognize that slavery and a restricted franchise rendered the South more stable politically than the North, but that was hardly a justification for slavery. To the contrary, Madison reflected, "In proportion as slavery prevails in a State, the Government, however democratic in name, must be aristocratic in fact." Using such a standard, Madison judged even the republics of antiquity defective. "All the antient popular governments," he observed, "were for this reason aristocracies," as were the states of the American South.[6] So powerful was the egalitarian logic of Revolutionary doctrine that it could be used to challenge not only slavery but the classical republics as well.

Although southerners at the time of the Revolution were unable to mount a republican defense of slavery, they found the rhetoric of republicanism useful for other purposes, in particular for talking about their society and other power relations in it. When they discussed the economy and slavery, however, they used the language of liberalism. In the Revolutionary South, the languages of liberalism and republicanism existed side by side, and while they might be spoken simultaneously, each was most useful in particular contexts. In the decades after the Revolution, southerners remained bilingual, but their usages changed. We are, however, getting ahead of our story.

≺ I ≻
Slavery and Revolutionary Republicanism

When American revolutionaries spoke about slavery in republican terms, they almost always did so to indict it. Sometimes southerners themselves framed the charge; more often, they were called upon to offer a defense, to justify an institution that seemed on its face contradictory to republican notions of equality. The ways in which slaveholders attempted to reconcile slavery with their Revolutionary ideals tells us a great deal not only about those ideals themselves, their reach and their limitations, but also about the kind of society they were trying to create.

"All men are created equal," the Declaration of Independence proclaimed, and whatever inequalities the nation that subscribed to that motto maintained, the universalist implications of the words themselves were difficult to evade. St. George Tucker, for one, was certain that they applied to slaves. In 1796 the Virginia jurist set out "to demonstrate the incompatibility of a state of slavery with the principles of our government, and of that revolution upon which it is founded." Tucker accused his fellow patriots of inconsistency and blindness, of weakness and self-love. "Whilst we were offering up vows at the shrine of Liberty . . . whilst we swore irreconcilable hostility to her enemies, and hurled defiance in their faces; whilst we adjured the God of Hosts to witness our resolution to live free, or die, and imprecated curses on their heads who refused to unite with us in establishing the empire of freedom; we were imposing upon our fellow men . . . a *slavery* ten thousand times more cruel than the utmost extremity of those grievances and oppressions, of which we complained." American revolutionaries stood indicted by their own words. Tucker held up a mirror to "a people who have declared, 'That *all men* are by nature *equally free* and *independent*.'" True patriots must seek the abolition of slavery. "If ever there was a cause, if ever an occasion, in which all hearts should be united, every nerve strained, and every power exerted, surely the restoration of human nature to its inalienable right is such."[7]

Tucker was not alone. In the decades just after the Revolution, virtually all Americans who spoke publicly on the issue expressed a hope for slavery's eventual demise. All of the states north of Maryland embarked upon plans for its termination,[8] and a number of thoughtful southerners such as Tucker offered schemes for its eventual elimination. Nonetheless, slavery persisted in the South; and in the absence of a convincing defense slaveholders offered excuses, attempting to explain why, if slavery were indeed incompatible with republican ideals, it could not be eliminated quite yet.

The family correspondence of Virginia's Lee family illustrates the problem. In what was perhaps the earliest formal, republican critique of the institution of slavery, Richard Henry Lee addressed the Virginia Assembly in 1759, excoriating a traffic in "our fellow-creatures, who are no longer to be considered as created in the image of God as well as ourselves, and equally entitled to liberty and freedom by the great law of nature."[9] Several years later, Lee's brothers Arthur and William were living in London and trying to purchase slaves for their brother when they heard that he had joined with the burgesses in petitioning the king to curtail the slave trade. Arthur reminded Richard Henry that "it will certainly wear an awkward appearance, that a strenuous opposer of this trade should be an agent in it." In response Richard Henry protested—somewhat unconvincingly— that he had played no role in the assembly's petition. "You know in general I have always thought the Trade bad; but since it will be carried on, I do not see how I could in justice to my family refuse any advantage that might arise from the selling of them."[10] In principle opposed to slavery, Lee could not see how he could "in justice" to his family decline "an advantage."

Thomas Jefferson's tortured efforts to reconcile his commitment to liberty with slaveholding are well known. Throughout his long life he considered slavery "a great moral and political evil." He believed that those who loved liberty must hate slavery and assumed that the primary impediment to emancipation in his native state was an insufficient attachment to liberty on the part of his fellow Virginians. He used the language of republicanism to oppose slavery, associating the preservation of the institution with the sort of narrow self-interest that republicanism condemned. In 1785 he observed to the English philosopher Richard Price that debates over the future of slavery in Virginia presented "the interesting spectacle of justice, in conflict with avarice and oppression." Thirty years later, deeply disappointed that slavery had not somehow been eliminated, he used similar language in his famous letter to Edward Coles: "I had always hoped that the younger generation receiving their early impressions after the flame of liberty had been kindled in every breast . . . and above the suggestions of avarice, would have sympathized with oppression wherever found, and proved their love of liberty beyond their own share of it." Not republicanism, but naked self-interest—avarice—explained the persistence of slavery.[11]

Much has been written about Jefferson's views on slavery, whether his opposition to the institution was sincere, and whether he himself had done enough to eliminate it. As he aged, his optimism faltered, and his language shifted accordingly. The public debates about the future of slavery he had once welcomed, even spurred, now frightened him. The Missouri question was "like a fire-bell in the night." Although he still favored some sort of emancipation, "as it is, we have the wolf by the ears, and we can neither hold him, nor safely let him go. Justice is in the one hand, and self-preservation in the other."[12] Justice was still on the side of the slave, but by 1820 Jefferson had come to identify himself with the interests of the slaveholder. Tellingly, however, the only justifications offered for maintaining slavery—self-interest and expedience—came from outside the realm of republican discourse.

If Jefferson agonized more deeply and expressed himself more eloquently, other republican slaveholders faced a similar dilemma and resolved it in much the same way. Even defenders of the institution recognized its incompatibility with certain of their ideals. Charles Cotesworth Pinckney, for example, explained to his fellow South Carolinians that the Constitution he had helped to draft could not include a bill of rights because "such bills generally begin with declaring that all men are by nature free. Now we should make that declaration with a very bad grace, when a large part of our property consists in men who are actually born slaves."[13] So powerful was the challenge to slavery presented by Revolutionary ideology that it made virtually impossible any sort of coherent, elaborated proslavery defense.[14]

Still, certain occasions demanded if not a full justification of slavery, at least an effective response to those who wished to end it. Unable to mount a defense of slavery, its supporters, trapped in what they acknowledged was an awkward position, were able to make only two moves: the resort to inexpedience and the justification of self-interest. How supporters of slavery offered these justifications seems to have been determined primarily by the place where, at a particular moment, they stood. The southern discourse on slavery, in other words, was site specific. In the state ratifying conventions in the South, for example, the defense of slavery was often linked rhetorically to an almost obligatory republican condemnation of the institution. In the North Carolina debates, for example, a number of delegates deplored simultaneously both slavery and any suggestions for immediate termination. James Iredell declared that the slave trade was "utterly inconsistent with the rights of humanity." Indeed, he looked forward to the happy day "when the entire abolition of slavery takes place." "But," he mused, "we often wish for things which are not attainable," and, as if to make certain that was the case, he asked rhetorically, later in the debate, "Is there anything in this Constitution which says that Congress shall have it in their power to abolish the slavery of those slaves who are now in the country?" William R. Davie noted that slaves were "an unhappy species of population; but we cannot at present alter their situation."[15]

In Virginia, a theoretical opposition to slavery was insufficient to overcome a practical reliance on the institution, and it led many delegates to the state convention to oppose ratification of the Constitution. Describing slavery as a "detested" institution that could be abolished "at some future period," Patrick Henry explained that for the present, however, "As much as I deplore slavery, I see that prudence forbids its abolition." Fearing a strong centralized government that would threaten slavery, he spoke against ratification. Like Henry, George Mason voiced his opposition to the Constitution and to slavery both. "It is far from being a desirable Property," he acknowledged, "but it will involve us in great difficulties and infelicity to be now deprived of them."[16] The issue is not whether the Constitution supported or undermined slavery—although both Edmund Randolph and James Madison, who, like Mason, had been at the Convention, were confident that the document protected southern slave property.[17] What is significant in this context is that both Mason and Henry, who proclaimed themselves opponents of slavery, argued that its abolition was inexpedient, and they considered this line of reasoning not only an objection to the Constitution, but also adequate for the institution's defense.

At the Federal Convention[18] representatives from the slaveholding states generally dispensed with the reflexive lament about the impossibility of terminating slavery. The task was to protect the institution constitutionally, not rhetorically, and the discussions were couched almost wholly in pragmatic terms. After the Convention, Charles Cotesworth Pinckney was able to claim, "We have made the best terms for the security of this species of property it was in our power to make."[19] In that successful endeavor Pinckney and his fellow southerners most often used the language of "interest." In arguing for the right to import slaves, John Rutledge had scoffed that the southernmost states would "never be such fools as to give up so important an interest." Rutledge believed that he was articulating a fundamental and readily-understood principle. "Religion & humanity [have] nothing to do with this question. Interest alone is the governing principle with nations."[20]

Slavery was an interest, one that distinguished the southern states from those to the north, and such differences among the states were critical. Madison, for example, noted that "the States were divided into different interests . . . principally from their having or not having slaves," and in debate Charles Pinckney argued that there was "a solid distinction as to interest between the southern and northern states." And although Edmund Randolph revealed his misgivings about slavery, and even "lamented that such a species of property existed," he defended southern interests by insisting that slaves be counted in apportioning representation.[21] Like Randolph, southerners described slaves as property and insisted that the Constitution secure their investment. Again and again, southerners defined slaves as property that must be protected because, as Pierce Butler put it, the central government "was instituted principally for the protection of property." Charles Cotesworth Pinckney might have been articulating a general principle when he announced that "property in slaves should not be exposed to danger under a Govt. instituted for the protection of property."[22]

The "protection of property": in the Philadelphia convention, delegates from the slaveholding states asserted, even if they did not elaborate, a property right in slaves. In the decades just after the establishment of the national government, some slaveholders would qualify that claim, while others would attempt to ground it in the available political ideologies. Yet always the operative word was "property." Sometimes the argument was that it was inexpedient or unwise for the government to impinge upon the ownership of slaves.

In the Third Congress, for example, Virginia's William Branch Giles objected to a bill that would bar immigrants from owning slaves. Naturally he "lamented and detested" the institution of slavery, and regretted that he himself owned slaves, but "from the existing state of the country, it was impossible at present to help it," and he had to oppose legislation that "was calculated to injure the property of gentlemen."[23]

On other occasions, slaveholders, particularly those from the lower South, would assert their right to slave property without equivocation. Charles Pinckney, now governor of South Carolina, in 1798 tied the defense of slavery to a vision of political economy when he urged a strengthening of the slave code in order to give "all the security and protection in our power to this species of property. As they are the instruments of our cultivation, and of the first importance to our wealth and commercial consequence." A year earlier John Rutledge had explained to the Fifth Congress that in the South "most of [the] property consisted of slaves, and . . . the rest was of no value without them."[24]

Other southerners justified the institution in ideological terms. In the sixth Congress, Virginia Representative Henry Lee made his political philosophy clear when he observed that "gentlemen were sent to that House to protect the rights of the people and the rights of property. That property which the people of the southern states possess consisted of slaves, and therefore Congress had no authority but to protect it, and not take measures to deprive the citizens of it."[25] Likewise, when some of the residents of Virginia's Pittsylvania County objected to a petition for emancipation, they protested that such an action would reverse the accomplishments of the Revolution. "When the British parliament usurped a right to dispose of our property without our consent," they explained, "we dissolved the union with our parent state, and established a constitution of our own, that our property might be secured in the future." Now "our rights to liberty and property are as well secured to us as they can be by any human form of government."[26] Southerners could link liberty and slavery only by invoking the rights of property.

When southerners crafted their first post-Revolutionary rationales for slavery, their first line of defense was expedience, typically used not as an absolute, but more as a delaying tactic, as when Madison assured his fellow Congressmen that the elimination of slavery was "going on as quickly as possible."[27] After that they fell back upon the right of property. In other words, they turned to Locke. Pierce Butler's claim that the federal government had been created "principally for the protection of property" was an almost verbatim quotation from *Two Treatises of Government*. While there is some debate among scholars about whether Locke considered property a natural right—in his theory the right to hold property is adventitious, although the right to acquire it seems to be fundamental—he clearly thought that the chief end of government was the protection of property.[28]

The invocation of Locke, however, raises questions about the ongoing debate among historians about the relative significance of republican and liberal themes in Revolutionary discourse.[29] Recent studies of Revolutionary ideology have accustomed us to think of republicanism and liberalism as two coherent, competing ideologies, "separate tunnels" through the thought of the eighteenth century.[30] It may be more useful to think of Revolutionary thought as a series of unstable syntheses of several different but overlapping philosophical strands.[31] "Republicanism" and "liberalism" should be considered not so much as antithetical doctrines but as positions on particular issues, vocabularies to be used for certain situations and in special settings. That an individual might draw upon Locke for one purpose and Harrington for another demonstrates not simply the complexity and occasional inconsistency of Revolutionary thought, but the array of problems to be addressed and the variety of sites in which those discussions took place. Yet in specific locations, the terms that were used had precise meanings and clear implications.

To defend slavery as an interest and in terms of a right to property, then, was to select from the lexicon of liberalism, just as surely as Luther Martin's condemnation of slavery was grounded in the republican vocabulary. In 1788 the Maryland antifederalist argued against ratification of a Constitution that permitted the importation of slaves. "*Slavery*," he wrote, "is *inconsistent* with the *genius* of *republicanism* . . . it *lessens the sense* of the *equal rights* of *mankind*, and habituates us to *tyranny* and *oppression*."[32] Incapable of rearranging those terms into a justification of slavery, southerners would turn instead to an alternate body of thought, one that reflected a different area of their experience.

It should not be surprising that southerners found their first Revolutionary era defense of slavery among the principles of liberalism, for the circumstances of southern life over the past century and a half had inculcated in white southerners a strong attachment to property rights and individual freedom—as well as to slavery.[33] Indeed, Locke's own defense of slavery seems to have derived from his involvement in Shaftesbury's Carolina venture.[34] The development of a possessive individualism in the southern colonies was certainly not planned; as Edmund Burke put it, "The settlement of *our* colonies was never pursued upon any regular plan; but they were formed, grew, and flourished, as accidents, the nature of the climate, or the dispositions of private men happened to operate."[35] Nor did it reflect contemporary explicit political discourse, which was yet to privilege such extensive rights to property and self-government for ordinary white men. But it did reflect the lived experience of several generations of American colonists, and perhaps nowhere more than in the South. Indeed, Jack P. Greene says that the development of the southern colonies in the colonial period was "normative" and that they were "for their free populations, the very embodiment of what was arguably the single most important element in the emerging American mind—the ideal of the pursuit of happiness by independent people in a setting that provided significant opportunities for success."[36]

Moreover, the development of this notion of freedom, tied as it was to the ideal of economic opportunity, marked the southern colonies as both liberal and capitalist. Nor, as Peter A. Coclanis and James Oakes have recently argued, was slavery necessarily an anomaly in such a system. Indeed, the "very being" of modern slave societies was, as Oakes has put it, "inconceivable except as a function of capitalist development." Oakes has noted that the capitalist transformation of seventeenth- and eighteenth-century England created a growing population of consumers who, with their nearly insatiable demands, created the markets for the products of new world plantations. In that sense, the plantation economies, along with their slave labor, were the creation of a profound transformation in European society. The markets of the old world and the plantations of the new were bound reciprocally, opposite sides of the same coin.[37]

Furthermore, liberal capitalism permeated the slave societies themselves. Coclanis has demonstrated that colonial South Carolina planters were economically rational, that the market informed their values and behavior both. Nor was the colony's economy, as some historians have suggested, "some rough economic beast slouching toward capitalism"; it was capitalism itself. South Carolinians demonstrated "a strong desire for wealth and a ready disposition to exploit others."[38] Slavery was one expression of the ruthless drive for profit, and if it would eventually become anathema in the West, it was not sufficiently troubling at the time it was established in the new world colonies to attract anyone's notice. It developed alongside increasing freedom for whites. The same proprietors who would, to use Coclanis's words, "encourage, promote, [and] defend" the enslavement of Africans, attracted white settlers by offering "cheap land . . . generous headrights, the waiver of quitrents for twenty years . . . representative government, religious toleration, land registration, ease of naturalization, and a waiver of duties on imports and exports." South Carolina was established by "a curious coupling of lure and lash."[39] And that is why, when southerners at the time of the Revolution were first called upon to defend what was beginning to seem a peculiar institution they drew from the language of liberal capitalism, for it was under the aegis of that system that slavery had developed.[40]

If the source of planters' wealth and their resort to enslavement came from the realm of liberal capitalism, their genteel pretensions inclined them to republicanism. Aping the refinement of the English gentry and transforming their own naked power into the responsibility of that class, the southern gentry found their social fulfillment in the republican ideal of disinterested service and virtuous sacrifice for the common good. Moreover, a series of revolts and pressures from the poorer whites of the piedmont, the backwoods, and the upcountry made it clear that the political stability of the colonial elite depended upon its ability to assure economic opportunity to those who had not yet made good.[41] So the planters came to republicanism out of necessity as well, as they exercised leadership in colonies in which the majority of whites came to share the similar interest of producing a staple crop with the labor of black slaves. Slavery was the glue that held this system together.

Yet slavery had no place in republican rhetoric; it was never effectively integrated into the doctrine that formed the basis for discourse about the relations of power. Some have suggested that republicanism in early America worked as a rhetoric of denial, which pasted

over the divisions and developments that were rending colonial society.[42] Those who spoke the language of republicanism could pre-
tend that the seaboard cities did not each have a growing lower class,
that tenancy was not on the rise, that the gap between rich and poor
was not increasing, and that "enslavement" described the relationship between the British government and its American subjects. Republicanism served to externalize colonial problems, to make them
a function of imperial policies, rather than domestic social or political development.

    The only source for slavery in such a schematic was London. So
Jefferson, in his first draft of the Declaration of Independence, blamed
American slavery on George III; the British monarch, not southern
planters or northern slave merchants, had "waged cruel war against
human nature itself, violating the most sacred right of life and liberty
in the persons of a distant people who never offended him, captivating and carrying them into slavery in another hemisphere."[43] Other
Revolutionaries imagined that the British were trying to reduce them
to slavery.[44] Southern Revolutionaries who sought a justification for
slavery would be unable to find it in the language of American republicanism, for that doctrine defined slavery as *not* American. And republicanism enabled southerners, at least for a while, to detach slavery from the circumstances of their society.

≺ II ≻

Colonization and Diffusion

Although rooted in a legitimate contemporary political discourse,
the property defense of slavery would, in the decades after the Revolution, prove highly vulnerable to both external and internal threats.
Southerners acknowledged as much when they conceded that slavery was an evil and pleaded for time to eliminate it in their own way.
They made these appeals when, as early as the second session of the
First Congress, northern opponents of slavery attempted to undermine the institution.[45] Southerners said that they thought the issue
had been settled; they reminded their northern countrymen that, as
William L. Smith put it in the 1790 debate about receiving an abolitionist petition from Pennsylvania Quakers, at the time the Constitution was written "there was then an implied compact between the

Northern and Southern people, that no step should be taken to injure the property of the latter, or to disturb their tranquillity."[46]

Fourteen years later, after South Carolina had reopened the slave trade and northern representatives to Congress were threatening to exercise the option to tax the importation of slaves, southern representatives were still calling for more time. South Carolina's Benjamin Huger assured the House that the "evil" of slavery was on the decline in his state. He urged the opponents of slavery to "let us alone, and we will pursue the best means the nature of the case admits of."[47] These were the terms of the unwritten compromise between North and South: if the slaveholders would acknowledge that the institution was wrong, northerners would let them discover their own means to eliminate it. Many southerners were, in fact, sincere in their distaste for slavery, and they formulated plans for and founded their hopes on its eventual abolition. The weaknesses in these schemes demonstrate the flaws in the dream of "conditional termination."[48]

Most plans for the elimination of slavery assumed that the primary problem to be solved was what to do with the freed slaves. St. George Tucker offered a plan for gradual emancipation that was "*expedient*, rather than *desirable*," one that Winthrop D. Jordan has described as "complicated and confusing." Tucker's objective was to emancipate the slaves but so restrict their political liberties as to induce them to emigrate from the South. Virtually the only rights left to the emancipated slaves would be the privileges of contracting for their own labor and marrying members of their own race.[49] Although their details certainly differed, most plans for conditional termination embraced racism and consequently contemplated restrictions upon blacks' liberties, prefiguring the sort of adjustment to emancipation that southerners eventually would make.[50]

Many southerners who disliked slavery seized upon schemes for colonization. Those with even less specific plans for the termination of slavery placed their hopes in the principle of diffusion. Both approaches, like Tucker's design for conditional termination, aimed, as Jordan has put it, to "rid" America "of the twin tyrannies of Negroes and slavery."[51] Colonizationists often had a particular destination in mind for the liberated slaves, while diffusionists believed that if only the number of slaves who were living in the United States could be spread out over a wider territory, then perhaps the institution itself might fade away. This was not an entirely unrealistic hope, for surely it was the relative sparseness of the slave population in the northern states that had made possible the elimination of slavery there after the Revolution. As early as the Federal Convention, Roger Sherman had observed that "the abolition of slavery seemed to be going on in the U.S.," and he predicted "that the good sense of the several States would probably by degrees compleat it." Northerners who disliked slavery but desired union could agree to protect slavery where it existed, believing that the institution was in an irreversible decline. Oliver Ellsworth was confident that "slavery in time will not be a speck in our country."[52]

Likewise, southerners who disliked both slavery and blacks could support the termination of the international slave trade, while opposing plans for abolition. Yet ostensibly anti-slavery arguments could also be twisted into a rationale for the introduction of slavery into new territories. In 1803 Allan B. Magruder offered a plan for delivering his country "from its greatest evil." If the young slaves in the eastern states could regularly be sent to the newly-acquired Louisiana territory, they "would be giving strength and population to the new colony, instead of remaining among the whites, to precipitate the evils of slavery." Similarly, as Paul Finkelman and Peter S. Onuf each have shown, inhabitants of what would become Indiana—where slavery was outlawed under the provisions of the Northwest Ordinance—petitioned to be allowed to bring in slaves, which they argued would draw them away from the more densely black old southern states. At the same time, the proponents of slavery in the northwest territories would argue that the use of slavery was an "improvement," a mark of progress analogous to a spinning machine. "If slavery was admitted," one of the institution's advocates argued in 1823, "our country would populate in abundance, wealth would be in our country, money would circulate for a while—it would put a new spring to business." Western advocates of slavery insisted, as they would continue to up until the Civil War, that slavery was vital to their prosperity; it should be tolerated because it could make ordinary white men rich.[53]

The early southern anti-slavery position, then, was not fixed. Some considered slavery poisonous wherever it existed, while others were willing to tolerate—or even welcome—it in a small enough dose. What all southern critics of slavery shared was the conviction that too many slaves in a particular location created a danger. Such southern fears were not entirely misplaced, for slaves—like their masters—recognized that the Revolutionaries' ideals of freedom were inconsistent with the practice of slavery. When, about to be executed for his role in leading the rebellion of 1800 that bears his name, Gabriel Prosser was allowed some final words, he compared himself to the father of the country whose ideals he claimed: "I have nothing more to offer than what General Washington would have had to offer, had he been taken by the British and put to trial by them. I have adventured my life in endeavouring to obtain the liberty of my countrymen, and am a willing sacrifice to their cause."[54] Many years later, Frederick Douglass would observe that the ideas of the abolitionist movement originated with the "patriots of the American Revolution . . . Washington, and Jefferson, Patrick Henry, and Luther Martin, Franklin, and Adams, Madison, and Monroe," all of whom had looked forward to the termination of slavery.[55] When slaves and abolitionists could depict themselves as the legitimate heirs of the Revolution, slaveholders faced a problem that attempts to curtail discussion could not solve.

≺ III ≻

The Evangelical Challenge

A solution of sorts would come from the most unlikely of quarters: a series of religious transformations that threatened to undermine the structure of southern society. Virginia, from the middle of the eighteenth century on, was swept by a series of revivals, first Presbyterian, then Baptist, and finally Methodist.[56] Rhys Isaac has argued that the social conflict engendered by the Baptist revival that began in 1765 "was not over the distribution of political power or economic wealth, but over the ways of men and the ways of God." The Baptists who led what Isaac has termed an "evangelical revolt" against the mores of the gentry rejected that group's arrogance, aggression, and display of lofty status. In its place they substituted a fellowship of the converted and an order based upon an almost ascetic self-control. Alienated by the competitive individualism of the planters, evangelicals sought a Christian communalism instead.[57] Yet the revivalists manifested a sort of individualist thrust; the basis of the revival, after all, was the individual's conversion. However, they anchored it in the community of believers. And each of the revivals, in its early years, extended the hand of fellowship to free blacks and slaves.

Mechal Sobel has observed that, in Virginia at least, spiritual revival "came when and where whites were in extensive and intensive contact with blacks."[58] In some places, without apparent forethought or discussion, slaves were allowed to attend revival meetings and, when churches were formed, to become church members and accept church discipline. The Baptists in particular welcomed blacks into their congregations. Blacks were members—and sometimes even the majority—in virtually all of the forty eighteenth-century Virginia Baptist congregations for which records are extant.[59] In other regions, revivalist ministers made it a point to preach to slaves. The great evangelist George Whitefield noted in his diary his "usual custom" of visiting the slaves whenever he went to a plantation, and he told his white followers that, in a spiritual sense, they were their slaves' equals: "Think you, your children are in any way better by nature than the poor negroes! No! In no wise! Blacks are just as much, and no more, conceived and born in sin, as white men are; and both, if born and bred up here, are naturally capable of the same improvement."[60] We have records of Presbyterian and Baptist ministers urging that slaves be provided with religious instruction and be brought to church. Methodist circuit riders may have been the most aggressive in reaching out to slaves, for their sermons were filled with references to the "sons and daughters of oppression," "poor distressed Africans," and the "poor Negroes."[61]

Evangelical religion changed the face of slavery, effectively converting the southern slave population to Christianity. That is not to say that slaves were encompassed by a hegemonic white culture, for not only was white Christianity itself in the process of change, but, as students of slave religion have demonstrated, blacks adapted evangelical Christianity to their own purposes. Indeed, the slaves' version of Protestantism became one of the bases of slave culture.[62] Recently Mechal Sobel has suggested that eighteenth-century slaves exerted a powerful influence upon white religion as well, and that the evangelical form of Protestantism that resulted from the revivals was created by blacks and whites together, as a product of their shared worship.[63]

One product of the cultural creation described by Sobel and others was the forging of new, strict standards of personal behavior.[64] Both slaves and whites were enjoined to maintain order in their families, according to similar, if not always identical, standards. Church discipline was used as a means to enforce the converts' new standards of family life. Thus South Carolina's Bush River Baptist Church excluded one Thomas Barlow from fellowship for "drunkenness and profanely swearing and for abusing his wife."[65] A Spottsylvania County, Virginia, church dealt similarly with one of its slave members, "Theo Coleman's Guice," in 1799. He was "Excommunicated for keeping two wives," but the next year was accepted back "by repentance," and, Mechal Sobel surmises, by getting rid of one of the wives.[66] Evangelical churches upheld a standard of monogamy for both blacks and whites and disciplined members of both races for committing adultery.[67]

Evangelical Protestantism had created a new image of the family that its followers were expected to uphold. At the same time, the elite and not necessarily evangelical planter family, much like its British gentry counterpart, was adopting new standards of affection and intimacy, which softened the patriarchal controls by which it had previously been shaped. The result was that, by the end of the eighteenth century, southerners both rich and poor and both slave and free shared a single standard of family behavior that emphasized monogamy, affection, and responsibility.[68]

To be sure, many southerners honored this new standard primarily in its breach. The wealthiest and the poorest, in particular the males of the family, often hewed to older standards, sometimes flaunting their drunkenness and infidelity.[69] Moreover, the ethos of evangelical Christianity would seem singularly inappropriate for those who were enslaved. It would appear to contradict the very basis of slavery to suggest that slaves might take personal responsibility for their own behavior, let alone join with whites on terms that approached equality. Yet those churches that accepted slaves as members asked them to act, essentially, as if they were in control of their own lives.[70]

But slaves who wanted to follow the ways of their masters' faith would sometimes complain about the masters who stood in their way. When the masters themselves belonged to the same church, the congregation would face difficult dilemmas. There are records of Virginia slaveholders who received church discipline for "using Barbarity toward their Slaves" and for separating slave families. The Upper King and Queen Church asked itself, "Is it agreeable to scripture for any member to part man & wife?" The answer was in the negative; moreover, "any member who Shall be guilty of such crimes shall be dealt with by the church for such ~~crimes~~ [*sic*] misconduct."[71] While it is true that slaves seem to have been censured more often than their masters, especially for theft, and that church discipline was a very effective tool for enforcing slave discipline, it is also true that evangelical Christianity could present a challenge to the very nature of slavery.

The English revivalist George Whitefield, distressed to see the religious indifference of whites in the South and the cruelty with which they treated their slaves, considered the brutality of the slaveholders evidence of their unconverted state. He endeavored to bring both blacks and whites to Christ and to change the nature of southern slavery. He told the slaveholders of South Carolina that "when . . . I have viewed your plantations cleared and cultivated, many spacious houses built, and the owners of them faring sumptuously every day, my blood had frequently almost run cold within me to consider how many of your slaves had neither convenient food to eat, nor proper raiment to put on, notwithstanding [that] most of the comforts you enjoy, were solely owing to their indefatigable labours." In 1740 Whitefield wrote "An Open Letter to the Inhabitants of Maryland, Virginia, North and South Carolina concerning the treatment of their Negroes." In it he castigated the slaveholders for working their slaves as if they were dogs, for punishing them barbarously, and for failing to Christianize them. He warned them that "it is sinful" to use slaves "as though they were brutes," and he reminded them that God "does not reject the prayer of the poor and destitute, nor disregard the cry of the meanest negroes." Slaveholders were told in no uncertain terms that they would have to answer to God for their cruelty.[72]

In South Carolina Whitefield's followers obeyed his injunctions, creating "Christian plantations" where slaves were offered religious instruction. They admitted slaves to membership in their churches, which entitled them to baptism, religious marriage, and Christian burial; and in some cases the physical treatment of slaves may have become less brutal. An occasional slave was allowed to preach, and

some were even freed.[73] A similar pattern seems to have followed
other eighteenth-century revivals. Some evangelical churches went
so far as to instruct their white members on how they ought to treat
their slaves. Congregations established standards of appropriate behavior and in the process created the ideal of the Christian master.
The members of South Carolina's Welsh Neck Baptist Church, for
example, resolved in 1785 to "act a truly Christian part" by their
slaves "by giving them good advice, laying our commands on them
to attend the worship of God in public on Lords day and in private in
our Families when convenient." They also promised not "to treat
them with cruelty, nor prevent their obtaining religious knowledge."
Similarly, the Baptist church at Mechanicsville urged its members to
provide religious instruction for their slaves and to "supply them
with food and raiment becoming their station."[74] Consulting Scripture, a majority of Virginia's Meherrin Baptist Church believed that
Matthew 18 required reasoning about a slave's offense and a full discussion in the presence of several church members before a master
could whip him.[75]

≺ IV ≻

The Domestication of Slavery

The process of Christianizing the slave population, recognizing slave
families, and establishing standards for humane treatment coincided
with dramatic changes in the demographic structure of the slave
population. By the end of the eighteenth century there was a vast
population of native-born slaves with extensive ties of kinship to
other African-Americans. Slaves began to live in what both they and
their masters recognized as families. This tendency was reenforced
when masters began to buy an increasing proportion of female slaves,
rather than primarily males. The result was a gender-balanced,
multi-generational slave force, which slaves and masters both came
to accept as the norm.[76]

While historians such as Herbert Gutman and Allan Kulikoff
have rightly focussed upon the slaves' role in establishing and maintaining their families and the ways in which slaves used their families as a source of strength and a means of resisting the cruelties of
slavery, the part of the masters in the establishment of slave families

should not be overlooked. By the latter half of the eighteenth century, masters increasingly were willing to recognize and even encourage the formation of slave families. Philip Morgan has discovered that a growing proportion of those South Carolina low country slaves who were inventoried at the time of their master's death lived in family groupings, and that advertisements for runaways detailed slaves' family relationships. He has also found that slaves were often sold and bought "in families." Prospective buyers might advertise to purchase slaves "in large families, the more so the more agreeable" or refuse to buy "any gang where any of the slaves have been separated from their families." One slaveholder, who was complying with his bondsman's desire to be sold, alerted prospective purchasers that they would have to take the slave's wife, as well, "for a principle of humanity *alone.*"[77]

Daniel Littlefield has uncovered similar evidence of planters' efforts to keep slave families together. Even before the slave population had begun to reproduce itself naturally, planters such as Henry Laurens tried to achieve what demographic trends would later accomplish on their own. In 1764 Laurens wrote to the overseer on one of his plantations that he was sending "up a stout young Woman to be a Wife to whom she shall like best amongst the single men. The rest of the Gentlemen shall be served as I have opportunity."[78] It is not always possible to determine the extent to which such planters were responding to evangelical injunction or increasingly sentimental models of elite family life. Moreover, by the end of the eighteenth century, a number of educated planters had absorbed Enlightenment ideas about the essential similarity of all human beings.[79] Whatever the precise origins of these developments, the result was the same: the assumption that blacks, like whites, should live in well-organized families.

In a very important article, Willie Lee Rose has denominated this transformation of slavery "the domestication of domestic slavery." Rose dates this process after the Revolution, and she sees it as an expression not only of evangelical religion but of the South's response to the anti-slavery sentiment aroused by the Revolution. She says that by the time these changes had taken place, slavery had become "a more regular and systematic labor system," that the use of violence "was considered to be a failure of diplomacy," and that "selling slaves apart from their immediate families incurred a social stigma."[80] While Rose is probably correct in saying that this transformation was not accomplished until the third decade of the nineteenth century, it is important to note that the process began several decades before the Revolution and has its earliest sources in evangelical Protestantism.

Each of the eighteenth century evangelical denominations would come to question the morality of slavery. They would ask whether slaves could be Christians and whether Christians could be slaveholders. Mechal Sobel reports that in Virginia "Church after church asked, 'Is it a Rituous [sic] thing for a Christian to hold or cause any of the human race to be held in slavery?' " In 1787 the Black Creek Baptist Church replied with an unequivocal "Unrighteous!!"[81] Ministers such as the Virginia Baptist John Leland and the Kentucky Presbyterian David Rice became outspoken opponents of slavery.[82] Some evangelicals even emancipated their slaves. In 1791 the wealthy Virginia planter Robert Carter, perhaps the most prominent of all Baptist converts, began the process of liberating his 422 slaves.[83] Although only a small minority of evangelical southerners would ultimately free their slaves, the egalitarianism of early evangelical congregations gave rise to serious and probing challenges to the legitimacy of the institution.[84]

It was for this reason in particular that southerners who were committed to the slave system were troubled by the evangelical movement. Fearing a wave of abolitionism, slaveholders challenged evangelicalism and its liberating potential. As early as 1742 the South Carolina House of Commons had taken efforts to squash the interracial revival led by George Whitefield's followers, the wealthy Bryan brothers. Accusing the Bryans of fomenting slave revolt—only a few years after the Stono revolt—the government had brought enormous pressures to bear, finally extracting apologies from both Hugh and Jonathan Bryan and crippling the South Carolina evangelical movement.[85] When the Baptist revival reappeared in the South Carolina backcountry in the decades just after the Revolution, the ministers this time were prepared to respond to the community's fears. Richard Furman and other leading Baptist ministers made it clear that, although they preached to blacks and whites both, they had no intention of undermining slavery. Rather, they argued that Christianity would make slaves more obedient. Over the opposition of representatives from the low country, they were able to persuade the House to pass a bill legalizing religious meetings that included slaves.[86] Evangelicals learned that their survival in a slave society depended upon their willingness to eschew any hint of abolitionism.

Everywhere the story was much the same. In the years after the Revolution, southern evangelical sects came to terms with the South's peculiar institution. So it was that the Virginia Baptist General Committee, which had in 1785 decried slavery as a "horrid evil," eight years later decided "by a large majority (after considering it a while) that the subject be dismissed from this committee, as it belongs to the legislative body." Thenceforth individuals could chart their own courses; no collective pressures would be brought to bear.[87] The other denominations made similar accommodations, with the Presbyterian General Assembly in 1818 characterizing slavery, to use Donald Mathews's term, as a "moral dilemma" and at the same time warning that abolitionists were "socially disruptive." Two years earlier the Methodist General Conference had admitted that "little can be done to abolish the practice so contrary to the principles of moral justice."[88]

Abandoning hopes of a general emancipation, evangelicals turned their eyes from the legislatures to the plantations, and sought instead individual solutions to the evils of slavery. As Francis Asbury explained to fellow Methodists in South Carolina, a year earlier he had visited "a tyrannical old Welshman" who treated his slaves "like dogs." Now the planter was "much softened, his people admitted into the house of prayer, the whole plantation, forty or fifty singing and praising God."[89] Evangelicals' retreat on the issue of slavery, however, "resolved once and for all the problem of whether or not the moral struggle of the Christian would be carried on in the world of power and traditional relationships or within the mind and psychology of the individual believer."[90] The encounter with slavery intensified the individualistic impulse inherent in evangelicalism, and at the same time it suppressed its communalism.

Yet by the time that the evangelicals had made their accommodation to slavery, the institution itself had been transformed. The adjustment to slaveholding enabled evangelicals to continue their mission to the slaves and to continue upholding Christian standards for slaveholding. And once the anti-slavery impulse had been checked, evangelicalism might serve as an instrument of slave discipline, accommodating slaves to their servitude and easing the consciences of their owners.[91] Those churches that had made their peace with slavery designated different responsibilities for their white and black members. Kentucky's Transylvania Presbytery, for example, urged slaveholders to "secure the religious instruction of slaves with a humane and christian treatment." At the same time, the state's South Concord Baptist Association was enumerating the duties of slaves, who were required "to shew all good fidelity."[92] The power relations of slavery were now obscured by the terms of evangelical Protestantism itself; slavery had been domesticated.

So had southern evangelical Protestantism. It turned its face on the public sphere by recognizing slavery as a civil institution, thereby acknowledging that politics was outside the church's realm.[93] As the Virginia Baptist General Committee put it, in responding to one church's questions about the righteousness of slavery, that was "an improper subject of investigation in a Baptist Association, whose only business is to give advice to the Churches respecting religious matters; and considering the subject of this query to be the business of government."[94] The abolition of slavery was no longer a "religious matter."

Evangelical religion thus was privatized, and in the process, slavery was defined, for evangelicals, as a fundamentally private—a domestic—institution. That is not to say that slavery was beyond the reach of the law or the state; as would become evident once "popular sovereignty" was proposed as a solution to the national problem of the expansion of slavery into the western territories, slavery could not exist without the positive protection of the law.[95] Yet at the same time that southerners were rewriting slave codes to make the institution of slavery more secure, they were describing it as a private and domestic institution, under the rule of the slaveholder, in order to protect it from anti-slavery assaults.[96] As early as 1804 Benjamin Huger explained to Congress why it should not meddle in the institution of slavery. "Do we not all know," he asked rhetorically, "that by interfering between a man and his wife, we only aggravate the difference; and do we not likewise know that any interference between a master and his slave induces the former to be more severe." Several years later, another South Carolinian, Senator Robert Y. Hayne, would try to protect slavery with the same logic: "The question of slavery must be considered and treated as entirely a DOMESTIC QUESTION . . . It is a matter . . . for ourselves."[97]

Evangelicalism, a number of historians have noted, served the vital purpose of accommodating nineteenth-century Americans to

liberalism and capitalism both.[98] It could do so, however, only by ex-
cluding certain of society's institutions from the realm of politics.
We are most familiar with the way this process operated in the first
decades of the nineteenth century to establish "separate" male and
female "spheres" of activity, which served to isolate the supposedly private sphere of the family from market forces and the self-
interested strivings of the political world. The family could serve,
ideologically at least, as a haven from or a counter to the more alien-
ating aspects of economic and political life. By the same token, all
that transpired within the family was by definition "private."[99]

The evangelical accommodation to slavery served in a similar
way to detach the institution from the public sphere. To be sure, it
was not, nor could it be, a complete severing. The function of slavery
was the enrichment of slaveholders; in that sense, slavery was fundamentally an economic institution, and because it depended upon
the use of force, it was a political one, as well. With very few exceptions, slaveholders put their economic needs first, sacrificing sentiment when need be—when, for example, debt seemed to require the
selling of slaves. Yet to the extent that slaveholders could relegate
slavery to the private sphere, the realm of love rather than work, they
could protect it from the threats presented by the egalitarian tenden-
cics of antebellum American politics. As one defender of slavery explained, the South's domestic institution was a form of "patriarchal"
government, that is, "the same form of government to which the abolitionists subject their wives and children."[100]

Southern historians have often interpreted slaveholders' claims
that their slaves were part of their families as evidence of a patriarchal worldview.[101] Supposedly a plantation master thought of himself
as a patriarch, a pater familias in charge of a plantation filled with
dependents both black and white. As early as 1726 the Virginia
planter William Byrd II had boasted to an English correspondent
about his preeminent position on his plantation. "Like one of the
patriarchs, I have my flocks and my herds, my bonds-men and bond
women, and every soart of trade amongst my own servants so that I
live in a kind of independence on every one but Providence." More
than a century later the South Carolinian Christopher Memminger
would create a similar image. "The Slave Institution at the South,"
he said, "increases the tendency to dignify the family. Each planter
in fact is a Patriarch—his position compels him to be a ruler in his
household."[102] Yet the fundamental nature of the southern family

had changed. What it meant to rule a household, even a plantation
household, early in the eighteenth century and at the mid-point of
the nineteenth were very different things. To put it most simply, unlike their colonial ancestors, southern planters expected to be loved.[103]

When southern planters put the best face on slavery they could
be as sentimental as any Victorian. Jeremiah Clemens, for example,
wrote in 1834 that "I love the sabbath. It is a time when slavery itself
is free—when it unlooses its shackles, forgets its horrors and tells its
tales of love."[104] The connection between the sentimentalization of
slavery and evangelical Protestantism is equally evident in the comments of a Virginia churchwoman who, according to Bertram Wyatt-
Brown, "declared 'it is in the interest of the master to observe to his
slave that kind of love which makes' the slave rejoice 'to serve and
obey his master; not with eye-service,' but with heartfelt, Christian
'willingness.' " Some slaveholders were able to convince themselves
that their slaves labored not out of obligation, but out of love. The
Mississippi planter Francis Terry Leak tried to persuade a former
neighbor to move back from the West by explaining, "He would then
have a permanent family—servants who would wait on him from
affection, & not for the sake of money—and who would never desire
his death in the hopes of getting a share of his estate, as is sometimes
the case where an old bachelor is dependent upon hirelings &c."[105]
That is not to say that slaveholders always described slavery in such
sentimental terms or that they regarded their slaves with affection.
Nor is it to suggest that the emotion slaves typically felt for their
masters was love. In the face of almost everything that we know
about the institution of slavery in the antebellum South, it would
have taken extraordinary efforts for southerners to maintain the belief that the relationship between master and slave was one based
upon love; the point is that many tried. And it was only by engaging
in this exercise that they would finally be able to adapt republicanism to the justification of slavery.

≺ V ≻

Republicanizing Slavery

By the third decade of the nineteenth century, slaveholders would
argue that the institution of slavery was mild and getting milder all
the time. That was what southerners told themselves, as when South

Carolinian James L. Petigru wrote his daughter in 1835, "The only thing to flatter my vanity as a proprietor is the evident and striking improvement in the moral and physical conditions of the negroes since they have been under my administration."[106] And that is what they told others. In 1836 the *Farmers' Register* asserted that in Virginia "the condition of negroes . . . has been greatly ameliorated," and thirteen years later *DeBow's Review* would say the same thing: slaves "are better treated now than formerly." James Oakes has discovered that throughout the nineteenth century, slaveholders would claim that slavery was now milder than it had been, and it was gentler wherever they happened to live than it was elsewhere.[107]

Such arguments were obviously self-serving, but they also reflected an application of the doctrine of progress to the institution of slavery. If those such as Jefferson who had subscribed to this quintessentially liberal creed in the eighteenth century had believed that it would eventuate in slavery's demise, later slaveholders could adapt it to an institution they hoped to preserve. The belief that slavery was getting better, that it was governed by the laws of progress, proved to be a necessary precondition for thinking of it as inherently and intrinsically good.

In 1832 Thomas Roderick Dew published an essay that many have seen as "the crucial connecting link between southern apologies for slavery and the emergence of a positive good argument throughout the South." If recent students of proslavery ideology have revised that judgment somewhat,[108] it is nonetheless true that Dew was the first to mount a formal and well-developed benevolence defense. Aroused by the Virginia legislative debates of 1831–32, Dew wanted to show that all plans for emancipation and colonization were impractical and unfair. He proceeded to answer those who argued that slavery was evil and unjust. Jefferson, he wrote, was wrong when he asserted that slavery undermined the morals of slave owners. Jefferson had believed that children learned to imitate the cruelties of their slaveholding fathers. But, asked Dew, "is not this master sometimes kind and indulgent to his slaves? does he not mete out to them, for faithful service, the reward of his cordial approbation?" Slavery could serve to school the young master in benevolence. Observing the interaction between the "good master" and his slave, "the exalted principles of morality and religion may thereby be sometimes indelibly inculcated upon his mind, and instead of being reared a selfish contracted being . . . he acquires a more exalted benevolence."

If earlier in his essay Dew had defended the property rights of slaveholders, and if later he would assert the profitability of the institution, now he was arguing that slaveholding was the essence of benevolence. Slaveholders were characterized by "noble and elevated sentiment, by humane and virtuous feelings. We do not find among them that cold, contracted, calculating *selfishness*, which . . . lessens or destroys all the multiplied enjoyments of social intercourse." In "national councils," the slaveholders were "the most disinterested, the most conscientious, and the least unjust and oppressive in their principles."[109] In other words, slaveholders were virtuous, and they were republicans.

In Dew we also see the outlines of a republican defense of slavery. To be sure, some of his arguments recalled those made half a century earlier. "The great object of government," he asserted, "is the protection of property."[110] Yet the benevolence defense, which said that slaveholding made the masters virtuous, was novel. To be disinterested and conscientious, to recoil from injustice and oppression— that was to exhibit the character that the Whigs had thought necessary for citizens in a republic. Here, almost fifty years after the beginning of the Revolution, a slaveholder was finally making the explicit connection between slaveholding and republicanism that we might have expected much earlier. Dew continued the analysis. It was simply untrue that "slavery is unfavourable to a republican spirit." Southerners were more attached to liberty than those who lived in the North, no doubt because of "the perfect spirit of equality so prevalent among whites of all the slave-holding states." Slavery had brought southern whites as close to "one common level . . . as nearly as can be expected or desired in this world. The menial and low offices being all performed by blacks, there is at once taken away the greatest cause of distinction and separation of the ranks of society." Slavery, then, was a condition of freedom, as it made for equality among whites, "and it is this spirit of equality which is both the generator and preserver of the genuine spirit of liberty."[111]

Not until the nineteenth century would slaveholders begin to formulate a republican defense of slavery; those who created it believed that they were carrying on the Revolutionary tradition, although all of them were too young to have participated in the ideological work of the Revolution itself. Dew had been born in 1802, John C. Calhoun in 1782, and John Taylor of Caroline in 1753. Unlike Dew, John Taylor cannot be considered a true apologist for slavery; he thought that the institution was "an evil that the United States must look in the face,"[112] and he approved of colonization to remove free blacks from the United States. He believed that the institution could and should be ameliorated, but that emancipation would be a disaster. His response to anti-slavery advocates was couched in republican terms.

Taylor feared that if masses of slaves were freed, they would remain ignorant and impoverished, liable to exploitation by "some interest or combination," possibly that of the North. In such an event he anticipated "miseries on both their owners and themselves, by the perpetual excitements to insurrection,"[113] just as republican theorists imagined that tyrants would mobilize the landless poor in their assaults upon the liberty of the virtuous citizenry. Ultimately "the blacks will be more enslaved than they are at present; and the whites in pursuit of an ideal of freedom for them, will create some vortex for engulphing the liberty left in the world and obtain real slavery for themselves."[114] Slavery, then, must be maintained in order to preserve freedom.

Slavery was better for blacks, as well. Not only were "well managed" slaves "docile, useful, and happy," but their masters were better able than was some self-serving political faction to secure their happiness. Unlike those who were driven by "superstition, cunning, or ambition," the individual master was "restrained by his property in the slave, and susceptible of humanity." Moreover, "religion assails him both with her blandishments and terrors. It indissolubly binds him, and his slave's happiness and misery together."[115] Taylor came close to saying that master and slave had a unity of interest.

It was left to John C. Calhoun to elaborate that argument. In a famous speech to Congress in 1837, the South Carolina senator defended the institution of slavery. He claimed that "it has been a great blessing to both of the races . . . The one has greatly improved, and the other has not deteriorated; while in a political point of view, it has been the great stay of the Union and our free institutions, and one of the main sources of the unbounded prosperity of the whole."[116] He continued to defend slavery in republican terms, although, as Lacy K. Ford has observed, this was a republicanism that—unlike Taylor's—had made an accommodation to "the realities of modern commercial capitalism."[117]

Like republican theorists, Calhoun believed that freedom was best preserved in a society in which men were economically independent. Yet, as Ford notes, Calhoun accepted commerce and insisted only that independent producers have easy access to the market. Slavery fit into his political economy by permitting men, as Ford puts it, "to expand their entrepreneurial endeavors without engendering the tension between labor and capital that naturally arose in a free-labor society as household production gave way to workshops and factories." Under the slave system, southern planters could expand the scale of their operations "without generating a white proletariat."[118] The slave system enabled the South to escape the sorts of conflicts that made it "so difficult to establish and maintain free institutions in all wealthy and highly civilized nations."[119] Calhoun had perfected the republican defense of slavery, arguing not only that slavery enabled whites to preserve their freedom, but—moving beyond Taylor—that the interests of master and slave were one and the same.

After Calhoun, other defenders of slavery would make the same argument. George Frederick Holmes would claim that under slavery "the interest of the labourer and the employer are absolutely identical," and William John Grayson would say that the southern system "is the only condition of society in which labor and capital are associated on a large scale—in which their interests are combined, and not in conflict."[120] And George McDuffie, of course, would announce that slavery was the "cornerstone of our republican edifice." Nineteenth-century proslavery apologists refashioned the language of republicanism to make it fit slavery. In the process they sometimes misrepresented the Revolutionary heritage, making it appear, as Kenneth S. Greenberg has noted, more egalitarian than it actually was. That does not mean, as Greenberg would have it, that proslavery ideologues such as Calhoun were "solidly within the tradition of [their] Revolutionary ancestors."[121] Rather, they discovered in the republican idiom a defense of the institution that their ancestors had never been able to find. And in their efforts to find a compelling justification for slavery, they would put republicanism to a new use.

With slavery protected by republicanism, it could be insulated from the language of liberalism that, for most occasions, characterized the southern vernacular.[122] So natural was the language of a possessive individualism that, occasionally, southern apologists defended slavery in terms of property rights and hitched it to the liberal worldview.[123] Yet the Lockean—that is, property-rights—defense of slavery that had been invoked at the time of the Revolution would never be developed fully into a rationale for slavery because the liberal political thought in which it was embedded led away from that institution's defense. Liberalism was founded upon the sanctity of property rights, but it also embodied a humanitarianism that was premised upon the fundamental similarity of all persons. "Benevolence is due from one to another, not as a return of advantage received, but as an essential mark of humanity," an anonymous Charlestonian wrote in 1783 in an address he entitled "Rudiments of Law and Government Deduced from the Law of Nature." This humanitarianism would find expression in the condemnation of cruelty, which would, in turn, lead both to an attack upon slavery and to schemes aimed at its reformation. The anonymous Charlestonian advocated "rescu[ing]" slaves "by purchasing them from less considerate owners."[124]

Moreover, the egalitarian impulse in southern political thought was so strong that for almost fifty years slaveholders overlooked justifications for slavery that appeared before their very eyes, in the texts they relied upon when crafting their ideology of revolution. Indeed, although Locke himself had accepted the institution of slavery, perhaps because his discussion of the subject was so ambiguous and ambivalent, southerners never cited his justification of enslavement or integrated it into their discussions of the topic.[125] Instead, when they read Locke they absorbed his contract theory of government and the passage in his *Second Treatise* in which he commented that "every Man has a *Property* in his own *Person*."[126] If it were granted that the slave were a *person*, then the logic against slavery seemed compelling.

A liberal defense of slavery, then, would have to deny the personhood of the slave. The increasingly well-articulated racism of the nineteenth century would work toward this end. As a result, antebellum property-rights justifications of slavery were accompanied by a fervent racism that attempted to place blacks outside the boundaries of those beings who were entitled to ownership of their very selves.[127] Yet liberalism also embodied a humanitarianism that posed a continual challenge to a racism that denied the personhood of the slave and that consequently made it very difficult to exclude slaves from the bounded world that the American Revolution had created.[128]

James Madison is a case in point. Much of his defense of slavery
derived from Locke, and he tried to work out the contradictions of
slavery in liberal terms. In *Federalist LIV* he attempted to justify the
three-fifths clause. Slaves, he concluded, were treated by the law as
"in some respects" persons and in others, property. Indeed, it was the
law itself that established the "mixt character" of the slave, treating
him at once as "degraded from the human rank, and classed with
those irrational animals, which fall under the denomination of property," and as "a member of society . . . a moral person." The calculus
of the three-fifths clause, Madison suggested, worked out the proportions between the slave's humanity and his status as property about
right. Yet Madison acknowledged that the position of the slave was
established not by nature, but by convention, and that "if the laws
were to restore the rights which have been taken away, the negroes
could no longer be refused an equal share of representation with the
other inhabitants."[129]

Madison's clever computation seems more a reflection of the
need to secure ratification than deep conviction; he put the words
into the mouth of "one of our" imagined "southern brethren."[130] He
must have been uncomfortable with the formulation, for he did not
repeat it in later years. Instead, he placed his hopes in diffusion and
then colonization. And while each of these programs, as we have
seen, could collapse into a defense of slavery, they were also expressions of the liberal impulse. Diffusion rested upon a faith in progress; for Madison, it represented, as Drew R. McCoy has put, "the
best hope that the Union would survive longer than slavery, long
enough, perhaps, to resolve the dilemma of slavery without violent
upheaval."[131]

Madison also joined the American Colonization Society and
argued vigorously for the removal of blacks to Africa. Although
colonization, like diffusion, may be regarded as "preposterously uto-
pian," and at best a "compelling fantasy,"[132] it also expressed a certain Lockean logic. When Madison laid out his plans for colonization, he returned time and again to the principle of consent. Not only
must slaveholders agree to the project, for, quite obviously, property
could not be taken without its owner's consent; the slaves themselves were required to accept the proposition, even to agree to their
own emancipation. Liberated slaves might return to Africa, where
they could found their own societies. Madison had high hopes that

an experiment in colonization would offer "a happy introduction to blessings for Africa," which might in turn "lead to other successful experiments, all founded on the *consent* of the Blacks."[133]

Like St. George Tucker, Madison believed that the prejudice of the whites was so great that the two races would be unable to live side-by-side and in harmony. And like Tucker, he believed that blacks would have to be induced voluntarily to depart and create elsewhere their own societies in Africa. In this light, the Revolutionaries' frequent complaint that the institution of slavery had been foisted upon them by the British appears somewhat less fatuous: It meant that the blacks, unlike the whites who had migrated voluntarily, were not part of the imaginary social compact that had created the American nation. Lockean consent theory required that freed blacks could and should create their own voluntary communities; an underlying racism dictated that they should do it somewhere else.

The Lockean liberalism that in the seventeenth century had acquiesced in the use of slavery in new colonies might lead in the opposite direction when its logic was applied to a liberal commercial republic, particularly when it was reenforced by a humanitarian sensibility.[134] Southerners needed a defense of slavery that would, at the very least, appear humane. The evangelical accommodation to slavery helped them to find one, and it was only after they had convinced themselves that their slaves were happy and they themselves were good Christians, that slaveholders could find in republicanism, with its insistence upon individual virtue and social harmony, a defense of their peculiar institution.

The republican defense of slavery depicted the institution as if it were a family, and like a family, free from conflict and bound by love. On the plantation, as in the family, interests, supposedly, were harmonized. Yet the analogy never quite worked. The role of the slaves was never adequately defined. Although often described as emotional and irrational, slaves were not accorded the disinterestedness and moral excellence of women; nor did they seem to have the capacity of children to mature into responsible adults. The inescapable fact was that slaves, no matter how happy, served to make their masters rich, and, when all was said and done, the southern ethos was individualist, not communal. Slavery was a system designed to serve the interests of the masters. As one southern woman would explain on the eve of the Civil War, the slave might soon "become imbued

with a sense of his position and with the assistance of real philan-
thropists perform his part so as to be classed among necessary blessings to the white race instead of being as many now think, a curse.
In truth he is even now numbered by true hearted Southern masters
as an auxiliary to happiness."[135] The claim to disinterestedness was
a sham. The republican defense of slavery, then, was doubly deceptive, for it misrepresented both the position of the slave and the motivation of his master as well.

To be sure, much of the discourse of republicanism in the nineteenth century may have worked the same way, not so much as a
language of opposition as one of deceit. The most self-interested of
actors, when challenged, might claim to have the good of the community at heart. Moreover, this rehabilitated republicanism pre-
tended to critique the liberal world that had made it possible. Slaveholders could not have crafted a republican defense of slavery outside
the world that evangelicalism and benevolence had created, with its
sentimentalized families and strong faith in progress. And because it
shifted the site of discourse and spoke in a different idiom, this new
version of republicanism could also conveniently evade the liberal
mandate to extend and secure the rights of the people.

The refashioned republican terminology would also prove particularly useful for rationalizing the apparent anomalies in a capitalist system. And slavery, by the middle of the nineteenth century, was
nothing if not an anomaly. In this sense, it was truly the South's peculiar institution. Its supporters were never able to ground it securely
in the dominant discourse of the day. The defense of slavery was always somewhat off the mark. And while generations of southerners
certainly behaved as if slavery were a condition of their freedom,
they were never able to explain that relationship in a way that
Americans who did not own slaves could fully grasp. Perhaps their
consciences got in the way; we would certainly like to think so. Or
perhaps southern political theorists were not as brilliant as we have
usually supposed. No matter how hard they tried, from the middle of
the eighteenth century slavery remained inconsistent with the prevailing concepts of freedom.

REFERENCE MATTER

≺ ≻

Abbreviations

AHR	*American Historical Review.*
Annals of Congress	U. S. Congress, *The Debates and Proceedings in the Congress of the United States . . . from March 3, 1789 to May 27, 1824, inclusive,* 42 vols. (Washington, 1834–56).
APSR	*American Political Science Review.*
APW	*American Political Writing During the Revolutionary Era,* ed. Charles S. Hyneman and Donald S. Lutz, 2 vols. paged successively (Indianapolis, 1983).
ASP	*American State Papers: Documents, Legislative and Executive of the United States. Class II: Indian Affairs* (Washington, 1832).
CWTP	*The Complete Writings of Thomas Paine,* ed. Philip S. Foner, 2 vols. (New York, 1945).
EIHC	*Essex Institute Historical Collections.*
FC	*The Founders' Constitution,* ed. Philip B. Kurland and Ralph Lerner, 5 vols. (Chicago, 1987).
Federalist	*The Federalist,* ed. Jacob E. Cooke (Middletown, CT, 1961). References to specific Federalist papers in the notes also are to this edition.
JAH	*Journal of American History.*
JSH	*Journal of Southern History.*
LC	Library of Congress.
PAH	*The Papers of Alexander Hamilton,* ed. Harold C. Syrett et al., 27 vols. (New York, 1961–87).
PJM	*The Papers of James Madison,* ed. William T. Hutchinson, now Robert A. Rutland (Chicago, now Charlottesville, VA, 1962–).
PTJ	*The Papers of Thomas Jefferson,* ed. Julian P. Boyd et al. (Princeton, NJ, 1950–).
WMQ	*William and Mary Quarterly,* 3d. Series.
Works	*The Works of Thomas Jefferson,* ed. Paul Leicester Ford, 12 vols. (New York, 1904).
Writings	*The Writings of Thomas Jefferson,* ed. Andrew A. Lipscomb and Albert Ellery Bergh, 20 vols. (Washington, 1903–5).

<><

Notes

INTRODUCTION

1. James Madison, *Federalist LI*, 349.
2. This contest is best described and analyzed in Bernard Bailyn, *The Ideological Origins of the American Revolution*, rev. ed. (Cambridge, MA, 1992), chap. 3, "Power and Liberty: A Theory of Politics."
3. John Jay, *Federalist IV*, 22.
4. David A. Hollinger, "Historians and the Discourse of Intellectuals," in David A. Hollinger, ed., *In the American Province. Studies in the History and Historiography of Ideas* (Bloomington, IN, 1985), 132.
5. Ibid., 134, 142.
6. The literature on the political dimensions of the Founding is voluminous, but current thinking on this process continues to be framed by Gordon S. Wood's classic, *The Creation of the American Republic, 1776–1787* (Chapel Hill, NC, 1969). For a recent evaluation of this work, see the "Forum" published in *WMQ* 44 (1987): 550–640. For an excellent collection of work extending the question, see *Beyond Confederation. Origins of the Constitution and American National Identity*, ed. Richard Beeman, Stephen Botein, and Edward C. Carter II (Chapel Hill, NC, 1987).
7. Joseph Galloway, cited by Bailyn, *Ideological Origins*, 223.
8. Madison, *Federalist LI*, 349.
9. Thomas Paine, *Common Sense* [1776], in *CWTP* 1:9.
10. Madison, *Federalist XXXIX*, 250.
11. Madison, *Federalist LI*, 351.

CHAPTER I

1. Scholarly landmarks include J. G. A. Pocock, *The Machiavellian Moment: Florentine Political Thought and the Atlantic Republican Tradition* (Princeton, NJ, 1975); Drew R. McCoy, *The Elusive Republic: Political Economy in Jeffersonian America* (Chapel Hill, NC, 1980); Joyce Appleby, *Capitalism and a New Social Order: The Republican Vision of the 1790s* (New York, 1984); Gordon S. Wood, "Interests and Disinterestedness in the Making of the Constitution," in Richard Beeman et al., eds., *Beyond Confederation: Origins of the Constitution and American National Identity* (Cha-

pel Hill, NC, 1987), 69–109; and Cathy D. Matson and Peter S. Onuf, *A Union of Interests: Political and Economic Thought in Revolutionary America* (Lawrence, KS, 1990).

2. This chapter's special debt to McCoy, *The Elusive Republic*, will be repeatedly apparent. It may be fairly read as an attempt to build on that and on my own earlier writings, especially *The Jeffersonian Persuasion: Evolution of a Party Ideology* (Ithaca, NY, 1978). It is compatible in most respects with Stanley Elkins and Eric McKitrick, *The Age of Federalism: The Early American Republic, 1788–1800* (New York, 1993), which appeared after it was written.

3. Richard H. Kohn, *Eagle and Sword: The Federalists and the Creation of the Military Establishment in America, 1783–1802* (New York, 1975), chap. 2; C. Edward Skeen, "The Newburgh Conspiracy Reconsidered," with a rebuttal by Richard H. Kohn, *WMQ* 31 (1974): 273–98; Clarence L. VerSteeg, *Robert Morris: Revolutionary Financier* (New York, 1954), especially 166–77.

4. Morris's report is in Worthington Chauncy Ford et al., eds., *Journals of the Continental Congress, 1774–1789*, 34 vols. (Washington, 1904–37), 22: 429–46. For the general situation and the evolution of his plans, I have relied especially on VerSteeg, *Robert Morris*, chap. 5 and pp. 123–29; E. James Ferguson, *The Power of the Purse: A History of American Public Finance, 1776–1790* (Chapel Hill, NC, 1961); id., "The Nationalists of 1781–1783 and the Economic Interpretation of the Constitution," *JAH* 41 (1969): 241–61; Edmund Cody Burnett, *The Continental Congress* (New York, 1941); H. James Henderson, *Party Politics in the Continental Congress* (New York, 1974); Jack N. Rakove, *The Beginnings of National Politics: An Interpretive History of the Continental Congress* (New York, 1979); Charles Royster, *A Revolutionary People at War: The Continental Army and American National Character, 1775–1783* (Chapel Hill, NC, 1979); and E. Wayne Carp, *To Starve the Army at Pleasure: Continental Army Administration and American Political Culture, 1775–1783* (Chapel Hill, NC, 1984).

5. Edmund Randolph to James Madison, 13 Dec. 1782, and "Notes on Debates," 24 Dec. 1782, in *PJM* 5:401, 441–42.

6. The crisis can be followed day by day in *Journals of the Continental Congress* and in Madison's notes on the congressional debates. My reconstruction, developed more fully in "James Madison and the Nationalists, 1780–1783," *WMQ* 40 (1983): 227–55, is based primarily on these as supplemented by the sources cited in note 4.

7. Madison, "Notes on Debates," 18 Feb. 1783, in *PJM* 6:251.

8. Madison, "Notes on Debates," 28 Jan. 1783, in ibid., 143.

9. Ibid. Entered by Madison as a long footnote to his record of Hamilton's speech.

10. Madison, "Notes on Debates," in *PJM* 6:259–61.

11. Ibid., 265–66.

12. Ibid., 270–72.

13. Ibid., 290–92.

14. Ibid., 375. Washington's report and the Newburgh Addresses themselves are in *Journals of the Continental Congress* 24:294–311.

15. Madison's plan of 26 Feb. appears as a long footnote in his "Notes on Debates." The "Report on Restoring Public Credit" as reported from the select committee of Madison, Hamilton, Gorham, FitzSimons, and Rutledge (6 March) is printed in *PJM* 6:311–14.

16. Speech of 27 Feb., "Notes on Debates," ibid., 297–98. This was in response to Mercer's charge that commutation tended "in common with the funding of other debts to establish and perpetuate a monied interest" which "would gain the ascendance of the landed interest . . . and by their example and influence become dangerous to our republican constitutions."

17. Speech of 21 Feb., ibid., 272.

18. Speech of 28 Jan., ibid., 143–47. Compare Madison to Jefferson, 6 May 1780, *PJM* 2:19–20.

19. For the full extent of Madison's discomfort with his allies, see Banning, "James Madison and the Nationalists," 249–51.

20. Report of 29 July 1782, *Journals of the Continental Congress* 22: 435–37.

21. Morris to John Jay, 13 July 1781, quoted in Ferguson, *Power of the Purse*, 123–24; report of 29 July, *Journals of the Continental Congress* 22: 432.

22. See, especially, the letters to an unknown recipient (n.d.), to James Duane (3 Sept. 1780), and to Robert Morris (30 April 1781), along with the conclusion of "The Continentalist," in *PAH* 2:234–51, 400–418, 604–35; 3:99–106. In the last, originally published 4 July 1782, Hamilton wrote: "The reason of allowing Congress to appoint its own officers of the customs, collectors of taxes, and military officers of every rank is to create in the interior of each state a mass of influence in favor of the federal government . . . interesting such a number of individuals in each state in support of the federal government as will be counterpoised to the ambition of others" (3:106).

23. Ferguson was first to see that the Morris nationalists understood and wished to replicate "the role of funded debt and national bank in stabilizing the regime founded in Britain after the revolution of 1689" (*Power of the Purse*, 289–90 and *passim*). See, further, Banning, *The Jeffersonian Persuasion*, 126–40 and *passim*; McCoy, *The Elusive Republic*; John M. Murrin, "The Great Inversion, or Court versus Country: A Comparison of the Revolution Settlements in England (1688–1721) and America (1776–1816)," in J. G. A. Pocock, ed., *Three British Revolutions: 1641, 1688, 1776* (Princeton, NJ, 1980), 368–453; and Ralph Ketcham, *Presidents Above Party: The First American Presidency, 1789–1829* (Chapel Hill, NC, 1984), 31–38 and chap. 10.

24. There are four superb biographies of nicely varied lengths: Irving Brant, *James Madison*, 6 vols. (Indianapolis, 1941–61); Ralph Ketcham, *James Madison: A Biography* (New York, 1971); Harold S. Schultz, *James Madison* (New York, 1970); and Jack N. Rakove, *James Madison and the Creation of the American Republic* (Glenview, IL, 1990).

25. The literature on British opposition thinking is extensive, but see, as a beginning, J. G. A. Pocock, "Machiavelli, Harrington, and English Political Ideologies in the Eighteenth Century," *WMQ* 22 (1965): 549–63; id., *The Machiavellian Moment;* Isaac Kramnick, *Bolingbroke and His Circle: The Politics of Nostalgia in the Age of Walpole* (Cambridge, MA, 1968); and Roger Durrell Parker, "The Gospel of Opposition" (Ph.D. diss., Wayne State Univ., 1975).

26. P. G. M. Dickson, *The Financial Revolution in England: A Study in the Development of Public Credit, 1688–1756* (New York, 1967); John Brewer, *The Sinews of Power: War, Money, and the English State, 1688– 1783* (New York, 1989).

27. Its stabilizing role is a central theme for J. H. Plumb, *The Growth of Political Stability in England, 1675–1725* (London, 1967).

28. See [John Trenchard and Thomas Gordon], *Cato's Letters, or Essays on Liberty, Civil and Religious, and other Important Subjects,* 4 vols., 3d ed. (London, 1733; orig. pub. 1720–23) and J[ames] B[urgh], *Political Disquisitions, or an Inquiry into Public Errors, Defects, and Abuses,* 3 vols. (London, 1774–75). Tory spokesmen, led by Viscount Bolingbroke, were more inclined to express the landed gentry's discontent with rising commerce in itself.

29. J. G. A. Pocock, ed., *The Political Works of James Harrington* (Cambridge, 1977), and id., "Machiavelli, Harrington, and English Political Ideologies."

30. The masterworks on the enormous influence of this thinking on the early Revolution are Bernard Bailyn, *The Ideological Origins of the American Revolution* (Cambridge, MA, 1967), and Gordon S. Wood, *The Creation of the American Republic, 1776–1787* (Chapel Hill, NC, 1969). Robert Shalhope, "Toward a Republican Synthesis: The Emergence of an Understanding of Republicanism in American Historiography," *WMQ* 29 (1972): 49–80, and id., "Republicanism and Early American Historiography," ibid., 39 (1982): 334–56, provide an introduction to the rapidly growing literature. For some of the most recent contributions, see Peter S. Onuf, "Reflections on the Founding: Constitutional Historiography in Bicentennial Perspective," *WMQ* 45 (1989): 341–75.

31. Hamilton drafted a congressional resolution calling for a federal convention shortly before he retired from Congress, then decided that there was too little support to introduce it (*PAH* 3:420–26). Ferguson, *The Power of the Purse,* believes that Morris also hoped for a structural transformation of the system, but this is doubted by VerSteeg, *Robert Morris,* and Rakove, *Beginnings of National Politics.*

32. Stephen Higginson to Henry Knox, 1787, in Edmund C. Burnett, ed., *Letters of Members of the Continental Congress,* 8 vols. (Washington, 1921– 36), 7:123n.

33. Ferguson, *Power of the Purse,* 292.

34. Curtis P. Nettels, *The Emergence of a National Economy, 1775–1815* (New York, 1962), 48–49.

35. Ibid., especially 46–63, remains the standard survey and accords with recent studies in suggesting that Progressive scholars, led by Merrill Jensen, minimized the troubles. See John J. McCusker and Russell R. Menard, *The Economy of British America, 1606–1789: Needs and Opportunities for Study* (Chapel Hill, NC, 1985), 367–77; and Richard B. Morris, *The Forging of the Union, 1781–1789* (New York, 1987), chap. 6.

36. For the early-revolutionary enthusiasm for free trade, see McCoy, *The Elusive Republic*, 86–90, and Matson and Onuf, *A Union of Interests*, 21–26. Frederick W. Marks III, *Independence on Trial: Foreign Affairs and the Making of the Constitution* (Baton Rouge, LA, 1973), chap. 2, is a convenient summary of the restrictions on American trade.

37. George Bancroft, *History of the Formation of the Constitution of the United States of America*, 2 vols. (New York, 1882), 1, bk ii, chap. 4; Nettles, *Emergence of a National Economy*, 72–75; Marks, *Independence*, 80–82. For the states' mercantile systems see, more fully, Matson and Onuf, *Union of Interests*, chap. 2, and Forrest McDonald, *Novus Ordo Seclorum: The Intellectual Origins of the Constitution* (Lawrence, KS, 1985), 102–6.

38. On this ambivalence, I have been influenced mostly by McCoy, *The Elusive Republic*, especially chap. 1, and by Pocock, *The Machiavellian Moment*.

39. Albert O. Hirschman, *The Passions and the Interests: Political Arguments for Capitalism before Its Triumph* (Princeton, NJ, 1977); Joyce O. Appleby, *Economic Thought and Ideology in Seventeenth-Century England* (Princeton, NJ, 1978); and the introductory essay in Istvan Hont and Michael Ignatieff, eds., *Wealth and Virtue: The Shaping of Political Economy in the Scottish Enlightenment* (Cambridge, 1983), an excellent recent collection.

40. Among the English, the most notorious example was Bernard Mandeville's *The Fable of the Bees: or Private Vices, Public Benefits* (London, 1714). See the excellent brief discussions in McCoy, *The Elusive Republic*, 25–27, and McDonald, *Novus Ordo Seclorum*, 109–10, 119–28. Far more moderate in tone, but also relatively unrestrained in their defense of commerce, were David Hume's influential essays "Of Commerce," "Of Luxury," and "Of Refinement in the Arts," originally published in 1752 and available in *Essays: Moral, Political, and Literary*, ed. Eugene F. Miller (Indianapolis, 1985).

41. See, most vividly, Adam Smith, *An Inquiry into the Nature and Causes of the Wealth of Nations*, ed. Edwin Canan (New York, 1937), 734–40; McCoy's superb discussion of Smith and other Scots, *The Elusive Republic*, 19–21, 35–40; and McDonald, *Novus Ordo Seclorum*, chap. 4.

42. Smith devoted much of book 4 of *Wealth of Nations* to a condemnation of policies designed "to enrich a great nation rather by trade and manufactures than by the improvement and cultivation of land, rather by the industry of the towns than by that of the country" (591).

43. "The Continentalist" No. 5, *PAH* 3:76.

44. McCoy, *Elusive Republic*, chap. 4; Matson and Onuf, *Union of Interests*, 46–47.

45. Perhaps the most famous came in "The Continentalist" No. 6, *PAH* 3:103.

46. For the unqualified defense of commercialization in the resolutions of public meetings and in the writings of William Barton, David Daggett, and William Vans Murray, see McCoy, *Elusive Republic*, 96–100, 118–19, and Matson and Onuf, *Union of Interests*, 91–97.

47. A central theme of Progressive and neo-Progressive scholarship from Orin G. Libby, *Geographical Distribution of the Vote of the Thirteen States on the Ratification of the Federal Constitution, 1787–1788* (Madison, WI, 1894) to Jackson Turner Main, *Political Parties before the Constitution* (Chapel Hill, NC, 1973).

48. For an argument that "thousands of [enterprising] ordinary traders, petty businessmen, aspiring artisans, and market farmers" opposed the Constitution, see Wood, "Interests and Disinterestedness in the Making of the Constitution," 80 and *passim*, together with Saul Abraham Cornell, "The Political Thought and Culture of the Anti-Federalists" (Ph.D. diss., Univ. of Pennsylvania, 1989), chaps. 5–6.

49. *Journals of the Continental Congress* 19:110–13; Banning, "James Madison and the Nationalists," 234.

50. Madison to Edmund Randolph, 20 May 1783, *PJM* 7:59–62. Compare Madison to Jefferson, 13 May 1783, ibid., 39.

51. Madison to Randolph, 30 Aug. 1783, ibid., 295–96.

52. Madison to Randolph, 13 Sept. 1783, ibid., 314–15.

53. For Madison's own, essentially unsuccessful campaign to free Virginia from British commercial domination, see Drew R. McCoy, "The Virginia Port Bill of 1784," *Virginia Magazine of History and Biography* 83 (1975): 288–303, and Robert B. Bittner, "Economic Independence and the Virginia Port Bill of 1784," in Richard A. Rutyna and Peter C. Stewart, *Virginia in the American Revolution* (Norfolk, VA, 1977), 73–92.

54. McCoy, *The Elusive Republic*, 121–32.

55. Madison to Jefferson, 18 Mar. 1786, *PJM* 8:502.

56. Madison to Monroe, 7 Aug. 1785, ibid., 333–36.

57. See Madison's speech supporting a federal power (ibid., 431–32), his letters to Washington of 11 Nov. and 9 Dec. 1785 (ibid., 404, 438–39); the editorial notes and legislative drafts in ibid., 406–10, 413–15; and Madison to Jefferson, 22 Jan. 1786, ibid., 476–77.

58. Contemporary information on the Annapolis Convention is extraordinarily scanty, which may explain the paucity and brevity of secondary studies (e.g., Burnett, *Continental Congress*, 665–68; Morris, *Forging of the Union*, 253–57). The text of the address is in *PAH* 3:686–90.

59. Banning, "Madison and the Nationalists," 232–33, and on the Mississippi more particularly, *PJM* 2:202–4, 224, 241–42, 302–3; 3:261–62.

60. Madison to Jefferson, 7 Sept. 1784, enclosing Madison to Jefferson, 20 Aug. 1784, *PJM* 8:113–14, 104–8. The adventure to Ft. Stanwix is recounted in Brant, *James Madison* 2, chap. 21.

61. Madison to Jefferson, 20 Aug. 1784, in *PJM* 8:108.

62. Madison to Lafayette, 20 Mar. 1785, ibid., 250–53. Useful background is in Madison to Jefferson, 20 Mar. 1785, ibid., 268–69.

63. Madison to Lafayette, ibid., 251.

64. Ibid.

65. These phrases are all but universal in the commentaries of contemporary political scientists, especially on *Federalist X*. They can be traced to the enormously influential essays of the late Martin Diamond, especially "Democracy and *The Federalist*: A Reconsideration of the Framers' Intent," *APSR* 53 (1959): 52–68.

66. Most explicitly, moreover, in the passage deleted from his letter to Jefferson and written before he met Lafayette. These thoughts were not developed simply for French consumption.

67. See n. 54 above.

68. Query 19 of *Notes on the State of Virginia*, written in 1781–82 and carefully read by Madison no later than the early fall of 1785 (*PJM* 8:415–16).

69. See the *National Gazette* essays on "Republican Distribution of Citizens" (3 Mar. 1792) and "Fashion" (20 Mar. 1792), reprinted in *PJM* 14:244–46, 257–59.

70. Jefferson to Madison, 28 Oct. 1785, *PJM* 8:285–88.

71. 19 June 1786, ibid. 9:76–77. See, further, Drew R. McCoy, "Jefferson and Madison on Malthus: Population Growth in Jeffersonian Political Economy," *Virginia Magazine of History and Biography* 88 (1980): 259–76.

72. Henderson, *Party Politics* 387–94; Burnett, *Continental Congress*, 654–59; Morris, *Forging of the Union*, 233–44; Marks, *Independence on Trial*, 24–45.

73. See, for example, Charles Thomson's report of the speech of Rufus King, 16 Aug. 1786, in *Letters of Members of Congress* 8:429.

74. Theodore Sedgwick to Caleb Strong, 6 Aug. 1786, quoted in Burnett, *Continental Congress*, 657. The best recent discussion of the widespread talk of separate regional confederations is in Matson and Onuf, *Union of Interests*, 82–90.

75. The point is powerfully developed in Drew R. McCoy, "James Madison and Visions of American Nationality in the Confederation Period," in Beeman et al., eds., *Beyond Confederation*, 226–58, which is essential for distinguishing Madison's views from those of other Virginians.

76. Thomson's report of Grayson's speech of 16 Aug. (*Letters of Members of Congress* 8:427–29) and Monroe to Governor Patrick Henry, 12 Aug. 1786 (ibid., 422–25).

77. Madison to Monroe, 21 June 1786, *PJM* 9:82–83.

78. *Journals of the Continental Congress* 31:494–97.

79. *PJM* 9:91–92.

80. 14 Aug. 1786, ibid., 104.

81. 17 Aug. 1786, ibid., 107–8.

82. Ibid., 109. Delaware was the only state unrepresented during the crisis.

83. Ibid., 113–14.

84. Madison to Monroe, 11 Sept. 1786, ibid., 121.

85. *The Federalist*, 91–92.

86. Isaac Kramnick, ed., *The Federalist Papers* (Harmondsworth, Eng., 1987), 67.

87. Madison to Monroe, 18 Mar. 1786, in *PJM* 8 : 502; Madison to Monroe, 5 Oct. 1786, in ibid. 9 : 140.

88. George W. Carey, "Publius—A Split Personality?" *Review of Politics* 46 (1984): 5–22; David F. Epstein, *The Political Theory of "The Federalist"* (Chicago, 1984); Albert Furtwangler, *The Authority of Publius: A Reading of the Federalist Papers* (Ithaca, NY, 1984); and Gary Wills, *Explaining America: The Federalist* (New York, 1981).

89. Some of these differences have been detected even in *The Federalist*. See Douglas Adair, "The Authorship of the Disputed Federalist Papers," in *Fame and the Founding Fathers: Essays by Douglas Adair*, ed. Trevor Colbourn (New York, 1974), 55–60; Alpheus Thomas Mason, "The Federalist— A Split Personality," *AHR* 57 (1952): 625–43; and Gottfried Dietze, *The Federalist: A Classic on Federalism and Free Government* (Baltimore, 1960), 150–51, 260–64, 267–71.

90. The most revealing document is an undated private memorandum written shortly after the adjournment of the Federal Convention: "Conjectures About the New Constitution," in *PAH* 4 : 275–77.

91. The critical documents here are Madison's speech of 29 June in Max Farrand, ed., *The Records of the Federal Convention of 1787*, rev. ed., 4 vols. (New Haven, CT, 1966), 1 : 464–65, and *Federalist XLI*, 259–60.

92. Jonathan Elliot, ed., *The Debates in the Several State Conventions on the Adoption of the Federal Constitution*, 2d ed., 5 vols. (Philadelphia, 1901), 3 : 47, 135.

93. For more on this distinction, see my essays "The Practicable Sphere of a Republic: James Madison, the Constitutional Convention, and the Emergence of Revolutionary Federalism," in Beeman et al., *Beyond Confederation*, 162–87; and "1787 and 1776: Patrick Henry, James Madison, the Constitution, and the Revolution," in Neil L. York, ed., *Toward a More Perfect Union: Six Essays on the Constitution* (Provo, UT, 1988), 59–89.

94. *Federalist*, 66–68.

95. For the central role of this fear in the decisions of Edmund Randolph and George Mason not to sign the Constitution, and among Virginia Antifederalists in general, see Lance Banning, "Virginia: Sectionalism and the General Good," in *Ratifying the Constitution*, ed. Michael Allen Gillespie and Michael Lienesch (Lawrence, KS, 1989), 261–99. But note that, even so, these critics almost always argued that commercial treaties and regulations should require a two-thirds vote in Congress, not that these commercial powers should not be placed in federal hands.

96. For the stance of "bourgeois radicals" among the Antifederalists, see Cornell, "The Political Thought and Culture of the Anti-Federalists," chap. 5. A few examples might include "A Plebeian" (perhaps Melancton Smith), in Herbert J. Storing, ed., *The Complete Anti-Federalist*, 7 vols. (Chicago,

1981), 6:131–32, 140; and the essays collected in chap. 4 of W. B. Allen and Gordon Lloyd, eds., *The Essential Antifederalist* (Lanham, MD, 1985), especially "Aggrippa" at 235, 240–41, and "Centinel" at 253–54.

97. Banning, "Virginia," 274–76, 281–82; McCoy, "Madison and Visions of American Nationality," 245–48.

98. Speech of 8 Apr. 1789, in *PJM* 12:64–66; supporting speeches of 21 and 25 Apr. and 4 May in ibid., 97–103, 109–13, 125–30.

99. See, especially, the Report on Manufactures, *PAH* 10:287–90, which McCoy rightly calls "Hamilton's answer to Madison's defense of commercial discrimination" (*Elusive Republic*, 150).

100. Madison's advocacy of commercial discrimination in congressional speeches of the early 1790s is superbly summarized in McCoy, *Elusive Republic* 140–45, 162–63. The most important public expositions of his thinking came in his *National Gazette* essays on "Parties," "Republican Distribution of Citizens," and "Fashion" (*PJM* 14:197–98, 244–46, 257–59), together with his "Political Observations" of 20 Apr. 1795 (ibid. 15:511–34). For Jefferson, see Merrill Peterson, "Thomas Jefferson and Commercial Policy, 1783–1793," *WMQ* 22 (1965): 584–610. On the Jeffersonians in power, McCoy, *Elusive Republic*, chaps. 8–10, and Banning, *The Jeffersonian Persuasion*, chap. 10, should be supplemented by J. C. A. Stagg, "James Madison and the Coercion of Great Britain: Canada, the West Indies, and the War of 1812," *WMQ* 38 (1981): 3–34, and Donald R. Hickey, "American Trade Restrictions during the War of 1812," *JAH* 68 (1981): 517–38.

101. Hamilton's indebtedness to Hume was well established in John C. Miller, *Alexander Hamilton: Portrait in Paradox* (New York, 1959), 46–51 and *passim*, and in Gerald Stourzh, *Alexander Hamilton and the Idea of Republican Government* (Stanford, 1970), 70–75 and *passim*. For the influence of the Scottish mercantilist James Steuart (*An Inquiry into the Principles of Political Oeconomy* [1767]), see McDonald, *Novus Ordo Seclorum*, 119–28, 135–42, which summarizes the important, longer discussion of Hamilton's political economy in id., *Alexander Hamilton: A Biography* (New York, 1979).

102. For Hamilton's grand vision, in addition to the essential works just cited, see McCoy, *The Elusive Republic*, 146–52; Banning, *The Jeffersonian Persuasion*, 129–40. Also useful for contrasting party understandings of America's position in the world is Jerald A. Combs, *The Jay Treaty: Political Battleground of the Founding Fathers* (Berkeley, 1970). Hamilton's relationships with George Beckwith and George Hammond were not as sinister as they appear in Julian P. Boyd, *Number Seven: Alexander Hamilton's Secret Attempts to Control American Foreign Policy* (Princeton, NJ, 1964), but it is generally agreed that they occasionally torpedoed the administration's stance in Anglo-American negotiations.

103. *PAH* 6:80–81.

104. See, further, "Notes on the Advantages of a National Bank," in *PAH* 8:223.

105. The clearest explanations of the workings of this system are in McDonald, *Alexander Hamilton*, chap. 8; id., *The Presidency of George*

Washington (Lawrence, KS, 1974), 47–65; and Ferguson, *The Power of the Purse*, 292–96. See also Donald F. Swanson, *The Origins of Hamilton's Fiscal Policies* (Gainesville, FL, 1963).

106. Report on Manufactures, *PAH* 10:255–56.

107. Again, the Report on Manufactures, *PAH* 10:230–340, is the major text.

108. Banning, *The Jeffersonian Persuasion*, 153–55 and chap. 6; id., "The Hamiltonian Madison," 20–28.

109. Ferguson, *Power of the Purse*, 329–30; Whitney K. Bates, "Northern Speculators and Southern State Debts, 1790," *WMQ* 19 (1962): 32–34, 39.

110. Madison to Jefferson, 10 July and 8 Aug. 1791, *PJM* 14:43, 69.

111. John R. Nelson, "Alexander Hamilton and American Manufacturing: A Reexamination," *JAH* 65 (1979): 971–95; id., *Liberty and Property: Political Economy and Policymaking in the New Nation, 1789–1812* (Baltimore, 1987), 81–90; Alfred F. Young, *The Democratic Republicans of New York: The Origins, 1763–1797* (Chapel Hill, NC, 1967).

112. Nelson, *Liberty and Property*, 10, 93.

113. Ibid., 90–96; Murrin, "The Great Inversion," 412, 419–21; and sources cited by both.

114. Here, without accepting their interpretive positions, I draw especially on Appleby, *Capitalism and a New Social Order*; Steven Watts, *The Republic Reborn: War and the Making of Liberal America, 1790–1820* (Baltimore, 1987); and Michael Durey, "Thomas Paine's Apostles: Radical Emigres and the Triumph of Jeffersonian Republicanism," *WMQ* 44 (1987): 661–86. Years ago, in *Tom Paine and Revolutionary America* (New York, 1976), Eric Foner suggested that the author of "Common Sense" and many of the artisans to whom he most appealed were sympathetic to both of the great transformations of the age: popular participation in political affairs, *and* the advent of an advanced market economy. The influence of this thinking, both democratic and profoundly pro-developmental, has only recently become a subject of close inquiry.

115. Jefferson to William H. Crawford, in *Works* 11:537–39.

116. For the debates on the carrying trade, see McCoy, *The Elusive Republic*, 174–78, 212–16.

117. Ibid., chap. 10; Stagg, "James Madison and the Coercion of Great Britain." Madison, who had been willing even in 1790 to protect manufactories which had already emerged, though not to foster new ones, now specifically endorsed protection for some "manufacturing establishments ... of the more complicated kind" (quoted in McCoy, *Elusive Republic*, 245). Jefferson was more reluctant. See his letter to Benjamin Austin, 9 Jan. 1816, *Works* 11: 502–5; and Merrill Peterson, *Thomas Jefferson and the New Nation* (New York, 1970), 940–41.

CHAPTER 2

1. The standard accounts of the retrocession crisis are Arthur P. Whitaker, *The Mississippi Question, 1795–1803* (New York, 1934), 189–236, and

Alexander DeConde, *This Affair of Louisiana* (New York, 1976), 127–92. For a persuasive critical account of Jefferson's diplomacy see Robert W. Tucker and David C. Hendrickson, *Empire of Liberty: The Statecraft of Thomas Jefferson* (New York, 1990), 87–171.

2. Cathy D. Matson and Peter S. Onuf, *A Union of Interests: Political and Economic Thought in Revolutionary America* (Lawrence, KS, 1990), 64–66, 84–85; Thomas P. Slaughter, *The Whiskey Rebellion: Frontier Epilogue to the American Revolution* (New York, 1986), 36–45; Peter S. Onuf, *Origins of the Federal Republic: Jurisdictional Controversies in the United States, 1775–1787* (Philadelphia, 1983), 33–41; Joseph L. Davis, *Sectionalism in American Politics, 1774–1787* (Madison, WI, 1977), 109–26; Frederick W. Marks III, *Independence on Trial: Foreign Affairs and the Making of the Constitution* (Baton Rouge, LA, 1973), 24–36; Arthur P. Whitaker, *The Spanish-American Frontier: 1783–1795: The Westward Movement and the Spanish Retreat in the Mississippi Valley* (Boston, 1927), 63–77.

3. Livingston and Monroe to James Madison, dated Paris, 13 May 1803, *Annals of Congress,* 7th Cong., 2d Sess., app., 1146–47.

4. Orasmus Cook Merrill, *The Happiness of America. An Oration Delivered at Shaftsbury, on the Fourth of July, 1804* (Bennington, VT, 1804), 10, 20.

5. Rep. John Clopton (VA), 24 Feb. 1804, Noble Cunningham, ed., *Circular Letters of Congressmen to their Constituents, 1789–1829*, 3 vols. (Chapel Hill, NC, 1978), 1:367–69, at 367.

6. Sen. Robert Wright (MD), speech of 24 Feb. 1803, *Annals of Congress,* 7th Cong., 2d Sess., 165.

7. Report of House Committee on resolution to appropriate two million dollars for possible purchase of New Orleans, 12 Jan. 1803, ibid., 373. The best account of the sources and development of Jeffersonian ideology is Lance Banning, *The Jeffersonian Persuasion: Evolution of a Party Ideology* (Ithaca, NY, 1978); see esp. 246–70.

8. David Ramsay, *Oration on the Cession of Louisiana, to the United States* (Charleston, SC, 1804), 14.

9. Sen. DeWitt Clinton speech of 23 Feb. 1803, *Annals of Congress,* 7th Cong., 2d Sess., 132.

10. Pericles [Alexander Hamilton], *Evening Post* (NY), 8 Feb. 1803, in *PAH* 26:82–85, at 83. See the discussion in Whitaker, *Mississippi Question,* 209–14.

11. [Charles Brockden Brown], *An Address to the Government of the United States, on the Cession of Louisiana to the French,* new and rev. ed. (Philadelphia, 1803), 49.

12. Sen. William Wells (DE), speech of 24 Feb. 1803, *Annals of Congress,* 7th Cong., 2d Sess., 155.

13. James Ross (PA), speech of 14 Feb. 1803, ibid., 87. The Ross resolutions (16 Feb.) would have authorized Jefferson "to take immediate possession" of New Orleans and to augment "the military and naval forces of the Union" with up to 50,000 militiamen from neighboring states; they were defeated (25 Feb.), by a straight partisan vote, 15–11. Ibid., 95–96, 255.

14. Wells speech of 24 Feb. 1803, *Annals of Congress*, 7th Cong., 2d Sess., 156.

15. Rep. Samuel Purviance (NC), speech of 25 Oct. 1803, *Annals of Congress*, 8th Cong., 1st Sess., 444.

16. Marshall Smelser, "The Federalist Period as an Age of Passion," *American Quarterly* 10 (1958): 391–419; John R. Howe, "Republican Political Thought and the Political Violence of the 1790s," ibid., 19 (1967): 147–65.

17. Sen. Gouverneur Morris (NY), speech of 24 Feb. 1803, *Annals of Congress*, 7th Cong., 2d Sess., 192.

18. Sen. James Jackson (GA), speech of 25 Feb. 1803, *Annals of Congress*, 7th Cong., 2d sess., 243, my emphasis.

19. Sen. DeWitt Clinton (NY), speech of 23 Feb. 1803, *Annals of Congress*, 7th Cong., 2d Sess., 134.

20. "Algernon Sidney" [Gideon Granger], *A Vindication of the Measures of the Present Administration* (Portsmouth, NH, 1803), 21.

21. Rep. Joseph Nicholson (MD), speech of 25 Oct. 1803, *Annals of Congress*, 8th Cong., 1st Sess., 466.

22. Joseph Winston (NC), 20 Mar. 1804, Cunningham, ed., *Circular Letters* 1:369–72, at 369–70.

23. Ramsay, *Oration on the Cession*, 16.

24. "Sylvestris," *Reflections on the Cession of Louisiana to the United States* (Washington City, 1803), 11, 13.

25. "Camillus" [William Duane], *The Mississippi Question Fairly Stated, and the Views and Arguments of those who Clamor for War, Examined* (Philadelphia, 1803), 37.

26. Merrill, *The Happiness of America*, 9.

27. Allan Boure Magruder, *Political, Commercial, and Moral Reflections, on the Late Cession of Louisiana, to the United States* (Lexington, KY, 1803), 35–36. "Sylvestris," *Reflections on the Cession of Louisiana*, 14.

28. Ramsay, *Oration on the Cession of Louisiana*, 24.

29. Merrill, *The Happiness of America*, 9.

30. Magruder, *Reflections on the Late Cession of Louisiana*, 37. For an earlier discussion of the American federal republic as a "peace plan," see Joel Barlow, *To His Fellow Citizens of the United States of America* (Philadelphia, 1801), Letter 2, dated Paris, 20 Dec. 1799, 9–11.

31. Ramsay, *Oration on the Cession of Louisiana*, 21.

32. David Augustus Leonard, *An Oration, Delivered at Raynham, Friday, May 11th, 1804, on the Late Acquisition of Louisiana* (Newport, RI, 1804), 20.

33. Rep. Samuel Mitchill (NY), speech of 25 Oct. 1803, *Annals of Congress*, 8th Cong., 1st Sess., 483.

34. Chapman Johnson, *An Oration on the Late Treaty with France, by which Louisiana was Acquired* (Staunton, VA, 1804), 14.

35. Ezra Stiles, *The United States Elevated to Glory and Honour*, 2d ed. (Worcester, MA, 1785), 84, 49–50. On early American foreign policy see

Felix Gilbert, *To the Farewell Address: Ideas of Early American Foreign Policy* (Princeton, NJ, 1961) and James H. Hutson, *John Adams and the Diplomacy of the American Revolution* (Lexington, KY, 1980).

36. Albert O. Hirschman, *The Passions and the Interests: Political Arguments for Capitalism before its Triumph* (Princeton, NJ, 1977); Ralph Lerner, "Commerce and Character: The Anglo-American as a New-Model Man," *WMQ* 36 (1979): 3–26. On liberalism see Joyce Appleby, *Capitalism and a New Social Order* (New York, 1984).

37. Stiles, *United States Elevated*, 85, 84–85, 60. The population in 1880 was 50,155,783.

38. T[homas] Pownall, *A Memorial Addressed to the Sovereigns of America* (London, 1783), 138. See also [Anon.], *A Translation of the Memorial to the Sovereigns of Europe upon the Present State of Affairs, Between the Old and the New World, Into Common Sense and Intelligible English* (London, 1781).

39. Richard Price, *Observations on the Importance of the American Revolution, and the Means of Making it a Benefit to the World. To which is Added a letter from M. Turgot* (2d ed., London, 1785), repr. in Bernard Leach, ed., *Richard Price and the Ethical Foundations of the American Revolution* (Durham, NC, 1979), 177–224, at 210.

40. Stiles, *United States Elevated*, 86.

41. Thomas Paine, *Letter Addressed to the Abbe Raynal, on the Affairs of North-America* (Philadelphia, 1782), postscript, 72. For similar thinking see John Brown Cutting to Thomas Jefferson, 16 Sept. 1788, in *PTJ* 13:608–13, at 609–10: "the mildness of our laws and the wisdom of our political institutions . . . might tempt the subjects of any arbitrary potentates in our vicinity to voluntarily commute themselves into free citizens and thus become attached to the first empire that mankind has ever erected on the solid foundation of truth, reason or common sense."

42. Drew R. McCoy, *The Elusive Republic: Political Economy in Jeffersonian America* (Chapel Hill, NC, 1980).

43. "Extract of a Letter from Louisville," dated 4 Dec. 1786, in *Cumberland Gazette* (Portland, MA), 19 July 1787.

44. Earl of Sheffield [John B. Holroyd], *Observations on the Commerce of the American States* (London, 1783), 103, 105, 104–5.

45. Peter S. Onuf, "Liberty, Development, and Union: Visions of the West in the 1780s," *WMQ* 43 (1986): 179–213.

46. Price, *Observations on the Revolution*, 187, my emphasis.

47. Abbe de Mably, *Observations on the Government and Laws of the United States* (Eng. ed., Amsterdam, 1784), 121.

48. Josiah Tucker, *Cui Bono? Or, An Inquiry, what Benefits Can Arise Either to the English or the Americans, the French, Spaniards, or Dutch, From the Present War? Being a Series of Letters, Addressed to Monsieur Necker* (2d ed., Gloucester, MA, 1782), 118–19.

49. Peter S. Onuf, "State Sovereignty and the Making of the Constitution," in Terence Ball and J. G. A. Pocock, eds., *Conceptual Change and the Constitution* (Lawrence, KS, 1988), 79–98.

50. Thomas Dawes speech, Massachusetts Convention, 21 Jan. 1788, in Jonathan Elliot, ed., *The Debates in the Several State Conventions on the Adoption of the Federal Constitution*, 5 vols. (Philadelphia, 1876), 2:58.

51. Edmund Randolph speech, Virginia Convention, 24 June 1788, in ibid. 3:603. See also Randolph's speech of 4 June for a full discussion of the implications of disunion. John P. Kaminski, et al., eds., *The Documentary History of the Ratification of the Constitution* (Madison, WI, 1976–), 9: 931–36.

52. [John Jay], *An Address to the People of the State of New York* (New York, 1788), in Paul Leicester Ford, ed., *Pamphlets on the Constitution of the United States* (Brooklyn, 1888), 67–86, at 84.

53. *Federalist* VIII (Hamilton): 49. See the excellent discussion in Gerald Stourzh, *Alexander Hamilton and the Idea of Republican Government* (Stanford, 1970), 149–53.

54. "Cato," "To the Public," *New-Haven Gazette*, 25 Jan. 1787.

55. Emmerich de Vattel, *The Law of Nations, or the Principles of Natural Law Applied to the Conduct and Affairs of Nations and Sovereigns* (trans. of 1758 ed., Washington, 1916), bk. 1, chap. 2. On Vattel's influence in America see Charles G. Fenwick, "The Authority of Vattel," *APSR* 7 (1913): 370–424, and Daniel George Lang, *Foreign Policy in the Early Republic* (Baton Rouge, LA, 1985), 13–33.

56. Barlow, *To His Fellow Citizens*, letter 2, dated Paris, 8n.

57. William Wiecek, *The Guarantee Clause of the U.S. Constitution* (Ithaca, NY, 1972), 11–77.

58. Barlow, *To His Fellow Citizens*, letter 2, 28.

59. "A Calm Observer," *Letters on the Subject of the Concert of Princes, and the Dismemberment of Poland and France* (London, 1794), letter 11, dated 21 and 23 May 1793, 206.

60. Cession of Louisiana, Art. 3, Charles I. Bevans, comp., *Treaties and other International Agreements of the United States of America, 1776– 1949*, 13 vols. (Washington, 1968–76), 7:812–15, at 813.

61. [Granger], *Vindication of the Present Administration*, 22.

62. Sen. James Jackson (GA), speech of 25 Feb. 1803, *Annals of Congress*, 7th Cong., 2d Sess., 243.

63. Calm Observer, *Letters on the Concert of Princes*, letter 12, dated 7 June 1793, 229.

64. [Anon.], *Peace and Reform Against War and Corruption. In Answer to a Pamphlet Written by Arthur Young* (London, 1794), 25–26.

65. Nathaniel Chipman, *Sketches of the Principles of Government* (Rutland, VT, 1793), 278. On the acceptance of the Constitution see Lance Banning, "Republican Ideology and the Triumph of the Constitution," *WMQ* 31 (1974): 167–88.

66. Calm Observer, *Letters on the Concert of Princes*, letter 12, dated 7 June 1793, 229.

67. David F. Epstein, *The Political Theory of the Federalist* (Chicago, 1984); Richard B. Bernstein, "*The Federalist* on Energetic Government," in

Stephen Schecter, ed., *Roots of the Republic: American Founding Documents Interpreted* (Madison, WI, 1990), 335–54.

68. Barlow, *To His Fellow Citizens*, letter 2, 35, 25, 24.

69. Sen. George Nicholas (VA), speech of 25 Feb. 1803, *Annals of Congress*, 7th Cong., 2d Sess., 236.

70. Rep. John Rhea (TN), 8 Apr. 1806, Cunningham, ed., *Circular Letters of Congressmen* 1:425–29, at 429.

71. Rep. Marmaduke Williams (NC), 26 Feb. ibid., 502–4, at 503, explaining to his constituents why the Burr Conspiracy was so easily suppressed.

72. Sen. John Breckinridge (KY), speech of 23 Feb. 1803, *Annals of Congress*, 7th Cong., 2d Sess., 118.

73. Ramsay, *Oration on the Cession of Louisiana*, 18. As long as Governor William Claiborne treated them as *"vassals,"* disgruntled Louisianans would offer no guarantee of their loyalty. But *"how different it would be, if liberty, if self government was given to them." Reflections on the Cause of the Louisianans, Carefully Submitted by their Agents* (Washington, 1804), 9, 11. See George Dargo, *Jefferson's Louisiana: Politics and the Clash of Legal Traditions* (Cambridge, 1975), esp. 23–50.

74. Magruder, *Reflections on the Late Cession of Louisiana*, 73.

75. On state equality see John Taylor, *An Inquiry into the Principles of Policy of the Government of the United States* (Fredericksburg, VA, 1814), 504–5, and the discussion in Peter S. Onuf, "New State Equality: The Ambiguous History of a Constitutional Principle," *Publius* 18 (1988): 53–69.

76. Granger, *Vindication of the Present Administration*, 21.

77. Magruder, *Reflections on the Late Cession of Louisiana*, 72, 74.

78. Ramsay, *Oration on the Cession of Louisiana*, 19. For a similar argument see Merrill, *The Happiness of America*, 19.

79. Rep. John Rhea (TN), 12 Feb. 1805, Cunningham, ed., *Circular Letters of Congressmen* 1:377–82, at 380.

80. "Sylvestris," *Reflections on the Cession of Louisiana*, 14.

81. Richard Law speech, Connecticut Convention, 9 Jan. 1788, in Kaminski et al., eds., *Documentary History of the Ratification* 3:559.

82. Magruder, *Reflections on the Late Cession of Louisiana*, 38.

83. Peter S. Onuf, *Statehood and Union: A History of the Northwest Ordinance* (Bloomington, IN, 1987), 1–66.

84. Onuf, *Origins of the Federal Republic*, 126–45; Paul S. Gillies, "Adjusting to Union: An Assessment of Statehood, 1791–1816," in Michael Sherman, ed., *A More Perfect Union: Vermont Becomes a State, 1777–1816* (Montpelier, VT, 1991), 114–49.

85. Charles Cummings to the President of Congress, on behalf of residents of Washington Co., VA, 7 Apr. 1785, Papers of the Continental Congress (National Archives, Washington) 48:297; "Extract of a letter from Virginia," dated Washington Co., 1 June 1785, *Pennsylvania Packet* (Philadelphia), 3 Oct. 1785. On early separatist movements see Onuf, *Origins of the Federal Republic*, 33–41, and, on settlers' motives, chap. 3 below.

86. On the territorial system see Robert F. Berkhofer, Jr., "The Northwest

Ordinance and the Principle of Territorial Evolution," in John Porter Bloom, ed., *The American Territorial System* (Athens, OH, 1973), 45–55; Peter S. Onuf, "Territories and Statehood," in Jack P. Greene, ed., *Encyclopedia of American Political History*, 3 vols. (New York, 1984), 3:1283–1304; Onuf, *Statehood and Union*, 44–66.

87. Rep. Albert Gallatin (PA), speech of 6 May 1796, *Annals of Congress*, 4th Cong., 1st Sess., 1327.

88. "An Address of New Market Township to their fellow citizens," *Western Spy* (Cincinnati), 21 Aug. 1802.

89. *Journals of Congress* 32:334–43. The most comprehensive treatment of the state-making process is Jack Ericson Eblen, *The First and Second United States Empires: Governors and Territorial Government, 1784–1912* (Pittsburgh, PA, 1968), 201–36.

90. On the Ohio statehood movement see Onuf, *Statehood and Union*, 67–87, and Andrew R. L. Cayton, *The Frontier Republic: Ideology and Politics in the Ohio Country, 1780–1825* (Kent, OH, 1986), 68–80.

91. Meeting at Marietta, 12 Jan. 1801, *Western Spy*, 11 Feb. 1801.

92. Address dated Cincinnati, 30 Dec. 1797, excerpted in Randolph Chandler Downes, *Frontier Ohio, 1788–1803* (Columbus, OH, 1935), 184.

93. *Annals of Congress*, 7th Cong., 1st Sess., Senate (9–27 Apr. 1803), 258, 259, 268, 275, 294–95, 296–97; House (29 Jan.-30 Apr.), 470–71, 814, 985, 1017, 1097–1118, 1123–26, 1128, 1155–56, 1158–62, 1252, 1349–51 (text of enabling act). For the Ohio Constitution see Francis Newton Thorpe, ed., *The Federal and State Constitutions*, 7 vols. (Washington, 1909), 5: 2901–13.

94. "Frank Stubblefield" [William McMillan], No. 4, *Western Spy*, 21 Aug. 1802, my emphasis.

95. "Extract of a Letter from a member of the Senate," *Western Spy*, 12 June 1802.

96. If Congress refused to accept the new state on its own terms, St. Clair told the constitutional convention, it could follow the example of Vermont which had remained outside the union "eight years after" the people "had formed their government." St. Clair's speech [3 Nov. 1802], in William Henry Smith, ed., *The St. Clair Papers: The Life and Public Services of Arthur St. Clair*, 2 vols. (Cincinnati, 1882), 2:592–97, at 594.

97. Rep. Samuel Mitchill (NY), speech of 25 Oct. 1803, *Annals of Congress*, 8th Cong., 1st Sess., 480, 482. As Supreme Court Justice Levi Woodbury later wrote (in 1847), "the acknowledgement of a domestic state is like the *recognition* of the independence or existence *of a foreign state."* Scott et al. v. Jones, 5 Howard 343 (1847), my emphasis.

98. Rep. Laban Wheaton (MA), speech of 4 Jan. 1811, *Annals of Congress*, 11th Cong., 3d Sess., 494.

99. Sen. Uriah Tracy (CT), speech of 3 Nov. 1803, *Annals of Congress*, 8th Cong., 1st Sess., 56. For a typical prediction of the imminent "subversion of our Union," see Rep. Matthew Griswold (CT), speech of 25 Oct. 1803, ibid., 465.

100. "Memorandums of a Tour made by Joseph Espy in the States of Ohio and Kentucky and Indiana Territory in 1805," *Ohio Valley Historical Series,* no. 7 (Cincinnati, 1870), 25.

101. Gould Francis Lecky, *An Historical Survey of the Foreign Affairs of Great Britain, with a View to Explain the Causes of the Disasters of the Late and Present Wars* (London, 1808), 150–51.

102. [Joseph Hamilton Daveiss], *An Essay on Federalism* [Frankfort, KY?, 1810?], 46.

103. Rep. Josiah Quincy (MA), speech of 14 Jan. 1811, *Annals of Congress,* 11th Cong., 3d Sess., 540.

104. For the "consolidationist" charge and an interesting discussion of Federalist efforts "to annihilate the sovereignty of the respective States," see Benjamin Austin, Jr., *Constitutional Republicanism, in Opposition to Fallacious Federalism* (Boston, 1803), 54, and *passim.*

105. Rep. Robert Goodloe Harper (SC), 5 Mar. 1801, Cunningham, ed., *Circular Letters of Congressmen* 1:247–65, at 252.

106. Malcolm Rohrbough, *The Land Office Business: The Settlement and Administration of American Public Lands, 1789–1837* (New York, 1968), 3–136.

107. James Madison to Thomas Jefferson, 20 Aug. 1784, in *PJM* 8:108.

108. Barlow, *Advice to the Privileged Orders, in the Several States of Europe* (London; repr. New York, 1792), 36, 64–65.

109. "Friend to the People" [Tiffin], "To the Inhabitants," *Scioto Gazette,* 24 Sept. 1801.

110. See James H. Kettner, *The Development of American Citizenship, 1608–1870* (Chapel Hill, NC, 1978).

111. [Madison], "Consolidation," dated 3 Dec. 1791, *National Gazette* (Philadelphia), 5 Dec. 1791. Jefferson expressed similar sentiments in a letter to John Dickinson, 6 Mar. 1801: "I hope to see shortly a perfect consolidation, to affect which, nothing shall be spared on my part, short of the abandonment of the principles of our revolution." Paul Leicester Ford, ed., *The Writings of Thomas Jefferson,* 10 vols. (New York, 1892–99), 8:7–8.

112. [Charles Brockden Brown], *An Address to the Government of the United States, on the Cession of Louisiana to the French,* rev. ed. (Philadelphia, 1803), 37. The quotation is from a translation of a French document urging French colonization of Louisiana and emphasizing American vulnerability.

113. Concern was often focussed on prospects for continuing public land sales. For example, see Rep. John Stratton (VA), 3 Mar. 1803, in Cunningham, ed., *Circular Letters of Congressmen* 1:352–61, at 355: with the creation of a new state in the Northwest Territory, "little controul . . . will now be left to the National Government" over the public lands within its boundaries. Sen. James Ross (PA) warned that, without free navigation of the Mississippi, westerners "will rob you of your public lands." Speech of 14 Feb. 1803, *Annals of Congress,* 7th Cong., 2d Sess., 88.

114. Rep. Josiah Quincy (MA), speech of 14 Jan. 1811, *Annals of Congress,*

11th Cong., 3rd Sess., 525, 535, 540. For a comprehensive recapitulation of congressional debates on Louisiana see Everett Somerville Brown, *The Constitutional History of the Louisiana Purchase, 1803–1812* (Berkeley, 1920). On Quincy and Federalist "anti-expansionism," see Robert A. McCaughey, *Josiah Quincy, 1772–1864: The Last Federalist* (Cambridge, MA, 1974), 29–33, 68: the 14 Jan. speech, writes McCaughey, was one of Quincy's "petulant outbursts," and caused considerable embarrassment to his Federalist colleagues. See also the excellent study by James M. Banner, Jr., *To the Hartford Convention: The Federalists and the Origins of Party Politics in Massachusetts, 1789–1815* (New York, 1970), esp. at 110–14.

115. Johnson, *Oration on the Treaty with France,* 10. The Louisiana Purchase inspired colonization proposals, e.g., Magruder, *Reflections on the Late Cession,* 150; "Sylvestris," *Reflections on the Cession,* 25. Sylvestris also suggested that Indian nations might be induced to move across the Mississippi, ibid., 24. On the slavery problem in this period see Donald L. Robinson, *Slavery in the Structure of American Politics, 1765–1820* (New York, 1971), esp. 378–423 on "Slavery and the Territories." For further discussion and citations see chap. 9 below.

116. On the comity issue, see Paul Finkelman, *An Imperfect Union: Slavery, Federalism, and Comity* (Chapel Hill, NC, 1981).

117. For an eloquent defense of the Jeffersonian idea of union see Julian P. Boyd, "Thomas Jefferson's Empire of Liberty," *Virginia Quarterly Review* 24 (1948): 538–54. For a less favorable assessment, underscoring Jefferson's "ambiguity" about the new nation's role as "exemplar" or "crusader," see Tucker and Hendrickson, *Empire of Liberty,* 249–56.

CHAPTER 3

I am grateful to the editors, the other authors in this volume, and the commentators at the initial conference for their careful reading and helpful criticism. I also benefitted from insightful suggestions offered by Stephen Aron, Wayne Bodle, Robert Gross, and Peter Mancall. I was especially fortunate that Richard White was so generous in sharing his (then) unpublished scholarship, in criticizing my drafts, and in responding so thoughtfully to my queries.

1. Frederick Jackson Turner, *The Frontier in American History* (New York, 1920), 1–38, 243–66.

2. Richard Hofstadter, *The Progressive Historians: Turner, Beard, Parrington* (Chicago, 1968), 118–64; Cecelia Tichy, *New World, New Earth: Environmental Reform in American Literature from the Puritans through Whitman* (New Haven, CT, 1979), 1–113; William Cronon, *Changes in the Land: Indians, Colonists, and the Ecology of New England* (New York, 1983); William Cronon, "Revisiting the Vanishing Frontier: The Legacy of Frederick Jackson Turner," *Western Historical Quarterly* 18 (Apr. 1987): 157–76; Patricia Nelson Limerick, *The Legacy of Conquest: The Unbroken Past of the American West* (New York, 1987), 17–32.

3. Peter S. Onuf, "Settlers, Settlements, and New States," and James H.

Merrell, "Declarations of Independence: Indian White Relations in the New Nation," in Jack P. Greene, ed., *The American Revolution: Its Character and Limits* (New York, 1987), 171–96 and 197–223; Dorothy V. Jones, *License for Empire: Colonialism by Treaty in Early America* (Chicago, 1982), 162.

4. Jeremiah Crabb, 5 Apr. 1796, *Annals of Congress*, 4th Congress, 1st Session, 861. Gregory Stiverson has shown that penurious farmers who had to rent land composed almost half of Maryland's population—a larger proportion than of any other state—and that thousands of those tenants sought a refuge in the West during the 1790s. Poor migrants sought "independence" by emigrating West. See Gregory Stiverson, *Poverty in a Land of Plenty: Tenancy in Eighteenth-Century Maryland* (Baltimore, 1977), 140–42.

5. Cathy Matson and Peter Onuf, "Toward a Republican Empire: Interest and Ideology in Revolutionary America," *American Quarterly* 37 (1985): 498, 519; Gordon S. Wood, *The Creation of the American Republic, 1776–1787* (Chapel Hill, NC, 1969), 64; Daniel Vickers, "Competency and Competition: Economic Culture in Early America," *WMQ* 47 (1990): 3–29.

6. James Holland, 5 Apr. 1796, *Annals of Congress*, 4th Congress, 1st Sess., 858–59.

7. Jeremiah Crabb, 5 Apr. 1796, *Annals of Congress*, 4th Congress, 1st Sess., 860; Richard L. Bushman, *King and People in Provincial Massachusetts* (Chapel Hill, NC, 1985), 62–63; Drew R. McCoy, *The Elusive Republic: Political Economy in Jeffersonian America* (Chapel Hill, NC, 1980), 14, 68.

8. Joseph Doddridge, *Notes on the Settlement and Indian Wars of the Western Parts of Virginia and Pennsylvania, From 1763 to 1783, Inclusive* (New York, 1972 repr. of 1876 edition), 190, 194.

9. For the radical implications of "independence," see Ruth Bogin, "New Jersey's True Policy: the Radical Republican Vision of Abraham Clark," *WMQ* 35 (1978): 100–109; Ruth Bogin, "Petitioning and the New Moral Economy of Post-Revolutionary America," *WMQ* 45 (1988): 391–425; Stanley N. Katz, "Thomas Jefferson and the Right to Property in Revolutionary America," *Journal of Law and Economics* 19 (1976): 467–88; James P. Walsh, "'Mechanics and Citizens': The Connecticut Artisan Protest of 1792," *WMQ* 42 (1985): 66–89.

10. Wood, *The Creation of the American Republic*, 70–75; Jack P. Greene, *Pursuits of Happiness: The Social Development of Early Modern British Colonies and the Formation of American Culture* (Chapel Hill, NC, 1988), 187–89; Jackson Turner Main, *The Social Structure of Revolutionary America* (Princeton, NJ, 1965), 30–35, 45–67, 221–39. For the Congressmen see Alfred F. Young, *The Democratic Republicans of New York: The Origins, 1763–1797* (Chapel Hill, NC, 1967), 554–58.

11. Daniel Scott Smith, "A Malthusian-Frontier Interpretation of United States Demographic History Before c. 1815," in Woodrow Borah et al., eds., *Urbanization in the Americas: The Background in Comparative Perspective* (Ottawa, 1980), 15–20; Jim Potter, "Demographic Development and Family Structure," in Jack P. Greene and J. R. Pole, eds., *Colonial British America: Essays in the New History of the Early Modern Era* (Baltimore, 1984), 136, 149.

12. James H. Merrell, *The Indians' New World: Catawbas and Their Neighbors from European Contact through the Era of Removal* (Chapel Hill, NC, 1989), 167–225; Greene, *Pursuits of Happiness*, 190–91.

13. Stephen Anthony Aron, "How the West was Lost: The Transformation of Kentucky from Daniel Boone to Henry Clay," (Ph.D. diss., Univ. of California, Berkeley, 1990), 81–85; Onuf, "Settlers, Settlements, and New States," 176–80, 184 (Kentuckian quoted); Samuel Preston, "Journey to Harmony," in Patricia H. Christian, ed., *Samuel Preston, 1789–1989* (Equinunk, PA, 1989), 82–83.

14. "Petition of Inhabitants West of the Ohio River," to the Continental Congress, 11 Apr. 1785, in Archer B. Hulbert, ed., *Ohio in the Time of the Confederation* (Marietta, OH, 1918), vol. 3 of Marietta College Historical Commission, *Collections*, 103–5.

15. "Petition of Kentuckians for Lands North of Ohio River," to the Continental Congress, n.d. (c. 1786), in Hulbert, ed., *Ohio in the Time of the Confederation*, 137–38. See also "Petition to Settle Ohio Lands," to the Continental Congress, 30 Oct. 1784, in Hulbert, ed., *Ohio in the Time of the Confederation*, 95; Doddridge, *Notes on the Settlement*, 130–31. For the legal troubles of Kentucky settlers in the 1780s and 1790s, see Aron, "How the West was Lost," 235–59; for Pennsylvania see Dorothy E. Fennell, "From Rebelliousness to Insurrection: A Social History of the Whiskey Rebellion, 1765–1802" (Ph.D. diss., Univ. of Pittsburgh, 1981), 183–84; Robert E. Harper, "The Class Structure of Western Pennsylvania in the late Eighteenth Century," (Ph.D. diss., Univ. of Pittsburgh, 1969), 118–26.

16. Harper, "The Class Structure of Western Pennsylvania," 36–39, 55, 62–66, 74–80; Lee Soltow, "Housing Characteristics on the Pennsylvania Frontier: Mifflin County Dwelling Values in 1798," *Pennsylvania History* 47 (1980): 57–70; Lee Soltow, "Kentucky Wealth at the End of the Eighteenth Century," *Journal of Economic History* 43 (1983): 617–33; Aron, "How the West was Lost," 266. Soltow estimates Kentucky landlessness at 43 to 46 percent in 1800; Stephen Aron sets the landlessness in Kentucky during the 1780s and 1790s at over 50 percent.

17. "Petition of Inhabitants West of the Ohio River," to the Continental Congress, 11 Apr. 1785 (quotation), and "Petition of Kentuckians for Lands North of the Ohio River," to the Continental Congress, n.d. (c. 1786), in Hulbert, ed., *Ohio in the Time of the Confederation*, 105, 139–40; Doddridge, *Notes on the Settlement*, 130, 132 (quotation), 134; for the possession speculators of Kentucky see Aron, "How the West was Lost," 86, 181–82, 227–28, 233–34; Neal O. Hammon, "Land Acquisition on the Kentucky Frontier," *The Register of the Kentucky Historical Society* 78 (1980): 297–321. Aron points out that Daniel Boone was one land-grabber who claimed far more than his family needed. R. E. Harper found that over 90 percent of the landholdings in western Pennsylvania were under 400 acres. See Harper, "The Class Structure of Western Pennsylvania," 45.

18. Gen. Richard Butler, "Journal of General Butler," in Neville B. Craig, ed., *The Olden Time*, 2 vols. (Cincinnati, 1876), 2:437; "Extracts From an Address to the Western Inhabitants," n.d. (c. 1785, quotation), and "Petition

of Kentuckians for Lands North of Ohio River," to Continental Congress, n.d. (c. 1786), in Hulbert, ed., *Ohio in the Time of the Confederation,* 128. On settler localism see also Richard White, *The Middle Ground: Indians, Empires, and Republics in the Great Lakes Region* (New York, 1991), 366–412.

19. Randolph C. Downes, "Ohio's Squatter Governor: William Hogland of Hoglandstown," Ohio State Archaeological and Historical Society, *Quarterly* 43 (1934): 273–82; "Proclamation of Congress on Western Lands," in Hulbert, ed., *Ohio in the Time of the Confederation,* 112; John Emerson, "Advertisement," 12 Mar. 1785, in William H. Smith, ed., *The St. Clair Papers: The Life and Public Services of Arthur St. Clair . . . With his Correspondence and other Papers,* 2 vols. (Cincinnati, 1882), 2:5n.

20. John D. Barnhart, *Valley of Democracy: The Frontier Versus the Plantation in the Ohio Valley, 1775–1818* (Bloomington, IN, 1953), 129–30; Charles A. Hanna, *Historical Collections of Harrison County in the State of Ohio* (New York, 1900), 49–53; John Armstrong to Josiah Harmar, 12 Apr. 1785, in Hulbert, ed., *Ohio in the Time of the Confederation,* 107; White, *The Middle Ground,* 413–68.

21. Aron, "How the West was Lost," 63–72, 82–84; White, *The Middle Ground,* 366–412; Merrell, "Declarations of Independence," 199; Speech of Half King and Captain Pipes, 2 Sept. 1787, Lyman Draper Collection, Series 23U (reel 59), State Historical Society of Wisconsin; Indians quoted in Hendrick Aupaumut, "A Narrative of an Embassy to the Western Indians," Historical Society of Pennsylvania, *Memoirs* 2 (Philadelphia, 1827): 127–28.

22. "Report of the Committee Appointed to Visit the Indians of Oneida & New Stockbridge, 1796," Jeremy Belknap Papers, Massachusetts Historical Society; Nicholas B. Wainwright, ed., "The Opinions of George Croghan on the American Indian," *Pennsylvania Magazine of History and Biography* 71 (1947): 152–59; James H. Howard, *Shawnee! The Ceremonialism of a Native Indian Tribe and Its Cultural Background* (Athens, OH, 1981), 1–60; Michael N. McConnell, "Peoples 'In Between': The Iroquois and the Ohio Indians, 1720–1768," in Daniel K. Richter and James H. Merrell, eds., *Beyond the Covenant Chain: The Iroquois and Their Neighbors in Indian North America, 1600–1800* (Syracuse, NY, 1987), 93–112; Randolph C. Downes, *Council Fires on the Upper Ohio: A Narrative of Indian Affairs in the Upper Ohio Valley until 1795* (Pittsburgh, 1940), 1–41.

23. Anthony F. C. Wallace, *The Death and Rebirth of the Seneca* (New York, 1973), 23–25, 28–39 (Jackson quotation, 38), 49, 125; Merrell, "Declarations of Independence," 206.

24. White, *The Middle Ground,* 366–468; Wallace, *The Death and Rebirth of the Seneca,* 39–45; Merrell, "Declarations of Independence," 201; McConnell, "Peoples 'In Between,' " 101–6; Bert Anson, *The Miami Indians* (Norman, OK, 1970), 3–28; Harvey Lewis Carter, *The Life and Times of Little Turtle: First Sagamore of the Wabash* (Chicago, 1987), 3–64.

25. John Heckewelder, *History, Manners, and Customs of the Indian Nations Who Once Inhabited Pennsylvania and the Neighboring States* (Philadelphia, 1876, repr. of 1819 edition), 101; Wainwright, ed., "The Opin-

ions of George Croghan," 156; White, *The Middle Ground;* Wallace, *The Death and Rebirth of the Seneca,* 46, 49–103.

26. Wallace, *The Death and Rebirth of the Seneca,* 24; Merrell, *The Indians' New World: Catawbas and Their Neighbors from European Contact Through the Era of Removal,* 167–81.

27. Heckewelder, *History, Manners, and Customs of the Indian Nations,* 189; Wainwright, ed., "The Opinions of George Croghan," 158; George S. Snyderman, "Concepts of Land Ownership Among the Iroquois and Their Neighbors," in William N. Fenton, ed., *Symposium on Local Diversity in Iroquois Culture* (Bureau of American Ethnology, *Bulletin Number 149* [Washington, 1951]), 16–18.

28. Heckewelder, *History, Manners, and Customs of the Indian Nations,* 81. For the Indians' ominous sense of identity with the plight of black slaves, see also Aupaumut, "A Narrative of an Embasssy to the Western Indians," 89.

29. Benjamin Lincoln, "Journal of a Treaty Held in 1793, with the Indian Tribes North-West of the Ohio, By Commissioners of the United States," Massachusetts Historical Society, *Collections,* 3d ser., 5 (1836): 139–41; General Henry Knox, Secretary of War, Report to the President, 7 July 1789, U.S. Congress, *ASP* 1:53–54; Shawnee speech, 20 Mar. 1785, in Lyman Draper Collection, Series 23U (reel 59), the State Historical Society of Wisconsin; Heckewelder, *History, Manners, and Customs of the Indian Nations,* 187, 316; Messquakenoe's speech, 7 Oct. 1792, in E. A. Cruikshank, ed., *The Correspondence of Lieut. Governor John Graves Simcoe,* 5 vols. (Toronto, 1923–31), 1:227.

30. Anson, *The Miami Indians,* 20–22, 27–29; Howard, *Shawnee!,* 49–54; Anthony Wayne to the Secretary of War, 14 Aug. 1794, *ASP* 1:490.

31. Wallace, *The Death and Rebirth of the Seneca,* 25; Heckewelder, *History, Manners, and Customs of the Indian Nations,* 102; Lincoln, "Journal of a Treaty Held in 1793," 151–53.

32. Speech of the Five Nations to the Western Indians, Nov. 1786, and Speech of the Shawnee Chiefs, 7 Sept. 1789, Lyman Draper Collection, Series 23U (reel 59), State Historical Society of Wisconsin; Speech of The Snake, 28 Oct. 1792, in Cruikshank, ed., *The Correspondence of Simcoe* 2:242 (quotation regarding the Mohicans); Isabel Thompson Kelsay, *Joseph Brant, 1743–1807: Man of Two Worlds* (Syracuse, NY, 1984), 403; "Address of the Indian Confederacy," 16 Nov. 1792, *ASP* 1:323–24; White, *The Middle Ground,* 413–68; Downes, *Council Fires on the Upper Ohio,* 277–309.

33. White, *The Middle Ground,* 413–68; Downes, *Council Fires on the Upper Ohio,* 179–340; "Speech of the United Indian Nations," 18 Dec. 1786, *ASP* 1:8–9; Carter, *The Life and Times of Little Turtle,* 65–121; Anson, *The Miami Indians,* 58–138; James H. Merrell, "Declarations of Independence," 201–3; Kelsay, *Joseph Brant,* 344–46.

34. Wallace, *The Death and Rebirth of the Seneca,* 155–56; Kelsay, *Joseph Brant,* 295–414; White, *The Middle Ground,* 413–68; Downes, *Council Fires on the Upper Ohio,* 328–29.

35. Downes, *Council Fires on the Upper Ohio*, 317–20; White, *The Middle Ground*, 413–68; Thomas P. Slaughter, *The Whiskey Rebellion: Frontier Epilogue to the American Revolution* (New York, 1986), 105–8.

36. Downes, *Council Fires on the Upper Ohio*, 321–22; "Address of the Indian Confederacy," 16 Nov. 1792, *ASP* 2:323–24. For the Indians' use of kinship terms in diplomacy see Heckewelder, *History, Manners, and Customs of the Indian Nations*, 326; Aupaumut, "A Narrative of an Embassy," 76–77. The Indians were willing to apply kinship terms of superiority to other tribes of longest standing in the region (especially the Delaware and the Wyandot) or to the French and the British, but they balked at conceding inferiority to the Americans who were perceived as unable or unwilling to perform the responsibilities of older brothers or fathers.

37. Henry Knox as Secretary of War, report to President George Washington, 22 Jan. 1791, *ASP* 1:112; Col. Josiah Harmar to Secretary of War Knox, 15 Nov. 1786, in W. H. Smith, *St. Clair Papers* 2:18–19; Slaughter, *The Whiskey Rebellion*, 28–60; Onuf, "Settlers, Settlements, and New States," 171–72.

38. E. James Ferguson, *The Power of the Purse: A History of American Public Finance, 1776–1790* (Chapel Hill, NC, 1961), 289–343; John J. McCusker and Russell R. Menard, *The Economy of British America, 1607–1789* (Chapel Hill, NC, 1985), 373; John C. Miller, *The Federalist Era: 1789–1801* (New York, 1960), 183; Randolph C. Downes, *Frontier Ohio, 1788–1803* (Columbus, OH, 1935), 47–54; Malcolm J. Rohrbough, *The Land Office Business: The Settlement and Administration of American Public Lands, 1789–1837* (New York, 1968), 15; Andrew R. L. Cayton, *The Frontier Republic: Ideology and Politics in the Ohio Country, 1780–1825* (Kent, OH, 1986), 12–32. For the revenue figures see Jones, *License for Empire*, 163.

39. Richard Buel, Jr., *Securing the Revolution: Ideology in American Politics, 1789–1815* (Ithaca, NY, 1972), 94–109.

40. Jack N. Rakove, *The Beginnings of National Politics: An Interpretive History of the Continental Congress* (New York, 1979), 354; Governor Arthur St. Clair to President George Washington, Aug. 1789, and Judge Rufus Putnam to President Washington, 28 Feb. 1791, in Clarence E. Carter, ed., *The Territorial Papers of the United States*, 26 vols. (Washington, DC, 1934–62), 2:209, 338; John Jay to Thomas Jefferson, 24 Apr. 1787, in Henry P. Johnston, ed., *The Correspondence and Public Papers of John Jay*, 4 vols. (New York, 1891), 3:245; Thomas Jefferson to James Monroe, 9 July 1786, *PTJ* 10: 112–13.

41. Federal surveyor quoted in Onuf, "Settlers, Settlements, and New States," 183; Richard Butler, "Journal of General Butler," in Neville B. Craig, ed., *The Olden Time*, 2 vols. (Cincinnati, 1876), 2:507; Arthur St. Clair to John Jay, 13 Dec. 1788, in Carter, ed., *Territorial Papers* 2:168. See also Col. Josiah Harmar to the Secretary of War, Henry Knox, 4 Aug. 1786, and 14 May 1787, in William Henry Smith, ed., *The Life and Public Services of Arthur St. Clair*, 2 vols. (Cincinnati, 1882), 2:16, 22.

42. Henry Knox, Secretary of War, report to President Washington, 7 July

1789, *ASP* 1:53; Merrell, "Declarations of Independence," 210; Onuf, "Settlers, Settlements, and New States," 173–80, 185–87, 190–91.

43. Secretary of War Henry Knox to President George Washington, 22 Jan. 1791, *ASP* 1:112–13; Secretary of War Knox to Congress, 10 July 1787, in Carter, ed., *Territorial Papers* 2:31. President Washington had long subscribed to the ideas articulated in Knox's reports. See George Washington to James Duane, 7 Sept. 1783, in John C. Fitzpatrick, ed., *The Writings of George Washington from the Original Manuscript Sources, 1745–1799*, 39 vols. (Washington, 1931–44), 27:133–39.

44. Arthur St. Clair to President George Washington, Aug. 1789, in Carter, ed., *Territorial Papers* 2:212; Cayton, *The Frontier Republic*, 12–50; Peter S. Onuf, "Liberty, Development, and Union: Visions of the West in the 1780s," *WMQ* 43 (1986): 179–213.

45. Onuf, "Liberty, Development and Union," 179–83; Andrew R. L. Cayton, "The Northwest Ordinance from the Perspective of the Frontier," in Robert M. Taylor, Jr., ed., *The Northwest Ordinance, 1787: A Bicentennial Handbook* (Indianapolis, 1987), 1–23; Peletiah Webster, *Political Essays on the Nature and Operation of Money, Public Finances, and Other Subjects* (Philadelphia, 1791), 494–500.

46. Secretary of War Henry Knox, Reports to the President, 15 June 1789, 7 July 1789, 4 Jan. 1790, and 29 Dec. 1794, in *ASP* 1:12–14 (quotations), 53–54, 60, 543–44; Merrell, "Declarations of Independence," 201–8; Jones, *License for Empire*, 157–79; Wallace, *The Death and Rebirth of the Seneca*, 149–51, 160–62; Francis Paul Prucha, *The Great Father: The United States Government and the American Indians* (Lincoln, NE, 1984), 59–61.

47. Jeanne Ronda and James P. Ronda, "'As They Were Faithful': Chief Hendrick Aupaumut and the Struggle for Stockbridge Survival, 1757–1830," *American Indian Culture and Research Journal* 3 (1979): 43–55; William N. Fenton, ed., "The Journal of James Emlen Kept on a Trip to Canandaigua, New York, September 15 to October 30, 1794 to Attend the Treaty between the United States and The Six Nations," *Ethnohistory* 12 (1965): 279–342. For Henry Knox as a case study of the Federalist world-view see Alan Taylor, *Liberty Men and Great Proprietors: The Revolutionary Settlement on the Maine Frontier, 1760–1820* (Chapel Hill, NC, 1990), 37–47.

48. Secretary of War Henry Knox to President Washington, 7 July 1789, and 4 Jan. 1790, in *ASP* 1:53 (quotation), 60.

49. Secretary of War Henry Knox, Reports to the President, 15 June 1789, and 7 July 1789, in *ASP* 1:12–14 (first two quotations), 53–54 (third quotation); Prucha, *The Great Father*, 60.

50. Downes, *Council Fires on the Upper Ohio*, 322; Henry Knox, as Secretary of War, to the Indian Commissioners, 26 Apr. 1793, *ASP* 1:340; Address of the United States Indian Commissioners to the General Indian Council, 31 July 1793, in *ASP* 1:352–54; Anson, *The Miami Indians*, 122–25.

51. Address of the General Indian Council to the United States Commissioners, 13 Aug. 1793, *ASP* 1:356–57. It is significant that similar senti-

ments were expressed by Messquakenoe, a Shawnee orator speaking on be-half of the Indian confederation in 1792. Messquakenoe's speech, 7 Oct. 1792, in Cruikshank, ed., *The Correspondence of Simcoe* 1:227.

52. For the relationship of class conflict to frontier expansion see Morgan, *American Slavery, American Freedom*, 328–32.

53. Downes, *Council Fires on the Upper Ohio*, 322–23; The United States Commissioners to the Indian Council, 16 Aug. 1793, in *ASP* 1:357; Slaughter, *The Whiskey Rebellion*, 133–42.

54. Downes, *Council Fires on the Upper Ohio*, 323–24; Carter, *The Life and Times of Little Turtle*, 124–55; Anson, *The Miami Indians*, 125–37; Kelsay, *Joseph Brant*, 507–10.

55. "Treaty of Greenville," 3 Aug. 1795, and "Minutes of the Treaty of Greenville," 16 June-10 Aug. 1795, in *ASP* 1:562–63, 564–82.

56. "Treaty of Greenville," 3 Aug. 1795, in *ASP* 1:562–63; Jones, *License for Empire*, 174–75.

57. Malcolm J. Rohrbough, *The Trans-Appalachian Frontier: People, Societies, and Institutions, 1775–1850* (New York, 1978), 63–65.

58. Prucha, *The Great Father*, 31 (Jefferson quotation), 76–78, 191–200; Merrell, "Declarations of Independence," 212–13; Bernard W. Sheehan, *Seeds of Extinction: Jeffersonian Philanthropy and the American Indian* (Chapel Hill, NC, 1973).

59. Rohrbough, *The Land Office Business*, 177–98.

60. Soltow, "Inequality Amidst Abundance," 133–51 (quotation 147).

CHAPTER 4

1. Paul A. Gilje, "The Common People and the Constitution: Popular Culture in Late Eighteenth-Century New York City," in Paul A. Gilje and William Pencak, eds., *New York in the Age of the Constitution 1775–1800* (Rutherford, NJ, 1992), 48–73; Alfred F. Young, "English Plebeian Culture and Eighteenth-Century American Radicalism," in Margaret Jacob and James Jacob, eds., *The Origins of Anglo-American Radicalism* (London, 1984), 185–212.

2. Douglass C. North, *The Economic Growth of the United States, 1790– 1860* (Englewood Cliffs, NJ, 1961), 24–58.

3. *Works* 4:85–86, 449–50.

4. *PJM* 14:168, 244–46.

5. Richard Henry Dana, *Two Years Before the Mast* (New York, 1936; orig. pub. 1840), 118–19.

6. Herman Melville, *White Jacket: or The World in a Man-of-War*, Harrison Hayford et al., eds. (Evanston, IL, 1970; orig. pub. 1850), 226.

7. George Little, *Life on the Ocean; or Twenty Years at Sea*, 14th ed. (New York, 1843), 369–77.

8. Ibid., 374.

9. Horace Lane, *The Wandering Boy, Careless Sailor, and Result of Inconsideration. A True Narrative* (Skaneateles, NY, 1839), 27.

10. Samuel Leech, *Thirty Years From Home, or A Voice From the Main Deck* (Boston, 1843), 230.

11. Joshua Penny, *The Life and Adventures of Joshua Penny* (New York, 1815), 39.

12. Nathaniel Ames, *Nautical Reminiscences* (Providence, RI, 1832), 38.

13. William Widger, "The Diary of William Widger of Marblehead, Kept at Mill Prison, England, 1781," *EIHC* 73 (1937): 347. See also Jesse Lemisch, "Listening to the 'Inarticulate': William Widger's Dream and the Loyalties of American Revolutionary Seamen in British Prisons," *Journal of Social History* 3 (1969): 1–29.

14. Thomas Gerry to Helen Gerry, 26 Sept. 1816, Gerry-Knight Papers II, 1768–1853, Massachusetts Historical Society.

15. Christopher Hawkins, *The Adventures of Christopher Hawkins*, Introduction and Notes by Charles I. Bushnell (New York, 1864), 37.

16. Penny, *Life and Adventures*, 39.

17. *Sailor's Magazine and Naval Journal* 2 (Dec. 1829): 112.

18. Leech, *Thirty Years From Home*, 65, 110–11.

19. *Sailor's Magazine and Naval Journal* 2: 111–13.

20. Ames, *Nautical Reminiscences*, 38.

21. *A Full and Particular Account of the Trial of Francisco Dos Santos* (New York, 1806).

22. Henry Chase, "Visits to families of mariners From 18 Dec. 1821 to 18 Jan. 1822," Diary, ms., New-York Historical Society.

23. Daniel Vickers, "Nantucket Whalemen in the Deep-Sea Fishery: The Changing Anatomy of an Early American Labor Force," *JAH* 72 (1985): 277–96; W. Jeffrey Bolster, "'To Feel like a Man': Black Seamen in the Northern States, 1800–1860," *JAH* 76 (1990): 1173–99.

24. Benjamin Morrell, Jr., *A Narrative of Four Voyages* (New York, 1832), xi.

25. Dana, *Two Years Before The Mast*, 53.

26. Herman Melville, *Redburn, His First Voyage: Being the Sailor-boy Confessions and Reminiscences of the Son-of-a-Gentleman in the Merchant Service*, Harrison Hayford et al., eds. (Evanston, IL, 1969; orig. pub. 1849), 52, 56–62, 66, 257–58.

27. J. Ross Browne, *Etchings of a Whaling Cruise*, John Seelye, ed., (Cambridge, MA, 1968; orig. pub. New York, 1846), 24, 305–16.

28. Ames, *Nautical Reminiscences*, 73–74.

29. Browne, *Etchings of a Whaling Cruise*, 315, 356; Leech, *Thirty Years From Home*, 74; William McNally, *Evils and Abuses in the Naval and Merchant Service, Exposed* (Boston, 1839), 121; Melville, *Redburn*, 66; Moses Smith, *Naval Scenes in the Last War* (Boston, 1846), 42.

30. McNally, *Evils and Abuses*, 71.

31. For good discussion of relationships and conditions aboard ship see Marcus Rediker, *Between the Devil and the Deep Blue Sea: Merchant Seamen, Pirates, and the Anglo-American Maritime World, 1700–1750* (Cam-

bridge, 1987); and Margaret Scott Creighton, "The Private Life of Jack Tar: Sailors at Sea in the Nineteenth Century," (Ph.D. diss., Boston Univ., 1985).

32. James Durand, *An Able Seaman of 1812: His Adventures on "Old Ironsides" and as an Impressed Sailor in the British Navy,* George S. Brooks, ed. (New Haven, CT, 1926; orig. pub. Rochester, NY, 1820), 38.

33. Caleb Foote, ed., "Reminiscences of the Revolution: Prison Letters and Sea Journal of Caleb Foot: Born, 1750; Died 1787," *EIHC* 26 (1889): 90–122.

34. Lane, *The Wandering Boy,* 105; McNally, *Evils and Abuses,* 71–72, 76–77.

35. Dana, *Two Years Before the Mast,* 75–76.

36. Capt. John Manly to Hector McNeal, Boston, 6 May 1777, Boston Marine Society, ms., Massachusetts Historical Society.

37. Robert Wilden Neeser, ed., *Letters and Papers Relating to the Cruises of Gustavus Conyngham, Captain of the Continental Navy, 1777–1779* 1 (New York, 1915): 6.

38. Amos A. Evans, *Journal Kept on Board the Frigate Constitution, 1812* (Lincoln, MA, 1967; orig. pub. 1895), 382, 472–73.

39. William James Morgan, ed., *Naval Documents of the American Revolution* 7 (Washington, 1976): 1004–5.

40. [Sir John Barrow], *The Eventful History of the Mutiny and Piratical Seizure of H.M.S. Bounty: Its Causes and Consequences* (London, 1831); Little, *Life on the Ocean,* 132.

41. Rediker, *Between the Devil and the Deep Blue Sea,* 254–87; Rediker, "'Under the Banner of King Death': The Social World of Anglo-American Pirates, 1716 to 1726," *WMQ* 38 (1981): 203–27.

42. Little, *Life on the Ocean,* 172.

43. McNally, *Evils and Abuses,* 71–72; William Lay and Cyrus M. Hussey, *A Narrative of the Mutiny On Board the Whaleship Globe,* intro. by Edouard A. Stackpole (New York, 1963; orig. pub. New London, CT, 1828).

44. [George Jones], *Sketches of Naval Life, With Notices of Men, Manners and Scenery . . . By A "Civilian"* 1 (New Haven, 1829): 218.

45. Dana, *Two Years Before the Mast,* 323–25.

46. [Joseph Valpey, Jr.], *Journal of Joseph Valpey, Jr. of Salem, November 1813-April 1815: With Other Papers Relating to His Experience in Dartmoor Prison* (n.p., 1922), 7, 9, 10.

47. [Josiah Cobb], *A Green Hand's First Cruise* 1 (Boston, 1841): 104–17, 175; Ebenezer Fox, *The Adventures of Ebenezer Fox in the Revolutionary War* (Boston, 1838), 87; [Valpey], *Journal,* 9; [Benjamin Waterhouse], *A Journal of a Young Man of Massachusetts* (Lexington, KY, 1816), 9.

48. Little, *Life on the Ocean,* 125.

49. Edward Cutbush, *Observations on the Means of Preserving the Health of Soldiers and Sailors* (Philadelphia, 1808), 127–28.

50. For a discussion of this ritual see Knut Weibust, *Deep Sea Sailors: A Study in Maritime Ethnology,* 2d ed. (Stockholm, 1976), 169–82; Henning

Henningsen, *Crossing the Equator: Sailor's Baptism and Other Initiation Rites* (Copenhagen, 1961); Creighton, "The Private Life of Jack Tar," 119–38. For an example of this ritual see Samuel Curson, "Journal on Voyage to the Northwest Coast, 1798–1799," photocopy, Massachusetts Historical Society. For a general discussion of ritual and further citations see Paul A. Gilje, *The Road to Mobocracy: Popular Disorder in New York City, 1763–1834* (Chapel Hill, NC, 1987), 16–30.

51. John Lax and William Pencak, "The Knowles Riot and the Crisis of the 1740's in Massachusetts," *Perspectives in American History* 10 (Cambridge, MA, 1976): 163–214; Gary B. Nash, *The Urban Crucible: Social Change, Political Consciousness, and the Origins of the American Revolution* (Cambridge, MA, 1979), 221–24, 229, 239, 261, 266, 371; Gilje, *Road to Mobocracy*, 12–13, 21, 23–24. See also Dora Mae Clark, "The Impressment of Seamen in the American Colonies," in *Essays in Colonial American History Presented to C. M. Andrews* (New Haven, CT, 1931), 198–224.

52. Penny, *Life and Adventures*, 39–42.

53. Clement Cleveland Sawtell, "Impressment of American Seamen by the British," *EIHC* 76 (1940): 314–41; George Selement, "Impressment and the American Merchant Marine, 1782–1812," *Mariner's Mirror* 59 (1973): 409–18; James Fulton Zimmerman, *Impressment of American Seaman* (Port Washington, NY, 1966; orig. pub. New York, 1925). Poor records and polyglot crews make it almost impossible to determine how many American sailors were pressed into the British navy. Zimmerman discussed the issue in detail. He believed almost 10,000 men were taken from American ships between 1793 and 1815. Zimmermann, *Impressment*, 259–75.

54. Penny, *Life and Adventures*, 11–12.

55. Durand, *An Able Seaman of 1812*, 49–86.

56. Ibid., 75–76.

57. Charles Andrews, *The Prisoner's Memoirs, or Dartmoor Prison* (New York, 1815), 121, 138–39, 141–42.

58. Albert Greene, *Recollections of the Jersey Prison Ship: From the Manuscript of Capt. Thomas Dring*, intro. by Lawrence H. Leder (New York, 1961; orig. pub. Providence, RI, 1829), 14–20, 39, 84–88.

59. Lemisch, "Listening to the 'Inarticulate'," 1–29; Lemisch, "Jack Tar in the Streets: Merchant Seamen in the Politics of Revolutionary America," *WMQ* 25 (1968): 371–407.

60. Andrews, *The Prisoner's Memoirs*, 74–75.

61. Ibid., 39, 44–45; [Cobb], *A Green Hand's First Cruise* 2:137; Leech, *Thirty Years From Home*, 202; Benjamin F. Palmer, *The Diary of Benjamin F. Palmer: While a Prisoner on Board English War Ships at Sea, in the Prison at Melville Island and at Dartmoor* (n.p., 1914), 19–23, 244–47; Jeduthun Upton, "Log of Jeduthun Upton, 'Schooner *Polly*', Salem, Massachusetts, 1812–1813," 19, typescript, Massachusetts Historical Society; [Waterhouse], *A Journal of a Young Man of Massachusetts*, 54–56, 174–81. See also Reginald Horseman, "The Paradox of Dartmoor Prison," *American Heritage* 26 (1975): 12–17, 85; and Robin Fabel, "Self-Help in Dartmoor: Black and

White Prisoners in the War of 1812," *Journal of the Early Republic* 9 (1989): 165–90.

62. Andrews, *The Prisoner's Memoirs*, 137–324; Anonymous, *Dartmoor Massacre* (Pittsfield, MA, 1815); [Cobb], *A Green Hand's First Cruise* 2: 188–281; [Simeon Coleman], *A Concise Narrative of the Barbarous Treatment Experienced By American Prisoners in England and the West Indies, &c.* (Danville, VT, 1816); John Melish, *A Description of Dartmoor Prison with an Account of the Massacre of the Prisoners* (Philadelphia, 1816); Palmer, *The Diary*, 155–200, 240–66; Nathaniel Pierce, "Journal of Nathaniel Pierce of Newburyport, Kept at Dartmoor Prison, 1814–1815," *EIHC* 73 (1937): 24–59; [John Hunter Waddell], *The Dartmoor Massacre* [Boston?, 1815?]; [Waterhouse], *A Journal of a Young Man of Massachusetts*, 192–234.

63. Norman S. Cohen, "The Philadelphia Election Riot of 1742," *Pennsylvania Magazine of History and Biography* 92 (1968): 306–19; William T. Parsons, "The Bloody Election of 1742," *Pennsylvania History* 36 (1969): 290–306.

64. Gilje, *Road to Mobocracy*, 30–35, 47–48; Lemisch, "Jack Tar in the Streets," *WMQ* 25 (1968): 371–407.

65. Steven J. Rosswurm, "'That They were Grown Unruly': The Crowd and Lower-Classes in Philadelphia, 1765–1780" (M.A. thesis, Northern Illinois Univ., 1974), 58–61; Rosswurm, *Arms, Country, and Class: The Philadelphia Militia and "Lower Sort" During the American Revolution, 1775–1783* (New Brunswick, NJ, 1987), 30–34.

66. Lemisch, "Jack Tar in the Streets," 371–407; Gilje, *Road to Mobocracy*, 52–58; Dirk Hoerder, *Crowd Action in Revolutionary Massachusetts, 1765–1780* (New York, 1977), 223–34.

67. Gilje, *Road to Mobocracy*, 37–68; Lemisch, "Jack Tar in the Streets," 371–407; Hoerder, *Crowd Action, passim*; Nash, *Urban Crucible*, 292–384.

68. Alfred F. Young, "George Robert Twelves Hewes (1742–1840): A Boston Shoemaker and the Memory of the American Revolution," *WMQ* 38 (1981): 561–623.

69. Gilje, *Road to Mobocracy*, 178–88.

70. Hawkins, *Adventures*, 24.

71. Penny, *Life and Adventures*, 26.

72. Smith, *Naval Scenes*, 6.

73. Leech, *Thirty Years From Home*, 183, 191.

74. *A Narrative of the Capture of the United States Brig Vixen* (New York, 1813), 26–30; Andrews, *The Prisoner's Memoirs*, 44–45, 66, 114–15; [Cobb], *A Green Hand's First Cruise* 2:137, 191; [Charles Calvert Egerton], *The Journal of an Unfortunate Prisoner, on Board the British Prison Ship Loyalist* (Baltimore, 1813), 12; Leech, *Thirty Years From Home*, 202; Palmer, *The Diary*, 20–32, 109, 117, 244–47; [Waterhouse], *A Journal of a Young Man of Massachusetts*, 58, 90–94, 174–81; Paul A. Gilje, ed., "A Sailor Prisoner of War During the War of 1812," *Maryland Historical Magazine* 85 (1990): 58–72.

75. [Waterhouse], *A Journal of a Young Man of Massachusetts*, 84–85, 239.

76. Ibid., 239.

77. Eugene Jackman, "Efforts Made Before 1825 to Ameliorate the Lot of the American Seaman: With Emphasis on His Moral Regeneration," *American Neptune* 24 (1964): 109–18; Hugh H. Davis, "The American Seamen's Friend Society and the American Sailor, 1828–1838, *American Neptune* 39 (1979): 45–57; George Sidney Webster, *The Seamen's Friend: A Sketch of the American Seamen's Friend Society, By Its Secretary* (New York, 1932); Harold D. Langley, *Social Reform in the United States Navy, 1798–1862* (Urbana, IL, 1967).

78. Ibid., 55, 57.

79. *Sailor's Magazine and Naval Journal* 1–6 (1828–1834): *passim*.

80. Lane, *The Wandering Boy*, 210–11.

81. Fox, *The Adventures*, vi.

82. Richard M. Dorson, ed., *America Rebels: Narratives of the Patriots* (New York, 1953); see also Young, "George Robert Twelves Hewes," 561–623.

83. Dana, *Two Years Before the Mast*; James Fenimore Cooper, *The Pilot: A Tale of the Sea*, Kay Seymour House, ed. (Albany, NY, 1986; orig. pub. New York, 1824); id., *Ned Myers: or, A life Before the Mast* (Philadelphia, 1843); Nathaniel Hawthorne, ed., [Benjamin F. Browne], *The Yarn of a Yankee Privateer* (New York, 1926); Herman Melville, *Israel Potter: His Fifty Years Exile*, Harrison Hayford et al., eds. (Evanston, IL, 1982); Melville, *White-Jacket*.

84. J. Ross Browne to Richard Henry Dana, Jr., 9 Nov. 1846, Dana Family Papers, I, Box 10, 1845–48, Massachusetts Historical Society.

85. J. G. Hodge to Richard Henry Dana, Jr., 15 Oct. 1842, Dana Family Papers, I, Box 8, 1841–42, Massachusetts Historical Society.

86. Joseph G. Clark, *Lights and Shadows of Sailor Life, As Exemplified in Fifteen Years' Experience* (Boston, 1848), 311.

87. McNally, *Evils and Abuses*, 130–31, 95.

CHAPTER 5

1. Thomas Paine, *Common Sense and The Crisis* (Garden City, NY, 1960), 18.

2. Quoted in Merrill D. Peterson, *Thomas Jefferson and the New Nation* (New York, 1970), 145.

3. Letter to W. T. Barry, 4 Aug. 1522, in William C. Rives and Philip R. Fendall, eds., *Letters and Other Writing of James Madison* (Philadelphia, 1865), 3:276.

4. Bernard Bailyn, *The Ideological Origins of the American Revolution* (Cambridge, MA, 1967); Caroline Robbins, *The Eighteenth Century Commonwealthman: Studies in the Transmission, Development, and Circumstance of English Liberal Thought from the Restoration of Charles II until the War with the Thirteen Colonies* (Cambridge, MA, 1959); Isaac Kram-

nick, *Republicanism and bourgeois radicalism: political ideology in late eighteenth-century England and America* (Ithaca, NY, 1990).

5. Arthur B. Ferguson, *The Articulate Citizen and the English Renaissance* (Durham, NC, 1965); Clyde Augustus Duniway, *The Development of Freedom of the Press in Massachusetts* (Cambridge, MA, 1906), 5n.

6. Ferguson, *Articulate Citizen*, 142–43.

7. Duniway, *Development of Freedom of the Press*, 32.

8. Ferguson, *Articulate Citizen*, 157.

9. Letter to Commissioners of Trade and Plantations, in William Waller Hening, ed., *The Statutes at Large; Being a Collection of All the Laws of Virginia, from the First Session of the Legislature, in the Year 1619*, 13 vols. (New York, 1810–23), 2:517.

10. James Sutherland, *The Restoration Newspaper and its Development* (Cambridge, 1986), 1–2; J.R. Pole, *The Gift of Government: Political Responsibility from the English Restoration to American Independence* (Athens, GA, 1983), chap. 4.

11. David Johnston, *The Rhetoric of Leviathan: Thomas Hobbes and the Politics of Cultural Transformation* (Princeton, 1986), 125, 127–29.

12. R. Astbury, "The Renewal of the Licensing Act in 1693 and its Lapse in 1695," *Library*, 5th ser., 33 (1978): 296–322.

13. Jeremy Black, *The English Press in the Eighteenth Century* (Philadelphia, 1987), 8, 10, 11; Graham Gibbs, "Press and Public Opinion: Perspective," in *Liberty Secured? Britain Before and After 1688*, J. R. Jones, ed. (Stanford, 1992), 231–64.

14. J. L. DeLolme, *The Constitution of England; or an Account of the English Government; in which it is Compared both with the Republican Form of Government, and the Other Monarchies of Europe* (new ed., corrected, London, 1800 [first pub. 1775]), 410; Duniway, *The Development of Freedom of the Press*, 83; Larry D. Eldridge, *A Distant Heritage: The Growth of Free Speech in Early America* (New York, 1994). On the early history of American newspapers see Charles E. Clark, *The Public Prints: The Newspaper in Anglo-American Culture, 1665–1740* (New York, 1994).

15. Quoted in Black, *The English Press*, 298, 303.

16. Quoted in Richard D. Altick, *The English Common Reader: A Social History of the Mass Reading Public, 1800–1900* (Chicago, 1957), 31–32.

17. M. G. Jones, *The Charity School Movement* (Cambridge, 1938), 102.

18. Bernard Mandeville, *The Fable of the Bees: Or, Private Vices, Public Benefits*, in 2 vols., with a commentary, critical, historical, and explanatory by F. B. Kaye (Oxford, 1924), 1:269.

19. Ibid., 311.

20. Ibid., 269.

21. R. A. Houston, *Scottish Literacy and Scottish Identity* (Cambridge, 1985), chaps. 4, 6, 7.

22. [Richard Steele], *The Spectator*, No. 294, 6 Feb. 1712, in Donald F. Bond, ed., *The Spectator* (Oxford, 1965), 3:48, 49. According to the bishop of Peterborough, who was recalling the Civil War of the 1640s, a "Forerunner

of Ruin, [was] the Spiriting up the common People into Riots and Tumults, and so pushing them forward to Insurrections and Rebellion; *they were taught Grievances, and a Right to have them redressed* in their own Way: Justice was to be a Demand in the Streets; *the meanest of the People were instructed* and managed to gather in the Night, and to appear at Noon-Day; and to besiege Palaces and Parliament-Houses." (White, Lord Bishop of Peterborough, *A Sermon Preached before the Lords Spiritual and Temporal, in the Abbey-Church at Westminster, the 30th of January 1719* [London, 1720], 25–26, italics added).

23. Isaac Kramnick, *Republicanism and Bourgeois Radicalism*, and his "Republicanism Revisited: The Case of James Burgh," *The Republican Synthesis Revisited*, Milton M. Klein et al., eds. (Worcester, MA 1992), 19–36.

24. Lawrence A. Cremin, *American Education: The Colonial Experience, 1607–1783* (New York, 1970), 421–41.

25. Quoted in *The Oxford Dictionary of Quotations*, 2d ed. (London, 1962), 352.

26. William Livingston and Others, *The Independent Reflector*, Milton M. Klein, ed. (Cambridge, MA, 1963), 419–20. See also Richard Buel, Jr., "Freedom of the Press in Revolutionary America: The Evolution of Libertarianism, 1760–1820," in Bernard Bailyn and John Hench, eds., *The Press and the American Revolution* (Worcester, MA, 1980), 59–97.

27. Livingston, *Independent Reflector*, 420–21.

28. Boston Town Meeting, 24 May 1764, in *A Report of the Record Commissioners of the City of Boston, Containing the Boston Town Records, 1758 to 1769* (Boston, 1886), 121–22.

29. The political mobilization of the people has been treated extensively in the scholarly literature, most recently by Gordon S. Wood in *The Radicalism of the American Revolution* (New York, 1992), pt. 3. See also Richard D. Brown, *Revolutionary Politics in Massachusetts: The Boston Committee of Correspondence and the Towns, 1772–1774* (Cambridge, MA, 1970); Ronald P. Formisano, *The Transformation of Political Culture: Massachusetts Parties, 1790s-1840s* (New York, 1983); Edmund S. Morgan, *Inventing the People: The Rise of Popular Sovereignty in England and America* (New York, 1988); J. R. Pole, *The Gift of Government: Political Responsibility from the English Restoration to American Independence* (Athens, GA, 1983) and *Political Representation in England and the Origins of the American Republic* (New York, 1966); Richard Alan Ryerson, *The Revolution is Now Begun: The Radical Committees of Philadelphia, 1765–1776* (Philadelphia, 1978); Chilton Williamson, *American Suffrage: From Property to Democracy, 1760–1860* (Princeton, NJ, 1960).

30. See Lois G. Schwoerer, "Liberty of the Press and Public Opinion: 1660–1695," and Gibbs, "Press and Public Opinion," in Jones, ed., *Liberty Secured?*, 199–230 and 231–64.

31. Young to Hugh Hughes, Boston, 21 Dec. 1772, Miscellaneous Bound Manuscript Collection, Massachusetts Historical Society.

32. Pole, *Gift of Government*, 130.

33. See John C. Davenport, "Making Public Matters Public: The Construction of the Spectators' Gallery in the Colonial Massachusetts House of Representatives," *Retrospection* 6, no. 2 (1993): 6-22. Adams quoted in Brown, *Revolutionary Politics in Massachusetts*, 43.

34. Harry S. Stout, "Religion, Communications, and the Ideological Origins of the American Revolution," *WMQ* 34 (1977): 519-41.

35. Ibid., 36; Bernard Bailyn, *The Ordeal of Thomas Hutchinson* (Cambridge, MA, 1974), 199-201.

36. Bailyn, *Ordeal*, 218-19.

37. Pauline Maier, *From Resistance to Revolution: Colonial Radicals and the Development of American Opposition to Britain, 1765-1776* (New York, 1972).

38. Richard Alan Ryerson, *The Revolution is Now Begun: The Radical Committees of Philadelphia, 1765-1776* (Philadelphia, 1978); Gary B. Nash, *The Urban Crucible: Social Change, Political Consciousness, and the Origins of the American Revolution* (Cambridge, MA, 1979), 148-54.

39. Eric Foner, *Tom Paine and Revolutionary America* (New York, 1976).

40. Peter Shaw, *The Character of John Adams* (Chapel Hill, NC, 1976); Page Smith, *John Adams* (New York, 1962).

41. Philadelphia, 31 May 1787, James Madison's notes, in Max Farrand, ed., *The Records of the Federal Convention of 1787*, rev. ed. (New Haven, 1937), 1:48.

42. Barbara Clark Smith, "Food Rioters and the American Revolution," *WMQ* 51 (1994): 3-38.

43. London *Public Ledger*, quoted in *Connecticut Courant* (Hartford), 20 Jan. 1766, 1:1.

44. *General Advertiser, and Political, Commercial, Agricultural and Literary Journal*, 1st issue, 1790, ed. Benjamin Franklin Bache, who was raised under the supervision of his grandfather Benjamin Franklin. Quoted in Jeffrey A. Smith, *Printers and Press Freedom: The Ideology of Early American Journalism* (New York, 1988), 158.

45. Letter of 1792 to Washington quoted in Smith, *Printers and Press Freedom*, 40.

46. 1794. Quoted in ibid., 89.

47. John Adams to Samuel Adams, New York, 18 Oct. 1790, in Charles Francis Adams, ed., *The Works of John Adams* (Boston, 1851), 6:414-16.

48. Samuel Adams to John Adams, Boston, 25 Nov. 1790, in Harry A. Cushing, ed., *The Writings of Samuel Adams* (repr. New York, 1968), 4:347, 349.

49. *PJM* 14:170.

50. The law is reprinted in James Morton Smith, *Freedom's Fetters: The Alien and Sedition Laws and American Civil Liberties* (Ithaca, NY, 1966), 442.

51. Zephaniah S. Moore, *An Oration on the Anniversary of the Independence of the United States of America . . . July 5, 1802* (Worcester, MA, 1802), 16.

52. Massachusetts Constitution of 1780, in *The Popular Sources of Political Authority: Documents on the Massachusetts Constitution of 1780*, Oscar and Mary F. Handlin, eds. (Cambridge, MA., 1966), 442–43.

53. Ibid., 446.

54. Ibid., 446.

55. Ibid., 465.

56. Ibid., 467.

57. *PTJ* 2:526–35.

58. Ibid., 526–27.

59. *Notes on the State of Virginia*, in Paul Leicester Ford, ed., *The Writings of Thomas Jefferson* (New York, 1904), 4:61, 64.

60. The bill which Jefferson drafted provided that in alternate years the visitors of each of the two regions would select from all of the "seniors" (one in each school), "one among the said seniors of the best learning and most hopeful disposition . . . to proceed to William and Mary College, there to be educated, boarded, and clothed, three years . . . paid by the Treasurer." (*PTJ* 2:533.) Later, when Jefferson described the plan in his *Notes on the State of Virginia*, he said that the plan aimed to send 10 students to William and Mary each year. (*Writings* 2:203–4.) James Madison to Thomas Jefferson, New York, 15 Feb. 1787, *PTJ* 11:152.

61. Madison to Jefferson, 15 Feb. 1787; also *PTJ* 2:535n.

62. Rhys Isaac, *The Transformation of Virginia, 1740–1790* (Chapel Hill, NC, 1982), 294–95; Peterson, *Thomas Jefferson*, 150. In Georgia a plan similar to Virginia's met an even more unfortunate fate. See Keith Whitescarver, "Creating Citizens for the Republic: Education in Georgia, 1776–1810," *Journal of the Early Republic 13* (Winter, 1993): 455–79.

63. Henry Steele Commager and Milton Cantor, eds., *Documents of American History*, 10th ed., vol. 1 to 1898 (Englewood Cliffs, NJ, 1988), 124, 131.

64. Quoted in Frederick Rudolph, ed., *Essays on Education in the Early Republic* (Cambridge, MA, 1965), xv.

65. Ibid., xv; Samuel Harrison Smith, *Remarks on Education* (1798), in ibid., 190, 210; Samuel Knox, *An Essay on the Best System of Liberal Education* (1799), ibid., 311.

66. James McLachlan, "Classical Names, American Identities: Some Notes on College Students and the Classical Tradition in the 1770s," in *Classical Traditions in Early America*, John W. Eadie, ed. (Ann Arbor, MI, 1976), 81–98; Stephen Botein, "Cicero as a Role Model for Early American Lawyers: A Case Study in Classical Influence," *Classical Journal 73* (1977–78): 313–21; James M. Farrell, "*Pro Militibus Oratio*: John Adams's Imitation of Cicero in the Boston Massacre Trial," *Rhetorica 9* (Summer 1991): 233–49.

67. Benjamin Rush, *A Plan for The Establishment of Public Schools and the Diffusion of Knowledge in Pennsylvania* (Philadelphia, 1786), in Rudolph, ed., *Essays on Education in the Early Republic*, 21–22; Linda K. Ker-

ber, *Women of the Republic: Intellect and Ideology in Revolutionary America* (Chapel Hill, NC, 1980), chap. 7; Jan Lewis, "The Republican Wife: Virtue and Seduction in the Early Republic," *WMQ* 44 (1987): 689–721. The problematic understanding of women's citizenship status is discussed in Linda K. Kerber, "The Paradox of Women's Citizenship in the Early Republic: The Case of *Martin vs. Massachusetts*, 1805," *AHR* 97, no. 2 (Apr. 1992): 349–78, and in her "The Revolutionary Generation: Ideology, Politics, and Culture in the Early Republic," in Eric Foner, ed., *The New American History* (Philadelphia, 1990), 30.

68. Carl F. Kaestle, *Pillars of The Republic: Common Schools and American Society, 1780–1860* (New York, 1983), chaps. 1–3.

69. Ibid.

70. Peter Onuf, "State Politics and Republican Virtue: Religion, Education and Morality in Early American Federalism," in Paul Finkelman and Stephen E. Gottlieb, eds., *Toward a Usable Past: An Examination of the Origins and Duplications of State Protections of Liberty* (Athens, GA, 1991), 91–116.

71. *PTJ* 2:535n.

72. Peterson, *Thomas Jefferson*, 981.

73. See James Willard Hurst, "The Release of Energy," in his *Law and the Conditions of Freedom* (Madison, WI, 1956), 3–32; Richard B. Kielbowicz, *News in the Mail: The Press, Post Office, and Public Information, 1700–1860s* (New York, 1989); Richard R. John, *Spreading the Word: The American Postal System from Franklin to Morse* (Cambridge, MA, 1995), chap. 2.

74. Quoted in Sherman Williams, "Jedidiah Peck: The Father of the Public School System of the State of New York," *Quarterly Journal of the New York State Historial Association* 1 (1920): 221, 222.

75. Ibid., 226, 236–39.

76. Ibid., 236.

77. Richard D. Brown, *Knowledge is Power: The Diffusion of Information in Early America, 1700–1865* (New York, 1989), conclusion.

78. Ibid.

79. Marian Barber Stowell, *Early American Almanacs: The Colonial Weekday Bible* (New York, 1977); James A. Bear, Jr., and Mary Caperton Bear, *A Checklist of Virginia Almanacs, 1732–1850* (Charlottesville, VA, 1962). See also George L. Kittredge, *The Old Farmer and His Almanac* (Boston, 1904).

80. James D. Watkinson, "Useful Knowledge? Concepts, Values, and Access in American Education, 1776–1840," *History of Education Quarterly* 30 (1990): 351–70; the reference to *The Christian Herald and Seaman's Magazine* was provided by Paul Gilje.

81. Gordon S. Wood, "The Democratization of Mind in the American Revolution," *Leadership in The American Revolution* (Washington, 1974); id., *Radicalism of the American Revolution* (New York, 1992); Neil McKendrick, "Commercialization and the Economy," in McKendrick, John Brewer, and J. H. Plumb, *The Birth of a Consumer Society: The Commer-*

cialization of Eighteenth-Century England (Bloomington, IN, 1982), 9–194. Richard L. Bushman, *The Refinement of America: Persons, Houses, Cities* (New York, 1992), xv, xvi, and pt. 2 ("Respectability, 1790–1850."): *passim.*

82. Watkinson, "Useful Knowledge? Concepts, Values, and Access in American Education, 1776–1840," 355.

83. Ibid., 352.

84. Brown, *Knowledge is Power*, chap. 8; Louise Chipley, "William Bentley, Journalist of the Early Republic," *Essex Institute Historical Collections* 123 (1987): 331–47.

85. Watkinson, "Useful Knowledge?," 359–62, 366, 370.

86. *Papers of Benjamin Franklin*, Leonard W. Labaree et al., eds. (New Haven, CT, 1960), 2:380–83. This proposal would soon lead to the formation of the American Philosophical Society.

87. Nathan O. Hatch, "Elias Smith and the Rise of Religious Journalism in the Early Republic," in William L. Joyce et al., eds., *Printing and Society in Early America* (Worcester, MA, 1983), 250–77; Nathan O. Hatch, *The Democratization of American Christianity* (New Haven, CT, 1989), chaps. 2, 3, 5, 6; David Paul Nord, "The Evangelical Origins of Mass Media in America, 1815–1835," *Journalism Monographs*, no. 88 (May 1984); Peter J. Wosh, *Spreading the Word: The Bible Business in Nineteenth-Century America* (Ithaca, NY, 1994).

88. William J. Gilmore, *Reading Becomes a Necessity of Life: Material and Cultural Life in Rural New England, 1780–1835* (Knoxville, TN, 1989); Richard D. Brown, *Knowledge is Power*, conclusion.

89. Bacon's general influence, and his impact on Thomas Jefferson and the idea of "useful knowledge," is discussed in Joseph F. Kett, "Education," in *Thomas Jefferson: A Reference Biography*, Merrill D. Peterson, ed. (New York, 1986), 244. Richard D. Brown, "The Emergence of Urban Society in Rural Massachusetts, 1760–1820," *JAH* 61 (1974): 29–51; Alexis de Tocqueville, *Democracy in America*, Phillips Bradley, ed., 2 vols. (New York, 1945).

90. Joseph F. Kett and Patricia A. McClung, "Book Culture in Post-Revolutionary Virginia," *Proceedings of the American Antiquarian Society* 94, pt. 1 (1984): 97–147.

91. American Bible Society, *Resolutions of the American Bible Society, and an Address to the Christian Public, on the subject of supplying the Whole World with the Sacred Scripture; within a Definite Period* (New York, 1833), 1, 5.

92. Aaron Bancroft, *The Importance of Education, Illustrated in an Oration, Delivered before the Trustees, Preceptors, and Students of Leicester Academy, on the 4th of July, 1806* (Worcester, MA, 1806), 11.

93. Moore, *An Oration on the Anniversary*, 24.

94. Janet Duitsman Cornelius, *When I Can Read My Title Clear: Literacy, Slavery, and Religion in the Antebellum South* (Columbia, SC, 1991).

95. Ibid., 14, 16–17.

96. Harlow Sheidley, "Sectional Nationalism: The Culture and Politics of the Massachusetts Conservative Elite, 1815–1836" (Ph.D. diss., Univ. of

Conn., 1990). *American Oratory, or Selections from the Speeches of Eminent Americans.* Compiled by a Member of the Philadelphia Bar (Philadelphia, 1836).

97. Daniel Webster, in *American Oratory*, 449.

98. Ibid., 447.

99. Ibid., 444–45.

100. Story, *A Discourse, Pronounced at Cambridge, before the Phi Beta Kappa Society . . . on the thirty-first day of August, 1826*, in *American Oratory*, 507–8.

101. Ibid., 508.

102. Reverend Samuel Stillman, 6 Feb. 1788, quoted in *Connecticut Courant*, 31 Mar. 1788, 2; O[rsamus] C[ook] Merrill, *The Happiness of America. An Oration Delivered at Shaftesbury, Vermont* (Bennington, VT, 1804), 13. This reference courtesy of Peter Onuf.

103. Ibid., 509.

CHAPTER 6

1. Cited by Stephen A. Conrad, "Polite Foundation: Citizenship and Common Sense in James Wilson's Republican Theory," *The Supreme Court Review* (1984), 374.

2. Ibid.

3. James Kent, *An Introductory Lecture to a Course of Law Lectures* (New York, 1794), 3–4.

4. Ibid., 4.

5. Thomas Jefferson, "Autobiography," in *Works* 1:66–67.

6. It remains a commonplace of historians that the Revolution had little or no impact on private law, especially compared with public law. For the classic statement that independence "had virtually no effect upon the system of private law" in one region, see Richard B. Morris, "Legalism *versus* Revolutionary Doctrine in New England," *New England Quarterly* 4 (1931): 215. A useful corrective is George Dargo, *Law in the New Republic. Private Law in the Public Estate* (New York, 1983).

7. Alexander Hamilton, *Federalist LXVIII*, 522.

8. John Jay, *Federalist IV*, 22.

9. Jefferson, "Autobiography," *Works* 1:57.

10. Hamilton, *Federalist VI*, 31.

11. Adam Smith, "Report Dated 1766," in *Lectures on Jurisprudence* [1762–63, 1766], ed. R. L. Meek, D. D. Raphael, and P. G. Stein (Indianapolis, 1978), 397.

12. Jesse Root, *Reports of Cases Adjudged in the Superior Court and in the Supreme Court of Errors in the State of Connecticut, from July, A.D. 1789, to June, A.D. 1798* (Hartford, 1798), xliv.

13. James Wilson, "Lectures on Law," in *The Works of James Wilson*, ed. Robert Green McCloskey, 2 vols. paged successively (Cambridge, MA, 1967), 302.

14. John Jay, *A Charge of Chief Justice John Jay to the Grand Juries on the Eastern Circuit* (Portsmouth, NH, 1790), 8.

15. James Kent, *Memoirs and Letters of James Kent, LL.D.*, ed. William Kent (Boston, 1898), 112–13, 58–59, 157–58.

16. Wilson, "Lectures on Law," 79, 121.

17. *Blackstone's Commentaries: with Notes and References to the Constitution of the Federal Government of the United States; and of the Commonwealth of Virginia*, ed. St. George Tucker, 5 vols. (Philadelphia, 1803), 1: app. 10 [hereinafter, *Tucker's Blackstone*]. For this effort, see Robert Morton Scott, "St. George Tucker and the Development of American Culture in Early Federal Virginia" (Ph.D. diss., George Washington University, 1991), 101–30.

18. Jefferson to James Madison, 17 Feb. 1826, in *Writings* 16:156. Jefferson to Phillip Mazzei, 28 Nov. 1785, in *PTJ* 9:71. For Hamilton's criticism of Mansfield, see *The Law Practice of Alexander Hamilton. Documents and Commentary*, ed. Julius Goebel, Jr., 5 vols. (New York, 1964–81), 1:798, 832.

19. Jefferson to Skelton Jones, 28 July 1809, in *Writings* 12:298–300, cited by Edward Dumbauld, *Thomas Jefferson and the Law* (Norman, 1978), 134.

20. Wilson, "Lectures on Law," 82.

21. Madison to Washington, 18 Oct. 1787, *PTJ* 10:197. Jefferson shared Madison's fear that some might argue that the common law included ecclesiastical law. See his vigorous refutation of this point in "Whether Christianity is a part of the common law?" in *Reports of Cases Determined in the General Court of Virginia. From 1730, to 1740; and From 1768, to 1772*, comp. Thomas Jefferson (1829, repr. Buffalo, 1981), 137, 142.

22. Massachusetts Constitution of 1780, chap. 6, article 6.

23. Root, *Reports*, xiv.

24. John Smilie at Pennsylvania constitutional ratification convention, in *Documentary History of the Ratification of the Constitution*, ed. Merrill Jensen et al. (Madison, 1976–), 2:385.

25. Jay, *Charge to Grand Jury*, 4–5.

26. Wilson, "Lectures on Law," 821.

27. Jay, *Charge to Grand Jury*, 5.

28. Wilson, "Lectures on Law," 354.

29. *Tucker's Blackstone* 1:app., 4.

30. Wilson, "Speech, 1789," in *Works*, 784–85.

31. Nathaniel Chipman, *Reports and Dissertations in Two Parts. Part I, Reports of Cases Determined in the Superior Court of Vermont, in the Years 1789, 1790, and 1791. Part II, Dissertations on the Statute Adopting the Common Law of England the Statute of Conveyances the Statute of Offsets, and on the Negotiability of Notes* (Rutland, VT, 1793), 123–24, 125.

32. Continental Congress to Quebec, 26 Oct. 1774, in *FC* 1:442.

33. David Spadafora, *The Idea of Progress in Eighteenth-Century Britain* (New Haven, CT, 1990), 246.

34. Ibid. Congress invited Price to accept American citizenship and residence in 1778, but he declined. *Richard Price and the Ethical Foundations of the American Revolution*, ed. Bernard Peach (Durham, NC, 1979), 10.

NOTES TO PAGES 183–89

NOTES TO PAGES 183 – 89   341

35. Adam Smith, *The Theory of Moral Sentiments*, ed. D. D. Raphael and A. L. Macfie ([1759] Indianapolis, 1982), 234; Smith, *Lectures on Jurisprudence*, 16, 5.

36. Smith, *Theory of Moral Sentiments*, 234. Smith labeled this attitude "Tory" as opposed to its reverse, "whig," in his *Lectures on Jurisprudence*, 319.

37. Joseph Story, *Commentaries*, III, sec. 1822 [1833], in *FC* 4:584.

38. John Locke, *The Second Treatise of Government* [1689], in *Two Treatises of Government. A Critical Edition with an Introduction and Apparatus Criticus*, ed. Peter Laslett (New York, 1963), 343.

39. Simeon Howard, "A Sermon preached to the Ancient and Honorable Artillery Company in Boston" [1773], in *APW*, 187.

40. On this concept, and its distinction from social contract, see John Phillip Reid, *Constitutional History of the American Revolution. The Authority of Rights* (Madison, WI, 1986), 130–38.

41. Howard, "Sermon," 188.

42. Reid, *Rights*, 90–92, 88.

43. Thomas Paine, "Candid and Critical Remarks on a Letter Signed Ludlow" [1777], in *CWTP* 2:274.

44. *Calder v. Bull*, 3 Dallas 386 (1798), at 398–99.

45. Arthur Lord, "The Mayflower Compact," *American Antiquarian Society Proceedings* 30 (1920): 280–82.

46. Wilson, "Lectures on Law," 361.

47. Theophilus Parsons, *The Essex Result* [1778], in *The Popular Sources of Political Authority. Documents on the Massachusetts Constitution of 1780*, ed. Oscar Handlin (Cambridge, MA, 1966), 331, 339.

48. William E. Nelson, *Americanization of the Common Law. The Impact of Legal Change on Massachusetts Society, 1760–1830* (Cambridge, MA, 1975), 36–63.

49. Alexander Hamilton, *The Farmer Refuted* [1775], in *PAH* 1:88.

50. Parsons, *Essex Result*, 330.

51. Though he does not name his target as Hobbes, Wilson is clearly attacking him in his "Lectures on Law," 228–29.

52. Thomas Jefferson, *The Commonplace Book of Thomas Jefferson, a Repertory of His Ideas on Government*, ed. Gilbert Chinard (Baltimore, 1926), 107–8.

53. Ibid., 103. John Adams read passages of the *Historical Law Tracts* aloud at his meetings of the Boston "Sodalitas, a Clubb of Friends." *Diary and Autobiography of John Adams*, ed. Lyman Butterfield, 3 vols. (Cambridge, MA, 1962), 1:251, 254. Adams also owned a copy of the *Tracts* autographed by Kames. On Kames's influence in America, see William C. Lehmann, *Scottish and Scottish-Irish Contributions to Early American Life and Culture* (Port Washington, NY, 1978), chap. 9. Lehmann notes that Wilson cited the *Tracts* 45 times in his law lectures. Ibid., 153.

54. Anonymous, "An Alarm: or, an Address to the people of Pennsylvania on the Late Resolve of Congress" [1776], in *APW*, 325–26.

55. Patrick Henry, "Resolutions" on the Stamp Act [1765], in Edmund S.

Morgan, ed., *Prologue to Revolution. Sources and Documents on the Stamp Act Crisis* (Chapel Hill, NC, 1959), 48.

56. See Luther Martin, *The Genuine Information Delivered to the Legislature of Maryland Relative to the Proceedings of the General Convention Lately Held in Philadelphia* [1788], in Herbert J. Storing, ed., *The Complete Anti-Federalist,* 7 vols. (Chicago, 1981), 2 : 35 – 36.

57. "Americanus" [Timothy Ford], "The Constitutionalist: Or, An Inquiry How Far It Is Expedient and proper to Alter the Constitution of South Carolina" [1794], in *APW,* 929.

58. *Federalist X,* 58, 65. Madison's arguments here closely resemble those of John Millar of Glasgow, in his *Origin of the Distinction of Ranks; or, An Enquiry into the Circumstances which Give Rise to Influence and Authority in the Different Members of Society* (London, 1779), which set out Millar's theory on the inevitability of ranks, their necessity for social order, and the danger of trying to abolish them. Caroline Robbins, *The Eighteenth-Century Commonwealthman. Studies in the Transmission, Development and Circumstance of English Liberal Thought from the Restoration of Charles II until the War with the Thirteen Colonies* (New York, 1968), 214 – 15. Lehmann, *Contributions,* 219n. Madison owned a copy of Millar's work.

59. On the fear of government aid to the powerful as an impediment to equality, see J. R. Pole, *The Pursuit of Equality in American History* (Berkeley, 1978), 122.

60. Joseph Priestley, *Lectures on History and General Policy* (Philadelphia, 1803), 259.

61. Locke, *Second Treatise,* 344, 205.

62. Smith, *Theory of Moral Sentiments,* 308 – 9.

63. Richard Price, *Observations on the Importance of the American Revolution, and the Means of Making it a Benefit to the World* [1785], in *Richard Price and Ethical Foundations,* ed. Peach, 208 – 9.

64. Peter Stein, "Law and Society in Eighteenth-Century Scottish Thought," in *Scotland in the Age of Improvement. Essays in Scottish History in the Eighteenth Century,* ed. N. T. Phillipson and Rosalind Mitchison (Edinburgh, 1970), 148 – 68. This paragraph draws heavily on Professor Stein's article.

65. Ibid., 153.

66. Ibid., 164.

67. Neil MacCormick, "Law and Enlightenment," in *The Origins and Nature of the Scottish Enlightenment,* ed. R. H. Campbell and Andrew S. Skinner (Edinburgh, 1982), 157 – 58.

68. Knud Haakonssen, *The Science of a Legislator. The Natural Jurisprudence of David Hume and Adam Smith* (Cambridge, 1981), 43 – 44.

69. In the apt phrasing of Duncan Forbes, the Scots' effort was "an attempt to construct an empirically based natural law," by first understanding "the social human nature which was the empirical ground of natural law." Forbes, "Natural Law and the Scottish Enlightenment," in *Origins and Nature of the Scottish Enlightenment,* ed. Campbell and Skinner, 189, 192.

70. Wilson, "Lectures on Law," 84.

71. Madison, "Speech in the Virginia Constitutional Convention," 2 Dec. 1829, in *The Writings of James Madison*, ed. Gaillard Hunt, 9 vols. (New York, 1900–1910), 9:361.

72. Jefferson to Isaac McPherson, 13 Aug. 1813, *Writings* 13:333–34.

73. Robert Coram, *Political Inquiries, to which is Added a Plan for the Establishment of Schools Throughout the United States* [1791], in *APW*, 782.

74. Ibid., 791. Coram was quoting "Dr. [Samuel] Garth" (1661–1719), Whig poet and friend of Alexander Pope.

75. Samuel Blodget, *Thoughts on the Increasing Wealth and National Economy of the United States* (Washington, DC, 1801), 36. Jefferson to James Madison, 28 Oct. 1785, *PTJ* 8:682.

76. *Tucker's Blackstone* 1:x–xi.

77. James Madison, "Parties" [1792], in *PJM* 14:197–98.

78. Nathaniel Chipman, *Sketches of the Principles of Government* [1793], in *FC* 1:557–58.

79. Noah Webster, *An Examination into the Leading Principles of the Federal Constitution* [1787], ibid., 597.

80. *Body of Liberties*, 51. *Acts and Resolves, Public and Private, of the Province of the Massachusetts Bay, Volume I: 1692–1714* (Boston, 1869), 43–45.

81. Laws of 1791, chap. 61, in *The Perpetual Laws of the Commonwealth of Massachusetts, From the Establishment of its Constitution, in the Year 1780, to the End of the Year 1800*, 3 vols. (Boston, 1801), 2:131–32.

82. *The Statutes at Large: Being a Collection of All the Laws of Virginia From the First Session of the Legislature in the Year 1619*, ed. William Waller Hening, 13 vols. (Richmond, VA, and Philadelphia, 1809–23), 9:226, 12:138–40.

83. Willi Paul Adams, *The First American Constitutions. Republican Ideology and the Making of the State Constitutions in the Revolutionary Era*, trans. Rita Kimber and Robert Kimber (Chapel Hill, NC, 1980), 194–96.

84. Henry Chipman, *An Oration on the Study and Profession of the Law* (Middlebury, VT, 1806), 6, 17. On Smith, see Ronald Hamowy, *The Scottish Enlightenment and the Theory of Spontaneous Order* (Carbondale, IL, 1987), 21; and, especially, Jacob Viner's analysis of how Smith's opposition to governmental interference in the economy was firmly rooted in protests against specific abuses of the time, in "Adam Smith and Laissez-faire," in *Adam Smith: Critical Assessments*, ed. John Cunningham Wood, 4 vols. (London, 1984), 1:155–65.

85. Nathaniel Chipman, *Reports and Dissertations*, 129–30.

86. *Tucker's Blackstone* 1:x–xi.

87. Thomas Paine, "Letters on the Bank" [20 June 1786], in *CWTP* 2:429.

88. Adam Smith, *Wealth of Nations*, 424.

89. James Kent, *Dissertations. Being the First Part of a Course of Law Lectures* (New York, 1795), 19, 20. In part based on "the writings of Adam

Smith," Kent also supported the incorporating of a New York State bank in 1791. Kent, *Memoirs*, 42.

90. Adams, *First American Constitutions*, 194.

91. Cited in Cathy D. Matson and Peter S. Onuf, *A Union of Interests. Political and Economic Thought in Revolutionary America* (Lawrence, KS, 1990), 36–37.

92. Lee to Henry Laurens, 6 June 1779, *FC* 1:672. Adam Smith harshly criticized Mandeville and described his presentation of the theory that "private vices are public benefits" as "profligate audaciousness." Smith, *Theory of Moral Sentiments*, 312–13.

93. *Calder* v. *Bull*, 3 Dall. 386 (1798).

94. James Madison, "Parties," *National Gazette*, ca. 23 Jan. 1792, *PJM* 14: 197–98.

95. *FC* 1:442.

96. Noah Webster, *Effects of Slavery on Morals and Industry* [1793], cited by Pole, *Equality*, 118.

97. Madison to Jefferson, 15 Oct. 1788, in *FC* 1:650.

98. James Madison, note on speech to Virginia constitutional convention, ibid., 601.

99. The Scottish concept of unanticipated consequences is the subject of Hamowy, *Spontaneous Order*.

100. *The Records of the Federal Convention of 1787*, ed. Max Farrand, 4 vols. (New Haven, CT, 1937), 1:422–23.

101. Madison to Jefferson, 17 Oct. 1788, *PJM* 11:297–98.

102. Madison discussed the benefits of enlarging the republic in *Federalist IX and X*, but it was not until XIV that he used the term "extended republic." *Federalist*, 88. The dangers of coalitions are in his *Vices of the Political System of the United States* [1787], *FC* 1:168–69.

103. Cited by Isaac Kramnick, *Republicanism and Bourgeois Radicalism. Political Ideology in Late Eighteenth-Century England and America* (Ithaca, NY, 1990), 10.

104. For a sensitive portrait of this fact, see Bernard Bailyn, *The Ordeal of Thomas Hutchinson* (Cambridge, MA, 1974), esp. 106–7.

105. See, generally, Merrill Jensen, *The New Nation* (New York, 1950), 179–93. For a more specific and illuminating family portrait, see Emory S. Evans, "The Rise and Decline of the Virginia Aristocracy in the Eighteenth Century: The Nelsons," in *The Old Dominion. Essays for Thomas Perkins Abernethy*, ed. Darret Rutman (Charlottesville, VA, 1964), 62–78. This fear of falling was widespread among Virginians. See Gordon S. Wood, "Rhetoric and Reality in the American Revolution," *WMQ* 23 (1966): 3–32.

106. Thomas Paine, *Dissertation on the First Principles of Government* [1795], *FC* 1:419.

107. Farrand, *Federal Convention* 1:422.

108. Ibid., 49.

109. *Cato's Letters*, no. 45 (16 Nov. 1721), *FC* 1:511.

110. Priestley, *First Principles*, 29–30.

111. Gouverneur Morris, *Political Enquiries* [1776], *FC* 1:588.

112. Thomas Jefferson, "First Inaugural Address," *FC* 1:141.

113. Thomas Paine, "A Serious Address to the People of Pennsylvania on the Present State of their Affairs" [1778], in *CWTP* 2:285. See also Joseph Priestley, *Lectures on History and General Policy*, 49; Tunis Wortman, *A Treatise Concerning Political Enquiry and the Liberty of the Press* (New York, 1800, repr. New York, 1970), 198.

114. See chap. 3 above.

115. [Alexander Hamilton], *Federalist*, 528–29.

116. James Madison, "Memorial and Remonstrance Against Religious Assessments" [1785], *PJM* 8:303.

117. Massachusetts Constitution of 1780, chap. 5, sec. 2.

118. Jefferson, First Inaugural. See also Jefferson's citing the importance of "Agreeable society" to Madison, 8 Dec. 1784, in *PTJ* 7:559.

119. Wortman, *Treatise*, 175.

120. Carter Braxton, "An Address to the Convention of the Colony and Ancient Dominion of Virginia on the Subject of Government in General, and Recommending a Particular Form to Their Attention" [1776], in *APW*, 334–35.

121. Kames, *Historical Law Tracts*, iii.

122. Jefferson to Washington, 15 Mar. 1784, *PTJ* 7:26.

123. Phillips Payson, "A Sermon" [1778], in *APW*, 526–30, 532, 536.

124. Zabdiel Adams, "An Election Sermon" [1782], in *APW*, 561.

125. Henry May notes the widespread appeal of the Scots in *The Enlightenment in America* (New York, 1976), 19, 83, 121, 293, 343.

126. These writers and teachers are especially well treated by Richard B. Sher, "Introduction: Scottish-American Cultural Studies, Past and Present," in *Scotland and America in the Age of Enlightenment*, ed. Richard B. Sher and Jeffery R. Smitten (Princeton, NJ, 1990), 1–28; by Peter J. Diamond, "Witherspoon, William Smith and the Scottish Philosophy in Revolutionary America," ibid., 115–32; and by Lehmann, *Scottish and Scottish-Irish Contributions*, chap. 9.

127. Nicholas Phillipson stresses the impact of 1707 on eighteenth-century Scottish thought in "Scottish Public Opinion and the Union in the Age of the Association," in *Scotland in the Age of Improvement*, ed. Nicholas Phillipson and Rosalind Mitchison (Edinburgh, 1970), 125–47. See also Nicholas Phillipson, "The Scottish Enlightenment," in *The Enlightenment in National Context*, ed. Roy Porter and Mikulas Teich (Cambridge, 1981), 19–40.

128. Ned C. Landsman, "Witherspoon and the Problem of Provincial Identity in Scottish Evangelical Culture," in *Scotland and America*, ed. Sher and Smitten, 29–45. John Adams, *Diary and Autobiography* 2:248.

129. Jefferson, "Autobiography," in *Works* 1:52. The question came up during the Continental Congress's debate on representation for large and small states, and Franklin made the analogy with Scotland, too. Ibid., 50–51.

130. Adams, *Diary and Autobiography* 3:122.

131. John Brewer, *The Sinews of Power. War, Money and the English State, 1688–1783* (Cambridge, MA, 1990), xviii–xix.

132. Madison, "Influence of the size of a nation on Government" [ca. 19 Dec. 1791–3 Mar. 1792], *PJM* 14:160.

133. Although constitutional interpretations of its meaning differ, historical treatments of the Second Amendment are abundant. Most useful are Lawrence Delbert Cress, *Citizens in Arms: The Army and the Militia in American Society to the War of 1812* (Chapel Hill, NC, 1982); Robert E. Shalhope, "The Ideological Origins of the Second Amendment," *JAH* 69 (1982): 599–614; Cress and Shalhope, "The Second Amendment and the Right to Bear Arms: An Exchange," ibid. 71 (1984): 587–93; and Joyce Malcolm, "The Right to Keep and Bear Arms: The Common Law Tradition," *Hastings Law Quarterly* 10 (1983): 285–314.

134. Phillipson, "Scottish Public Opinion," 141. On Scots' complaints about the Militia Act of 1757, which did not apply to Scotland, see Janet Adam Smith, "Eighteenth-Century Ideas About Scotland," in Phillipson and Mitchison, *Improvement*, 109.

135. Reid, *Constitutional History: Tax*, 24. Phillipson, "Scottish Public Opinion," 141. The English ban derived from the Petition of Right. Blackstone, *Commentaries* 1:400.

136. Bruce P. Lenman, "Aristocratic 'Country' Whiggery in Scotland and the American Revolution," in *Scotland and America*, ed. Sher and Smitten, 180–92.

137. Robbins, *Eighteenth-Century Commonwealthman*, chap. 6. It is noteworthy that Montesquieu, whom the Scots cited repeatedly in support of the link between social factors and liberty, became the most widely cited Enlightenment authority during the creative period of constitution making of the late 1780s. Donald S. Lutz, *The Origins of American Constitutionalism* (Baton Rouge, LA, 1988), 143.

138. Wilson, "Lectures on Law," 131–32.

139. K. A. B. Mackinnon notes that Turnbull used the term in his *Discourse upon the Nature and Origine of Moral and Civil Laws*, 273, appended to his translation of Heineccius's *Elementa Juris Naturae et Gentium*, published as *A Methodical System of Universal Law* (1738). "George Turnbull's Common Sense Jurisprudence," in *Aberdeen and the Enlightenment*, ed. Jennifer J. Carter and Joan H. Pittock (Aberdeen, 1987), 107–8. John Adams read Turnbull's Heineccius and cited it in his interview for admission to the bar. Adams, *Diary and Autobiography* 3:271.

140. British writers in the first part of the century had called for an ideal of "politeness" to serve as "an antidote" to the corruptions of party. Nicholas Phillipson, "Propriety, Property, and Politeness in Early Eighteenth-Century Britain" (paper delivered at the UCLA Center for Seventeenth and Eighteenth-Century Studies, 16 Mar. 1990). I am grateful to Professor Phillipson for his helpful remarks, and for his permission to cite his suggestive paper.

141. Gordon S. Wood, *The Creation of the American Republic, 1776–1787* (Chapel Hill, NC, 1969), 383, 368, 411.

142. Coram, "Political Inquiries" [1791], in *APW*, 787.

143. Paine, *Common Sense* [1776], in *CWTP* 1:9.

144. Payson, "Sermon," 526.

145. Wortman, "Oration," 30.

146. Wilson, "Lectures on Law," 240–41.

147. For the contrasting French revolutionary aversion to "activities or social relationships that encourage differentiation," and its preference for an undifferentiated society that would be more vulnerable to the will of its leaders, see Richard E. Flathman, *The Practice of Rights* (Cambridge, 1976), 188. Kent criticized Rousseau by name for this. *Dissertations*, 7.

148. Thomas Paine, "Dissertations on Government" [1786], in *CWTP* 2:372.

149. Root, *Reports*, i, xvi.

150. For a trenchant critique of this definition of "politeness" in political thought, see Isaac Kramnick, *Republicanism and Bourgeois Radicalism. Political Ideology in Late Eighteenth-Century England and America* (Ithaca, NY, 1990), 277.

151. Smith, *Wealth of Nations* 1:26.

152. Blodget, *Thoughts on Increasing Wealth* (Washington, DC, 1801), 10, 20–21.

153. Wilson, "Considerations on the Bank of North America" [1785], in *Works*, 836. See also Richard Price, "Importance of the American Revolution," 186; Paine, "Rights of Man," in *CWTP* 1:427.

154. Paine, "A Serious Address to the People of Pennsylvania on the Present Situation of Their Affairs" [1778], in *CWTP* 2:295.

155. Cited by Adams, *First Constitutions*, 224.

156. *Documentary History of the Ratification*, ed. Kaminski and Saladino, 2:345.

157. Jefferson to Charles Thomson, 29 Jan. 1817, in *The Life and Selected Writings of Thomas Jefferson*, ed. Adrienne Koch and William Peden (New York, 1944), 620.

158. Madison, "Memorial and Remonstrance Against Religious Assessments" [1785], *PJM* 8:299.

159. On the continuity of collective goals as justification for corporations, see Pauline Maier, "The Revolutionary Origins of the American Corporation," *WMQ* 50 (1993): 51–84; and Rowland T. Berthoff, "Conventional Mentality: Free Blacks, Women, and Business Corporations as Unequal Persons, 1820–1870," *JAH* 76 (1989): 760, 762–63, 775.

160. The treatise was *A Treatise on the Law of Private Corporations Aggregate* by James K. Angell and Samuel Ames. The legal aspects of this development are ably described by Edwin Merrick Dodd, *American Business Corporations until 1860* (Cambridge, MA, 1954). On the social and political aspects, see Oscar Handlin and Mary Flug Handlin, *Commonwealth. A Study of the Role of Government in the American Economy, Massachusetts 1774–1861*, rev. ed. (Cambridge, MA, 1969).

161. The First Amendment has generated a corpus of contentious schol-

arly writing concerning its colonial and Revolutionary backgrounds. For the most recent stage of the debate, see Leonard W. Levy, *Emergence of a Free Press* (New York, 1985), along with David M. Rabban, *Printers and Press Freedom: The Ideology of Early American Journalism* (New York, 1988).

162. Reid, *Constitutional History: Rights*, 7–8.

163. *Tucker's Blackstone* 1:app., 297.

164. Levy, *Free Press*, 220–81.

165. Wortman, *Treatise*, 123.

166. Price, "Importance of the American Revolution," 190–94.

167. W. S. Howell, "Adam Smith's Lectures on Rhetoric: an Historical Assessment," in *Essays on Adam Smith*, ed. Andrew S. Skinner and Thomas Wilson (Oxford, 1975), 21.

168. James Otis, *The Rudiments of Latin Prosody: with a Dissertation on letters, and the Principles of harmony in Poetic and prosaic Composition* (Boston, 1760), 25, 66.

169. Wilson, "Lectures on Law," 231.

170. Wortman, *Treatise*, 123.

171. Ibid., 34.

172. Ibid., 46.

173. Ibid., 140.

174. Rush was educated at a Scot's "country School" in Cecil County, Maryland, before going on to Princeton and the University of Edinburgh. *Autobiography of Benjamin Rush. His "Travels Through Life Together with his Commonplace Book"* [1792–1813], ed. George W. Corner (Princeton, NJ, 1948), 398. According to medical knowledge of the day, chyle was a less-than-nutritious fatty substance produced in digestion.

175. Letter from Jefferson to Thomas Cooper, 2 November 1822, *Works* 12:272.

176. Root, *Reports*, xx.

177. Madison, "Public Opinion" [ca. 19 Dec. 1791], in *PJM* 14:170.

178. "Influence of the size of a nation on Government," ca. 19 Dec. 1791–3 Mar. 1792, in *PJM* 14:159.

179. Joel Barlow, "To His Fellow Citizens of the United States" [1801], in *APW*, 1120.

180. Rush, "A Plan for the Establishment of Public Schools and the Diffusion of Knowledge in Pennsylvania" [1786], in *APW*, 680.

181. Wilson, "Lectures on Law," 528.

182. Jeremiah Atwater, "A Sermon" [1801], in *APW*, 1178–79.

183. Reid, *Constitutional History: Tax*, 174–75.

184. [Anonymous], "Rudiments of Law and Government Deduced from the Law of Nature" [1783], in *APW*, 598, 601.

185. "Lectures on Law," 235. Defoe's novel was widely popular in late eighteenth-century America.

186. William Fessenden, *An Essay on the Law of Patents for New Inventions* (Boston, 1810), ix.

187. Fessenden, *Essay*, xi, xxxvii.

188. Wilson, "Lectures on Law," 392.

189. Madison, *Federalist XLIV*, 288.

190. United States Constitution, art. 1, sec. 8, clause 8. Irah Donner, "The Copyright Clause of the United States Constitution: Why Did the Framers Include It with Unanimous Approval?" *American Journal of Legal History* 36 (1992): 361–78.

191. Paine, *Rights of Man* [1791], in *CWTP* 1:406n.

192. Frank D. Prager, "Historic Background and Foundation of American Patent Law," *American Journal of Legal History* 5 (1961): 309–25; Prager, "Trends and Developments in American Patent Law from Jefferson to Clifford (1790–1870)," ibid. 6 (1962): 45–62.

193. John Locke, *An Essay Concerning Human Understanding* [1689], ed. Peter H. Nidditch (Oxford, 1975), 659–60, cited by Lola Blardinelli, "Thomas Jefferson: The Making of a Republican" (Ph.D. diss., Washington University in St. Louis, 1992), 119. Wortman, *Treatise*, 255.

194. *Tucker's Blackstone* 3:app. 66.

195. Chipman, *Reports and Dissertations*, 141–66.

196. *People v. Croswell*, 3 Johnson's Cas. [New York], 337. *New York Laws*, 28 Sess. 1805, chap. 90. The fullest account of this episode is to be found in Julius G. Goebel, Jr., ed., *The Law Practice of Alexander Hamilton. Documents and Commentary*, 5 vols. (New York, 1964–81), 1:775–848.

197. Donald Roper, "James Kent and the Emergence of New York's Libel Law," *American Journal of Legal History* 17 (1973): 223–31.

198. James Kent, *Commentaries on American Law*, 2d ed. (New York, 1832), 2:20. The case was *Commonwealth v. Chase* (4 Mass. Rep. 163).

199. *Spencer v. Croswell* (1804), cited in Goebel, *Law Practice of Alexander Hamilton* 1:844.

200. Ibid., 837, 841.

201. Jack N. Rakove, "The Structure of Politics at the Accession of George Washington," in Richard Beeman, Stephen Botein, and Edward C. Carter II, eds., *Beyond Confederation: Origins of the Constitution and American National Identity* (Chapel Hill, NC, 1987), 261–94.

202. Kent, *Commentaries* 2:25.

203. Wilson, "Lectures on Law," 622.

204. Ibid., 596.

205. On Kentucky, Francis N. Thorpe, ed., *The Federal and State Constitutions, Colonial Charters, and Other Organic Laws of the States, Territories, and Colonies now or heretofore forming the United States of America*, 7 vols. (Washington, DC, 1909), 3:1274. See also New Hampshire (ibid. 4:2457), Pennsylvania (ibid. 5:3099), Delaware (ibid. 1:568).

206. Wilson, "Lectures on Law," 231–32.

207. The crisis is described and analyzed more than capably in Wood, *Creation of the American Republic*, 393–429.

208. Madison used the phrase in *Federalist XLIV*, 300, in deploring the "pestilent effects of paper money."

209. Francis Hutcheson, *A Short Introduction to Moral Philosophy*, 2d

ed. (Glasgow, 1753), 168, cited by Stein, "Law and Society," 153. John Adams records a winter day in 1756 spent "Reading Hutcheson's Introduction to moral Phylosophy." Adams, *Diary and Autobiography* 1:2.

210. Nathaniel Niles, "Two Discourses on Liberty" [1774], in *APW*, 267–68.

211. Rev. James Madison to Thomas Madison, 1 Oct. 1787, in *Documentary History of the Ratification* 8:30–31.

212. *Maryland Gazette*, 8 Feb. 1787, cited by Steven R. Boyd, "The Contract Clause and the Evolution of American Federalism," *WMQ* 44 (1987): 545.

213. This transition is described by Rowland T. Berthoff and John M. Murrin, "Feudalism, Communalism, and the Yeoman Freeholder: The American Revolution Considered as a Social Accident," in *Essays on the American Revolution*, ed. Stephen G. Kurtz and James H. Hutson (Chapel Hill, NC, 1973), 256–88.

214. *Federalist XLII*, 287.

215. *Annals of Congress, Eighth Congress* (Washington, DC, 1852), 618.

216. Charles Warren, *Bankruptcy in United States History* (Cambridge, MA, 1935), 5–10, 14, 19–20, 34, 49–92.

217. Kent to Joseph Story, 23 June 1837, cited by R. Kent Newmyer, *Supreme Court Justice Joseph Story, Statesman of the Old Republic* (Chapel Hill, NC, 1985), 228. For an evocative description of Story's disenchantment with the justices who replaced the appointees of Presidents Adams, Jefferson, and Madison, see ibid., 196–235.

CHAPTER 7

1. Master's Report, Sarah Everitt v. William Everitt (1787), BA,E-1, Archives of the Supreme Court of New York County.

2. Decree, in ibid.

3. On the links between marriage and government, see especially Carole Pateman, *The Sexual Contract* (Stanford, 1988).

4. Studies of self-divorce, customary divorce, "besom divorce," and wife-sale include: Samuel Pyeatt Menefee, *Wives for Sale: An Ethnographic Study of British Popular Divorce* (New York, 1981); Gerhard O. W. Mueller, "Inquiry into the State of a Divorceless Society: Domestic Relations, Law and Morals in England from 1660 to 1857," *University of Pittsburgh Law Review* 18 (1957): 545–78; and John R. Gillis, *For Better, For Worse: British Marriages, 1600 to the Present* (New York, 1985).

5. Evidence of such alternatives appears in the file papers of legal divorces. Thus witnesses who describe an extralegal union as "passing" as man and wife were underscoring the permanence and outward respectability of the union while simultaneously acknowledging its illegality.

6. With the single ground of adultery, New York was restrictive with regard to grounds. Nonetheless, I am referring here also to other states that

first recognized divorce in the post-Revolutionary era and to other litigants without significant property or assets.

7. Roderick Phillips, *Putting Asunder: A History of Divorce in Western Society* (New York, 1988), 176.

8. Ibid., 175–84, citation on 176; Joan B. Landes, *Women and the Public Sphere in the Age of the French Revolution* (Ithaca, NY, 1988).

9. On Connecticut, see Cornelia Hughes Dayton, "Women before the Bar: Gender, Law, and Society in Connecticut, 1710–1790" (Ph.D. diss., Princeton Univ., 1986), chap. 3; Henry S. Cohn, "Connecticut's Divorce Mechanism, 1636–1969," *American Journal of Legal History* 14 (1970): 35–55; and Marylynn Salmon, *Women and the Law Of Property in Early America* (Chapel Hill, NC, 1986), 60–70.

10. Linda K. Kerber, *Women of the Republic: Intellect and Ideology in Revolutionary America* (Chapel Hill, NC, 1980), 161; Salmon, *Women and the Law of Property*, 61.

11. William Renwick Riddell, "Legislative Divorce in Colonial Pennsylvania," *Pennsylvania Magazine of History and Biography* 57 (1933): 175–80; Thomas Meehan, "Not Made Out of Levity," *Pennsylvania Magazine of History and Biography* 92 (1968): 442–43; Phillips, *Putting Asunder*, 149–50.

12. Jefferson's notes supporting divorce were developed in conjunction with the possible legislative divorce of Dr. James Blair of Williamsburg, who retained him as a lawyer-legislator in the event that his wife, from whom he was separated, should insist on a separate maintenance. Blair, however, died in December of 1772. Frank L. Dewey, "Thomas Jefferson's Notes on Divorce," *WMQ* 39 (1982): 212–23.

13. Cursory guidelines were laid down for alimony and the distribution of marital property. See *Laws of the Northwest Territory, 1788–1800*, ed. Theodore Calvin Pease (Springfield, IL, 1925), 258–59.

14. *Acts of Tennessee, 1799*, chap. 19. The Alabama Territories provided for divorce in 1803, Arkansas in 1807, and Kentucky in 1809.

15. Phillips, *Putting Asunder*, 154–55.

16. Ibid., 230–31; on the suit for criminal conversation and the shifting social status of the men who petitioned Parliament, see Lawrence Stone, *Road to Divorce: England 1530–1987* (New York, 1990), 231–345.

17. Natalie Zemon Davis, *Society and Culture in Early Modern France* (Stanford, 1975), 127; Jean Jacques Rousseau, *The Social Contract*, trans. and ed. Charles Frankel (New York, 1947), 6.

18. Pateman, *The Sexual Contract, passim*; on divorce, see 183–84.

19. Explorations of the familial paradigm include Philip J. Greven, Jr., *Four Generations: Population, Land, and Family in Colonial Andover, Massachusetts* (Ithaca, NY, 1970); Winthrop D. Jordan, "Familial Politics: Thomas Paine and the Killing of the King, 1776," *JAH* 60 (1973): 294–308; Jack P. Greene, "An Uneasy Connection: An Analysis of the Preconditions of the American Revolution," in Stephn G. Kurtz and James H. Hutson, eds., *Essays on the American Revolution* (Chapel Hill, NC, 1973), 32–80; Jay

Fliegelman, *Prodigals and Pilgrims: The American Revolution against Patriarchal Authority* (New York, 1982); Melvin Yazawa, *From Colonies to Commonwealth: Familial Ideology and the Beginnings of the American Republic* (Baltimore, 1985); Jan Lewis, "The Republican Wife: Virtue and Seduction in the Early Republic," *WMQ* 44 (1987): 689–721; Cynthia S. Jordan, "'Old Words' in New Circumstances: Language and Leadership in Post-Revolutionary America," *American Quarterly* 40 (1988): 491–521; and Kerber, *Women of the Republic.* These interpretations vary considerably. Whereas Yazawa argues that the bonds of filial affection gave way to a new emphasis on individual attachment to the state, and thus posits an erosion of the familial paradigm, both Fliegelman and Lewis find a new emphasis on matrimonial bonds. Lewis, moreover, notes as Kerber does, that republicanism presented women with a quasi-political role, but she locates that role primarily in wifehood while Kerber underscores motherhood. Cynthia Jordan, however, views the post-Revolutionary projection of the paradigm as a manipulative variant of patriarchy. On the status of women, see also Nancy F. Cott, "Divorce and the Changing Status of Women in Eighteenth-Century Massachusetts," *WMQ* 33 (1976): 20–43; Mary Beth Norton, *Liberty's Daughters: The Revolutionary Experience of American Women* (New York, 1980), and Joan Hoff Wilson, "The Illusion of Change: Women and the American Revolution," in Alfred F. Young, ed., *The American Revolution: Explorations in the History of American Radicalism* (DeKalb, IL, 1976), 383–445.

20. Sir William Blackstone, *Commentaries on the Laws of England in Four Books,* ed. Thomas Cooley, 2 vols., 4th ed. (Chicago, 1899), 1:374–75.

21. Henry Ferne, *Conscience Satisfied that there is No Warrant for the Armes Taken up by Subjects* (Oxford, 1643), 12, cited in Phillips, *Putting Asunder,* 117. See also Mary Lyndon Shanley, "Marriage Contract and Social Contract in Seventeenth-Century English Thought," *Western Political Quarterly* 32 (1979): 79–91; and Gordon Schochet, *Patriarchalism in Political Thought* (New York, 1975).

22. For an analysis of metaphor, I have relied on Clifford Geertz, *The Interpretation of Cultures* (New York, 1973), 210–11.

23. The quotation is from John Lind, *An Answer to the Declaration of the American Congress* (London, 1776), cited in Carl L. Becker, *The Declaration of Independence: A Study in the History of Political Ideas* (New York, 1922, 1942), 229.

24. Gordon S. Wood, *The Creation of the American Republic, 1776–1787* (Chapel Hill, NC, 1969), 259–73; Peter Charles Hoffer, *The Law's Conscience: Equitable Constitutionalism in America* (Chapel Hill, NC, 1990), 71–76, citation on 72; John W. Gough, *The Social Contract: A Critical Study of its Development* (London, 1957), 142–44.

25. Becker, *The Declaration of Independence,* 237–38.

26. John Milton, *Doctrine and Discipline of Divorce,* 2d ed. (London, 1644), 3–4; John Locke, *Two Treatises of Government,* ed. Peter Laslett (Cambridge, 1963), 339; Kerber, *Women of the Republic,* 18; Lawrence

Stone, *The Family, Sex and Marriage in England, 1500 to 1800* (abr. ed., New York, 1979), 164.

27. Sheldon S. Cohen, "To Parts of the World Unknown: The Circumstances of Divorce in Connecticut, 1750–1787," *Canadian Review of American Studies* 11 (1980): 289.

28. Andrew Jackson Davis, *The Great Harmonia; concerning Physiological Vices and Virtues, and the Seven Phases of Marriage*, 4 vols. (Boston, 1856), 4:404.

29. For a fine description of this literature, some of which was English in its origins, and for its specific meanings in the Revolutionary context, see Lewis, "The Republican Wife," 691–93.

30. Gilbert Imlay, *The Emigrants* (1793, repr. ed. Gainesville, FL, 1964), ii. There is a good chance that this novel attributed to Imlay, Mary Wollstonecraft's American lover, was written by Wollstonecraft herself.

31. Cathy N. Davidson, *Revolution and the Word: The Rise of the Novel in America* (New York, 1986), 45–46.

32. Fliegelman, *Prodigals and Pilgrims*, 126.

33. "Cupid and Hymen," *Pennsylvania Magazine*, Apr. 1775, 159–61.

34. "Reflections on Unhappy Marriages," ibid., June 1775, 264–65. On the role of Genesis in marriage and divorce, see Elaine Pagels, *Adam, Eve, and the Serpent* (New York, 1988), 8,13–14, 22. According to the New Testament, Jesus drew on Genesis to respond to the Pharisees' queries about the legitimate grounds for divorce. Not only did he rule out divorce altogether, thereby departing from Mosaic law, but he went on to suggest that celibacy may be preferable to marriage. Reinterpretations of the doctrine of divorcelessness focussed on Matthew, especially 5 : 27–31 and 9 : 10–13.

35. "On Marriage," *The General Magazine and Impartial Review of Knowledge and Entertainment*, July 1778, 41–45.

36. "Essay on Love and Marriage," *Boston Magazine*, Sept. 1785, 338; "Some Considerations on the Question Are Sensible Women the Best Wives," *Desert to the True American*, 12 Jan. 1799, n.p.; "The Difference Between Love and Friendship," *Gentlemen and Ladies Town and Country Magazine*, Nov. 1789, 550; "Panegyric on Marriage," *Desert to the True American*, 15 Dec. 1798, n.p.

37. "Essay on Love and Marriage," *Boston Magazine*, Nov. 1783, 15–17; "The Unreasonableness of the Law in Regard to Wives," *Columbian Magazine*, May 1788, 243–46, continued from Jan., 22–27, Feb., 61–65, Mar., 126–30, Apr., 186–89; and "Expostulation with the Married," *Desert to the True American*, 21 July 1798, n.p.

38. "The Matron," *Gentlemen and Ladies Town and Country Magazine*, Dec. 1784, 581–83.

39. A person's happiness, asserted one essayist, "is frequently ensured or destroyed by the proper or improper choice of a partner for life." "On Marriage," *The General Magazine and Impartial Review of Knowledge and Entertainment*, July 1778, 41.

40. "The Bad Effects of an Improvident Matrimonial Connection," *Desert*

to the True American, 12 Jan. 1799, n.p. See also "Three Days after Marriage, or the History of Ned Easy and Mrs. Manlove," *Gentlemen and Ladies Town and Country Magazine*, Feb. 1789, 19–21.

41. "The Directory of Love," *Royal American Magazine*, May 1774, 190.

42. On the centrality of marriage in women's lives and the significance of choosing a mate, see Phyllis Rose, *Parallel Lives: Five Victorian Marriages* (New York, 1984), 5–6.

43. Imlay, *The Emigrants*, v–vi, 35; on licentiousness, seduction, and the double standard, see "Unhappy Women," *Gentlemen and Ladies Town and Country Magazine*, July 1789, 311–12; "The Seduction of Young Women," *Boston Magazine*, Oct. 1783, 18–19; and "Suicide," *Desert to the True American*, 20 Apr. 1799, n.p.

44. "Curious Queries with regard to Bigamy," *Gentlemen and Ladies Town and Country Magazine*, July 1784, 116.

45. On the problem of desertion in early America and its role as a ground under early Pennsylvania divorce statutes, see Merrill D. Smith, "Breaking the Bonds: Marital Discord in Pennsylvania, 1730–1830" (Ph.D. diss., Temple Univ., 1989).

46. "Divorce in Pennsylvania," *Portfolio* 10 (1813): 489; on bigamy and shifting identity, see "Trial for Bigamy," *American Law Journal* 1 (1808): 70–80.

47. An Act for the relief of Catherine Moore, *Laws of Indiana Territory*, 1808, chap. 3.

48. Anon., *Amelia; or The Faithless Briton* (Boston, 1798); Kenneth Silverman, *A Cultural History of the American Revolution* (New York, 1976), 497–99.

49. "Answers to the Queries on Marriage," *Pennsylvania Magazine*, Dec. 1775, 558; "The Marriage Ceremonies of Different Countries Compared," *Columbian Magazine*, June 1787, 491–97; on statutory concerns, see Address of Thomas M'Kean, *Pennsylvania Archives*, 4th ser. (1802), 4:500–506, which advised the Pennsylvania Assembly on the "utility of revising the ancient laws relative to clandestine marriages"; see also "A Law to prevent forcible and stolen marriages, and for punishment of the crime of Bigomy [sic], Adopted from the Virginia code," *Laws of Indiana Territory*, 1803, chap. 6. On links between the emergence of divorce and the decline in marriage as an exchange of property, see Randolph Trumbach, *The Rise of the Egalitarian Family* (New York, 1978), 290.

50. On common law marriage and other redefinitions of marriage, see Michael Grossberg, *Governing the Hearth: Law and the Family in Nineteenth-Century America* (Chapel Hill, NC, 1985), 69–102.

51. On contract, see Patrick S. Atiyah, *Promises, Morals, and Law* (New York, 1981), 142.

52. The Rhode Island statute of 1798, for example, gave courts the authority to decree a divorce for "gross behavior and wickedness in either of the parties, repugnant to and in violation of the marriage covenant." Nelson Manfred Blake, *The Road to Reno: A History of Divorce in the United States*

(New York, 1962), 50. On the importance of causality in Revolutionary thinking, see also Gordon S. Wood, "Conspiracy and the Paranoid Style: Causality and Deceit in the Eighteenth Century," *WMQ* 39 (1982): 401–41.

53. Anon, *Essay on Marriage, or the Lawfulness of Divorce* (Philadelphia, 1788), 17–24; Trumbull, *An Appeal to the Public.*

54. Hannah Foster, *The Coquette; or, The History of Eliza Wharton* (Boston, 1797), 28, 254.

55. See especially "The Marriage Ceremonies of Different Countries Compared," *Columbian Magazine,* June 1787, 491–97.

56. "Original System of Laws in Massachusetts-Bay," *Columbian Magazine,* May 1788, 573.

57. *Boston Magazine,* Jan. 1784, 133–34.

58. "Selling of Wives," *Mirror of Taste* 2 (1810): 432–34.

59. New York *Daily Advertiser,* 25 June 1817.

60. See, for example, the petition from 50 "sundry citizens" of Warren County, Ohio, praying that Richard M' Donald might be divorced from Jane M'Donald, *Ohio House Journal 1835/6,* 339–40. For a retrospective view of legislative divorce petitions in New Jersey, see Governor's Annual Message, *General Assembly Journal 1829–31,* 77–83.

61. Gale W. Bamman and Debbie W. Spero, *Tennessee Divorces, 1791–1858* (Nashville, TN, 1985).

62. Salmon, *Women and the Law of Property,* 59.

63. As Michael A. Bellesisles has written, "Traditionally historians have seen law and order as generated principally from above. More recently some have written of the direct transportation of common law to the American frontier as though every settler carried a copy of Blackstone in his luggage." See "The Establishment of Legal Structures on the Frontier: The Case of Revolutionary Vermont," *JAH* 73 (1987): 895–915. On the lawfulness of settlers, see John P. Reid, *Law for the Elephant: Property and Social Behavior on the Overland Trail* (San Marino, CA, 1980). There is good reason to believe that the transition from divorcelessness to divorce in the post-Revolutionary era embodied many of the same issues of "frontier justice" regardless of the locale.

64. *Laws of New York,* chap. 69; forfeiture of property by the guilty spouse was spelled out in *Laws of New York 1813,* chap. 102. On the decline of prosecution for adultery, see William E. Nelson, "Emerging Notions of Modern Criminal Law in the Revolutionary Era: An Historical Perspective," in *American Law and the Constitutional Order,* ed. Lawrence M. Friedman and Harry N. Scheiber (Cambridge, MA, 1978),163–72.

65. Benjamin Trumbull, *An Appeal to the Public, Especially to the Learned, with Respect to the Unlawfulness of Divorces (in all cases except Incontinency)* (New Haven, CT, 1788), 45.

66. Meehan, "Not Made out of Levity."

67. On the inherent ambivalence and necessary hypocrisy of Victorian divorce, see Lawrence M. Friedman, "Notes Toward a History of American Justice," in *American Law and the Constitutional Order,* 17–18.

68. On the economic problems of divorce for women that unfolded over the course of the nineteenth century, see Norma Basch, "Relief in the Premises: Divorce as a Woman's Remedy in New York and Indiana, 1815–1870," *Law and History Review* 8 (1990): 1–24.

69. On the symbolic import of the right of divorce for the women of the Revolutionary era, see Cott, "Divorce and the Changing Status of Women."

CHAPTER 8

1. Several recent books are superb on these themes: Robert H. Wiebe, *The Opening of American Society: From the Adoption of the Constitution to the Eve of Disunion* (New York, 1984); Sean Wilentz, *Chants Democratic: New York City and the Rise of the American Working Class, 1788–1850* (New York, 1984); Joyce Appleby, *Capitalism and a New Social Order: The Republican Vision of the 1790s* (New York, 1984); Alan Taylor, *Liberty Men and Great Proprietors: The Revolutionary Settlement on the Maine Frontier, 1760–1820* (Chapel Hill, NC, 1990); Charles Sellers, *The Market Revolution: Jacksonian America 1815–1846* (New York, 1991); and Gordon S. Wood, *The Radicalism of the American Revolution* (New York, 1992).

2. Michael Zuckerman, "Holy Wars, Civil Wars: Religion and Economics in Nineteenth Century America," *Prospects* 16 (1991): 205–6.

3. Two intriguing studies that reflect these questions are Richard Bushman, *From Puritan to Yankee: Character and the Social Order in Connecticut, 1690–1765* (Cambridge, MA, 1967) and E. Digby Baltzell, *Puritan Boston and Quaker Philadelphia: Two Protestant Ethics and the Spirit of Class Authority and Leadership* (New York, 1979).

4. A recent symposium by the Society for Historians of the Early American Republic attempted a synthetic approach to the topics of labor, ideology, class, and gender, but omitted religion entirely as a variable in their analysis. See "Labor, Ideology, Class, and Gender in the Early Republic: Essays from a SHEAR Symposium," *Journal of the Early Republic* 10 (Fall, 1990): 311–13. Zuckerman, "Holy Wars, Civil Wars," 230. Two excellent studies of early American economic development that omit any attention to religion are John McCusker and Russell Menard, *The Economy of British America, 1607–1789* (Chapel Hill, NC, 1985) and Ronald Hoffman et al., eds., *The Economy of Early America: The Revolutionary Period, 1763–1790* (Charlottesville, VA, 1988).

5. The issue of religious culture is only incidental in Christopher Clark, *The Roots of Rural Capitalism: Western Massachusetts, 1780–1860* (Ithaca, NY, 1990) and Steven Hahn and Jonathan Prude, eds., *The Countryside in the Age of Capitalist Transformation: Essays in the Social History of Rural America* (Chapel Hill, NC, 1987).

6. Jon Butler, *Awash in a Sea of Faith: Christianizing the American People* (Cambridge, MA, 1990) and Nathan O. Hatch, *The Democratization of American Christianity* (New Haven, CT, 1989).

7. For an insightful treatment of the ways in which three decades of po-

litical debate mobilized common people, culminating in the 1790s, see
Appleby, *Capitalism and a New Social Order*, especially 51–104.

8. Wood, *The Radicalism of the American Revolution*, 232.

9. Roger Finke and Rodney Stark, "How the Upstart Sects Won America:
1776–1850," *Journal for the Scientific Study of Religion* 28 (1989): 27–44.

10. George M. Thomas, *Revivalism and Cultural Change: Christianity,
Nation Building, and the Market in the Nineteenth-Century United States*
(Chicago, 1989).

11. David Martin, *Tongues of Fire: The Explosion of Protestantism in
Latin America* (Oxford, 1990), 21, 43. On these themes, see also Mark
Chaves and David E. Cann, "Regulation, Pluralism, and Religious Market
Structure: Explaining Religion's Vitality," *Rationality and Society* 4 (1992):
272–90; and R. Stephen Warner, "Work in Progress Toward a New Paradigm
for the Sociological Study of Religion in the United States," *American Journal of Sociology*, vol. 95 n.s. (Mar. 1993).

12. Richard Hofstadter, *Anti-Intellectualism in American Life* (New
York, 1962), 84.

13. Clifford S. Griffin, *Their Brothers' Keepers: Moral Stewardship in the
United States, 1800–1865* (New Brunswick, NJ, 1960); John R. Bodo, *The
Protestant Clergy and Public Issues, 1812–1848* (Princeton, 1954); Charles
I. Foster, *An Errand of Mercy: The Evangelical United Front, 1790–1837*
(Chapel Hill, NC, 1960); and Charles C. Cole, Jr., *The Social Ideas of the
Northern Evangelists, 1820–1860* (New York, 1954).

14. E. Brooks Holifield, *The Gentlemen Theologians: American Theology
in Southern Culture, 1795–1860* (Durham, NC, 1978), 36–49; Donald M.
Scott, *From Office to Profession: The New England Ministry, 1750–1850*
(Philadelphia, 1978).

15. Ann Douglas, *The Feminization of American Culture* (New York,
1977).

16. Frederick V. Mills, Sr., "Mentors of Methodism, 1784–1844," *Methodist History* 12 (1973): 43. William W. Sweet, *Religion on the American
Frontier, 1783–1840* (Chicago, 1946), 11, 45–46.

17. See, for example, Bernard Semmel, *The Methodist Revolution* (New
York, 1973); David Hempton, *Methodism and Politics in British Society
1750–1850* (Stanford, 1984); W. R. Ward, *Religion and Society in England
1790–1850* (New York, 1973); and John Walsh, "Methodism at the End of the
Eighteenth Century," in *A History of the Methodist Church in Great Britain*, Rupert Davies and Gordon Rupp, eds., (London, 1965), 275–315.

18. Typical is Laurence Moore, *Religious Outsiders and the Making of
Americans* (New York, 1986). A clear exception is Butler, *Awash in a Sea of
Faith*.

19. For examples of the focus on cities and industrial workers, see Alan
Dawley, *Class and Community: The Industrial Revolution in Lynn* (Cam-
bridge, MA, 1976); Paul G. Faler, *Mechanics and Manufacturers in the Early
Industrial Revolution: Lynn Massachusetts 1780–1860* (Albany, NY, 1981);
Charles G. Steffen, *The Mechanics of Baltimore: Workers and Politics in the*

Age of the Revolution, 1763–1812 (Urbana, IL, 1984); and Sean Wilentz, *Chants Democratic.* Wilentz is perceptive and judicious in treating the role of popular religion in New York City, particularly the role of Methodism; but it is only incidental to the purposes of his work. A good example of what might be called the "new rural history" is Hahn and Prude, eds., *The Countryside in the Age of Capitalist Transformation.*

20. David Hempton notes this about the work of E. P. Thompson in Hempton, *Methodism and Politics* (Stanford, 1984), 75–76.

21. See Wood, *The Radicalism of the American Revolution,* 312.

22. Francis Asbury, *The Journal and Letters of Francis Asbury,* Elmer C. Clark, J. Manning Potts, and Jacob S. Payton, eds., 3 vols. (Nashville, TN, 1958), 3 : 332.

23. Bruce Laurie, *Working People of Philadelphia, 1800–1850* (Philadelphia, 1980); Paul E. Johnson, *A Shopkeeper's Millennium: Society and Revivals in Rochester, New York, 1815–1837* (New York, 1978), 9, 136–41. For an insightful discussion of these interpretations, see Zuckerman, "Holy Wars, Civil Wars," 208–10.

24. Sellers, *The Market Revolution,* 211, 31.

25. Paul E. Johnson, "Democracy, Patriarchy, and American Revivals, 1780–1830," *Journal of Social History* 24 (1991): 843–49.

26. See E. P. Thompson, *Customs in Common* (New York, 1992) and the perceptive review by Roy Porter in *The New Republic,* 4 May 1992, 35–38.

27. Laurie, *Working People of Philadelphia,* 46–48.

28. Harry S. Stout, *The Divine Dramatist: George Whitefield and the Rise of Modern Evangelicalism* (Grand Rapids, MI, 1991).

29. Mark Valeri, "The Economic Thought of Jonathan Edwards," *Church History* 60 (1991): 37–54.

30. David Jaffee, "The Village Enlightenment in New England, 1760–1820," *WMQ* 47 (1990): 327–46.

31. Michael Zuckerman, "A Different Thermidor: The Revolution Beyond the American Revolution," in James A. Henretta, Michael Kammen, and Stanley N. Katz, eds., *The Transformation of Early American History: Society, Authority, and Ideology* (New York, 1991), 188–89.

32. W. R. Ward, "The Legacy of John Wesley: The Pastoral Office in Britain and America," in Anne Whiteman, J. S. Bromley, and P. G. M. Dickson, eds., *Statesmen, Scholars and Merchants* (Oxford, 1973), 346–48.

33. Ralph E. Morrow, "The Great Revival, the West, and the Crisis of the Church," in *The Frontier Re-examined,* ed. John F. McDermott (Urbana, IL, 1967), 72.

34. F. Mark McKeirnan, *The Voice of One Crying in the Wilderness: Sidney Rigdon, Religious Reformer, 1793–1876* (Lawrence, KS, 1971), quote on 13.

35. Parsons Cooke, *A Century of Puritanism and a Century of Its Opposites* (Boston, 1855), 258; quoted in Faler, *Mechanics and Manufacturers in the Early Industrial Revolution,* 47.

36. Richard Cawardine has argued that many of the so-called "new measures" supposedly introduced by the revivalist Charles Finney (the "anxious

bench," women praying in public, colloquial preaching, protracted meetings) had been widely employed by the Methodists before Finney. See Richard Cawardine, "The Second Great Awakening in the Urban Centers: An Examination of Methodism and the 'New Measures,' " *JAH* 59 (1972): 327–40. For the innovative techniques of the Methodists, see also Terry D. Bilhartz, *Urban Religion and the Second Great Awakening: Church and Society in Early National Baltimore* (Rutherford, NJ, 1986).

37. William J. Gilmore, *Reading Becomes a Necessity of Life: Material and Cultural Life in Rural New England, 1780–1835* (Knoxville, TN, 1989), 84–113. See also chap. 5 above.

38. Thomas Andros, *The Scriptures Liable to be Wrested to Men's Own Destruction, and an Instance of This Found, in the Writings of Elias Smith* (Taunton, MA, 1817), 6.

39. Adam Smith, *The Wealth of Nations* (New York, 1933), 746.

40. Wood, *The Radicalism of the American Revolution*, 320–21.

41. Randolph A. Roth, *The Democratic Dilemma: Religion, Reform, and the Social Order in the Connecticut River Valley of Vermont, 1781–1850* (Cambridge, MA, 1987), 55.

42. The phrase is that of Joseph Smith, who reacted strongly to the sectarian competition he knew as a young man. Joseph Smith, *The Pearl of Great Price* (Salt Lake City, 1891), 56–70.

43. *Julian M. Sturtevant: An Autobiography*, ed. J. M. Sturtevant, Jr. (New York, 1896), 160–61. By 1860, Jacksonville had eighteen Protestant churches for a town of fewer than 10,000 people. See Don Harrison Doyle, *The Social Order of a Frontier Community: Jacksonville, Illinois, 1825–70* (Urbana, IL, 1978), 39–61.

44. Lawrence Foster, "Free Love and Feminism: John Humphrey Noyes and the Oneida Community," *Journal of the Early Republic* 1 (1981): 170.

45. David G. Hackett, *The Rude Hand of Innovation: Religion and Social Order in Albany, New York, 1652–1836* (New York, 1991), 98–99.

46. Lorenzo Dow, *Hint to the Public, or Thoughts on the Fulfillment of Prophecy* (Boston and Salisbury, NC, 1811); *Analects; or, Reflections upon Natural, Moral and Political Philosophy, Including the Rights, Interest and Duties of Man, Addressed to the Different Ranks and Societies Throughout the U.S. of America* (Alexandria, 1813).

47. Lorenzo Dow, *Omnifarious Law Exemplified. How to Curse and Swear, Lie, Cheat and Kill; according to Law* (New London, CT, 1829), 49–52.

48. Wood, *The Radicalism of the American Revolution*, 243–70.

49. Jonathan Edwards, Sermons 8 [untitled], June 1749, in *Selections from the Unpublished Writings of Jonathan Edwards*, ed. Alexander B. Grossart (Edinburgh, 1865), 208. Quoted in Valeri, "The Economic Thought of Jonathan Edwards," 49.

50. *Herald of Gospel Liberty*, 8 Dec. 1808, 29–30.

51. Alan Taylor, *Liberty Men and Great Proprietors*, 8.

52. See a lively discussion on these issues in the forum of essays on Wood's *Creation of the American Republic* in *WMQ* 44 (1987): 549–640,

particularly the essays by Gary B. Nash, John M. Murrin, and Gordon S. Wood.

53. Lucy Smith, *Biographical Sketches of Joseph Smith, the Prophet* (Liverpool, 1853; repr. New York, 1969), 37, 46–49.

54. *The Autobiography of Parley Parker Pratt, One of the Twelve Apostles*, ed. Parley P. Pratt (New York, 1874), 17.

55. *Autobiography of Rev. Tobias Spicer* (Boston, 1851), 32–33.

56. *The Biography of Barton W. Stone, Written by Himself with Additions and Reflections*, ed. John Rodgers (Cincinnati, 1847), 44–45.

57. See Leland's discussion of "The Right and Bonds of Conscience" in his pamphlet *The Virginia Chronicle* (Fredericksburg, VA, 1790), 45. "Conscience," Leland wrote in 1830, "is a court of judicature, erected in every breast, to take cognizance of every action in the home department, but has nothing to do with another man's conduct. My best judgment tells me that my neighbor does wrong, but my conscience has nothing to say of it. Were I to do as he does, my conscience would arrest and condemn me, but guilt is not transferable. Every one must give an account of himself." See "Transportation of the Mail," in *The Writings of the Late Elder John Leland*, ed. L. F. Greene (New York, 1845), 565.

58. Greene, *Writings of John Leland*, 78.

59. Asbury, *The Journal and Letters of Francis Asbury* 3:341–45, 453.

60. Deborah Valenze, *Prophetic Sons and Daughters: Female Preaching and Popular Religion in Industrial England* (Princeton, 1985), 89–93.

61. The itinerant Methodist Joshua Thomas reports two such incidents with Dow. See Adam Wallace, *The Parson of the Islands: A Biography of the Rev. Joshua Thomas* (Philadelphia, 1861), 76, 59.

62. John Williamson Nevin, "Antichrist and the Sect," in *The Mercersburg Theology*, ed. James Hastings Nichols (New York, 1966), 93–119; quote on 98–99.

63. Curtis D. Johnson, *Islands of Holiness: Rural Religion in Upstate New York, 1790–1860* (Ithaca, NY, 1989), 157.

64. Finke and Stark, "How the Upstart Sects Won America," 42.

65. Emil Pocock, "Popular Roots of Jacksonian Democracy: The Case of Dayton, Ohio, 1815–1830," *Journal of the Early Republic* 9 (1989): 489–515.

66. See Roy Porter, "The Heart of the Country," a review of E. P. Thompson, *Customs in Common*, in *The New Republic*, 4 May 1992, 35–38.

67. Wood, *The Radicalism of the American Revolution*, 347–69.

68. Alexis de Tocqueville, *Democracy in America*, trans. Henry Reeve, 2 vols. (New York, 1945), 1:53, 314.

69. Zuckerman, "A Different Thermidor," 174.

70. Philip Schaff, *The Principle of Protestantism*, Bard Thompson and George H. Bricker, eds. (1845; Philadelphia, 1964), 150.

CHAPTER 9

I would like to thank the Center for the History of Freedom and its marvelous director and staff: Richard Davis, Elisabeth Davis, Elisabeth Case, and

Becky Rauvola; all of the other fellows and amigos, in particular David Konig, the volume editor, and Peter Onuf; and James Oakes, Barry Bienstock, and James Grimmelmann.

1. "Governor McDuffie's Message on the Slavery Question, 1835," in Albert Bushnell Hart and Edward Channing, eds., *American History Leaflets*, No. 10 (New York, 1893), quotations on 3, 4, 5, 8, 9, 10. For McDuffie, see J. William Harris, *Plain Folk and Gentry in a Slave Society: White Liberty and Black Slavery in Augusta's Hinterlands* (Middletown, CT, 1985), 36–39.

2. My understanding of republicanism is informed particularly by Gordon S. Wood, *The Creation of the American Republic, 1776–1787* (Chapel Hill, NC, 1969). For a useful summary of the literature on this topic see Robert E. Shalhope, "Republicanism and Early American Historiography," *WMQ* 39 (1982): 334–56.

3. Harris, *Plain Folk and Gentry*, 219, n.72.

4. Edmund S. Morgan, *American Slavery, American Freedom: The Ordeal of Colonial Virginia* (New York, 1975), 385.

5. In *Notes of Debates in the Federal Convention of 1787 Reported by James Madison*, ed. Adrienne Koch (Athens, OH, 1966), 281. When Pinckney compared the American and British social structures and rejected the British Constitution as an appropriate model for imitation, he made no mention of slavery or an American peasantry. (See 181–87.) See also Mark D. Kaplanoff, "Charles Pinckney and the American Republican Tradition," in Michael O'Brien and David Moltke-Hansen, *Intellectual Life in Antebellum Charleston* (Knoxville, TN, 1986), 98.

6. Notes for the *National Gazette* Essays, 19 Dec. 1791–3 Mar. 1792, in *PJM* 14:163–64. Madison never published these reflections. See also Paul A. Rahe, *Republics Ancient and Modern: Classical Republicanism and the American Revolution* (Chapel Hill, NC, 1992), 695–96. For a somewhat different interpretation, see Drew R. McCoy, *The Last of the Fathers: James Madison and the Republican Legacy* (Cambridge, 1989), 234–35.

7. St. George Tucker, *A Dissertation on Slavery with a Proposal for the Gradual Abolition of It, in the State of Virginia* (Philadelphia, 1796; repr., Westport, CT, 1970), 9, 7, 27–28.

8. For the incompatibility of slavery and the natural rights philosophy of the Revolution, see Gary B. Nash, *Race and Revolution* (Madison, WI, 1990); for the elimination of slavery in the North see Arthur Zilversmit, *The First Emancipation: The Abolition of Slavery in the North* (Chicago, 1967).

9. In Richard Henry Lee, *Memoir of the Life of Richard Henry Lee and His Correspondence*, 2 vols. (1825), 1:17–19, quoted in Oliver Perry Chitwood, *Richard Henry Lee: Statesman of the Revolution* (Morgantown, WV, 1967), 18.

10. Arthur Lee to Richard Henry Lee, 14 Feb. 1773, and Richard Henry Lee to William Lee, 13 May 1773, quoted in Chitwood, *Lee*, 20–21.

11. Thomas Jefferson, *Notes on Virginia*, in *The Life and Selected Writings of Thomas Jefferson*, ed. Adrienne Koch and William Peden (New York, 1944), 219; letter to Dr. Price, 7 Aug. 1785, in ibid., 368; letter to Edward Coles, 25 Aug. 1814, in ibid., 642.

12. Letter to John Holmes, 22 Apr. 1820, in ibid., 698. Of course it is possible to equate "self-preservation" with the natural right to life, as Duncan J. MacLeod does in another context. See his *Slavery, Race and the American Revolution* (Cambridge, 1974), 74. To be sure, Jefferson feared a black revolution, but he also wanted to preserve southern society as it had developed. He assured Holmes that he continued to welcome emancipation if it could be accomplished "in any *practicable* way." For Jefferson's views on slavery see also Charles L. Griswold, Jr., "Rights and Wrongs: Jefferson, Slavery, and Philosophical Quandaries," in Michael J. Lacey and Knud Haakonssen, eds., *A Culture of Rights: The Bill of Rights in Philosophy, Politics, and Law, 1791–1991* (New York, 1991), 144–214; J. David Greenstone, *The Lincoln Persuasion: Remaking American Liberalism* (Princeton, NJ, 1993), pt. 2; Robert McColley, *Slavery and Jeffersonian Virginia*, 2d ed. (Urbana, IL, 1973); William W. Freehling, "The Founding Fathers and Slavery," *AHR* 77 (1972): 81–93; Winthrop Jordan, *White Over Black: American Attitudes Toward the Negro, 1550–1812* (Chapel Hill, NC, 1968), chap. 12; John Chester Miller, *The Wolf by the Ears: Thomas Jefferson and Slavery* (New York, 1977). See also Drew R. McCoy, *The Elusive Republic: Political Economy in Jeffersonian Virginia* (Chapel Hill, NC, 1980), 250–52.

13. "Speech in South Carolina House of Representatives," 18 Jan. 1788, in Max Farrand, ed., *The Records of the Federal Convention of 1787*, 4 vols., rev. ed. (New Haven, 1966), 3:256. See also MacLeod, *Slavery, Race, and Revolution*; and William W. Freehling, *The Road to Disunion: Volume I, Secessionists at Bay, 1776–1854* (New York, 1990), chap. 7.

14. See also Larry Tise, *Proslavery: A History of the Defense of Slavery in America, 1701–1840* (Athens, GA, 1987), 33.

15. Jonathan Elliot, ed., *The Debates in the Several State Conventions*, 5 vols. (Washington, 1836), 4:100, 102, 31, 101.

16. Ibid. 3:270, 590. For Henry's earlier acknowledgement of "the general Inconvenience of living without" slaves, see Rahe, *Republics Ancient and Modern*, 620. The source is a letter from Henry to Robert Pleasants, 18 Jan. 1773, in George S. Brooks, *Friend Anthony Benezet* (Philadelphia, 1937), 443–44.

17. For Madison, see Farrand, ed., *Records* 3:324–26; for Randolph, see ibid., 334. See also McColley, *Slavery and Jeffersonian Virginia*, 169–70.

18. For the southern defense of slavery at the Federal Convention see in particular Paul Finkelman, "Slavery and the Constitutional Convention: Making a Covenant with Death," in Richard Beeman, Stephen Botein, and Edward C. Carter II, eds., *Beyond Confederation: Origins of the Constitution and American National Identity* (Chapel Hill, NC, 1987), 188–225; William M. Wiecek, "The Witch at the Christening: Slavery and the Constitution's Origins," in Leonard W. Levy and Dennis J. Mahoney, eds., *The Framing and Ratification of the Constitution* (New York, 1987), 167–84; and William M. Wiecek, *The Sources of Antislavery Constitutionalism in America, 1760–1848* (Ithaca, NY, 1977), chap. 3, and Rahe, *Republics Ancient and Modern*, 617–47.

19. Elliot, ed., *Debates* 4:285–86, quoted in Finkelman, "Slavery and the Constitutional Convention." See also Wiecek, "Witch at the Christening."

20. Koch, *Notes of Debates*, 507, 502. See Rahe, *Republics Ancient and Modern*, 633–35. In the debates over restriction of the slave trade, southerners Luther Martin, George Mason, and Hugh Williamson characterized slavery as wrong in principle (*Notes of Debates*, 502–9, 530–31).

21. Farrand, ed., *Records* 1:486, 516, 594.

22. Ibid. 1:581, 594. Pinckney was addressing the question of the means and basis for apportioning representation.

23. See *Annals of Congress*, 3d Cong., 2d sess., 1 Jan. 1795, 1039; and ibid., 5th Cong., 2d sess., 30 Nov. 1797, 1:665.

24. Governor's Message, no. 1, South Carolina Senate Journal, 29 Nov. 1798, SCSA, quoted in Mark D. Kaplanoff, "Charles Pinckney and the American Republican Tradition," 98; *Annals of Congress*, 5th Cong., 2d sess., 30 Nov. 1797, 1:667.

25. *Annals of Congress*, 6th Cong., 2d sess., 2 Jan. 1800, 231. See similarly, 235.

26. James Hugo Johnston, *Race Relations in Virginia and Miscegenation in the South* (Amherst, MA, 1970), 110–11, quoted in MacLeod, *Slavery, Race and Revolution*, 75.

27. *Annals of Congress*, 3d Cong., 2d sess., 1 Jan. 1795, 1040; Rahe, *Republics Ancient and Modern*, 636–41. See also Charles Griswold's discussion of Jefferson's philosophic commitment to "prudence" ("Rights and Wrongs," 163, 189–214).

28. In his *Second Treatise* John Locke wrote that "the great and *chief end* of Men's uniting into Commonwealths, and putting themselves under Government, *is the Preservation of their Property*" (in *Two Treatises of Government*, ed. Peter Laslett [Cambridge, 1960], 2:124 [350–51]). For a variety of recent views about the meaning and influence in America of Locke's views on property, see Ellen Frank Paul and Howard Dickman, eds., *Liberty, Property, and the Foundations of the American Constitution* (Albany, NY, 1989). See also David Brion Davis, *The Problem of Slavery in Western Culture* (Ithaca, NY, 1966), 118–21.

29. For recent discussions about the sources of Revolutionary ideology see Greenstone, *Lincoln Persuasion*; Rahe, *Republics Ancient and Modern*; David F. Ericson, *The Shaping of American Liberalism: The Debates Over Ratification, Nullification, and Slavery* (Chicago, 1993); Peter Onuf and Nicholas Onuf, *Federal Union, Modern World: The Law of Nations in an Age of Revolutions, 1776–1814* (Madison, WI, 1993); Lance Banning, "Jeffersonian Ideology Revisited: Liberal and Classical Ideas in the New American Republic," *WMQ* 43 (1986): 3–19; Joyce Appleby, "What is Still American in the Political Philosophy of Thomas Jefferson?" *WMQ* 39 (1982): 287–309; id., *Capitalism and a New Social Order: The Republican Vision of the 1790s* (New York, 1984); id., "Republicanism in Old and New Contexts," *WMQ* 43 (1986): 20–34; and id., "Republicanism and Ideology," *American Quarterly*

37 (1985): 461–73; John P. Diggins, *The Lost Soul of American Politics: Virtue, Self-Interest, and the Foundations of Liberalism* (New York, 1984); Isaac Kramnick, "Republican Revisionism," and "The 'Great National Discussion': The Discourse of Politics in 1787," *WMQ* 45 (1988): 3–32; and John Ashworth, "The Jeffersonians: Classical Republicans or Liberal Capitalists?" *Journal of American Studies* 18 (1984): 425–35. For the meaning of "happiness" see Garry Wills, *Inventing America: Jefferson's Declaration of Independence* (New York, 1978); and Jan Lewis, "Happiness," in Jack P. Greene and J. R. Pole, eds., *The Blackwell Encyclopedia of the American Revolution* (Oxford, 1991), 641–47. The republican—in contrast to the liberal—construction of the related terms of property and interest is revealed in Pennsylvania Representative David Bard's comments in the 1804 Congressional debate on taxing the importation of slaves: "South Carolina . . . has a right to consult and pursue her own interest, so far as the general good will permit . . . when the powers of a State, though Constitutional, operate against the general interest, then the exercise of those powers are politically wrong, because it is contrary to the fundamental principle of society, the public good." (14 Feb. 1804, *Annals of Congress*, 8th Cong., 1st Sess. 1:995).

30. This is how Lance Banning characterizes the work of John Pocock in "Some Second Thoughts on Virtue and the Course of Revolutionary Thinking," in Terence Ball and J. G. A. Pocock, eds., *Conceptual Change and the Constitution* (Lawrence, KS, 1988), 204.

31. See Peter S. Onuf, "Reflections on the Founding: Constitutional Historiography in Bicentennial Perspective," *WMQ* 46 (1989): 350–56. Several recent studies situate the conflict or instability of ideas within liberalism itself. See Ericson, *Shaping of American Liberalism*; Greenstone, *Lincoln Persuasion*; and, implicitly, Griswold, "Rights and Wrongs."

32. "The Genuine Information Delivered to the Legislature of the State of Maryland Relative to the Proceedings of the General Convention Lately Held at Philadelphia," (1788), in Herbert J. Storing, ed., *The Complete Anti-Federalist* 2 (Chicago, 1981): 62.

33. For a compelling analysis of the propulsive force in the colonies of what C. B. McPherson termed "possessive individualism," see Jack P. Greene's "Introduction" to his *Great Britain and the American Colonies, 1606–1763* (Columbia, SC, 1970), xi–xlvii.

34. See Locke, *Two Treatises of Government*, ed. Laslett, 2:22–24, (283–85) and editor's note, 284–85.

35. Quoted in Greene, *Britain and the Colonies*, xi (orig. *An Account of the European Settlements in America* [2 vols., London, 1757], 2:288).

36. Jack P. Greene, *Pursuits of Happiness: The Social Development of Early Modern British Colonies and the Formation of American Culture* (Chapel Hill, NC, 1988), quotations on 207.

37. James Oakes, *Slavery and Freedom: An Interpretation of the Old South* (New York, 1990), chap. 2, quotation on 52.

38. Peter A. Coclanis, *The Shadow of a Dream: Economic Life and Death in the South Carolina Low Country, 1670–1920* (New York, 1989), quota-

tions on 60, 56. See also Joyce E. Chaplin, *An Anxious Pursuit: Agricultural Innovation and Modernity in the Lower South, 1730–1815* (Chapel Hill, NC, 1993).

39. Ibid., 26.

40. See Rhys Isaac, *The Transformation of Virginia* (Chapel Hill, NC, 1982), and Jan Lewis, *The Pursuit of Happiness: Family and Values in Jefferson's Virginia* (New York, 1983), chap. 1.

41. See Isaac, *Transformation*; Morgan, *American Slavery, American Freedom*; and Lewis, *The Pursuit of Happiness*, chap. 1.

42. See for example Gordon S. Wood, "Rhetoric and Reality in the American Revolution," *WMQ* 23 (1966): 3–32. For a useful summary see also Wood's section of *The Great Republic: A History of the American People*, 1st ed. (Lexington, MA, 1977), pt. 2.

43. Quoted in Miller, *Wolf by the Ears*, 8. See similarly Tucker, *Dissertation on Slavery*, 39–45; and George Mason, in the Virginia Debates on ratification, in Elliot, ed., *Debates* 3:452.

44. Bernard Bailyn, *The Ideological Origins of the American Revolution* (Cambridge, MA, 1967), 233; Jack P. Greene, "'Slavery or Independence': Some Reflections on the Relationship Among Liberty, Black Bondage, and Equality in Revolutionary South Carolina," *South Carolina Historical Magazine* 80 (1979): 193–214; and Kenneth Greenberg, "Revolutionary Ideology and the Proslavery Argument: The Abolition of Slavery in Antebellum South Carolina," *JSH* 42 (1976): 366.

45. Donald L. Robinson, *Slavery in the Structure of American Politics, 1765–1820* (New York, 1971), chap. 7.

46. Debate in House of Representatives, 17 Mar. 1790, *Annals of Congress*, 1st Cong., 2d Sess., 2:1458.

47. Debate in Congress, 14 Feb. 1804, *Annals of Congress*, 8th Cong., 1st Sess., 1:1006. It should be noted that, in these early Congressional debates on slavery and the slave trade, southern representatives did not work as a bloc; the most vocal opposition to restrictions upon the institution came from South Carolina, which was often joined by representatives of New England. See Robinson, *Slavery and Structure of Politics*, chaps. 7 and 8.

48. The term is William W. Freehling's; see his *Road to Disunion*, chap. 7.

49. Tucker, *Dissertation*, 87, 92, 89, 91 and *passim*. Winthrop D. Jordan, *White Over Black: American Attitudes Toward the Negro, 1550–1812* (Chapel Hill, NC, 1968), 559.

50. For other plans for emancipation, including colonization, see Jordan, *White Over Black*, chap. 15.

51. Ibid., 546–69; quotation on 549.

52. Farrand, ed., *Records* 2:369–70, 371. See also John Adams, quoted in Rahe, *Republics Ancient and Modern*, 636.

53. Allen B. Magruder, *Political, Commercial and Moral Reflections, on the Late Cession of La.* (Lexington, KY, 1803), 150; Peter S. Onuf, *Statehood and Union: A History of the Northwest Ordinance* (Bloomington, IN, 1987), chap. 6, quotations on 120, 125; Paul Finkelman, "Evading the Ordinance:

The Persistence of Bondage in Indiana and Illinois," *Journal of the Early Republic* 9 (1989): 21–51; James Oakes, *The Ruling Race: A History of American Slaveholders* (New York, 1982), chap. 5. Oakes notes that "in practical terms, property rights represented little more than the slaveholders' assertion of their intent to make as much money as possible from the labor of their slaves" (134). For an elaboration of the diffusionist scheme, see Drew R. McCoy, *The Elusive Republic: Political Economy in Jeffersonian America* (Chapel Hill, NC, 1980) and *Last of the Fathers*, 267–86.

54. As reported by Robert Sutcliff, *Travels in Some Parts of North America*, 50, quoted in Herbert Aptheker, *American Negro Slave Revolts* (New York, 1969 ed.), 223–24.

55. Frederick Douglass, "The Anti-Slavery Movement," lecture delivered before the Rochester Ladies' Anti-Slavery Society, Jan. 1855, in *The Life and Writings of Frederick Douglass*, Philip S. Foner, ed. (New York, 1950), 2:337. In his *Appeal*, David Walker reprinted the Declaration of Independence and commanded whites: "See your declaration, Americans!! Do you understand your own language?" *Walker's Appeal in Four Articles* (New York, 1969; orig. pub. 1830), 85.

56. See Wesley M. Gewehr, *The Great Awakening in Virginia* (Durham, NC, 1930).

57. Isaac, *Transformation of Virginia*, esp. chap. 8. The discussion that follows is based upon Gewehr, *Awakening in Virginia*; Isaac, *Transformation of Virginia*; Richard R. Beeman, *The Evolution of the Southern Backcountry: A Case Study of Lunenberg County, Virginia, 1746–1832* (Philadelphia, 1984); Donald G. Mathews, *Religion in the Old South* (Chicago, 1977); Mechal Sobel, *The World They Made Together: Black and White Values in Eighteenth-Century Virginia* (Princeton, NJ, 1987), chaps. 14, 15; Rachel N. Klein, *Unification of a Slave State: The Rise of the Planter Class in the South Carolina Backcountry, 1760–1808* (Chapel Hill, NC, 1990), chap. 9; Lacy K. Ford, *Origins of Southern Radicalism: The South Carolina Upcountry, 1800–1860* (New York, 1988), chap. 1; Alan Gallay, "The Origins of Slaveholders' Paternalism: George Whitefield, the Bryan Family, and the Great Awakening in the South," *JSH* 53 (1987): 370–94; "The Great Sellout: George Whitefield on Slavery," in Winfred B. Moore, Jr., and Joseph F. Tripp, *Looking South: Chapters in the Story of an American Region* (Westport, CT, 1989), 17–30, and *The Formation of a Planter Elite: Jonathan Bryan and the Southern Colonial Frontier* (Athens, GA, 1989); Harvey H. Jackson, "Hugh Bryan and the Evangelical Movement in Colonial South Carolina," *WMQ* 43 (1986): 594–614; David T. Bailey, *Shadow on the Church: Southwestern Evangelical Religion and the Issue of Slavery, 1783–1860* (Ithaca, NY, 1985); and James D. Essig, *The Bonds of Wickedness: American Evangelicals Against Slavery, 1770–1808* (Philadelphia, 1982).

58. Sobel, *World They Made Together*, 180.

59. Ibid., 189.

60. Quoted in ibid., 182.

61. Mathews, *Religion in Old South*, 66. As early as the 1740s the Vir-

ginia Presbyterian Samuel Davies was preaching to slaves. See Essig, *Bonds of Wickedness*, 12–15.

62. See, for example, Albert J. Raboteau, *Slave Religion: The 'Invisible Institution' in the Antebellum South* (New York, 1978); Eugene D. Genovese, *Roll, Jordan, Roll: The World The Slaves Made* (New York, 1974), bk. 2; Mechal Sobel, *Trabelin' On: The Slave Journey to an Afro-Baptist Faith* (Princeton, NJ, 1988, orig. 1979).

63. Sobel, *World They Made Together*.

64. In addition to Sobel, *World They Made Together*, see Beeman, *Evolution of the Backcountry*, 108–11; Klein, *Unification of a Slave State*, 294–95; and Ford, *Origins of Southern Radicalism*, chap. 1.

65. Klein, *Unification of a Slave State*, 295.

66. Sobel, *World They Made Together*, 193.

67. For examples, see Ford, *Origins of Southern Radicalism*, 34, and Beeman, *Evolution of the Backcountry*, 110.

68. For changing family standards in the South see Lewis, *Pursuit of Happiness*; Daniel Blake Smith, *Inside the Great House: Planter Family Life in Eighteenth-Century Chesapeake Society* (Ithaca, NY, 1980); Philip Greven, *The Protestant Temperament: Patterns of Child-Rearing, Religious Experience, and the Self in Early America* (New York, 1977); and Isaac, *Transformation of Virginia*, 301–8. Consider also Jay Fliegelman, *Prodigals and Pilgrims: The American Revolution Against Patriarchal Authority, 1750–1800* (New York, 1982). For the southern family in the nineteenth century, see Jane Turner Censer, *North Carolina Planters and their Children* (Baton Rouge, LA, 1984); and Steven M. Stowe, *Intimacy and Power in the Old South: Ritual in the Lives of the Planters* (Baltimore, 1987). For different views see Allan Kulikoff, *Tobacco and Slaves: The Development of Southern Cultures in the Chesapeake, 1680–1800* (Chapel Hill, NC, 1986); Bertram Wyatt-Brown, *Southern Honor: Ethics and Behavior in the Old South* (New York, 1982); and Elizabeth Fox-Genovese, *Within the Plantation Household: Black and White Women of the Old South* (Chapel Hill, NC, 1988). For a similar transformation of the northern family see especially Mary Ryan, *Cradle of the Middle Class: The Family in Oneida County* (New York, 1981).

69. For examples, see Wyatt-Brown, *Southern Honor*.

70. Lacy K. Ford has noted that evangelical Christianity was "voluntary and intensely personal," and, as a consequence, ideally suited for those southerners "who maintained independent households whose heads were suspicious of outside authority and jealous of their own autonomy." Ford, *Origins of Southern Radicalism*, 37.

71. Sobel, *World They Made Together*, 192–97, quotations on 197, 193.

72. Gallay, "Great Sellout" and "Origin of Slaveholders' Paternalism"; first and third quotations in "Sellout," 21, 22; second quotation in "Paternalism," 381. For Whitefield's views on slavery see also Essig, *Bonds of Wickedness*, 3–15.

73. Gallay, "Great Sellout," 24.

74. Quoted in Klein, *Unification of a Slave State*, 287.

75. Sobel, *World They Made Together*, 195.

76. This process is described by Allan Kulikoff, "The Beginnings of the Afro-American Family in Maryland," in Aubrey Land et al., eds., *Law, Society, and Politics in Early Maryland* (Baltimore, 1977), 171–96; Herbert G. Gutman, *The Black Family in Slavery and Freedom, 1750–1925* (New York, 1977); Mary Beth Norton, Herbert G. Gutman, and Ira Berlin, "The Afro-American Family in the Age of the Revolution," and Philip D. Morgan, "Black Society in the Lowcountry, 1760–1810," in Ira Berlin and Ronald Hoffman, eds., *Slavery and Freedom in the Age of the American Revolution* (Charlottesville, VA, 1983), 175–91 and 83–141; Daniel Littlefield, "Plantations, Paternalism, and Profitability: Factors Affecting African Demography in the Old British Empire," *JSH* 47 (1981): 167–82; Sarah S. Hughes, "Immigrant Generations: African Women in Eighteenth-Century Virginia," paper presented at Eighth Berkshire Conference on the History of Women, Douglass College, June 1990.

77. Morgan, "Black Society in Lowcountry," quotations on 124–25.

78. Littlefield, "Plantations, Paternalism and Profitability," quotation on 180. See also Chaplin, *Anxious Pursuit*, 55–58.

79. Joyce E. Chaplin, "Slavery and the Principle of Humanity: A Modern Idea in the Early Lower South," *Journal of Social History* (1990): 299–315, and *Anxious Pursuit*. David Brion Davis ably describes the relationship among developing notions of benevolence in religious and philosophical thought (Davis, *Slavery in Western Culture*, 348–90).

80. That is the title of her essay, published in Rose, *Slavery and Freedom*, ed. William W. Freehling (New York, 1982), 18–36, quotations from 27.

81. Sobel, *World They Made Together*, 197.

82. For Leland, Rice, and other antislavery ministers see Essig, *Bonds of Wickedness, passim*. For Leland see also Sobel, *Trabelin' On*, 86; for Rice see also Bailey, *Shadow on the Church*, 43–49.

83. See Sobel, *Trabelin' On*, 86, and Louis Morton, *Robert Carter of Nomini Hall* (Williamsburg, VA, 1941).

84. See Sobel, *Trabelin' On*, 86–90; Bailey, *Shadow on the Church*; McColley, *Slavery and Virginia*, esp. 148–53; Mathews, *Religion in Old South*, 66–80, and *Slavery and Methodism: A Chapter in American Morality, 1780–1845* (Princeton, NJ, 1965).

85. Jackson, "Hugh Bryan," and Gallay, "Origins of Paternalism." See also Rahe, *Republics Ancient and Modern*, 622.

86. Klein, *Unification of a Slave State*, chap. 9.

87. Sobel, *World They Made Together*, 209.

88. Mathews, *Religion in Old South*, 75. See also Essig, *Bonds of Wickedness*, chap. 6.

89. Asbury to George Roberts, 11 Feb. 1797, in Elmer T. Clark et. al., eds., *The Journal and Letters of Francis Asbury* (Nashville, TN, 1958), 3:160, quoted in Essig, *Bonds of Wickedness*, 125. See also Ford, *Origins of Southern Radicalism*, 24, and Essig, *Bonds of Wickedness*, 125–26.

90. Mathews, *Religion in Old South*, 77.

91. For a summary see Mathews, *Religion in Old South*, chap. 4. See also Bailey, *Shadow on the Church*, 128–30. But it is important to remember that, as James Oakes has observed, the evangelical accommodation to slavery was by no means a proslavery apology; evangelicalism had contained its opposition to slavery, rather than erasing it. As a consequence, conscientious slaveholders might still have unsettling qualms about the morality of slavery. See Oakes, *Ruling Race*, chap. 4.

92. Bailey, *Shadow on the Church*, quotations on 128, 129. See also Essig, *Bonds of Wickedness*, 134.

93. Mathews, *Religion in Old South*, 157. The evangelical retreat from politics should be seen as part of the "increased detachment of religion from the state" in the early national era, which was reflected in the Constitution, described by Stephen Botein as "a perfectly secular text." (Botein, "Religious Dimensions of the Early American State," in Beeman, Botein, and Carter, *Beyond Confederation*, 317.) The first phrase is from Ruth H. Bloch, "Religion and Ideological Change in the American Revolution," in Mark A. Noll, ed., *Religion and American Politics: From the Colonial Period to the 1980s* (New York, 1990), 56; see *passim*, 44–61.

94. Quoted in Essig, *Bonds of Wickedness*, 117.

95. See, for example, David Potter, *The Impending Crisis: 1848–1861* (New York, 1976). See also Bertram Wyatt-Brown, "Modernizing Southern Slavery: The Proslavery Argument Reinterpreted," in J. Morgan Kousser and James M. McPherson, eds., *Region, Race, and Reconstruction: Essays in Honor of C. Vann Woodward* (New York, 1982), 27–49 for the southern proslavery redefinition of slavery as "an agency of the state" in the 1850s (quotation on 38).

96. See Rose, "Domestication of Slavery," 23–25. Establishing just such a separation between the public and private realms, was, as Morton J. Horwitz has recently suggested, precisely the objective of nineteenth-century American political, social, and economic thought, which "sought to establish a separate, 'natural' realm of non-coercive and non-political transactions free from the dangers of state interference and redistribution." *The Transformation of American Law, 1870–1960: The Crisis of Legal Orthodoxy* (New York, 1992), 11.

97. Debate, 14 Feb. 1804, *Annals of Congress*, 8th Cong., 1st Sess., 1: 1006–7; Hayne quoted in MacLeod, *Slavery, Race, and Revolution*, 90.

98. See Ryan, *Cradle of the Middle Class*; Ford, *Origins of Southern Radicalism*, chap. 2; Lewis, *Pursuit of Happiness*; Oakes, *Ruling Race*, chap. 4; Paul E. Johnson, *A Shopkeeper's Millenium: Society and Revivals in Rochester, New York, 1815–1837* (New York, 1978); and Susan Mary Juster, "Sinners and Saints: The Evangelical Construction of Gender and Authority in New England, 1740–1830" (Ph.D. diss., Univ. of Michigan, 1990).

99. See Nancy F. Cott, *The Bonds of Womanhood: "Woman's Sphere" in New England, 1780–1835* (New Haven, CT, 1977), and Kathryn Kish Sklar, *Catharine Beecher: A Study in American Domesticity* (New Haven, CT,

1973) for the doctrine of "separate spheres." See Linda K. Kerber, "Separate Spheres, Female Worlds, Woman's Place: The Rhetoric of Women's History," *JAH* 75 (1988): 9–39 for a critique of historians' use of the paradigm. Consider also Joan B. Landes, *Women and the Public Sphere in the Age of the French Revolution* (Ithaca, NY, 1988) for an analysis of the way that bourgeois liberalism constructed gender in France.

    100. *Southern Quarterly Review* 2 (Oct. 1842): 364–65, quoted in Kenneth S. Greenberg, "Revolutionary Ideology," 384.

    101. See, for example, Michael P. Johnson, "Planters and Patriarchy: Charleston, 1800–1860," *JSH* 46 (1980): 45–72. For recent reformulations of this thesis see Fox-Genovese, *Within the Plantation Household*, and Stephanie McCurry, "The Two Faces of Republicanism: Gender and Proslavery Politics in Antebellum South Carolina," *JAH* 78 (1992): 1245–64.

    102. Byrd to the earl of Orrery, 5 July 1726, quoted in Michael Mullin, ed., *American Negro Slavery: A Documentary History* (New York, 1976), 57–58. Memminger quoted in Eugene D. Genovese, *The World the Slaveholders Made: Two Essays in Interpretation* (Middletown, CT, 1988, orig. pub. 1969), 195.

    103. The transformation of the southern family is described by Smith, *Great House*; Lewis, *Pursuit of Happiness*; Censer, *North Carolina Planters*; Stowe, *Intimacy and Power*; and Russell Lindley Blake, "Ties of Intimacy: Social Values and Personal Relationships of Antebellum Slaveholders" (Ph.D. diss., University of Michigan, 1978). For Byrd see Michael Zuckerman, "William Byrd's Family," *Perspectives in American History* 12 (1979): 253–311.

    104. Quoted in Oakes, *Ruling Race*, 102.

    105. Wyatt-Brown, "Modernizing Southern Slavery," 33; Leak quoted in Blake, "Ties of Intimacy," 122. For Leak's public statements see Genovese, *World the Slaveholders Made*, 120–22.

    106. James L. Petigru to his daughter Jane North, 24 Dec. 1835, James L. Petigru MSS, LC, quoted in Wyatt-Brown, "Modernizing Southern Slavery," 30.

    107. Oakes, *Ruling Race*, 135–36; quotations on 136; see also 127–28.

    108. Tise, *Proslavery*, 69–74, quotation on 71; Drew Gilpin Faust, ed., *The Ideology of Slavery: Proslavery Thought in the Antebellum South, 1830–1860* (Baton Rouge, LA, 1981), intro. 1–21.

    109. Thomas Roderick Dew, "Abolition of Negro Slavery," *American Quarterly Review* 12 (1832), in Faust, ed., *Ideology of Slavery*, 63–64. It might be noted that both Jefferson and Dew subscribed to a sensationalist psychology. See Daniel W. Howe, "The Political Philosophy of *The Federalist*," *WMQ* 44 (1987): 485–509.

    110. Dew, "Abolition of Negro Slavery," in Faust, ed., *Ideology of Slavery*, 40.

    111. Ibid., 66–67.

    112. *Arator* (Petersburg, VA, 1818; orig. pub. 1813), 6th ed., 93, quoted in Shalhope, 145. For Taylor see Robert Shalhope, *John Taylor of Caroline: Pastoral Republican* (Columbia, SC, 1980). For his views on slavery see also

MacLeod, *Slavery, Race and Revolution*, 82–89. MacLeod notes that Taylor's theories about slavery assumed both the mental and the physical inferiority of blacks.

113. *Arator*, quoted in MacLeod, *Slavery, Race, and Revolution*, 86–87.

114. *Arator*, 94, quoted in Shalhope, *John Taylor*, 146–47.

115. *Arator*, 94–95, quoted in Shalhope, *John Taylor*, 146–47. Taylor may well have been responding also to the rapid growth in Virginia's free black population, which had mushroomed from 3000 in 1782 to over 30,000 by 1810, leading in 1806 to the state's passing a law that required manumitted slaves to leave the state (Rose, "Domestication of Slavery," 26). See also Douglas R. Egerton, " 'It's Origin is Not a Little Curious': A New Look at the American Colonization Society," *Journal of the Early Republic* 5 (1985): 468–70.

116. Quoted in Tise, *Proslavery*, 101.

117. Lacy K. Ford, "Republican Ideology in a Slave Society: The Political Economy of John C. Calhoun," *JSH* 54 (August 1988): 422. See also, Kenneth S. Greenberg, "Revolutionary Ideology and the Proslavery Argument: The Abolition of Slavery in Antebellum South Carolina," *JSH* 42 (Aug. 1976): 365–84, and *Masters and Statesmen: The Political Culture of American Slavery* (Baltimore, 1985).

118. Ford, "Political Economy of Calhoun," 422.

119. Quoted in ibid., 421; see also 422–23.

120. Quoted in Greenberg, *Masters and Statesmen*, 96. For other examples of a republican defense of slavery and how they were repeated in the decades before the Civil War, see J. William Harris, *Plain Folk and Gentry*, 36–39.

121. Greenberg, "Revolutionary Ideology and Proslavery Argument," 372.

122. See for example, James Oakes, "From Republicanism to Liberalism: Ideological Change and the Crisis of the Old South," *American Quarterly* 37 (1985): 551–71.

123. Lacy K. Ford uses the phrase "the antimercantilist economic liberalism of Adam Smith" to characterize Calhoun's economic philosophy; and while there were certainly disagreements among southern politicians, a large proportion of them shared a similar economic philosophy. See Ford, "Political Economy of Calhoun"; quotation is from 413. See also Oakes, "Republicanism to Liberalism," and *Slavery and Freedom*; Laurence Shore, *Southern Capitalists: The Ideological Leadership of an Elite, 1832–1885* (Chapel Hill, NC, 1986); J. Mills Thornton III, *Politics and Power in a Slave Society: Alabama, 1800–1860* (Baton Rouge, LA, 1978); and Diggins, *Lost Soul*, 140–43.

124. "Rudiments of Law and Government Deduced from the Law of Nature" (Charleston, 1783), printed in Charles S. Hyneman and Donald S. Lutz, *American Political Writing During the Founding Era, 1760–1805*, 2 vols. (Indianapolis, 1983), 1:583. See also Judith N. Shklar, *Ordinary Vices* (Cambridge, MA, 1984), esp. 3–5.

125. For Locke's justification of slavery see *Two Treatises*, ed. Laslett, 2:

22–24 (283–85). See also Davis, *Slavery in Western Culture*, 118–21. Francis Hutcheson also justified perpetual servitude in certain limited cases (see Davis, *Slavery in Western Culture*, 374–78), yet American defenders of slavery never drew from his arguments, either.

126. Laslett, ed., *Two Treatises* 2:27 (287).

127. George Fredrickson, *The Black Image in the White Mind: The Debate on Afro-American Character and Destiny, 1817–1914* (New York, 1971). Fredrickson has noted that "it was . . . in tandem with the concept of slavery as 'a positive good' that the doctrine of permanent black inferiority began its career." (47) An extended discussion of the development of racism and its use as a defense of slavery lies beyond the scope of this chapter. My thinking, however, has been informed by James Oakes, "Why Slaves Can't Read: The Political Significance of Jefferson's Racism," paper presented at conference on Thomas Jefferson and the Education of a Citizen, LC, 14 May 1993.

128. Griswold, "Rights and Wrongs"; Michael Walzer, *Spheres of Justice: A Defense of Pluralism and Equality* (New York, 1983).

129. *Federalist*, 367–68.

130. Ibid.

131. McCoy, *Last of the Fathers*, 274.

132. Jordan, *White Over Black*, 567.

133. Madison to William Turpin, 9 Aug. 1833, in Madison Papers, LC, quoted in McCoy, *Last of the Fathers*, 307. For Jefferson, see Griswold, "Rights and Wrongs."

134. For the rise of a humanitarian sensibility see Davis, *Problem of Slavery*, and Thomas Haskell, "Capitalism and the Origins of the Humanitarian Sensibility, pt. 1," *AHR* 90 (1985): 339–61, and "pt. 2," ibid., 547–66. Haskell suggests that the humanitarian sensibility itself was a product of capitalism. This proposition has been challenged by Davis and John Ashworth. See their replies to Haskell and his response: John Ashworth, "The Relationship between Capitalism and Humanitarianism," *AHR* 92 (Oct. 1987): 813–28; David Brion Davis, "Reflections on Abolitionism and Ideological Hegemony," 797–812; and Thomas Haskell, "Convention and Hegemonic Interest in the Debate over Antislavery: A Reply to Davis and Ashworth," 829–78.

135. Susan Cornwall Diary, 31 Jan. 1861, quoted in Blake, "Ties of Intimacy," 120.

Index

In this index an "f" after a number indicates a separate reference on the next page, and an "ff" indicates separate references on the next two pages. A continuous discussion over two or more pages is indicated by a span of page numbers, e.g., "57–59." *Passim* is used for a cluster of references in close but not consecutive sequence.

Library of Congress Cataloging-in-Publication Data

Devising liberty : preserving and creating freedom
in the new American Republic / edited by David
Thomas Konig
    p. cm.—(The making of modern freedom)
Includes bibliographical references and index.
ISBN 0-8047-2536-5 (acid-free paper)
    1. Civil rights—United States—History.   2. United
States—Politics and government—1789–1815.
3. United States—Economic policy—To 1933.
4. United States—Social policy.   I. Konig, David
Thomas, 1947–   . II. Series.
JC599.U5D48 1995
323.0972—dc20   94-35979
                                                      CIP

DATE DUE